Paul Valéry's work is a unique Odyssey in the universe of ideas and mental forms. The most recently acknowledged – and the most private – of the masters of modernity, Valéry is perhaps the most radical and wide-ranging. He navigates freely within the mental galaxies known to scientists, poets, literary theorists, musicians, philosophers, historians and social anthropologists, always concerned to explore the potential and limits of the human mind.

The present volume of essays by internationally recognised scholars offers the first comprehensive account of Valéry's work in English or French. It provides a series of readings bringing into focus the deeper coherence that animates what Valéry called his 'unitary mind in a thousand pieces', and offers new perspectives on the immense range of his experimental and fragmentary writings. This book moves forward the frontiers of our understanding of Valéry's work, and substantially alters the way in which he is perceived.

PAUL GIFFORD is Buchanan Professor of French at the University of St Andrews. He is author of *Valéry – le dialogue des choses divines* (1989) and *Valéry – 'Charmes'* (1997), and editor with Brian Stimpson of *Paul Valéry: Musique, mystique, mathématique* (1993).

BRIAN STIMPSON is Professor of Twentieth-Century French Literature at the Roehampton Institute, London. He is author of *Paul Valéry and Music: A Study of the Techniques of Composition in Valéry's Poetry* (1984), and editor of a number of books including with Nicole Celeyrette-Pietri *Un nouveau regard sur Paul Valéry* (1995), and with Lieve Spaas *Robinson Crusoe: Myths and Metamorphoses* (1996).

Paul Gifford and Brian Stimpson are both collaborating editors in the ongoing edition of Paul Valéry's *Cahiers* 1894–1914 (Paris, Gallimard, 1988–   ) and in the English translation *Paul Valéry: 'Cahiers'/Notebooks* (New York, Peter Lang, 1999–   ).

CAMBRIDGE STUDIES IN FRENCH 58

READING PAUL VALERY

CAMBRIDGE STUDIES IN FRENCH

GENERAL EDITOR: Michael Sheringham (*Royal Holloway, London*)
EDITORIAL BOARD: R. Howard Bloch (*Columbia University*),
Malcolm Bowie (*All Souls College, Oxford*), Terence Cave (*St John's College,
Oxford*), Ross Chambers (*University of Michigan*), Antoine Compagnon
(*Columbia University*), Peter France (*University of Edinburgh*),
Christie McDonald (*Harvard University*), Toril Moi (*Duke University*), Naomi
Schor (*Harvard University*)

*Recent titles in this series include*

SIMON GAUNT
*Gender and Genre in Medieval French Literature*

JEFFREY MEHLMAN
*Genealogies of the Text: Literature, Psychoanalysis, and Politics in Modern France*

LEWIS C. SEIFERT
*Fairy Tales, Sexuality and Gender in France 1690–1715: Nostalgic Utopias*

ELZA ADAMOWICZ
*Surrealist Collage in Text and Image: Dissecting the Exquisite Corpse*

NICHOLAS WHITE
*The Family in Crisis in Late Nineteenth-Century French Fiction*

A complete list of books in the series is given at the end of the volume.

# READING PAUL VALÉRY

*Universe in Mind*

EDITOR
PAUL GIFFORD

ASSOCIATE EDITOR
BRIAN STIMPSON

CAMBRIDGE
UNIVERSITY PRESS

PUBLISHED BY THE PRESS SYNDICATE OF THE UNIVERSITY OF CAMBRIDGE
The Pitt Building, Trumpington Street, Cambridge CB2 IRP, United Kingdom

CAMBRIDGE UNIVERSITY PRESS
The Edinburgh Building, Cambridge CB2 2RU, UK   http://www.cup.cam.ac.uk
40 West 20th Street, New York, NY 10011–4211, USA   http://www.cup.org
10 Stamford Road, Oakleigh, Melbourne 3166, Australia

First published 1998

Printed in the United Kingdom at the University Press, Cambridge

Typeset in 11/12½ pt Baskerville [CE]

*A catalogue record for this book is available from the British Library*

*Library of Congress cataloging in publication data*
Reading Paul Valéry: universe in mind / editor, Paul Gifford; associate editor, Brian Stimpson.
p.   cm. – (Cambridge Studies in French: 58)
Includes bibliographical references and index.
ISBN 0 521 58494 9 (hardback)
1. Valéry, Paul, 1871–1945 – Criticism and interpretation.
I. Gifford, Paul, 1944–   . II. Stimpson, Brian, 1944–   . III. Series.
PQ2643.A26Z7415   1998
841'.912 – dc21   98–15179
CIP

ISBN 0 521 58494 9 hardback

# Contents

# Contributors

KIRSTEEN ANDERSON – Senior Lecturer in French, Queen Mary and Westfield College, University of London.

NED BASTET – Professeur émerite, Université de Nice.

MALCOLM BOWIE – Marshal Foch Professor of French, All Souls College, University of Oxford.

NICOLE CELEYRETTE-PIETRI – Professeur de littérature française, Université de Paris-Val de Marne.

PAUL GIFFORD – Buchanan Professor of French, University of St Andrews.

MICHEL JARRETY – Professeur de littérature française, Université de Picardie, Amiens.

FLORENCE DE LUSSY – Conservateur en chef, Bibliothèque nationale de France.

WILLIAM MARX – Lecturer in French literature, University of Kyoto, Japan.

JEAN-MICHEL MAULPOIX – Professeur de littérature française, Ecole Normale Supérieure de Fontenay.

SUZANNE NASH – Professor of French literature, University of Princeton.

RÉGINE PIETRA – Professeur de philosophie, Université Mendès-France, Grenoble.

ROBERT PICKERING – Professeur de littérature française, Université Blaise Pascal, Clermont-Ferrand.

JUDITH ROBINSON-VALÉRY – Directeur de Recherche, Centre National de la Recherche Scientifique, Paris.

STEPHEN ROMER – Professeur d'anglais, Université de Tours.

BRIAN STIMPSON – Professor of French Literature, Roehampton Institute, London.

# *Abbreviations*

Source references to Valéry's published works, to his correspondence, to the *Cahiers* ('Notebooks') and to the unpublished manuscripts are given in the body of the text as follows:

| | |
|---|---|
| *Œ*, I (or II) | Paul Valéry, *Œuvres*, ed. Jean Hytier, 2 vols. (Paris, Gallimard, 'Bibliothèque de la Pléiade', new edn. 1992–3); (vol. I includes *JP*, 'La Jeune Parque'; *P*, 'La Pythie'; *FN*, 'Fragments du Narcisse'; *ES*, 'Ebauche d'un Serpent'; *CM*, 'Le Cimetière Marin'). |
| *VF* | *Gustave Fourment – Paul Valéry, Correspondance, 1887–1933, avec introduction, notes et documents par Octave Nadal* (Paris, Gallimard, *NRF*, 1957). |
| *LQ* | *Paul Valéry, Lettres à Quelques-uns* (Paris, Gallimard, *NRF*, 1952). |
| *GV* | *André Gide – Paul Valéry, Correspondance, 1890–1942, préface et notes par Robert Mallet* (Paris, Gallimard, *NRF*, 1955). |
| *C*1, *C*2 | Paul Valéry, *Cahiers*. ed. J. Robinson, 'Pléiade' (2 vols.). |
| *CI*, *CII*, etc. | Paul Valéry, *Cahiers 1894–1914* (Gallimard, 'integral' edition). |
| *C*, I, *C*, II, etc. | Paul Valéry, *Cahiers, 29 vols., in facsimile* (CNRS). (For a full description of editions of the *Cahiers*, please see Editors' note, p. 10). |
| *JP*, ms III, fo. 33 | *La Jeune Parque*, ms vol. III, fo. 33, Bibliothèque nationale. |
| *MF*, ms IV, fo. 26 v. | *Mon Faust*, ms vol. IV, fo. 26v, Bibliothèque nationale. |

| | |
|---|---|
| Cah. *Ch.* ii, fo. 21 | 2$^{e}$ cahier ms de *Charmes*, Bibliothèque nationale. |
| N.a.f. ms fo. 17 | Nouvelles acquisitions françaises, Bibliothèque nationale. |
| BN ms | Other manuscripts held at Bibliothèque nationale. |
| VRY | Valéryanum, manuscripts held at the Bibliothèque Jacques Doucet. |

# Introduction

## Paul Gifford and Brian Stimpson

The present volume brings together leading researchers from many countries in a concerted attempt, so far lacking in Valéry criticism, to view as a unitary whole a writer normally perceived as supremely diverse and fragmentary. On this novel basis, it is hoped to redraw the contours of recognition of Paul Valéry and to re-evaluate his standing some fifty years after his death.

This primary task implies two further objectives, which relate even more directly to the singular case of Valéry. It imposes on the one hand the need to re-examine and substantially re-present a major writer, since, for reasons which will appear, the vision of Valéry entertained by research specialists is markedly out of phase with perceptions current in the wider constituency of French Studies. No less significant, on the other hand, is the task of refracting the broader claims of Valéry, as now understood, to an audience outside the traditional field of French literature altogether, in the exact sciences, in parallel arts disciplines and in the social sciences.

Few would doubt that Valéry stands as one of the very greatest representative figures of French culture in the first half of the 20th century. His state funeral, decreed by General de Gaulle in the newly liberated Paris of 1945, may indeed be appropriately taken to symbolise the culmination and the end of an entire epoch of French cultural tradition; it marks, as nearly as one can date such large-scale phase-changes, the closing of an era of rationalistic anthropocentric European humanism, some four centuries old. Born in the second year of the Franco–Prussian war and writing his most central work *La Jeune Parque* during the Great War, within earshot of the artillery bombardments of Verdun, Valéry had been among the first to register earlier seismic tremors signalling the crisis of the culture and civilisation of that same era; and his work is profoundly seen as a reaction to such intimations of mortality.

If there are discrepant perceptions of his present standing, this has to do with the different ways in which Valéry is situated in relation to those larger changes. One might say that, since 1945, two inversely related processes of recognition and re-assessment have developed in paradoxical counterpoint to each other.

In France, the normal process of revisionist accountancy applied *post mortem* to major authors has not been especially kind to Valéry. Certainly, many of the respects in which he achieved pre-eminence during his lifetime have proved declining assets in the second half-century. In relation to the recognised Valéry – the public and pre-eminent humanist patriarch – largely unfavourable moments of readability have been defined successively by Surrealism, Existentialism, the *nouveau roman*, the *nouvelle critique*, structuralism, deconstructionism, and feminism, even though each of these presents, as we shall see, unsuspected and sometimes very striking common frontiers with Valéry. (It is also true that signs of the wheel turning and coming full circle appear in the wake of the official 'demise of ideologies').

Thus, in the fifty years following his death, the writer whom T. S. Eliot hailed as the finest poet of his generation was not infrequently dismissed as a neo-classical formalist, 'obscure', 'remote', 'difficult', entombed in his formal perfection; the more so since his particular perfection had, apparently, disdained to notice Cézanne and managed only slight and somewhat slighting reference to Picasso. The supremely lucid critic, essayist, aesthetic and political theorist of the inter-war years similarly attracted multiple dismissals: as official representative of a discredited Third Republic, as symbolic embodiment of an impotent intellectualism, as spokesman for a humanist inheritance that Sartre, Robbe-Grillet and Derrida proposed variously to denounce and destroy (often drawing their critiques, knowingly or unknowingly, on Valéryan lines). Avant-garde intellectuals frowned on his offical eloquence welcoming the victor of Verdun – and future head of the Vichy government – to the French Academy, on his failure to take note of the Russian Revolution, or on the absence of post-colonial geopolitical perspectives. 'Post-modernism', for its part, has sometimes doubted from afar his post-modern credentials, lauding his private Nietzschean iconoclasm but regretting a public bourgeois politeness, sometimes verging on political unrectitude, and mistrusting an obstinate and worrisome Judeo-Christian crease of origin . . .

In English-speaking countries, which remembered Eliot's praise and recalled the veneration registered by the award of an honorary doctorate at Oxford in 1931, this accountancy of negative assets was slower in asserting itself. Yet, as the statistics of Valéry's declining presence in the research and teaching activities in the universities of most English-speaking countries during the latter three decades of the century would sufficiently demonstrate, the same preventions and aversions intervened; and here, amnesia was often the deeper for the non-recognitions introduced by linguistic difficulty and inter-cultural distance.

Ironically, within the selfsame period, the advances made in Valéry scholarship initiated an exactly inverse trend: the shock of profound intellectual discovery, a new readability, new horizons of criticism and a sharply rising intellectual stock. One should perhaps speak of Valéry's stock as 'soaring', since, in the decade following the celebrations in 1971 of the centenary of his birth, he was hailed, not merely as the only modern French writer and intellectual to have profoundly understood modern science, but as the enviable holder of a generalised magisterium of modernity, derived from a private art of thinking which referred all questions to their genesis in mind and thus anticipated an impressive range of leading developments, not only in literary criticism and theory, but in most of the human sciences of our time.

Here, apparently at home in the new times, was the intellectuals' intellectual, invoked as such by the very titles of the reviews *Poétique* and *Tel Quel*; the subject of interdisciplinary research institutes founded under his name in a dozen countries of Europe and Asia; the interpreter of mind and world known to be the preferred author of French presidents of the Right (Pompidou) and of the Left (Mitterrand); the poet to whom repentent ex-Surrealists having once 'killed off the father' now returned (Bonnefoy).[1] A prescient and omni-pertinent Prophet, in excellent health, thus entered and took his place alongside his ailing traditionalist *doppelgänger*. 'Tel qu'en lui-même l'éternité le change'; but for *which* of these two essential Ideas was eternity, in fact, proposing to exchange him?

Between the downward curve of revisionist accountancy and the soaring counter-curve of research-based rediscovery, the difference is, indeed, one of identification. Which 'work' is being accounted for and considered as defining 'Valéry'? Remarkably, the pre-eminent humanist patriarch has continued to be identified, as he had originally come to exist, on the basis of a tiny fraction of his intellectual output – certainly less than one tenth of the total – which its author had published during his lifetime, often in a spirit of concession to the public, for reasons of alimentary necessity. (It is a biographical datum of some importance that, from the death in 1922 of his patron and employer Edouard Lebey, Director of the Agence Havas, Valéry lived, sometimes insecurely, from his pen.) Conversely, it is, of course, the 'reserved' nine-tenths of his work, which have become available and gradually understood only in the half-century since his death, which, proximately or more distantly, give rise to the antipodally different perceptions and estimates just recorded. These too were not always soundly based in fact and could be subject to distortions of judgment (as Michel Jarrety later shows in relation to the filiation claimed by the structuralists in respect of Valéry's poetics).

The *Cahiers* or Notebooks, were first published in the limited, 29 volume edition *in facsimile* of the CNRS between 1957 and 1961. As the sheer novelty (in point of form, content and significance) of these 26,600 pages of analytical notes came to be progressively assimilated, it became clear that they constituted the laboratory in which a powerfully experimental analyst and critical thinker had invested the essential part of himself. From 1972, the re-evaluation of Valéry accelerated and entered a second phase with the availability at the Bibliothèque Nationale of the almost equally voluminous collection of the classified manuscripts that constituted the workshop of the creative writer: one whose singularity lay in the fact that he was devoted more to writing itself, its multiple modes and possibilities, than to the finished work; and whose act of writing had no natural terminus for the – radical and sufficient – reason that what was involved was the exploration through writing of the reflexive subject of consciousness or 'self' and of all that was reflected and composed in the mirror of the mind.

The English-speaking world has in general not fully kept pace with the far-reaching and rapid changes involved in this re-discovery of Valéry, or in the re-evaluation which follows from it. This has not been for want of some interpreters and exegetes of the first rank, speaking in the relevant period of the 1960s, 70s and 80s across the interlinguistic and intercultural frontier: the eminent names of Judith Robinson, Christine Crow, James Lawler, Walter Ince come to mind ... Yet the play of many factors – the dimensions of the hidden part of the iceberg, the scale of the rethinking required, the time needed to create the appropriate tools with which to influence readability – has meant that the 'elapsed reaction time' has been considerable, and perhaps greater in the English-speaking world than elsewhere (for reasons of cultural predisposition, German-, Italian- or even Japanese-language speakers seem in practice to have adjusted rather more quickly to the novelty of 'another', experimental, Valéry).[2] The problems of forming any reliable and rounded view of a radically experimental writer of such remarkable diversity, one who spoke moreover of his 'unitary mind in a thousand pieces', were in any case formidable. Above all, the thousand pieces of Valéry's unitary mind were not, for a long time, materially available except to a handful of researchers able to make the quite exceptional investment of intellectual energy required to explore the iceberg in its hidden bulk. Symbolically, perhaps, for most of the period considered, the activity of 'reading Paul Valéry' has often been co-extensive, for most non-French readers, with the published and public literary works available in the English translation by Jackson Mathews.[3]

Naturally enough, the manuscripts still belong largely to a research culture and will doubtless long remain so (even if forms of electronic publication are envisaged that will make them more widely available). But the *Cahiers* have become progressively accessible, first in the invaluable classified selection ('choix de textes') in two volumes (1973, 1974) of the 'Pléiade' edition established by Judith Robinson-Valéry, and more recently (from 1987 onwards) in the critically annotated, 'Integral' edition, covering the formative years 1894–1914. As the present volume goes to press, an English translation of the 'Pléiade' *Cahiers* is being undertaken, publication of which will straddle the turn of the century[4]: it will appear, that is to say, some five years after the parallel German translation, some seven years after the Italian one, and fully ten years after its Japanese equivalent. This event will, it is hoped, open up frontiers closed by English-language monocompetency. A subtle and rigorous command of French will no longer be the sole key to entering a cosmos of the mind more diverse and more extensive than that of Nietzsche or Freud, and which has hitherto been the fabulous domain of a restricted community of research specialists.

Inevitably, therefore, the present volume stands, at least in part, in the considerable gap between the latest research-based understanding of Valéry and the very different recognitions of a wider public. In order to launch their own original act of rethinking and re-assessment, contributors have been asked to come at their specialist topic along axes of critical re-evaluation, incorporating a high-level synthesis of progress already acquired. There is some boldness, and perhaps some risk, in this conception: it invokes – and puts to the test – the belief that cutting-edge research, exploring the frontiers of Valéry's universe in mind, is not incompatible with the intention of opening that same universe to a broader generality of educated intelligence that Valéry seeks and requires. At least, this seems a necessary risk and a risk worth taking. 'Reading Paul Valéry' is, after all, the business, not of specialists alone, but of all those – whether academic colleagues and students, specialists of other university disciplines in arts and sciences or literate and curious minds in the wider public – who are willing to engage seriously with the range, novelty and penetration of this singular and outstanding representative of modern intelligence.

The metaphor or analogy of a 'universe in mind' which furnishes the sub-title of this volume is at once a pointer to the universalist vocation of Valéry's thought and writing, and an indication of its reflexive character (its preoccupation, that is, with mind-made constructions of meaning and value and with their genesis within the human subject or within the cultural polity of such subjects). Genetically speaking, it refers also to an important and little-known leitmotif in the formation of Valéry's famous 'System', the invention of which, resolving the crisis of 1891–2, initiated the 50-year adventure of the *Cahiers*.

The characteristic Valéryan analogy between the visible cosmos as known to the astrophysician and the cosmos of ideas and mental forms of which the human psyche is the locus and origin, was no doubt 'in the air' of the last decade of the nineteenth century. Spectacular advances in the science of the physical universe had created the expectation of homologous developments in the science of mind. The analogy is present, in some form, in Kant and in Mallarmé, even in Valéry's celebrated adversary, Pascal. Yet its particular resonance for the youthful Valéry derives most significantly from his illuminated reading, undertaken in his critical twenty-first year, before he engaged seriously with the exact sciences, of Edgar Allen Poe's lyrical cosmogony *Eureka*.

From the marginal annotations entered in his personal copy of this text,[5] which he read in Baudelaire's translation, it is clear that this act of reading triggered in Valéry a certain shock of objection and reactive self-recognition, illuminating his own original path. He is tremendously excited by the audacity of the Romantic poet's proposed decipherment of the cosmic 'text'; and yet he objects that Poe's attempt to comprehend the 'Poem of the material and spiritual universe', as conceived by the divine Artist, can only result in an illusory dream of Knowledge. The admirable epistemological principle and method of 'Consistency' invoked by Poe – the notion of a reciprocity of appropriation uniting the knowing mind and its objects – here overreaches itself. But – we hear the youthful reader murmur – let us just suppose a fully consistent Consistency, respecting the Copernican revolution introduced by Kant in philosophy. The self-reflecting subject would then become 'first Cause'; the thought-forms possible in mental space would become the system of constellations to be elucidated and plotted. Such a referral of mental formations to mental source would open up a path of discovery quite as majestic and far-reaching as that pursued in Poe's cosmogony. One might envisage – no longer the *poem* – but instead the lucid *poetics* of the starry heavens ...[6] The genesis of Valéry's 'System' is complex and still being elucidated; yet one is certain that here is, at least, the 'keynote' of his own original *eureka!* Some such 'maîtresse pensée' (cf. *Œ*, p. 1, 857) opens the space-time of the *Cahiers*, rather as, in Poe, the explosion of the 'primordial particle' opens the universe of material space and time. For this reason the mind–cosmos analogy haunts the conceptual language of Valéry's 'System'; and, even more clearly, it resonates in long echoes in his poetic imagination.[7]

What Valéry's 'System' in practice connotes epistemologically undoubtedly evolves in time. By 1908, it is probable that its inventor had, all but formally, forsaken his founding Overbid: the hope of a unitary, mathematically expressed model of mental functioning, commanding a single protocol language and providing the basis for a rigorous, universal and comprehensive analytics of the mind and its products. Thereafter, 'mon Système 92' becomes progressively equivalent to 'ma méthode'. It equates, that is, to a much more supple and empirically fruitful set of perspectives, procedures and mythical imperatives which amount to a personal 'system *for thinking*', rather than to something resembling *in ovo* a systematised sum, a totalising human science or a global critical theory. Not despite, but because of this epistemological modulation, the universe discovered by Valéry in the mind continues to expand and diversify exponentially. It is indicative that whereas the first twenty years of the 'System' occupy only four tomes of the CNRS edition, the remaining thirty-one years fill no less than twenty-five of them.

A single critical volume cannot hope to do more than suggest indicatively the sheer reach and diversity of this expanding cosmos of the mind. Many questions of prime importance for Valéry's thought – on the epistemological analysis of the System, for instance, or the hugely significant reflection on Language, or the construction of a 'mystique sans Dieu' – have already engendered their substantial exegeses. These must be taken here as read. Specialist and non-specialist readers alike are referred, in the final note of each chapter, to numbered items in the bibliography. It is hoped by this means both to fill in the inevitable gaps of 'coverage', and to supply the fundamental and most recent critical reading with which each author is in dialogue on a given question. It has seemed important nevertheless to reflect something of the versatility and range of a mind uniquely capable of espousing different viewpoints and 'turning around' central issues of the century ('Je tourne autour' is one of Valéry's mottos); in which respect, it has been possible and appropriate equally to give full play to a representative diversity of critical voices.

Part I attends to the founding *Self-science*. What this term portends is not, we have suggested, an objective and fully exact science, though the youthful Valéry did indeed dream of transposing the methods and aspirations of the natural sciences into the domain of mind, and of elucidating the productions of the human psyche impersonally. Rather, it signals a supremely practised art of self-attention and self-development, using his own subjectivity, as he says, agilely, methodically, advisedly, as the origin of universal co-ordinates (*C*, VI, p. 108). What emerges is a method of examining the entire range of creative and cognitive productions of the human psyche in the perspective of their genesis, in a way that transcends traditional disciplinary boundaries. Reciprocally, the same 'self-science', as it is here termed, engages a unique existential dialogue of the self as both subject and object, consciousness and sensibility, body and intellect – a dialogue of which Valéry's writing in all modes renders memorable account.

Successive contributions under this heading examine: the fruitful paradox of a Valéryan 'biography of the mind' (Ned Bastet); the régimes of thought and writing illustrated in the unique laboratory of the *Cahiers* (Paul Gifford); the mythical models that give force and intellectual focus to the project of 'self-science' at the moment of its conception (Robert Pickering); the role of Valéry's particular fascination with the exact sciences in shaping his own mental outlook, his science of mental functioning and the forms of the mind (Judith Robinson-Valéry); the revealing relationship between his art of (re-) thinking and traditional philosophy, against which it naturally reacts and defines itself (Régine Pietra).

Part 2 pursues the notion of a graphic and scriptural event at the heart of the adventure of 'perpetual lucidity'. Under the title *Self-writings*, it presents a series of essays exploring the remarkable range of form and genre generated, both within and beyond the *Cahiers*, by the unfolding in creative mode of Valéry's art of writing the self. Michel Jarrety examines the literary poetics, a form of enquiry largely defined by Valéry in its modern form, but also distinct from later developments under this name. We also encounter new contenders for a place in his literary corpus, and freshly evaluated old-ones. The poet Stephen Romer examines the vein of admirable and moving lyric utterance arising within the laboratory of abstract thought. Brian Stimpson studies the counter-fiction practised by this notorious contemner of the novel; while the staging and the politics of Valéry's inner voices in the Dialogues are explored by William Marx. Likewise following the golden thread of subject Voice, Jean-Michel Maulpoix revisits the major poetry and Suzanne Nash follows the creative transformation of other voices in the poetic writings on the theme of Narcissus. Florence de Lussy suggests in relation to 'Les Pas' how manuscript study can renew the options of the critic of the poetic text.

Part 3, devoted to *Body-mind-world*, explores interactions within Valéry's famous triad, constitutive of human subjectivity as such. These illustrate some of the most prescient and modern of his insights. Topics addressed here are, in order: the account of music and the visual arts offered by an analyst in search of a radically new aesthetics, an aesthetics of the subject (Brian Stimpson); the neglected and frequently impressive rubric 'History-Politics' of the *Cahiers*, which shows Valéry to be a mind conscious of history in the

making, possessed of far-ranging geopolitical vision and of considerable acumen in what is today considered the domain of the political
and social sciences (Nicole Celeyrette-Pietri); Valéry's encounter
with the symbolic-mythic feminine, which is a secret but major axis
of both self-science and self-writing (Kirsteen Anderson); the lifelong
fascination of this disciple of awakened intellect for the 'phase' of
consciousness represented by dreaming, integrating the non-rational
and even unconscious dimension of the psyche, in ways that
encounter Freud (Malcolm Bowie); the spiritual dynamics of a quest
for self-enfoldment, which, while proceeding within the intellectual
forms of an 'archi-pure rationalism', nevertheless originates, enigma-
tically, in a fundamental void of the desiring sensibility and a
multiform need for the Other (Paul Gifford).

It will be seen self-evidently that Valéry is profoundly our own
contemporary in the range and nature of his concerns; indeed, that
Valéry's science of the forms of the mind in many ways contains and
predicts most of the preoccupations and methodological emphases
making up our own landscape of the mind – the unconscious, the
elusive self, fragmentary writing, gender issues, the arts–science
divide, inter-textuality, counter-spirituality, to name but a few. Yet
despite this lively pertinence, contributors to the present volume
have avoided the temptation of merely 're-telling' Valéry retrospectively in 'post-modern' categories. The penalty of doing so would
have been to destroy the cardinal virtue of Valéry's particular form
of lucidity, in which acceptable conformity to the ever-changing
mindscape of intellectual fashion is strenuously set aside in favour of
a perpetually open and integrally relativistic tension of analytic
understanding, attentive to – and limited only by – the potential of
the human mind itself.

   An open conclusion seeks to reflect on the types of reading which
beckon to future research and on the strategic pertinence of Valéry's
universe in mind.

### EDITORS' NOTE ON EDITIONS OF VALÉRY'S *CAHIERS*

The term 'Cahiers' denotes the 260 original notebooks used by
Valéry in his dawn meditations: these are now part of the 'fonds
Valéry' of the Bibliothèque nationale de France (Département des
manuscrits).

To date, there have been three published editions of the *Cahiers*. It is a measure of the scale and difficulty of the editor's task that none can be considered complete and definitive. All, consequently, are referred to in the present volume in an order of priority determined by ease of consultation. Chronologically listed, they are:

*1 Cahiers, 29 vols, in facsimile, Paris, Centre National de la Recherche Scientifique (CNRS), 1957–61.*

This photographically reproduced edition made research into the 'reserved' bulk of Valéry's work possible. It has the twin advantages of being the most complete edition and of directly representing the graphic trace of the original 260 notebooks. It was however produced in 1,000 copies only and is therefore not usually available outside University libraries. Its sheer bulk makes it cumbersome to use; and it is entirely without critical apparatus. It also omits some authentic material, includes some extraneous material and exhibits errors of chronological ordering, particularly for the early period. The concern for economy in reproduction has led to some graphic misrepresentation of the original notebooks.

It remains the most basic tool, apart from the 260 original notebooks themselves, and is indispensable for advanced research. Given its restricted availability and low reader-friendliness, however, references to it in the present volume have been limited to the – considerable – quoted material which does not figure in either of the other editions. Source reference – (*C*, XXIX, p. 911), etc.

*2 Paul Valéry. Cahiers. Édition établie, ed. and intro. Judith Robinson, Paris, Gallimard, Bibliothèque de la Pléiade, vol. 1, 1973; vol. 2, 1974.*

This typographical edition offers in some 3,000 pages an excellent selection of material, covering approximately one tenth of the original notebooks. It follows the thirty-one thematic rubrics established by Valéry's own classification post-1921, giving date and cross-reference to the CNRS edition for all textual fragments reproduced. It has a first-rate critical apparatus, including introduction, notes and indexes of themes and proper names. Representative and easily accessible, this edition has been translated into many languages and has done most to promote the wider knowledge of the *Cahiers* in a scholarly but readable form.

Given its standing, availability and reader-friendliness, it is to this rubric-led or 'classified' edition that readers are first referred in the present volume, wherever the material discussed forms part of its selection. Source reference – (*C* 1, p. 1333), etc.

*3 Paul Valéry. Cahiers 1894–1914, integral edition, ed. and intro. Nicole Celeyrette-Pietri and Judith Robinson (vols. 1–3), ed. and intro. Nicole Celeyrette-Pietri (vols. 4–6), Paris, Gallimard, NRF, vol. 1, 1987; vol. 2, 1988; vol. 3, 1990; vol. 4, 1992; vol. 5, 1994; vol. 6, 1997*

This is a scholarly paperback edition designed to publish in twelve volumes the entirety of the material belonging to the first twenty years of Valéry's *Cahiers* and inspired by the – valid – notion that any reader who can decipher the 'difficult' formative period can cope with the bulk of the work thereafter. Prepared by an international team of specialists, it establishes the definitive content, ordering and chronology of the material and includes many hitherto unpublished texts casting light on the genesis of Valéry's enterprise of thought and writing. Notes are extensive and illuminating, incorporating the latest scholarship and setting Valéry expertly in his intellectual context. The attempt is made to maintain contact, as nearly as may be in typographical form, with the original manuscript presentation. Thematic indexes occur in every third volume. The principal disadvantage is that only four volumes of the twenty-nine comprising the CNRS edition, are covered; the finest of Valéry's mature thought is excluded. (The series may one day be completed, perhaps in computerised form.) This edition provides a stepping stone from the initial contact with the Pléiade edition to the encounter with the entire run of the *Cahiers* in the CNRS edition.

References to the 'Integral' edition (i.e. integral for the period 1894–1914) are given where the material discussed is not included in the Pléiade edition. Source reference – (*CIV,* p. 414), etc.

EDITORS' NOTE ON TRANSLATIONS

A note indicator immediately following material quoted from Valéry of more than one line in length refers to a translation given in the notes grouped at the end of each chapter; translation of quoted material under a line in length is given immediately in the body of the chapter. All translations of quoted material have been made by the editors.

No translation has been made of the manuscripts reproduced on pp. 205–6 since genetic criticism passes through the language of origin; for a French transcription, please see pp. 204 and 207.

Translation of all critical contributions written in French has been made by the editors.

NOTES

1 See Bonnefoy's preface to the seventh volume of the 'Integral' (1894–1914) edition of the *Cahiers* (Paris, Gallimard, 1998). For a full description of the editions of the *Cahiers* now available and referred to in the present volume, please see Editor's note following the Introduction.

2 The admirable review article by Richard Sieburth of the first volume of the 'Integral' edition (1894–1914) of the *Cahiers* remains the best general presentation to an English-speaking public. See 'Dawn Voyages', *Times Literary Supplement* (22–8 September), pp. 1019–20.

3 J. Mathews (ed.), *The Collected Works of Paul Valéry* (New York, Pantheon Books, Bollingen series, 45, 1956).

4 To be published by Peter Lang, under the editorship of B. Stimpson (executive editor), P. Gifford and R. Pickering, 1999–2002.

5 Valéry was a voracious reader, and his private book-collection is frequently most revealing. An edition of his library and annotations is being prepared by Judith Robinson-Valéry and Brian Stimpson, *Les Lectures de Valéry: Catalogue et corpus de notes marginales de la biblothèque personnelle de Paul Valéry.*

6 This genetic hypothesis is explored in P. Gifford, 'Perfection, poïétique, possibilité – Poe', *Remanences* 4–5 (June, 1995) and developed in 'Autour d'un "Livre stellaire": Paul Valéry et l'*Eureka* d'E. Poe', to appear in P. Signorile and P. Thibaud (eds.), *La Pensée, la Trace, Mélanges à la mémoire de Simon Lantieri* (Aix, Publications de l'Université de Provence), forthcoming 1998.

7 The leitmotif of the starry heavens is often evoked in terms that directly recall *Eureka*. It may be followed through the prelude of *La Jeune Parque*, 'Ebauche d'un Serpent', 'Ode secrète' (*Charmes*), the texts of *Variété* where Valéry wrestles with Pascal, the unpublished socratic dialogue 'Peri tôn toû theoû', the manuscript versions of the unfinished finale of 'Fragments du Narcisse', *Alphabet*, and 'Le Solitaire' (*Mon Faust*). See P. Gifford, 'Autour d'un "Livre stellaire"'.

# I

*Self-science*

CHAPTER I

# Towards a biography of the mind

## Ned Bastet

How can one conceive of a 'Valéryan biography'?[1] A biography, that is, which would remain faithful to a writer who unceasingly proclaimed: 'il m' ennuyerait trop d'écrire ce que je vis d'oublier' ('it would excessively bore me to write down what I live by forgetting') (*C*, XXIII, p. 8) and who systematically doubted the authenticity and usefulness of any such enquiry, whether in respect of himself or others?

We may recall the scenes in *Mon Faust* (1942) where Faust is observed dictating the 'Mémoires de Moi'. In the dancing play of parodic irony, Valéry offers a virtuoso exhibition of the pretentions and pretences of a whole autobiographical tradition, from Rousseau to Stendhal and Gide. Everywhere, he shows the impure contrivances of confession and 'sincerity': 'ce puissant effet ne s'obtient qu'en se chargeant soi-même de toutes les horreurs, ignominies intimes ou expériences exécrables – vraies ou fausses – dont un homme puisse s'être avisé' (*Œ*, II, p. 286).[2] To write one's life is to consent to the rule of appearances; it means peddling mythical images which, derisorily, fail to conceal the real ignorance and autographical incompetence of the subject. Taking the measure of a self's elusive authenticity, should one not perhaps label as purely and simply *imaginary* or *fictional* any enterprise which yields to the temptation of (auto)biography? 'Je vous ai dit et redit que ces mémoires ne sont pas des souvenirs, et que je tiens ce que j'imagine pour aussi digne d'être MOI que ce qui fut, et dont je doute ...' (*Œ*, II, p. 331).[3]

Such a *jeu de massacre* would appear to allow, at best, an abstract account of an *itinerarium mentis*, a life-story limited to the progress of an intellectual quest uncluttered of all incidents or accidents, all contingencies. *Vita Cartesii est simplicissima* ('the Cartesian life is simplest') (*Œ*, II, 15). In fact, the case is somewhat different. The

17

entire weight and density of experienced reality, the whole dimension
of lived time, is seen by Valéry to condition the manoeuvres of a
mind and to influence the shape of a personal destiny. As Faust is
made to say: 'je trouve que c'est une manière de falsification que de
séparer la pensée, même la plus abstraite, de la vie, même la plus ...
vécue' (Œ, II, p. 281).[4] The temptation of autobiography comes to
haunt his latter years, to the point of suggesting the abortive project,
at the very end of his life, of dictating his own memoirs –[5] a set of
'Mémoires de Moi', precisely. This latter title figures insistently in the
later Cahiers; and we know that some of the entries made under this
rubric found an at least partial form of publication in the Propos me
concernant (1944),[6] even if Valéry still firmly underlines his difference:
'Je n'écris, n'ai jamais écrit de journal de mes jours. Je prends note de
mes idées. Que me fait ma biographie? Et que me font mes jours
écoulés?' (Œ, II, p. 157).[7] Unquestionably, however, these confidences
intervowen with theoretical reflexions do offer the image of a
concrete and particular personality, one who comes over as a nexus
of reactions, desires, exaltations and anxieties; and their final effect is
to envelop this 'self' in a discreet complicity, a sort of tender
connivence in the most acute awareness of original singularity.

The biographical tools currently available to Valéry scholarship –
principally Agathe Rouart-Valéry's 'Introduction' to the Pléiade
edition of the Œuvres and the recent study by Denis Bertholet –[8] may
recount the events of a life, clarify a social and socialite 'trajectory',
and usefully illuminate the factual-psychological basis of many of his
attitudes and actions. Yet they hardly meet Valéry's own specification
for a 'biography of the mind'. The external details of an existence
convey little of what confers on that life its structural form, its inner
logic of development, its potential for creativity.

By contrast, the confidences and analyses of the rubric 'Ego' of
the Cahiers provide an illumination from within. Here Valéry himself
confronts the personal point of origin of his entire adventure of the
mind, scrutinising the fundamental co-ordinates of his human
personality, obsessively questioning the determining moments of
cataclysm that have caused his course of life to bifurcate. Tirelessly,
he explores the original context and real frame of his adventure, the
factors, invisible to third parties, which account for a singularity of
attitude and behaviour which he sees as diverging from human
normality. He undertakes also to identify that potential within
himself of which an actually lived existence should be concerned to

fulfil the programme. His ever more finely attuned, analytical self-recollection develops here from the intuitions of the unpublished youthful text 'Essai sur le mortel', which had distinguished between an 'interrupted life' and a 'finished existence' – one which would exhaust the inner law of maturation and fulfilment of what constitutes its unique individuality.

But the most passionate sense and tendency of this vast Valéryan anamnesis is to lay bare a 'fond de pensée et de sensibilité incomparable sur lequel on a vécu' ('ground of thought and sensibility on which one has lived') (*C*, XX, p. 239); specifically, it is to apprehend the 'secret sonority' of an ever-identical self, usually overlaid and veiled by the noises of existence, but which, far more than the simple evenmential tissue of things, engages the true and irreplaceable music of one's being.

This is to recognise that an all-powerful substratum operates in the secret places of the mind: no doubt technically distinguishable from the Freudian unconscious, yet still a place of those obscure forces which press upon the conscious subject. 'Le moi caché fait tout' ('the hidden self does everything') (*C*, XXVI, p. 24), as Valéry finally acknowledges. This central Unknown is revealed only after the event, when, to the surprise of consciousness, unsuspected 'latencies' and unforeseen selves declare their hand (*C2*, p. 1438). About ourselves we know only what circumstances have given us to know. 'Robespierre n'avait jamais imaginé qu'il guillotinerait à ce point – ni Léonard qu'il aimerait' (*ibid.*, p. 458).[9] Thus the Valéry of 1921 is stupefied to discover, new and radiant, within the depths of a consciousness he had never ceased to explore, 'la vraie demeure de mon âme' ('the true dwelling of my soul') (*C*, VIII, p. 778). It is this central obscurity within the self, linked to its unsuspected, potential forms of life, which challenge authentic biography and constitute its 'truth'. Whether or not they pass into the sphere of actually affirmed existence, the possible, the potential, the 'SI –' which are in us genuinely belong to the world of the self, as much as the 'events' so elegantly dismissed by Faust.

Furthermore, this play of forces seems to call up, perhaps even to create the event itself. The 'forme en creux' of what will happen is obscurely operative in advance of the event, preparing it, calling to it: and expectancy, still unclear about its object, will finally trigger the event, or at least, mobilise the energies which give the event its singular and resonant existence; at which point the 'accident' may happen. (If Valéry's 'music of being' is reminiscent of Proust, we here touch on an unsuspected kinship with the Breton of *Nadja* and *L'Amour fou*.) We shall see this figure drawn in the constant form of the affective crises which punctuate an existence apparently devoted to the intellect, but also, in a homologous way, in the intellectual 'coups d'état' which Valéry compares to the historical events of the Reformation or the Terror (*C*, XX, p. 122).

'The event' in fact presents, beyond its temporal realisation, both a 'before' and an 'after'. If it is too overwhelming, unleashing forces of unbearable intensity, then it must first be neutralised before it can be assimilated. Hence the characteristic double procedure of Valéry's reactive self-defence: we will constantly find an analytical distancing which accommodates the disturbing new fact to the discursive logic of the 'System'; but also a mythical sublimation, often bringing with it a quasi-musical 'catharsis' of immediate 'affects'. Yet the event will act nonetheless in a subsequent future time, 'educating' the sensibility 'once and for all', and reforming the expectant substance of a desire which tends obscurely to (re)discover its object (cf. *C*, XXIX, p. 750).

So it will be in the returns to poetry and to love, and indeed with the whole system of life-phases which Valéry himself sometimes compares to the periodic return of the same configurations of stars. He speaks of a 'mémoire ou une résonance de nous-mêmes à longue échéance, qui nous rapporte, et nous vient nous rendre à l'improviste nos tendances, nos puissances et même nos espoirs très anciens' (*Œ*, I, pp. 1491–2).[10] A life seems to proceed thus, by a series of phases, marked off by inner crises. Apparently contradictory, these phases are at bottom repetitive or cyclical, each seeming to trigger its antipode or complement as it exhausts its dynamic and runs out.

This periodic rhythm will involve large time-spans, succeeding each other by the process of 'modulation' which the poet of *La Jeune Parque* shows to be the fundamental texture-in-time of the psyche; and yet, slow transition accelerating towards an abrupt and devastating resolution, this process by no means excludes dramatic upheavals: 'j'ai voulu renverser mon âme comme un sablier' ('I attempted to turn my soul upside down like an hour-glass') (*C*, VIII, p. 180), he says in 1921 (but the same image eloquently evokes all his life crises).

Equipped with these principles and perspectives, the biographer of the mind can dream of plotting, in Valéry's own footsteps, the

organic development of a life, a development woven out of an
alternating play of primary forces, in which 'events' figure merely as
points of emergence and cristallisation and through which we may
identify the constant forms constituting Valéry's crises and life-
choices.

Valéry's childhood already reveals the operative tensions characteristic of his easily changeable personality. He is visited, as he sees it,
with a sensibility which counts as his most cruel and detestable gift.
He is anxious and self-defensive, apparently passive and reserved,
yet conflictually divided and inclined to extremes by a native
violence within.

The analyst of the rubric 'Ego' stresses a fearful vulnerability and
self-mistrust, felt from his earliest years: 'si craintif, si peu sûr de moi
– si défiant' ('so fearful, so unsure of myself – so mistrustful') (*Ci*,
pp. 42–3). He points to his astonishment and anguish at all things
external to his subject-consciousness (p. 48); and he underlines in his
make-up a desperate tenderness, curiously conjoined to an icily
exterminating fury (p. 111). This engenders in turn a nostalgia for a
primal fusion, a refuge against elemental threat.

From the earliest years too comes Valéry's reactive, self-defensive
attitude: either through a flight to an extreme, to a 'geometrical
point', signifying an abrupt reversion to the 'inner island' or a
violent and instantaneous suppression by the mind of the non-self; or
else, more confrontationally, it involves an icily objectifying gaze and
a labour of analysis which strips down the all-too-obvious – hence,
contemptible and negligible – mechanism of things. Such, we may
think, are the original faces of Valéry's 'two angels', as presented in
the famous text of 'La Révélation anagogique' (*Œ*, II, pp. 466–67)
which summarises the conflictual logic of an existence: *Noûs* (the
angel of the Intellect, who pierces all things with intelligible light),
but also *Erôs* (the angel of Desire who seeks the highest intensity, the
most blissful self-surrender).

These are the two antagonistic forces which give Valéry's long life
its coherence and its substantial truth; these forces call forth all his
choices and strategies, and undergird his politics of attempted
recreation of the self. For, no less than what man is by nature, his
concern will be with what man wishes to be, with 'la *plasticité*
humaine' ('human plasticity') (*Œ*, II, p. 18). This is the stuff of
M. Teste, hero and patron of Valéry's ambition to recreate himself

by a decisive act, and to affirm himself as an 'être refait' ('a remade being') (*C*, XXI, p. 46).

## THE FOUNDING CRISIS AND THE 'GRAND SILENCE'

Adolescence brings a concealed crisis which accumulates its charge secretly, preparing the thunderbolt. Its first moment shows a re-investment of inner energies: the native religiosity of a spirit athirst for exaltation attempts, by means of flight towards poetic, liturgical or musical Beauty, to find a compensation for the loss of religious references and the fin-de-siècle eclipse of Transcendence. And yet there are signs of the accumulating revolt. Amid the languid poses of the 'decadent' angel, Valéry's correspondence betrays sudden stir-rings of savage violence: the dream of a barbarian horseman 'fauchant tout sur son passage' ('scything down everything in his path') or the vision of volleys of shots and blood 'parmi le choc d'une Europe folle et rouge' ('amid the shock of a mad, blood-red Europe') (*GV*, pp. 82–3).

The great initiating crisis of the twenty-first year, which finds its culmination in the mythically remembered 'Nuit de Gênes', trans-forms this violence born of despair into a critical force, turned back against the attitudes of the young aesthete himself. What is the good of repeating what others (Poe, Mallarmé, Rimbaud, Wagner, the Catholic mass) have already carried to perfection? Why commit oneself to published works, when what counts is the secretly creative power of the mind, barely glimpsed, and the mechanisms of a mastered generality? Beyond the refusal to write poetry, an entire domain of virgin territory opens up before his conquering pride. The challenge: to understand the real functioning of the mind, its hidden mechanics, with the rigour of mathematics, no longer allowing himself to be trapped, like the philosophers and psychologists before him, by the approximations of language; to possess, in short, the fullness of the great human Instrument, elucidated and mastered ...

The intellectual revolution would not have been so decisive without the 'absurd' crisis of feeling that went with it: the delirious obsession, threatening to disrupt the entire psychic machine, with a woman he had barely glimpsed and who remained unaware of his passion; and the humiliation and rage, in a mind inured to freedom, at its impotence to escape the irrationality of the imaginary, and the destructive reactions of the body. To shine the icy light of analysis into this chaos, uncompromisingly, shaking off all illusions, and treating as a mechanics the sacralised inwardness of the Self, is, no doubt, an enterprise of knowledge and power; but it is also a work of salvation and of inalienable liberty. If the Intellect is henceforth revered as sole Idol, it is because it alone opens up this neutral field, and this space of sovereignty; this 'anti-vie' also – 'ce qui est spirituel fut toujours mon anti-vie, mon anesthésique' ('spiritual things were always my antidote to life, my anaesthetic') (*C*, XXIII, p. 590). By way of compensation, the energies and the *élans* evoked by former gods are re-invested in mental manoeuvre.

'Je me sens autre ce matin' ('I feel other this morning') (*Œ*, II, p. 1435), concludes his account of the Nuit de Gênes; or at least, 'I would like to be other'. Later, he will discern more acutely the ambiguities of the new cult of Intellect, its secret 'magisme':

Mon mouvement le plus désespéré, le plus certain, fut celui qu'exprimait pour moi seul et sans autre rigueur, ces mots: tout par l'intelligence ... – Ce nom, quel sens s'y attachait? / Il est certain que j'appelais d'abord ainsi le pouvoir de changer l'eau en vin / ... la volonté de supprimer ces formations ... [qui] étaient contre moi / Il y avait quelque chose d'une religion dans ce propos (*C*, V, p. 903).[11]

The long period of strict intellectual withdrawal opens at this point: an exclusive face-to-face with his 'cahiers' and a form of writing austerely distant from the Word of symbolist poetry. By a deliberate self-mutilation, Valéry now devotes himself to the ascesis of pure research, taking up residence in an impregnable island and tasting the fierce joy of mastering, as science and as gymnastics, the springs of the mind. Gratuitously so, out of the pure pride of the virtuoso. What work could ever equal this Power privately enjoyed? It was not, he imagined, too high a price to pay for all the sacrifices made (career, reputation, 'charms' of life). For some twenty years, in the private space of the 'cahiers', with minor compromises, he pursued this ascesis, these intellectual manoeuvres of the dawn hour, these preparatory traces of the 'System', sometimes dreaming of the work of three or four pages in which would be concentrated the lightening-flash of an intellectual life.

And yet, when so intense a personality reduces himself deliberately to the exclusive exercise of the intellect, and to the quest for a closed and mechanical system, with its fictive potentiality, how should he escape a sense of suffocation, of impasse? The 'System' began to mark time. In 1908, by a telling overreaction, Valéry feared

he has been intellectually forestalled (*GV*, pp. 415–16):[12] from this
point the régimes of writing in the 'cahiers' will, progressively,
diversify and change (anticipating the sea-change of the return to
poetic composition from 1912). As the horizon of his half-century
comes within view Valéry's life seems played out and the profit and
loss account looks dismal enough. The letters of 1915 to Albert Coste
render a doleful sound: 'une sorte d'intime froid' ('an inward chill') is
taking over (*LQ*, 105). Nostalgia for all he has renounced sets in
unobserved. External circumstances will of course play their part in
inflecting the course of things; yet they answer a subterranean
distress call. When, following the composition and publication of *La
Jeune Parque*, the opportunities and constraints of life are once more
assumed, there will remain nonetheless the indelible imprint of a
twenty-year self-education and of a (necessary) faith in the 'System'.

### THE 'RETURN OF THE REPRESSED' AND THE CRISIS OF VALÉRY'S MATURITY

From before the war of 1914, it is clear that all that has been
repressed is beginning to re-appear in the penumbra of Valéry's
consciousness, finding embodiment first in the imaginary domain of
the work of art, but then inflecting the course of his lived experience.
*La Jeune Parque* may, in this respect, be read as a revealing psycho-
drama. Externally solicited (but also reconnecting with an activity of
his youth), the poem incorporates the contributions of chance,
proceeding deliberately from formal exigencies and researches, and
finds an apparently arbitrary conclusion. For all that, it finally takes
on a 'figure' (a look and pattern) which escape their author's control;
it leads him, so he tells us, where he did not think to go; and, finally,
it looks back at him in turn (*Œ*, I, p. 1633).

From the earliest of the manuscripts *La Jeune Parque*, opens with
the anguished questioning of an identity from which all is abstracted
or lost save the onset of tears; progressively, it takes shape as the
quest for a birth or, alternatively, as the founding lack of an essence.
It is a confidence vouchsafed by a divided self who sees from a
distance her conflictual moments, without recognising herself in any
of them, save perhaps in the vain nostalgia for a 'transparente mort',
a definitive evanescence. Finally, in a brusque and decisive reversal –
this is the new structure of the second 'Act', which asserts itself in
1916 – the Parque consents to the obscure upsurge of the vital

impulses which constrain her. After sleep, an awakening, set between these two polarities: Teste and a feminine figure torn away from the night.

The poetic writing of this figure invites the emergence, beneath the most consciously developed of procedures of verbal articulation, of a diffuse sensuality, showing stable patterns of symbolic association. What emerges through the writing, what is liberated by means of the 'music' (always linked by Valéry to 'analysis') is a certain type of physiologically-rooted lyric emotion that the poet-analyst will always speak of in terms of Voice. However 'formal' his theory of poetic composition, he will confess that poetry is essentially a taming, by the play of language, of a latent music, an 'état chantant'; it is the transposing into resonant musical sound of a certain affective tension. It is also a decisive tearing open by which the lucid being in us accepts from within what speaks in the body and in Desire.

The specific character of Voice, says Valéry, is to move towards 'ce quelqu'un qu'elle crée' ('this somebody it creates') (*MF* ms IV, fo. 32). A poem sketched around 1916, 'Ovide au milieu des Barbares',[13] shows the poet anxious to find someone who will hear; and 'l'Ange et les hommes', an unpublished text of 1923 (after the affective crisis), expresses retrospectively the sadness of the Angel enclosed in his ipseity, weary of hearing the monotonous birdsong which is the voice of life at its most mechanical, and trembling at the call of 'la fille des hommes' ('the daughter of men'), in wild nostalgia for the human condition he has spurned for so long. The love crisis of 1921 can only burst like a thunderclap.

'In mezzo del cammin'[14] ('In the middle of life's course') (*C*2, p. 459), the encounter, by a Valéry 'las, blessé des choses de l'esprit' ('weary, wounded by the things of the mind') (*C*, VIII, p. 751), with a woman of high culture and passionate sensibility, Catherine Pozzi ('Béatrice', 'K[arin]' or 'CK') was the most sudden of earthquakes. 'Si je me regarde historiquement, je trouve deux événements formidables dans ma vie secrète. Un coup d'état en 92 et quelque chose d'immense, d'incommensurable en 1920. J'ai lancé la foudre sur ce que j'étais en 92. Vingt-huit ans après, elle est tombée sur moi de tes lèvres' (*C*, VIII, p. 762).[15] A total revelation ensued: a 'soleil' experienced by the senses, the acutest of dialogues between intelligences ('cahiers' were exchanged), an explosion of creative euphoria; most of all, a revelation of unknown spiritual depths, of strange and infinite inner spaces inviting discovery upon discovery, and an irresistible fusion of selves torn free from the fatality of their separate essences. 'Quel état. Quelle étrangeté ... A la vérité, qui n'y a pas été ne connaît pas sa profondeur' (C2, 457).[16]

Almost immediately, however, the destructive work of failure began also: the clash of two over-intense personalities, the long agony of successive *ruptures* and disappointments; impotent rage, traversing blindly the obscure grotto of tears (C2, pp. 426–7), and leaving in its wake the ravaged field of a disaster beyond the human. 'Voilà, leur dit le Réel, voilà ce qui ne peut être. Brisez-vous la tête contre ma substance de granit'.[17]

Yet the aftershock of this double revelation – 'enfer et paradis' ('hell and paradise') (C, VIII, p. 751) – re-echoes throughout the second half of Valéry's thinking and writing existence, propagating its 'potentiel énorme' ('enormous potential') (C, XXIX, p. 755) which will invisibly modify an entire structure of 'values'. True, the intellect takes over the 'aventure en profondeur' ('adventure in depth'), associating its own exigencies and turning it into a quest which seeks, thanks to the detour of the other, the intensest form of oneself.

Henceforth Valéry recognises the centrality of *desire*, seeing here an absolute 'note' in the self-sentient being, something deeper than the intelligence which emanates from it and stands as a mere modality of it. He will find here also energies at once desired and feared which, for a time, he attempts to use by controlling them to demystify *amour-passion*, by separating them from the illusory object which, illegitimately, they hypostasise. Love could thus resign itself to becoming 'Eros énergumène' (cf. Œ, II, p. 291ff.) – a supplier of vital energies, which a certain donjuanism in Valéry is entirely ready to capture to his own advantage.[18] Music reclaims its rights; so does the former cult of Wagner, the technician – but also the magician – of the irrational. The 'soul' is re-introduced as a feeling of super-abundance of consciousness; so is a sort of experimentation in the register of mysticism – a mysticism 'sans Dieu', no doubt, but not without its sense of 'le divin' which acts as a secret orient of Desire. 'Je pense en rationaliste archipur. Je sens en mystique' ('I think as the purest rationalist. I feel as a mystic') (C, VII, p. 855). Such are the 'valeurs irrationnelles' ('irrational values') which were to have been the subject of the 'Dialogue des choses divines', begun in 1921 and never renounced in intention.

What returns is in fact an 'Anima' too long suppressed, bringing with it all the secret stirrings of desire and a passionate hearing of all the deliverances of an inner music; a music of dereliction, of wonder, of the multiform influx of life, of the magic of the body and its senses in their ever fragile adjustment to the world, of the feverish invasion of a sensibility impatient to raise itself to the acutest point of its capacity for resonance – a whole world of poetry indissociable from music and from *eros*, that feeds an abundant creative output with a new sap, breaking the sealed fountains of desire (cf. *JP*, l. 226).

*Charmes* had already benefited from this new rising, though not without strategies of intellectual control; the same sap henceforth infuses many a prose poem (in the *Cahiers*, in *Mélanges* (1939), in *Tel Quel* (1941–3), even in the posthumously published *Histoires brisées* (1950), where the text 'L'esclave' mystically hymns the senses. The pseudo-platonic framework of the *Dialogues* (apart from the conveniences and constraints it offers) provides, through its diverse voices, a theatre of action for these same forces, directly and indirectly expressed, and celebrates the happiness and wisdom of the body: hence, the exalted lyricism of creation in *Eupalinos* (1921), the final ecstasy of *L'Ame et la Danse* (1921), pitted against a fundamental *taedium vitae*. The unfinished *Alphabet*[19] traces the curve of lyric emotion throughout the course of a day, until the stupor and awe of Night.

The other great mutation which occurs after the publication of *La Jeune Parque*, is a 'return to the century', with its multiple expressions: sudden literary fame, first confined to a limited if influential circle, then, following Valéry's election to the Académie française in 1925, spreading throughout the literary salons of Paris, in which he discharged a sociability curiously conjoined to inner solitude. These acceptances led in turn to a career of tasks, posts and honours in which he played a quasi-official role as the Bossuet of the Third Republic; they led also to an intense activity as polygraphic intellectual and artist, burdened by commissions at which he groaned, yet undertook out of financial necessity, at the expense of the *œuvre vraie* of the 'cahiers'. Yet are these servitudes not also the liberation of a thinker who experiences the need to ballast himself with a definite content, risking communicative expression and finding in the manifold aspects of the world a pasture for a versatile and devouring mind, secretly sustained by the 'System'?

His published work distributes the small change of the *Cahiers* (including actual borrowings), but hardly ever the directing principles. From this source comes his career as incisive *moraliste*, one

who remembers Nietzsche (*Tel Quel, Mauvaises Pensées et autres* (1941))
and also his reflexions on modern science, which he no longer views
as a model of rigorous thought, but instead questions for its own
sake, as an intellectual and social phenomenon, a 'pouvoir' rather
than a 'savoir', and one which is modifying the condition of men
radically – yet to what end? Here Valéry encounters the problem of
civilisation and its values which is broached in his abundant
'political' output (including *Regards sur le monde actuel* (1931)). Pointing
to the contemporary ruin of the old fiduciary myths, these writings
ponder the future of the 'human Adventure' and the irruption,
aberrant in relation to life, constituted by the advent of mind, a
morally ambiguous power which threatens to lead us to catastrophe
if it cannot find within itself the means to offer new finalities to a
lucid, active and creative humanity.

Last but not least, in the essays of the *Variété* series (1924–44), in
the *Pièces sur l'Art* (1938), in many a preface, and in his public lectures
at the Collège de France (1937–45), Valéry offers a general theory of
creative activity, literary and artistic: he studies the conditions of any
'poïetics', and those of the work in itself, and in its relations to
'producer' and 'consumer'. The implicit frame of reference is that of
a future literature fully conscious of its means and ends.

The mind thus consents for a time to a sort of compromise with
reality, as though on guard against the threat emanating from within
itself. 'Rien ne mène à la parfaite barbarie plus sûrement qu'un
attachement exclusif à l'esprit pur' (*Œ*,II, p. 1251).[20] Praise of action,
in its various forms, succeeds the earlier *mystique* of non-manifesta-
tion, as a 'proof' of the mind's powers and as remedy against the
void of consciousness. Valéry himself showed the way; surmounting
his innate scepticism, he turned his hand to defining a 'politics of the
mind', which he pursued at the 'Centre méditerranéen de Nice', in
the committees of the Society of Nations at Geneva, at the 'Institut
de co-opération intellectuelle', in European conferences, and during
his lecture tours abroad.

Throughout this wide range of activity, a unity nevertheless
emerges: that of a method of analysis based on a fresh and direct
vision, a determination to promote the intellect in its material
conditions of exercise; that also of a persevering construction of the
self through the artistic objects which fashion it, just as it fashions
them. The myth of the 'homme d'Univers' is embodied in 1935 in
the *Discours sur Goethe* in which Valéry projects the image of a man

(more than of a mind) who, through all the experiences – amorous, political, scientific, poetic – that he has in turn taken up, integrated and abandoned, never ceases to edify himself, not as a separate consciousness, but as a human totality, pursuing like the Gœthean Tree of the *Metamorphosis of Plants* the obstinate law of its 'entelechy'.

## THE FINAL CRISIS

Around 1935, at the height of his official celebrity, Valéry seems to reach a relative serenity, resting on the universality of his omni-active thought. In fact, this 'midi de l'esprit' was fissured by his self-destructive extremism and the anguish secreted by the mind itself. History-in-the-making brought increasing desolation; his scorn grew for the *débâcle* of contemporary civilisation; former cultures at least had an art of living. He saw old demons and new disorders preparing a conflagration which the efforts of intellectuals seemed absurdly impotent to check. He registered bitterly the failure of the intellectual co-operation which had fleetingly engaged him. The human Adventure appeared to be returning purely and simply to barbarism; and the Mind to be acting, after all, as a destructive force serving a blind death-wish.

Unable to save humanity, the Mind could not even quieten the anguish of the thinker. Acute awareness of ageing, increasing fatigue, the disturbing collapse of his ever-fragile health, were merely aggravated by a singular disaffection for the gratuitous play of thought, turning round and round in the same goldfish-bowl. Everything had, once already, conspired to bring about – but now in the mode of a bitter 'trop tard' – a new love-crisis, beginning in 1932. 'Te revoilà, coïncidence. Exquisite torsion et tension de l'être' (*C*2, pp. 501–2).[21] In a great west wind, amid the melancholy of autumn, season par excellence of Valéryan dereliction, had come the headlong need for the Other who might warm the inner chill of body and spirit. This time, the object of passion was a young sculptress (Renée Vauthier, 'Néère', 'NR') who declined him and forced Valéry to 'regarder le jamais plus en face' ('face up to the nevermore') (*C*2, p. 1228). A tender and desolate correspondence followed; so too did the project of a tragedy of classical technique, in which, in the fictional guise of King Seleucus who dramatically renounces his younger wife Stratonice, Valéry seeks to recover the grand Wagnerian music of the fateful and fated farewell, expressing the devastating loss of love and of the *vis viva* of youth. The same exacerbated anguish underlies the dizzying brio of *L'Idée fixe* (1932), in which the precipitously zigzagging conversational exchange exists in order to snatch the mind from its obsession.

Increasingly, Valéry the thinker is conscious of having circumnavigated what there is to be known and taken the measure of its nothingness. What comes to dominate, then, is the obsessive theme of 'non revivre' ('not living again'), of 'l'une fois pour toutes' ('once and for all'). Everything points to a new and radical crisis, an ultimate turning point. The disturbing approach, the onset of the war of 1939, in which he foresees the collapse of European civilisation, his despair at his fellow-humans who 'know not what they do' (the sombre conclusion of the last great public statement, the *Discours sur Voltaire* in 1944), all summon up a will to universal liquidation.

To have done with things, means – outrunning the general holocaust glimpsed on the horizon, and under pressure from his own shrinking span of life – to attempt to realise the ever-deferred synthesis of thought, a 'dernière pensée' summarising a lifetime of approaches. Never did Valéry's intellectual activity appear more intensive or his 'cahiers' more numerous and more dense. His writing projects pick up abortive attempts of his youth; the decisive essay expressing his debt to Mallarmé, 'Apocalypte Teste', concluding the Teste cycle with the revelation of Thought without object, killing its possessor . . . There is a late return to poetry, set off by a commissioned translation of the *Bucolics*, and producing in the *Cantate du Narcisse* a twilight echo of Valéry's most central theme, and the *Dialogue de l'Arbre* (1943), which gives alternating expression to the two voices, analytical and sensual, which co-exist in him.

Pre-eminently, however, it is the vast project of a 'Third Faust' which was intended to give form to the ambition of a definitive Book, unique in itself, in which would be delivered the essence of a life and its thought. Valéry had for years envisaged, although vaguely, a grand cycle uniting all dramatic forms, a work both polymorphous and unitary. Science, morality, politics would have their place, as would prose and verse, in this final reckoning of a life, and of human life as such – Faust-Valéry, first and last Man, recapitulatively assuming the Adventure which he would carry to its nihilistic conclusion.

Now comes a last affair of the heart, developing from 1938, contemporaneously with this project. Born of Valéry's generalised disgust for all Else, it restored presence and fascination to the hope, several times entertained, several times blasted, of a communion in love: a last tenderness from which he attempted in vain to protect himself, but which, progressively, submerged him to the point of delirium. His partner, a pragmatic, younger, career woman, Mme Jean Voilier, reciprocated only prudently.

Over against the will to have done with the painful illusion of life emerges the delirious thirst for a fusion of sensibilities, which Valéry's experience had always shown to be doomed to failure. This dramatic inner tension organises *Mon Faust*, a Faust no longer Gœthe's, but instead the most confidential and the most conflictual *alter ego* of a Valéry come to the extreme point of himself.

Fleeing the German invasion of 1940, morally crushed, Valéry took refuge for a few months at Dinard in Brittany. From his urgent attempt to escape the present moment emerged the entirely impro- vised first two Acts of the comedy *Lust* and Act I and the 'Intermède' of *Le Solitaire*. As with the *Idée fixe*, the shimmering play of ideas attempts to mask weightier concerns which nevertheless show through. Realising that this casual brio was at odds with the developments he already foresaw, Valéry notes: 'Tout ce qu'il y a d'imprimé est à reprendre dans les deux pièces'.[22] That he allowed himself in 1941 to be persuaded by bibliophile friends to publish these first 'ébauches', merely bespeaks his indifference towards them. Meanwhile, in his private laboratory, drafts, analyses, plans poured from his pen, keeping him mentally busy during the years of anguish and privation endured in occupied Paris. His *Faust* becomes the great 'work in progress', acquiring in its development a new weight of seriousness and lyric exaltation, in conformity with the rising intensity of the last amorous passion.

Initially, *Lust* and *Le Solitaire* seemed to open up two competing ways out of the Valéryan impasse: acceptance of a temperate and cautious tenderness uniting Faust's sovereign lucidity with an over- transparent 'demoiselle de cristal'; but also, a final 'Non!' thrown in the face of the universe, violently settling old scores with 'toute la Blague de l'Etre et du Non-Etre' ('the whole farce about Being and Non-Being') (*C*, XXIV, p. 673). ('Malédictions d'univers' is the sub- title of *Le Solitaire*, with its terrible vociferations uttered by a singular Old Man of the Mountain, a kind of rabid Zarathustra who casts Faust into the bottom of the abyss.)

These two competing dramatic hypotheses still show the twin

faces of a sensibility divided between its 'icy fury of extermination' and its 'infinitely tender tenderness'; specifically, they show Valéry's 'singularité de sensation intellectuelle et de sentiment tendre dans leur mélange et leur excès' (*MF* ms IV, fo. 128).[23] In practice, as Valéry explored these two hypotheses, both carried forward in tandem, the unseen linkage between them illumined and elucidated the sense of their apparently contradictory intentionalities and seems to settle the final word of a life lived.

Originally, the fourth Act of *Lust* was to have broken down, painfully, with grimly determined lucidity, the last illusory spells capable of holding Faust to existence: an existence which had, in all senses, 'exhausted' the temptation of passionate love and the infinity of its desire. It would have made out of a transfigured Lust an appeal to realise a life transcending life, a call to achieve a climax of two sensibilities mysteriously harmonised; only to show Faust, 'trop lucide', gently but implacably setting aside this temptation. 'Grande scène', notes Valéry, 'pathétique, adieux avec larmes' ('grand scene ... pathos, farewell in tears'); the model being, once again, Act 3 of *Die Walküre*, the scene representing the irremediable separation of Wotan – who renounces all in this supreme effort – from Brunne-hilde, daughter, lover, perfectly consonant and complementary *imago* of her father. This conclusion is, oddly, quite compatible with the third Act planned for *Le Solitaire*, which brings the strangest of mystically exalting transformations. In the depths of the abyss, the terrible Old Man, who has become all tenderness, revives Faust after his fall, only to reveal his true face: that of Faust himself, or rather, of the 'Moi pur' in Faust, the self which has observed the fading of life through its vicissitudes and has restored the purity of Faust's essence of desire; a self freed from all illusions and who, in a monologue where words catch fire, rises up one last time to cast his fullest, most devastating light in the very instant of his extinction.

The secret tenor of Valéry's own 'mystique sans Dieu' would thus have been affirmed in the grandiose and resonant idiom of myth: the need to touch some extreme, some fulguration, some ultimate 'note' of the sensibility of desire; a mysticism invented by a sensibility with no respondent in the world, lacking a Trancendence – since his rigorous critique is wont to reduce to illusion all claimants – and which had invested itself entirely in this alternative myth of the 'Moi pur'. Such is indeed the central point of Valéryan consciousness: the propensity to deny in turn each of its contingent and limited objects, the better to affirm its own inalienable presence; a mysticism of the 'Singular-Universal', fascinating yet fraught with menace, since it seemed to border on the horrified sensation of nothingness.

At precisely this point, the work took a new turn and changed direction radically, with a reversal of the fourth Act, undoing its determined obsession with 'not beginning again'. Lifted in turn by the lyrical current rising in its author, Faust answers the appeal of an increasingly sublime Lust; he abdicates his destructive lucidity and acknowledges the dream of an 'état béatifique d'échange' ('blissful state of exchange') (*C*2, p. 431), the secret pole towards which, throughout his life, he had been falling, his obscure 'ligne d'univers' ('direction of universality'). For the music of suffering inspired by the end of *Die Walküre* is substituted the rising curve of *Tristan*. The unfinished fourth Act,[24] forgetting the world and its all-too-human conclusions, offers suspended 'moments' of time, a hypnotic duo, a form of desire exacerbated to the limit of a cry: these superb fragments of a final mystico-lyrical starburst seem, in their very incompletion, to wish to carry language to some ecstatic beyond. We hear the angel *Erôs* at last victorious over *Noûs*, or rather, these two *élans* henceforth indistinguishable.

Such a transcendent hope was soon to be dashed by the treachery of the real Other, and Valéry did not survive the shock of it. Of all the inner voices of the Mind, the Heart and the Body which had in turn spoken so powerfully in him, in secret confrontation and in unexpected reversal – voices which his *œuvre*, so mistakenly reputed to be wholly intellectual – had not ceased to stage, there remained finally nothing more than the suffering which weighs down the final pages of the *Cahiers*.

Nothing remains but the gaping discrepancy between the assured, modestly self-justified intelligence, enclosed within its refringent sphere of self-seizure, and this painful irrationality, signified by the rising of tears from the depths of the deep, dark, all-powerful ground of the psyche. This is the tenor of the last of the writings, a short prose poem *L'Ange*, begun during the crisis of 1921 and now completed. The Intellect to which Valéry had appealed as a way of cancelling out reality, of giving himself the illusion of being an impersonal and incorruptible being, came to grief, at the last, on the reefs of desire and of death.

'Qui pleure là?' the Parque had asked on her awakening. At the end, the transparent consciousness of the Angel questions his own face in the mirror of the fountain; it is bathed in tears, mysteriously sprung from a source or sources unknown.[25]

NOTES

1 This question is more than theoretical: together with Mme Florence de Lussy, Mlle Jeannine Jallat and M. Jean Levaillant, M. Bastet is engaged in research for a biography, increasingly felt as necessary in Valéry studies (Editors' note).
2 'this powerful effect is only to be obtained by acccusing oneself of all the horrors and abominations a man ever thought of'
3 'I have said time and again that these memoirs are not memories, and that I hold what I imagine to be as worthy to be ME as what was and what I consider doubtful'
4 'and anyway, I reckon it is a kind of falsification to separate the most abstract thought from the most ... lived life'
5 Oral testimony given to the author by Mme Jean Voilier, model and inspiration for Faust's secretary, Lust.
6 See Œ, II, pp. 1507–38.
7 'I am not writing and have never written the journal of my days. I note my ideas. What does my biography matter to me? Of what interest to me are my spent days?'
8 Denis Bertholet, *Paul Valéry* (Paris, Plon, Coll. 'Biographies', 1995).
9 'Robespierre had never imagined he would guillotine so many people – nor Leonardo that he would love'. The latter name is probably a reference by Valéry to himself, 'Lionardo' being the pseudonym he bears in the relationship with Catherine Pozzi.
10 'a long-range memory or resonance of ourselves which brings back and suddenly restores to us our tendencies, our powers and even our very old hopes'
11 'My most desperate, most certain instinct, was that expressed for myself alone and without any other sanction in rigour, by the words: everything by intelligence ... – What sense did I attach to this noun? / Certain it is that what I first called by this name was the power to change water into wine / ... the determination to eliminate those formations ... which were against me / There was something of a religion in this purpose'
12 The origin of this impression remains a teasing enigma. One hypothesis envisaged by the editors of the 'integral' edition of the *Cahiers* is that Valéry may be reacting to a review registering the appearance in a French translation of a work by Ernst Mach, *La Connaissance et l'erreur* (Paris, Flammarion, 1908). Another candidate is an article by Pierre Duhem reviewing Abel Rey's thesis, 'La théorie physique' (See *Revue générale des sciences pures et appliquées*, January 1908.)

13 For a genetic study of this important manuscript, see H. Laurenti, ed., *Paul Valéry 'Ovide chez les Scythes'. Etude génétique d'un manuscrit de Paul Valéry par le groupe Paul Valéry de l'ITEM (CNRS)*, (Montpellier, Centre d'études du XXe siècle, 1997).

14 Allusion to the opening line in Dante's *Inferno*, 'Nel mezzo del cammin di nostra vita'.

15 'If I look at myself historically, I find two formidable events in my secret life. A coup d'état in 1892 and something immense, immeasurable, in 1920. I cast the thunderbolt on what I was in 92. Twenty-eight years later, it fell back upon me from your lips'.

16 'What a state. What a strange thing .... Truly, anyone who has not been there does not know his own depth'.

17 'There, says Reality, that is what cannot be. Now break your head on my granite substance' (ms dossier 'Orphée', Bibliothèque nationale).

18 The unpublished notebook 'Agar, Sophie Rachel' (Bibliothèque nationale) reflects significantly on this aspect of Valéry.

19 This text was published in a limited edition by Agathe Rouart-Valéry (Paris, Blaizot, 1976) and re-published in a dual-language (French-Italian) edition by Marina Giaveri (ed.), *Paul Valéry, Alphabet* (Pisa, Diabasis, 1993).

20 'Nothing leads to perfect barbarity more surely than an exclusive attachment to pure mind'

21 'There you are again, coincidence. Exquisite torsion and tension of being'

22 'Everything published is to be re-done in both plays'. For a full genetic account see my chapter 'Ulysse et la sirène', in A. Rouart-Valéry and J. Levaillant (eds.), *Cahiers Paul Valéry 2, 'Mes Théâtres'* (Paris, Gallimard, 1977).

23 'singularity of intellectual sensation and of tender feeling in their mixture and their excess'.

24 Extracts of Act 4 have been published in *Cahiers Paul Valéry 2, 'Mes Théâtres'*, pp. 51–88.

25 For further reading on the topic of this chapter, please see Bibliography, items 6, 7, 10, 18, 25, 39, 40, 61, 86, 104, 114, 129.

# CHAPTER 2

# Thinking-writing games of the 'Cahiers'

PAUL GIFFORD

'C'est à l'univers qu'il songe toujours, et à la rigueur' ('His constant thought is of everything and of rigour') (*Œ*, I, p. 1155): Valéry's characterisation of Leonardo's notebooks exactly prefigures his own *Cahiers*. Any one of the twenty-nine volumes of the in-facsimile edition opened at random (and even more so, the 26,600 pages of the series as a whole), attests a radicalism and a range of intellectual curiosity for which nothing else in twentieth century writing quite prepares us.

The mind-shift required in adjusting to the universalist vocation can be disconcerting, particularly if we open the 'difficult' early *Cahiers* (pre-1900) which plot the heroic beginnings of Valéry's 'System'. Algebraic equations attempting to model mental functioning jostle on the page with critical remarks on traditional psychology or philosophy or language science. The analysis of common mental operations invokes a strangely abstract imagery drawn from classical physics (force fields, crystals, degrees of symmetry, actions at a distance, reasoning by recurrence, 'ether'). These operations in turn connect, by subterranean webs of association, to analyses of Napoleon's exercise of power; or else, to remarks on dreaming or mysticism or the sexual act or the experience of battle as depicted in Stephen Crane's novel of the American Civil War, *The Red Badge of Courage*. Or they call up, within the sphere of abstraction, fleeting fragments of prose poetry or intellectual autobiography.

Visibly, the plurality of the possible forms and dimensions of intelligible mental space beckons to the young analyst, as to some kind of momentous awakening: 'Penser en algèbre, en Anglais, en politique, en marin, en poète, — en ornemaniste, en tout cela — en quelconque — en animal, en arbre — en pianiste, / C'est *aussi* exister dans un certain espace à q dimensions' (*CII*, p. 201).[1]An

Adventure has begun, daunting to the reader – but first of all to the writer himself – in its audacity and reach.

The mind itself is taken as the maker of all acts, all meanings. What can we know of this central, enigmatic instigator and orderer of the entire universe of representation within which we live and move and have our being? How far can we master it? A vast part of the intellectual life of the twentieth century in fact obeys the same curvature of psychologist reflexivity, the same persuasion of questioning and mastery. Here it is announced with the resolute simplicity of a set of founding axioms. 'L'esprit est le lieu géométrique ... de tout ce qu'il connaît' ('The mind is the geometric point ... of everything it knows') (*CI*, p. 67). 'La science des formes de l'esprit contient toute connaissance' ('The science of mental forms contains all knowledge') (*C*, I, p. 825). 'Ne cherche pas la "vérité" — Mais cherche à développer ces forces qui font et défont les vérités' (*C*I, p. 328).[2]

Consciousness of mental operations and of mind-body functioning is the key to the universe of the mind. There is a paradox or tension here, the first of many we shall come to recognise as characteristic of the texture of the *Cahiers* as a whole. For all his omnivorous reading, for all his unequalled range of eminent interlocutors in so many fields, Valéry's universalist vocation refers to an intimate, jealously guarded private practice of thought centred on the thinking-writing subject and his own resources. It passes, that is, through the acutest and most energetic particularity.

The unique character of the *Cahiers* as written document reflects this founding singularity. Uncompromisingly, these notebooks represent the antipode of the standard literary enterprise of writing for public consumption: 'Ici je ne tiens à charmer personne' ('Here, I'm not out to please anyone') (*CI*, p. 180). Writing here signifies the ethic of a research vocation espoused with radical integrity and recalled with terse insistence: 'Les autres font des livres. Moi, je fais mon esprit' ('Other people make books. I am making my mind') (*C*I, p. 30); 'Seule, la recherche — vaut la peine' ('Only research — is worthwhile') (*CI*, p. 277). Rather than as *journal intime* or as register of personal reflexions, the document itself is epitomised by the set of marine names given to the first four original 'cahiers' of 1894–6: fundamentally, all constitute the 'log book' of an immense journey of discovery of the mind, creating its own instruments of navigation, its own bearings and charts, its own observations, its own soundings, its own record of progress towards the unvisited 'extrême nord humain ... dernier point intelligible — imaginable' ('the extreme human North ... furthest intelligible — imaginable point') (p. 277). The handwriting – spidery, tense and irregular in the formative period until 1900 – settles thereafter into an amazingly regular, fine, legible copperplate; within which affective winds and storms nonetheless leave eddying traces, and voices of the deeper subject re-echo. Classificatory tables of all sorts, graphics, doodles, and, in the notebooks of Valéry's maturity, sumptuous water-colours (like those recording the poet-analyst's journey on board a cruiser of the French Mediterranean fleet from Toulon to Brest in 1925) attest the interaction with concrete imagination which the abstractive intellect seeks, and increasingly finds.

The document is essentially discontinuous. It is formed of hundreds of thousands of textual fragments, ranging from the most allusively or aphoristically brief to the sustained, recapitulative developments of two or three pages which figure in the later notebooks. All are idiosyncratically punctuated and paragraphed. Vigorous dashes articulate the often delicate and complex structures of thought, as in some gigantic mental 'draft copy', delivering spontaneous – but pre-focused and highly practised – pulses of self-dictated thinking. Erasures, variants, linking loops and marginal additions improvise continuity within and between fragments; they allow the writing hand to inscribe the darting mind, and hint at the strategy of review and dogged repetition which we shall come to see as central to Valéry's heuristic practice. There is total disconcern for surface continuities or transitions between fragments; one of the standing enigmas of the *Cahiers* is how and why the *scriptor* comes to think what he thinks in the attested sequence.

The fragmentary character of the notebooks is one of the greatest challenges to acquired habits of reading. Yet it is also the key to the endless fascination of this unique document. The Valéryan fragment is a natural pulse or unit of mental energy: enough to stimulate, enrich and direct the mind without exhausting it. Rewarding in its own right, it avoids closure in the guise of rigid development – something Valéry most deeply mistrusted in systems and ideologies. The mind, in his view, is authentic only in its rebounding, ever-renewed, always unfinished act; as achieved totality of understanding, it overreaches and falsifies itself. At the same time, as we come to know the thought of the *Cahiers* more intimately, the patterns of interconnection between fragments reveal an underlying consistency that is both massively coherent and immensely supple in operation; we begin to see and to savour the unitary mind informing the cosmos of fragments. Yet the fragmentary text still leaves us free to pick our own pathways of reading, to see our own patterns of interconnection and to establish our own dialogue with that informing mind. What is true of many modern works thus applies pre-eminently and in principle to this one: to read is to participate in making the text that is read, in the genesis of its ever-provisional sense-making.

These proliferating fragments, and the mounting pile of notebooks to which they were consigned, came inevitably to impose on Valéry some form of practical *a posteriori* systematisation. We know that three attempts at classification were made, with a view to consti-tuting a potential synthesis or sum, which might be putatively publishable. The first, in 1898, sought to consolidate the acquisitions of method and problematics of the formative years. The second in 1908, involved for the first time an attempt to revise and retype the accumulated mass of notes, and to classify them thematically. The last and most significant, begun in 1921 and carried on, with the help of successive secretaries until his death, generalised the typing and revision of the corpus and introduced a more comprehensive system of classification following the – by now classic – thirty-one subject rubrics. These same rubrics figure thereafter as 'sigles' identifying the themes of the work in progress; they are a valuable reading guide as we observe them in the in-facsimile CNRS edition, and they form the basis of the Pléiade selection.

Such attempts at classification never, within Valéry's own lifetime, reached the point of constituting a systematised sum delivered to the public. The material difficulty of processing the oceanic corpus of fragments was of course immense; Valéry famously lamented the lack of 'un Allemand qui achèverait mes idées' ('a German to finish off my ideas') (*C1*, p. 69). Even more inhibiting were the sacrifices involved in any determinate editing and ordering of the rubrics of his thought. The ethico-spiritual root of the matter lies, perhaps, in Valéry's Testian horror of self-publication. The whole notion of appearing before others in his most vitally authentic persona mobilised in reaction against it the nexus of dynamic instincts at work in his intellectual adventure as whole: acute perfectionism, proud singularity, a deep mistrust of the impurity involved in all 'anxiety of influence'; above all, an incoercible preference for the mind's potential over its actuality. No doubt there was also a fear of incomprehension, even a reluctance to expose himself to the same fiercely depreciatory judgments with which, in the privacy of his own laboratory of thought, he himself so readily demolishes the greatest minds. Certainly, we may discern a jealous intimacy or *pudeur*, with which he guarded his most valued treasure and potent secret weapon. Judith Robinson-Valéry is surely right in asserting that the *Cahiers* remained finally unsystematised, incomplete and unpublished for intrinsic, rather than contingent reasons.[3] They are 'des contre-œuvres, des contre-fini' ('counter-works', 'counter-finites') (*C*, XX, p. 678).

It would be a misjudgment of some magnitude, however, to conclude that this constitutes a 'failure' to systematise and publish; or that the lack of an authorially systematised sum diminishes the centrality, the importance or even the ultimate vocation to publication Valéry himself attributed to this reserved and ever-renewed work-in-progress. Precisely the reverse is true. For their self-writing subject, the *Cahiers*, constitute, rather than mere 'œuvres', the *Grand-Œuvre* itself, 'seul fil de ma vie, seul culte, seule morale, seul luxe, seul capital, et sans doute placement à fonds perdu' (*LQ*, p. 70).[4] At the most practical level, his notebooks packed into their famous grey postal sacks, were designated as the only objects to be saved, in case of bombardment or evacuation, in two wars – their possible loss judged an irreparable catastrophe. In the economy of a thinking life, they are strategically central; all else Valéry wrote and published is in some sense or other relative to his laboratory of self-cognisant thought: an application, a derivation, an annexe, an antidote, or an extract. We may be cautious, too, of drawing from his ironic self-depreciations the notion that the great investment might be literally misplaced or wasted. In the fear and trembling of the heroic beginnings of 1894, a strangely tenacious self-belief already persuades Valéry of his trail-blazing significance: 'Je travaille pour quelqu'un qui viendra après' ('I am writing for someone who will come after me') (*CI*, p. 60). That belief never wavered. In 1945, in the hour of his final summation reviewing a life-time of pure thought – 'pure' not only in its modality of perpetual lucidity, but in its uncompromising and sacrificial dedication to a supreme value – he writes movingly: 'ce que j'ai trouvé d'important — *je suis sûr de cette valeur* — ne sera pas facile à déchiffrer de mes notes' (*C*, XXIX,

p. 908).[5] The epic dimensions of the *Cahiers* – like the unfinished and unfinishable task of systematisation – indicate a universe of thought expanding over 50 years, an Odyssey in the cosmos of ideas and of mental forms.

It is a well-known part of the 'mythology' surrounding the unique document that the notebooks have their own space-time, the privileged interval 'entre la lampe et le soleil', from 5 to 7 o'clock (sometimes 4 or 3.30 to 8). The moment has its own lyrical charge, nourishing the 'aubades' or dawn songs of Valéry's 'poésie brute'. It also has its own pervasive logic of analogy and symbolism: the thought of the *Cahiers* is entirely described as a thought of awakening, of the coming of light and of the elucidation of the genesis in mind of the universe of the human subject or self. In terms of other metaphors used by their author, we may speak also of 'exercises' (*CIV,* p. 40) in awakening, or 'daily scales' (*C1*, p. 13) in the music of awakening: such are the metaphors used of the 'culture psychique sans objet entre 5 et 7' ('gratuitous mental fitness-training between 5 and 7') (*C1*, p. 10). Without object, that is, save perhaps the greatest: the analytical unfolding to conscious understanding of everything that is implied in 'mind' – that is, in the human psyche as such, with its inevitable axes and unfailing Valéryan correlatives of body and world (the famous 'C-E-M' of the *Cahiers* proclaims: 'Je suis corps, esprit et monde' ('I am body, mind and world') (cf. *C2*, pp. 853; 1119–49, etc.).

Perhaps we may think of the *Cahiers* as a strikingly singular sub-set of what Wittgenstein, in his *Philosophical Investigations* calls 'language games', and refers, pertinently, to the 'activities' or 'forms of life' which generate and explain them. The name of the most central thinking-writing game pursued in Valéry's dawn voyages is enunciated thus: 'Se servir agilement, sciemment et méthodiquement de son Moi comme origine de coordonnées universelle' (*CIV,* p. 108).[6] In one sense, the game is simple: 'Ma méthode, c'est moi. / Mais moi récapitulé, reconnu' ('My method is me. / But me summarised, recognised') (*C1*, p. 125); 'Mes deux questions: Que peut un homme? Comment cela 'marche-t-il?' ('My two questions: What is a man capable of? How does it 'work'?') (*C1*, p. 105). Certainly, the guiding idea has the simplicity of the great *évidences*: 'on ne pense pas éveillé plus souvent qu'endormi on ne rêve' ('people do not think when awake more often than they dream when asleep') (*CI*, p. 71). Yet what is implied in this design, and in the subject it elucidates, is a whole universe of questions which fifty years and 26,600 pages only begin to draw out; it is truly the unending text ...

The different modes and registers of writing to be found in the *Cahiers* suggest further 'sub-sets' of this activity, and help to outline the different but interlocking dimensions of the experiment / experience in train. What follows is an attempt to offer a novel typology of the writing and to reveal a 'pensée en acte'. The guidance offered here will, it is hoped, enable the reader to situate many of the themes to be treated later in the present volume in the perspective of the overall coherence they find within Valéry's enterprise as now understood.

(i) The first sub-set of the 'thinking-writing games' pursued in the *Cahiers* is that of a *functionalist psychology*, representing with scientific precision and objectivity the mechanisms of mind-body functioning. 'Mon idée est simple. Je suis sûr qu'il y a une mécanique de l'esprit dont dépend tout — de sorte que tout doit pouvoir s'exprimer en termes de fonctionnement' (*C*, XXVII, p. 216).[7] 'Comme l'homme respire, se meut, digère, ainsi doit-il sentir, connaître et penser' (*C1*, p. 809).[8] 'Mon système est une tentative de réduire en théorie de transformations (la plus générale) tout ce que nous pouvons nous représenter de l'*esprit* — et par là — de *tout*' (*C*, XXVI, p. 611).[9]

The primary horizon, leaving its traces in the algebraic equations, the models and concepts drawn from physics, and the extreme abstraction of style of the early *Cahiers*, was, historically, that of a calculus modelling the mind exactly. Hence the vaulting dream of 1897, moderating its claims subsequently, but never quite renounced in desire: 'essayer de construire la gamme et le système d'accords dont la pensée sera la musique' (*C1*, p. 334).[10] Mathematics in its purest branch is espoused as providing an ideal language: as offering to represent in purely formal terms, abstracted from the particular acts and contents of our mental life, that system of variations and transformations which, observably, constitutes subject-consciousness. 'Je pose que: La Science mathématique dégagée de ses applications ... réduite à l'algèbre, c'est-à-dire à l'analyse des transformations d'un être purement différentiel, c.-à-d., composé d'éléments homogènes — est le plus fidèle document des propriétés de groupement, de disjonction et de variation *de l'esprit*' (*ibid.*, p. 80).[11]

As an ideal, this guiding idea is far from absurd. Highly complex and irregular phenomena in nature, such as sunspots and the growth of cancerous tumours, are today successfully plotted by mathematical modelling. Why not, one day, human consciousness perceived as functional metamorphosis, differential, 'self-variance'? Yet the youthful inventor of the 'System' was, in this latter respect, precociously over-ambitious. Technically, he was unequal to the task of reducing mental functions (perception, imagination, memory, attention, dreaming, expecting, inventing, knowing, responding to poetry or music, etc.) to a set of rigorously homogeneous abstract data capable of being expressed algebraically; nor was his self-taught competence in algebraic calculus always equal to the advanced operations required.

Mathematics, for which his intelligence was nonetheless acute, leaves in his thinking a series of concepts which were analogically useful to him, together with a model of precise rigour exemplary for all intellectual acts. More secretly, it bequeaths an imprint of imaginative potency. Valéry is abidingly haunted by an epistemological form: that of the patterns of recurrence discernable in things, which can be 'integrated' into 'sets' admitting in turn of an 'invariant'. The form itself of the equation $(x + \ldots = 0)$ beckons like a semi-mythical symbol of epistemological closure and the promise of infinite self-awareness. 'La mathématique pure est une sorte de préfigure, de promesse et de modèle de l'état bienheureux de tous les possibles de l'esprit' (*C*, XII, p. 405).[12] A godlike power of lucidity would be self-coincident and self-cancelling, making the subject of consciousness equal to its own enigma ...

After 1900, the leading concepts of this same act of modelling or representation of mental phenomena are drawn rather from thermodynamics, like the fruitful idea of the 'phases' of consciousness (expressing the change of state through which we pass in moving, for instance, between sleep and waking) or the 'action complète' (describing the cycle accomplished by the psychic equivalents of such physiological functions as sexual arousal and release). In Valéry's maturity, such tools of representation and analysis are drawn from relativity theory, and, increasingly, from the living processes of physiology and biology. The style of the thinking-writing game is accordingly more imaged, concrete, 'realistic'; and Valéry's functional psychology itself becomes more self-relativising, a play of alternative metaphors and points of view. Throughout his life, Valéry continued to seek new instruments of analysis and representation. In a note of 1937 (*C*, XX, p. 291), he lists some fifteen theories, concepts and images which time has shown as successful contributions to the representational model he never ceased to explore and perfect. Always, the aim is to represent with adequate precision – rather than to 'explain' – the real functioning (observable or probable) of the body-mind-world continuum of human consciousness, considered as a finite system whose properties, acts, operations and potential are expressed in specialised but recognisable ways in whatever domain of human activity might be considered.

(ii) 'Grosso modo le Système a été la recherche d'un langage ou d'une notation qui permettrait de traiter de omni re comme la géométrie analytique de Des Cartes a permis de traiter toutes figures' (C1, p. 812).[13] The second subset of the 'thinking-writing games' of the *Cahiers* may be characterised as a *generalised psycho-poetics of the products of the mind*. Complete or incomplete, absolute or relativistic, Valéry's method of modelling body-mind functioning precisely provides a powerfully consistent method of examining all products of thought and culture in the perspective of their mental genesis. It is a formidable machine, if not for answering all problems, at least for revealing the hidden conditions and possibilities of our unthinking acts and for asking the ever-pertinent question. Consider the following notes, which figure respectively under the rubrics 'Psychology' and 'Eros': 'l'idée de *phase* est celle de possibilité immédiate' ('the idea of phases is that of immediate possibility') (C, XXVI, p. 401); '[l'amour] est le seul échantillon de mystique que tous ou presque tous connaissent (C2, p. 490).[14] Or this note from 'Poetics':

L'œuvre est une modification de l'auteur. A chacun des mouvements qui la tirent de lui, il subit une altération. Et quand elle est achevée, elle réagit encore une fois sur lui. Il se fait (par exemple) celui qui a été capable de l'engendrer. Il reconstruit en quelque sorte un formateur de l'ensemble réalisé, qui est un mythe – / De même un enfant finit par donner à son père, l'idée et comme la forme de la paternité (C, VI, p. 818).[15]

What is 'readiness', mobilisation for effective action? Is love – or do we mean 'passion'? – to be defined as a physiological need multiplied, in psychic refraction, by a form of mysticism? What does it mean to affirm authorship or paternity? If the thinker of the *Cahiers* so often shows piquancy, pertinence and savour, this is because he refers us with an unrivalled immediacy and precision, cutting through the often floundering verbalism of many legions of 'specialists', to the point in ourselves at which genuine problems arise. 'Mon objet est de faire penser — et de me faire penser moi-même, — à des choses auxquelles on ne pensait pas à cause de leur présence ou trop proche ou perpétuelle, — c'est-à-dire, de leur importance même' (*C*, XXIV, p. 876).[16]

(iii) The third, closely related sub-set of the thinking-writing activity pursued in the *Cahiers* is that of a *hermeneutic and critical reflection*, rethinking concepts, ideas, doctrines and theories from all horizons (and all time-zones) of the cultural mind-space. This game is frequently devastating. Its constant procedure is in the order of a 'rewriting' or 'translation', expressing received thought-forms in the protocol language of mental functioning, considered as 'pure' or 'absolute'. '*Absolu* est le langage qui est tout le Système (c'est d'ailleurs le langage du relatif déclaré)' (*C*, XVII, p. 671).[17] How is meaning constructed, how is value attributed – and with what degree of validity? The effect of such rewriting is to designate the tissue of confusion, self-mystification and arbitrary credence inhabiting nine-tenths of any and every human activity: philosophy, religion, morality, historiography, politics, literature, psychology, love, education, science itself . . .

Il y a des histoires où le type réflexe D[emande] R[éponse] intervient si naïvement! Le besoin de réponse crée l'événement-réponse. Goliath appelle David.
La 'vérité' peut se reconnaître à ceci qu'elle ne satisfait pas la sensibilité. (*C*, XXII, p. 406)[18]

The Valéryan terms for all such mental formations mortgaged to common language and to the naive, 'sleepwalking' creativity of the collective psyche are: 'myth', 'fiduciarity', 'idolatry'. As the rest of the present volume will amply demonstrate, the writer of the notebooks effects a grand purge of the entire mental space we inhabit as inheritors of Western culture; a purge in many ways more radical, despite its refusal of the rhetoric and theatrics of prophecy, than that of Nietzsche or of present-day deconstructionists.

(iv) Fourthly, the Notebooks resemble an immense chess game played, not so much externally, against the illegitimate meanings and values given currency by the 'language of the tribe' (Mallarmé's expression), as internally, against the infirmities of the thinking-writing mind itself. We may speak here of a *self-observing, self-theorising heuristics*, which is both pure (tending, that is, towards a general theory of mental creativity as such) and applied (illustrated in act by all the thinking-writing strategies through which Valéry seeks to activate and marshall his own resources of discovery). This is one of the most subtle and important dimensions of the *Cahiers*, intimately linked to the materiality of the graphic manuscript trace and of the manoeuvres of the writing hand within the space of the page; it is currently the object of intensive studies by teams of genetic critics of the CNRS.[19] Valéry views the inventive, thinking mind – the mind in its act – as an associative-relational-transformative capacity, registered as such in the language by the suffix '-BLE' (as in words such as 'combinable', 'conceivable', 'exprimable', 'possible' etc.). Its other great structural property is the ability to attend consciously to its own productions, correcting, developing, reworking, repeating them in modified forms: this is the function he refers to in personal shorthand as 'RE-' (from the prefix of such words as: 'retour', 'récurrence', 'revoir' etc.). The interaction of these properties gives it a latent, structurally inherent potential for forming new combinations (ideas, perspectives, images, forms, theories, strategies, answers, poems, etc.) which is rarely if ever actualised, but which he supposes finite in principle, and which he calls the 'implex' (a term usefully marking his originality in relation to the Freudian 'complex').[20]

It will be seen that the fragmentary, rebounding, provisional and ever-open form we have observed as characteristic of the *Cahiers* in fact represents Valéry's own epic attempt to explore – and, as far as may be, to exhaust – the implex. His writing practice, dynamised in desire by the educated intuition of what is gloriously possi-BLE, is of course founded on a certain methodic RE-currence: the same problems, regularly resurgent, are forever re-analysed, reformulated and reviewed, giving wider associations, sharper definition, renewed perspective, methodically soliciting and re-activating the implex of intellectual sensibilisation and energetic potential: 'Plus je pense, plus je pense' ('the more I think, the more I think') (*CII*, p. 39). It is the practice that best accommodates and transcends the infirmities of the psychic apparatus in all of us.

Of the latter, Valéry renders superbly lucid account: limited staying power, poor focus, unidimensionality, disorder, inconsequence, forgetfulness, wilful particularity, self-contradiction, affective warping, circular self-pleasing and chronic self-pacification ... At the same time, his particular gift is to prospect and ponder its positive resources: its 'sensibilité d'étonnement' (Newton asks why the moon does not fall like the apple); the marvellous webs of association and analogy that we call memory and imagination; the power of co-ordinated consequentiality introduced into mental time by the conscious 'I' which is projected from, or resolved out of, the pre-conscious nebula C-E-M; the mind's inherent inner dialogism; its ability to profit from the forcefield of its own creative tensions; its integrated creativity before all gaps of intelligibility and deficient resource; its world-transforming capacity for 'absent things' not given empirically; its vectorised thirst for self-transcendence and the unknown ... We cannot read the *Cahiers* without grasping the force of Valéry's contention that most of us are, most of the time, mental sleepwalkers; or his energising sense of what is possible to awakening. '*L'art de penser. Ars magna*' ('*The art of thinking. Ars magna*') (*CI*, p. 412).

(v) This founding persuasion has not only its transcription in objective analytic science, but also its resonance in poetic sensibility and lyric voice. The fifth recognisable subset of the 'thinking-writing games' of the *Cahiers* is the sentient human subject's own *drama of intellectual sensibility*. The personal voice is, from the first, present. Are we, for instance, reading poetry or psychopoetics when Valéry writes: 'L'univers n'est qu'un geste enveloppant et dans l'intérieur de ce geste — toutes les étoiles'? (*CV*, p. 272).[21] Yet it struggles to be heard, constrained and reduced to silence by the adventure of abstractive objectification. One of the earliest notebooks bears the eloquent title: 'Qui crie sans aucun bruit' ('Which cries out with no noise') (*CI*, p. 273). The truth behind the myth of the twenty-year 'Grand Silence' is no doubt allusively declared here: not that Valéry published nothing at all of his researches – he in fact published a good deal between 1894 and 1912, and projected the publication of much more – but that his most intimate sensibility was, for that period, contained (both muffled and repressed) within the circuits of analytical self-attention.

That the deeper and further reaches of psychic sensibility are to be sounded out, not by the seeing eye of the abstractive intellect, but by the hearing of the inward ear is one of Valéry's most important discoveries. 'O mes étranges personnages, — pourquoi ne seriez-vous pas une poésie? ... / après la recherche des éléments purs, les épouser, les être, les faire enfin vivre et revivre' (*C*, IV, p. 612),[22] he notes in 1910. Externally realised in the form of poetic voice in *La Jeune Parque* and *Charmes*, re-encountered devastatingly in the affective cataclysm of 1920–2, the deeper subjectivity is welcomed and integrated in the notebooks of Valéry's maturity as the essential complement of analytic self-writing and pyschogenetic science. The same *écriture de précision* which retraces abstract forms of mental functioning here consents to listen to the imaginative, affective, musical and spiritual particularity of those same functions of the psyche and to mould the expressive instrument to a second – 'other' – logic of subjectivity. Hence, within the laboratory of pure thought, the refreshing wellspring of the 'poésie brute'. Retracing the total modulation of sensibility, the lyric voice explores 'moments' of exultation, aspiration or dereliction, of delight in the natural world or of ethico-spiritual self-recognition, all exhibiting important links to the art of writing exemplified in Valéry's published dialogues, fictional narratives, theatre and poetry. In these unsurpassed examples of intellectual sensibility lyrically expressed may be found the most direct and appealing initiation to the world of the *Cahiers*.

(vi) To follow the logic of this second modality of utterance is to accede to the more elusive – but also more significantly human – dimensions of subject intentionality. Among these, we may distinguish, sixthly, the *spiritual exercise, part mental training in the 'ars magna', part strenuous mystique of self-construction and self-transcendence*, acknowledging its para-religious character in a remarkable cult of 'psalms' and 'prayers': '*Je ne suis que ton Dieu* — dit cette voix que je ne reconnus pas. Car je connais ma voix intérieure, et celle-ci était intérieure, mais non du tout *mienne*. Mais que veut dire *Mienne*?' (*C2*, p. 703).[23]

The master-construct pursued is an agnostic, psychologist, technically operative appropriation of 'the mystics' (Valéry has in mind a medley of essentialists and Catholics, the most significant being Plotinus, Ruysbroek, Loyola and John of the Cross), whom he views as pre-critical pioneers of the potential of the human psyche developed to its highest power. Such is, summarily expressed, the tenor of Valéry's celebrated, but still often poorly understood '*mystique sans Dieu*' (*Œ*, II, p. 34). 'Le problème capital dans la vie — est celui de l'ascèse, que j'entends comme possession de soi et aussi comme exploration. / Il n'y a pas à douter que la recherche du progrès intérieur (comme disent les mystiques) est le Seul objet possible, dont la poursuite des sciences n'est qu'un élément' (*C*, VI, p. 738).[24]

This master-game is the key to all the more elusive movements and horizons of the *Cahiers*: not least, their fascination with the extreme limits of the psychic capacity for sensation, feeling or intellection and the attempt – 'mon point *capital*' – to draw from a 'reconnaissance du réel psychique' ('recognition of psychic reality') a form of 'divinisation du possible psychique' ('divinisation of psychic possibility') (*C*1, p. 131). Under the names 'Gladiator' or 'l'Ange' or 'l'Apocalypte Teste' – but *all* his most dynamic myths refer sooner or later to this same strategic nerve-point – Valéry seeks to invent a supreme application of his pure self-science: at once a sporting or 'playful' ethic of mental development and an existential art of self-creation, standing in lieu of a transcendent faith and replacing the bankrupt 'métaphysiques-et-religions' of Western inheritance.

From 1921, this project of a parallel and rival construct of spirituality finds its fullest extension in the constantly reworked and expanded 'Dialogue of divine things' (noted θ or θθ). This unfinished Socratic dialogue explores Valéry's most central problematics of Desire – 'depuis le besoin du tendre jusqu'à l'appétit métaphysique' ('from the need for tenderness right up to metaphysical appetite') (*C*, XI, p. 808) – and of its 'divine' objects; a problematics set within the broader framework of the crisis of belief, value and finality which is increasingly seen to proceed from the rationalised and positive intellect of Western man, but to escape his control. 'Je lui dis [to P. Teilhard de Chardin] qu'il faudrait un travail type Einstein pour construire un *invariant* Dieu. N'est-ce pas l'objet primitif de θ, mon dialogue — de rebus divinis?' (*C*, XIV, p. 716).[25]

(vii) It will be seen, finally and most broadly, that the *Cahiers* constitute the log-book of an *existential quest for identity pursued in analytic self-comprehension, but also in reflective dialogue with the evolving adventure of the modern world*. The latter figures with increasing prominence in the mirror of the mind, often re-echoing its own drama, dramatising its own self-questioning: thus the premonitory tremors of the Sino–Japanese war, heralding the time of the 'finite world' and the end of European pre-eminence; the trauma of the Great War; the crisis of representation in science; the transformations of modern sensibility and political structures wrought by the

triumph of practical reason and the crisis of 'la Fiducia'; the rise of
the Dictatorships, preparing the defeat and occupation of France,
and its uncertain renaissance. Certainly, the symbol of Faust, in the
latter years of the *Cahiers*, fuses into one recapitulative symbol, the
symbiosis of the collective drama of the European Intellect and the
most intimate quest of an empirical self, whose human and intellectual personality is brilliantly analysed under the rubric Ego and in
the fragments of intellectual autobiography ('Mémoires de moi').

   This ultimate and framing subset of the thinking-writing games of
the *Cahiers* can perhaps be expressed as the attempt to comprehend,
in the fullest and most human sense of the term, the pre-rational,
irrational and trans-rational motivations, forces and values that
represent the intrinsic 'Other' of the human mind; hence, ambigu-
ously, both its perilous and demonic grandeur and its chances of
reconciling subject and object, knowledge and life. The ultimate
question: 'Que faire ... de l'Homme? Peut-on se faire de l'homme
une nouvelle idée? / Peut-on créer un nouveau but, un nouveau
désir?' (*C*, XXVI, p. 440)[26] merges here with the writer's own
recapitulative formula of existential self-definition: 'But d'une vie.
Arriver — (même sur le Tard) — à connaître nettement le fond de
pensée et de sensibilité incomparable sur lequel on a vécu' (*C*, XX,
p. 239).[27]

   'Mon vrai sujet est toi: amour de ce qui est enveloppé, impliqué
dans l'esprit' (*C*I, p. 103).[28] How the various thinking-writing games
we have distinguished relate to, qualify and enrich each other is a
matter of critical perspective and gives much scope to ongoing
research. As the 'dawn voyages' multiply in time, and as the grand
unfolding proceeds scripturally, so it becomes clearer that the true
subject of the *Cahiers* is ... the Subject. For what is implied in the
mind is the entirety of whatever is structurally implicit in the 'text' of
human subjectivity, taken as an unknown to be explored; and
explored precisely in its otherness ('mon vrai sujet est *toi* ...').

   Fundamentally, the reflexive form postulates and affirms a reciprocity of subject and object of consciousness, joined in an equation
of self-attention or self-presence of which the dawn act of writing is
at once the occasion, the stimulus, the mirror and the graphic trace.

   'Quand j'écris sur ces cahiers, *je m'écris*. / Mais je ne m'écris pas
tout.' (*C*I, p. 16).[29] The writing 'I' of the *Cahiers* is linked in
indefatigable curiosity to his own not-to-be-exhausted enigma,
relativistically but radically questioned: that of the human subject

henceforth devoid of any metaphysical essence or name, 'subjected'
only to its own 'sous-jet', to time and to the curvature of the mind-
generated universe to be discovered and explored . . .[30]

NOTES

1 'To think as an algebrist, an Englishman, a politician, a sailor, a poet,
an ornamentalist — as all of that — as anyone — as an animal, a tree,
a pianist / This is also to exist in a q-dimensional space'.
2 'Do not seek truth — But seek to develop those strengths which make
and unmake truths.'
3 See Preface, *Paul Valéry, Cahiers*, vol. 1, p. xvii.
4 'the one thread of my life, my only cult, only ethic, only luxury, only
capital and no doubt an investment to be written off '.
5 'The important things I have found — *I am sure of their value* — will not
be easy to decipher from my notes'.
6 'To use one's self agilely, advisedly, methodically as the universal origin
of co-ordinates'.
7 'My idea is simple: I am sure that there is a mechanics of the mind on
which everything depends — so that everything should be expressible
in terms of functioning'.
8 'As man breathes, moves, digests, so he must feel, know and think.'
9 'My system is an attempt to reduce to transformational theory (the most
general one possible) everything we can represent of the mind — and
hence — of everything.'
10 'to attempt to construct the scale and chord-system of which thought
will be the music'.
11 'I posit that mathematical science, disengaged from its applications and
reduced to algebra, i.e. to the analysis of a purely differential being
made up of homogeneous elements — is the most faithful document of
the properties of association, disjunction and variation *of the mind.*'
12 'Pure mathematics is a sort of prefiguration, a promise and model, of all
the possibilities of the mind'.
13 'Basically, the System was the search for a language or a notation which
would allow us to treat *de omni re* as DesCartes' analytic geometry has
allowed us to treat all figures'.
14 'love is the only sample of mysticism that everyone or nearly everyone
experiences'.
15 'The work is a modification of the author. At each of the movements
that draw it out of him, he undergoes a modification. And when it is
finished, it reacts once more upon him. He becomes (for instance), the
person capable of engendering it. He reconstructs, as it were, a shaper
of the realised whole, who is a myth — / in the same way, a child ends
up conferring on her father, the idea and, as it were, the form of
paternity'.

16 'My objective is to get people to think — and get myself to think — about things we didn't think about because they were too closely or too permanently present — i.e. because of their very importance . . .'

17 'What is *absolute* is the language, which is the whole of the System (it is, in fact, the language of the declared relative)'.

18 'There are cases where the reflex scheme Demand-Response operates so naively! the need for an answer creating the answer-event — Goliath calls for David'. Truth may be recognised in this, that it does not satisfy the sensibility'.

19 See, for example, R. Pickering (ed.), *Paul Valéry. Se faire ou se refaire. Lecture génétique d'un cahier (1943)* (Clermont-Ferrand, Centre de Recherche sur les littératures modernes et contemporaines, 1996).

20 Cf. *C1*, p. 1040: 'L'Implexe . . . est le *reste caché structural et fonctionnel* — (non le subconscient — ) d'une connaissance ou action consciente'.

21 'The universe is merely a gesture of enfoldment, catching within it — all the stars'.

22 'Oh, my strange characters — why would you not be a poetry . . . after the search for pure elements, why not espouse them, enact them, let them live and relive'.

23 '*I am only your God* — said the voice which I did not recognise. For I know my own inner voice, and this one was inward, but not *my own*. Yet what does *mine* mean?'

24 'Mysticism, without God.' 'The capital problem in life — is that of ascesis which I understand as self-possession and as exploration / There is no doubt that the search for inner progress (as the mystics say) is the only possible objective, of which the pursuit of the sciences is only one element'.

25 'I said to [P. Teilhard de Chardin] that it would take an Einstein-type labour to construct a God-invariant. Is that not the original objective of θ, my dialogue — *de rebus divinis?*'

26 'What is to be done . . . with Man. Can one create a new idea of man? / Can one create a new desire?'.

27 'Goal of a life. To manage — (even late in the day) to know clearly the substratum of thought and sensibility on which one has lived'.

28 'My true subject is you: love of what is enfolded, implied in the mind'.

29 'When I write these notebooks, I am writing myself / But I do not write myself out exhaustively . . .'

30 For further reading on the topic of this chapter, please see Bibliography, items 3, 4, 20, 24, 26, 27, 64, 66, 74, 83, 97, 98, 101, 108, 113, 116, 118, 122.

# CHAPTER 3

# Paradigms of the self: Valéry's mythical models

## Robert Pickering

'Je cherche mon secret' ('I'm looking for my secret') (*CIV*, p. 154): in a notebook of 1901 this arrestingly isolated statement indicates the central thrust of self-scrutiny and self-elucidation which had already, during the 1890's, provided the focus of Valéry's creative energies, and which underpins the entire framework of his subsequent thought and writing. Alongside this cognitive goal, reciprocal to it in reflexivity, runs an imperative of self-construction, which will equally remain constant; as late as 1943, the major motif is still '(se) Faire — ou (se) refaire' ('Making — or remaking — [oneself]') (*C*, XXVII, p. 731).

In the light of this continuity of reflexive reference, it might seem surprising that, from the earliest years of the 'System', Valéry should have sought models of action and thought externally, in a number of great artists, thinkers or statesmen (Leonardo da Vinci, Descartes, Tiberius and Napoleon), as well as in certain geographical points of reference (such as Bismarck's Germany or the Yalou river in China), and in certain invented myths (such as 'Monsieur Teste'). The recourse to these external sources creates a potentially uneasy relationship between the necessity of concentrating investigation on the self and the presence and persuasion of the various external reference points in which this enterprise is grounded. Yet from the earliest stages of Valéry's work, an acute self-awareness co-exists harmoniously with a quest for consciousness externally directed towards certain characteristic landmarks of Western civilisation.

In taking Leonardo da Vinci as a model of self-construction, or the vibrant efficiency of Germany at the turn-of-the-century as a paradigm of what a fully embraced method might be capable of achieving, Valéry highlights the universalising virtue of myth itself, albeit at some cost to the referential accuracy apparently promised in his titles (*Introduction à la méthode de Léonard de Vinci, La Conquête allemande*). Such figures of the universal indicate to Valéry the possibility of an elevated viewpoint; they allow a purification of consciousness transcending the all-too-human parameters of our condition which he detested in himself. The use of myth also permits him to express imaginatively the programmatic 'method', sometimes highly charged in desire, which underlies the entire process of self-construction. Teste, for example, like the richer, more encompassing framework of aspirations centred, during the final years of Valéry's life, on Faust, objectifies but also dramatises the search for a theory of the mind's functioning and for an ideal of pure consciousness; apparently distancing the self-referential focus, they yet admit simultaneously a complete imaginary investment.

This concomitance of potentially divergent inclinations, bringing together the internally and externally orientated energies arising from an equally powerful engagement with the self and with the world, is an aspect of Valéry's accomplishment which has been little studied. The creativity which it prompts is deeply generative, both in terms of an understanding of the mind and of the extra-mental world. Its mythical or paradigmatic bases call for reappraisal, since it is on such foundations and on the attitudes which they encapsulate that Valéry's emerging edifice of intellectual and existential choices is constructed. The imaginary recourse to great exponents of intellectual or political power is no merely local phenomenon: it allows the emergence of a field of analysis centred on a 'politics of thought' of which Leonardo, Teste or Bismarck are the first embodiments and which will later be explored in the political and ideological spheres of the *Regards sur le monde actuel*. As Valéry writes of Teste in 1901, 'M<sup>r</sup> T[este] ... serait le type de la politique de la pensée ... Le but de cette politique est le maintien et l'extension de l'idée qu'on a de soi. Préparer incessamment le moment de la chance, éloigner toute définition prématurée de soi-même, conquérir par toutes armes le mépris légitime d'autrui ... se servir de ses idées et non les servir' (*CIV*, p. 374).[1]

Valéry's stated determination to 'make use of one's ideas' is not a purely introspective concern. The tension between subjective and objective points of reference in his writing should be seen as enabling, rather than as conflictual. It engenders a genesis in self-construction which is constantly attuned to the challenges and insights of those great minds who have gone before, an attunement naturally expressed in encompassing or universal terms. Such is the

nature of Valéry's concerted quest for an '*Ars magna*'. In a comment
of 1900, he characteristically presents this art in terms of a conscious
striving towards a central nexus binding self to what stands beyond
it. He seeks an originating focus from which the power of perception
and understanding can radiate: 'Se servir agilement, sciemment, et
méthodiquement de son Moi comme origine de coordonnées universelle — tel est l'ars magna' (*ibid.*, p. 108).[2]

The geometrical image used here, pinpointing the 'co-ordinates'
of self and world in terms of a methodically pursued outward
extension, is apposite, and serves two functions. First, it affirms the
relationship between self and other, self and reality, in what is clearly
seen as a context of interaction, not of division or distancing.
Secondly, it serves to remind us that there is, alongside or within the
stability of the self taken as *origin*, a more hidden dynamic investing
the movement of self-enquiry and self-construction itself, a dynamic
perceptible from the earliest stages of Valéry's epistemological-
existential itinerary. In approaching some of the central figures
which are used by Valéry in the self-modelling process required by
his project in its foundational moment, it is important, therefore, to
remember that we are situated on the threshold of an 'édifice dans
l'âme' ('edifice in the soul') (*CM*, l. 17) to which private and public
writing alike will give expression. This critical vantage point opens
onto a consideration of the complex forms of creation in which the
origin of the mind's activity is embedded. Reciprocally, the strategy
of self-modelling acquires a singularly active status in the emerging
perspectives of Valéry's thought, foregrounding that programme of
intellectual training – agility, action consciously undertaken, and
method, according to his definition of an '*Ars magna*' – which he
elsewhere expresses by the analogy of the 'gladiator'.

When situated in relation to the genesis of his writing and
thought, Valéry's reworking of externally referred imaginary inputs
can be seen as belonging to the constitution of certain crucially
important themes and intellectual instruments, whose potential
echoes throughout his work. The radical *tabula rasa* which marks the
beginning of the great intellectual enterprise after the 'Nuit de
Gênes' prompts that characteristic, highly critical, scrutiny of the
'fiduciary' use of language and its attendant distortions in philosophical and even scientific debate. This radical revision in turn
prepares the way for a dynamics of the new: Valéry's various models
and paradigms are at this point appropriated and reworked in a

projective, exploratory context, enriching the entire architecture of the imaginary on which his later writing, spanning a complex range from the epistemological to the poetic, will draw.

These two dimensions – generative and universalising – of the mind's reworking of certain models are perhaps, in all of Valéry's work, most clearly to be seen in his *Introduction à la méthode de Léonard de Vinci* and the various pieces devoted to M. Teste. The work on Leonardo, published in 1895, proposes an 'introduction', echoing the context of beginning from which it springs. For the work places itself immediately in a domain which is investigative and exploratory. Imagination, which is just as important here as the rigour of analysis, has a central role to play in associating the particular with the universal (cf. *Œ*, I, p. 1155, 'Je me propose d'imaginer un homme de qui auraient paru des actions tellement distinctes que si je viens à leur supposer une pensée, il n'y en aura pas de plus étendue').[3] The provisional nature of the writing is confirmed by the remarkable dialogue written in 1929–30, which relativises in the margin the content of the original text,[4] sometimes confirming the accuracy of a previous insight, sometimes offering a refinement of viewpoint amounting to a disavowal. The model is thus imbued with a typically dual status : on the one hand, it is clearly held to be exemplary, while on the other this exemplary nature tends naturally to invite revision of the analysis devoted to it. This process is a pointer to a characteristic of Valéry's writing: to put pen to paper, as Valéry specifies in the preface to his *Analecta*, is to 'defer' any kind of definitive appraisal. This attitude has important links with a modern poetics of the indeterminate or 'open' work; but it is above all one of the crucial components defining the generative impulses of Valéry's creativity.

At the same time, his thrusting intelligence – positing as it does in the figure of Leonardo a link between the particularised and the universal – is aware of the naturally transgressive nature of the writing upon which it is engaged. One of the central tenets on which the *Introduction* is based, a tenet well-expressed in the later essay *Note et digression* (1919), involves what we may call the 'extensive propensities' of the text. It has the virtue, that is, of uniting a point of origin with an ever-radiating circle of reference: 'Je sentais que ce maître de ses moyens, ce possesseur du dessin, des images, du calcul, avait trouvé l'attitude centrale à partir de laquelle les entreprises de la connaissance et les opérations de l'art sont également possibles' (*Œ*, I, p. 1201).[5] It is also significant of the same extension that this introduction to Leonardo's method, which presupposes an epistemological and analytical orientation on the Cartesian model, should be classified in the *Œuvres* under 'Théorie poétique et esthétique': just as the Vincian 'central attitude' is plurivalent in its ramifications, so also does the writing move beyond a specific framework of functioning, to embrace a complex range of creative parameters.

Referring to the prestigious examples of the *Comédie Humaine* or the *Divine Comédie*, the essayist of *Note et Digression* looks back to the genesis in 1894 of the *Introduction* and to his attitude towards Leonardo at that time, intuitively positing the 'poetic' resonance of an 'Intellectual Comedy' (*ibid.*, p. 1201) in which Leonardo held the primary role. But, characteristically, the impact of this intuition – destined to provide a cornerstone of all Valéry's analysis of the mind in the form of the 'complete drama' of the life of the intellect, as he writes in one of his essays on Descartes (*ibid.*, p. 796) – is immediately relativised as a 'pensée bonne pour parler, non pour écrire' ('a thought suitable for speaking, not for writing') (*ibid.*, p. 1201). Writing itself, invested with singularly dynamic properties, becomes the focal point not just for analysis of Leonardo's 'Hostinato rigore' but also for *experimentation*, as the self simultaneously turns its objective enquiry towards the springs of its own activity, and adopts a mode of conceptualisation and of expression attuned to the provisional, constantly receding nature of its possibilities of intellection and imagination.

In aiming to define the elements of genius on which Leonardo's accomplishment was based, Valéry is thus engaged upon an enterprise of reconstitution, experimentation and creation in which the dynamics of writing are of an importance equal to a deepening grasp of method. The interdependence of these two perspectives provides the founding principle of the central ideas highlighted in Leonardo's intellectual and artistic creativity. Writing and its accompanying processes of re-reading and revision imply, as Valéry states in *Note et digression*, distanciation, estrangement (cf. *Œ*, I, p. 1200, 'l'air étranger') and a constant ability to displace habitual modes of perception or conventional ways of thinking, particularly as gelled in the written word (cf. p. 1162, 'Une pensée qui se fixe ... devient ... une idole' ('A thought which gets fixed ... becomes ... an idol')). So too, the mind of Leonardo: less fixed as a consecrated reference for

genius than posited from the outset as 'quelconque',[6] commonplace,
linked closely, in the special sense Valéry confers on the term, to the
'inhuman' (*ibid.*, p. 1157),[7] and to the relative. This singular dis-
position of mind is the one best suited to the 'construction' (*ibid.*, p.
1156) of self and world, since it remains constantly in touch with that
'otherness', that dimension of potentiality, according to which Man
and the universe function. This is a viewpoint safeguarding the
possibility that the existence conjectured under the name of Leonardo might itself be 'TOUT AUTRE', an imaginary projection of the
mind's own vast potential, tempered by the necessity of the highest
possible degree of awareness ('*le plus de* conscience *possible*' ('the
maximum possible consciousness')).

Logic and the imagination are the bases of the essay; it is from their
interaction that the study develops towards a 'logique imaginative'
(*Œ*, I, p. 1194), emphasising, in a style which sometimes comes very
close to mimetic empathy, the uncertainty of mental activity as it
now retreats from, now seizes, a given idea; a style remaining deeply
involved in the process whereby images vary and combine. An
understanding of Leonardo emerges as, above all, a radical re-
education of vision and observation: to circumscribe the mind's
movement and exercise it on the formless, on that experience of
undifferentiated perception preceding all rational or linguistic response (something in which Valéry was to see the source of Degas's
artistry) is to implement new 'ways of seeing' ('Manières de voir.
Batti l'occhio due volte' ('look and see afresh') writes Valéry in a
notebook of 1912 (*C*, IV, p. 702)), enlarging Leonardo's central
precept of perception. The inestimable merit of such an approach is
to inhabit imaginatively the models of production offered by Nature,
to examine the foundations of the apparently symmetrical and to
review the conventional opposition of regular and irregular forms,
uncovering their continuous interplay, the purely 'differential'
notion, as Valéry terms it, which separates them. Here lay the
essence of Leonardo's exceptional gifts : understanding derives from
imaginative investment in the passage from the formless to form,
presupposing a continuity of conceptualisation, in which the limits of
Euclidean geometry can be rethought, and surpassed. Countless
rearrangements and inventive designs are then made possible. The
many verbal forms used by Valéry to designate such activity not only
point to the ceaseless intervention practised by Leonardo on reality

but also project the movement of the mind itself (cf. *ibid.*, pp. 1176–7, 'Il fait ... Il passe ... Il vivifie ... Il reconstruit ... Il se joue, il s'enhardit, il traduit').[8]

Considerations bearing on form introduce the theme of transfer from the scientific to the artistic. The rest of the essay moves outwards from the internal considerations turning on the mind's capacity to see *beyond* the products of perception, and embraces the resources of artistic inventiveness based on the imperative of construction. The pages devoted to the status of ornament in composition, to the necessity in the observer of *non-recognition* when faced with the artist's canvas, or obliged to explore inductively the different conception of things thereby presented, are bent towards elucidating the founding necessity of 'communication' (*Œ*, I, p. 1187) between the diverse forms of activity in thought. Architecture also is adduced, in so far as it demonstrates in its reliance on theories of physics and mechanics, the principles of combination and linkage which are at work in normally independent domains of activity. Behind the figure of Leonardo there emerges a generalised spectrum of methodical enquiry, all-encompassing in its applicability, highlighting the 'continuity of operations' (*ibid.*, p. 1196) which, beyond *a* mind, lies potentially accessible in *the* mind; an enquiry capable in theory, like Leonardo, of integrating knowledge and generative or creative act, *Savoir* and *Pouvoir*. In this free flow between the play of individualised intelligence, the world on which it is brought to bear, and the mind whose task it is to communicate the whole, a central Valéryan model takes shape.

In 1919, *Note et digression* both confirms this highly influential reference in Valéry's scale of intellectual values, and modifies it. Tone and content are different: self-modelling and the imperative of method have long since been subjected to other forms of investigation and intense performance. One thinks in particular of the long gestation of *La Jeune Parque*, that centrally formative crucible of a 'MOI' which, far from being elucidated in its innermost constitution, is instead recognised in its alterity, as 'Mystérieuse' (*JP*, l. 325). A theory of self and of pure awareness is grafted onto the initial essay, in a way which both prolongs the essay's pertinence and modifies considerably its prime trajectory, that essentially extensive relationship between the particular and the general. The direction of the writing is no longer to suggest the fundamental principles of inventiveness, but, in a concerted drive towards the limits of self, to lay bare a pure act of being, close to an ideal absence of all recognisably human characteristics.

This negative dynamic turned against the human is, of course, not unrelated to the Teste cycle which, begun a year after the *Introduction*, forcefully initiates a powerfully reflexive return to the self as source and resource. It is important though to remember that *Note et digression* was published the same year as *La Crise de l'esprit*: the former essay's apparent break with the real world needs to be set against the latter's sombre vision of post-war Europe, divided from its former beliefs and ethical standards by the chasm of mortality which the implacable logic of destruction had opened up. By 1919 the emphasis placed in 1895 on the 'virtuality' (*Œ*, I, p. 1204) of a Leonardo removed from History has shifted towards a more fundamental detachment. In order to circumscribe the mind and consciousness, the text stresses the negating propensities of a conceptual process of extreme 'exhaustion' (p. 1225), stripping away the peripheral or contingent by means of a 'refus indéfini d'être quoi que ce soit'.

There is, in this progressive movement of reduction towards the '*moi pur*' (*Œ*, I, p. 1228), a tautness of conceptualisation which places the writing in a different register from that of the *Introduction*. The latter text brings to bear an imaginative empathy close to identification; now, reflection homes in on 'ce moi inqualifiable, qui n'a pas de nom, qui n'a pas d'histoire' ('this indescribable self, which has no name, no history'), which is irreducibly 'unique' (p. 1229) yet aspires to an all-powerful critical mass of extreme awareness. This model is re-imagined with such lyrical intensity that it tends to become eclipsed by the force of its own expectancy, rising inexorably towards a vision of integration and possession which seems at moments to be close to a vision of self-destruction. Towards the end of *Note et digression* the writing operates on a mystical threshold where antitheses are concatenated in a shared elevation, a 'contradictory coexistence' in which the limits of self-affirmation mingle with a self-consuming 'immolation' and 'conclusion'. To possess the self, to reach the purest realms of awareness, the text suggests, is to experience the limits of 'our being' as also of 'our body' (p. 1233). The moving quotation from Leonardo's manuscripts, penned by an unknown hand apostrophising 'lionardo mio', where 'suffering' is literally indistinguishable from 'thought' ('penate' / 'pensate'), indicates the extent to which the 'psychological model' of a 'theoretical being' has been surpassed, at the moment of its apparent omnipresence. It is not by chance that the text gravitates organically towards a lexis where the notion of movement *beyond* is dominant (cf. *Œ*, I, p. 1229, '[cette merveilleuse vie intellectuelle] a dépassé toutes créations, toutes œuvres').[9] Hence a prose style remarkable for its poetic density. One metaphor used to visualise the purity of consciousness, that of the centre of mass of a ring, unseen yet real, had already been developed in one of the most imaginatively resonant manuscript pages of *La Jeune Parque*.[10]

In 'digressing' from an investigation of the method permeating all of Leonardo's creativity, in highlighting the extremities of consciousness, Valéry has in fact taken up a number of themes developed in *La Soirée avec Monsieur Teste*, published in December 1896, enriching them with the imaginative depth of *La Jeune Parque* and the weight of this poem's war-time context. Teste's *raison d'être*, indeed, is to carry much further forward that internal exigency of experimentation previously personified in the 'virtual' or 'potential' Leonardo. Experimentation, in this case of self-modelling, works in the sense of pushing the power of mind to its extreme limits. If, in the case of Leonardo, Valéry characterises his enterprise in its audacity (cf. *Œ*, I, p. 1232, 'J'osai me considérer sous son nom, et utiliser ma personne' ('I dared to consider myself under his name, and to use my own person')), he turns in Teste to a fictional construct which has the benefit not just of encompassing the ability to create constantly inventive figures of the real world, but also of surpassing them, of penetrating into the depths of intellectual potential from which they originate.

Teste thus radicalises the power of mind, establishing a thematic continuity with the preceding model, yet simultaneously offering a new avenue of approach, that of the 'demon of possibility' (*Œ*, II, p. 14) to which Valéry refers in his preface written in 1925. The fictional context is vital, in that it both legitimises the experimental nature of the writing and impedes any facile identification with a self-portrait, realising a context of proximity yet of distance, essential to an investigation of potential. As a consequence, Teste hovers between hero and monster of the intellect. This constant interface ensures the absence of self-justification, and also lends the writing a singular indeterminateness of genre. For the text unfolds, during its first eight paragraphs, in a mould of apparent self-portraiture, mingling the ironic touch with a form of dramatic immediacy – exemplified by exclamation and typographical stress – close to that

intuition of the theatricality of the mind which had impressed itself
on Valéry from an early stage, and which, in this text, provides one
of the key décors framing Teste's existence. In this way, the
introductory 'Je' is at once given a leading role and left shrouded in
obscurity, never identified as one of the 'characters' in the uncertain
fictional world proposed. The result is to amplify the absence of
fixed parameters for conduct and thought, and to accentuate the
resources of intellectual potential focused in the primary figure
towards whom the writing directs us.

When memory eventually resurrects the character 'Edmond
Teste', this portrayal similarly avoids the overly realistic, despite its
objective mode and the demands of narrative representation. If
Teste lives before our eyes – an existence which is supported by the
various additions following the *Soirée* (letters written by his wife and a
close friend, extracts from his 'log-book', dialogue) – an ambiguity of
functioning insistently channels the writing towards the central axis
of an investigation of virtuality, materialised characteristically by the
question, 'Que peut un homme?' (*Œ*, II, p. 25). The interplay of past
and present, of internal and external perspectives, for which Teste's
room provides a spatial correlative (cf. p. 23, 'l'intérieur le plus
général'), is centred upon this founding dynamic.

The answer to Teste's question is: practically anything and
everything, the forms and experiences of life revealing their most
secret constitution under the illumination emanating from the
intellect. But the paradigm posited of the all-embracing possibility of
intellection encounters unexpected resistance from the very source
of its existence in the world, in many respects the supreme incarnation of the 'ordinary' (cf. *ibid.*, p. 23, 'l'impression du *quelconque*')
which, as in the case of Leonardo, is an essential appurtenance of
Teste's situation – that of the body, whose pain reinstates the finite in
an otherwise potentially limitless extension of mental power. Try as
it might, knowledge – epistemological, self-reflexive, or even carnal
– cannot plot its course beyond a 'geometry of suffering' (p. 24). The
exponential ability to withdraw from self, the better to understand
the latter's range of functioning, arrives at an irreducible dissociation
of being and awareness, expressed in a concluding remark where the
conjunction 'et' has less a connective role than that of a radical
hiatus (cf. *ibid.*, p. 25, 'Je suis étant, et me voyant' ('I am being, and
seeing myself')).

The towering importance of Teste in the formation of Valéry's 'mythologie intellectuelle' (*Œ*, II, p. 14) lies in the paradigm of intellectual domination which the character both asserts and destabilises. Etymologically, Teste (from the Latin *testis*) bears witness to a concerted quest for the full potential of creative mental activity. But to witness does not here imply the distance of mere self-observation, or the imitation of the visible world, even if these two parameters remain present in the continuing dialogue of the possible and the impossible. The innovatory significance of Teste's example lies in the type of writing which it solicits: present already in the *Introduction*, conjoining inner and outer perspectives in a theatre of the mind, which Jean Levaillant has aptly termed an '*écriture-pensée*'.[11] In this form of writing, the full depth, space and dynamics of thought are embodied in the play of metaphor, the interlocking equilibrium of inner and outer worlds, or the energies and tensions arising from a questioning of the limits of the intelligible and the imaginable. No doubt such a conception remains, as far as the *Soirée* is concerned, in the realm of the hypothetical, the digressive or the deferred. Yet it represents for Valéry no merely rhetorical ploy, safeguarding an author's line of escape in the face of the challenging epistemological advances of his time. Rather, it incorporates through the written word the mind's ceaseless activity; and it is the clearest possible materialisation, in the immediacy of the act of writing, of that intellectual potential which articulates the fundamental range of his own research.

The year following the publication of *La Soirée* was to consecrate what is, in the space of just three years, a remarkable trilogy of intellectual models and paradigms, of primary importance in Valéry's early production. As for the *Introduction*, commissioned by Madame Juliette Adam for the *Nouvelle Revue*, the origin of *La Conquête allemande*, published in 1897 and retitled *Une Conquête méthodique* in a new edition of 1924, is attributable to a request from the English poet and literary critic William Henley, director of *The New Review*. In studying the mechanisms and strategy underlying the economic and military rise of Germany at the turn of the century – a rapidly expanding sphere of influence which in 1896 had prompted Ernest Williams's '*Made in Germany*',[12] the primary source of *La Conquête allemande* – Valéry reorientates the central tenets of intellectual power and the functioning of mind towards an overtly political focus. But the objective remains the same, that of laying the foundations for an

'Art of Thinking' (Œ, I, p. 987), of charting the steps of a method capable of organising the mind and of generating the kind of ordered efficiency which had become a cause for concern in certain spheres of British and French public opinion.

The article develops a further model in the continuing dialectic of inner and outer considerations, placing emphasis now on the factual and the precise, inspired from the data adduced by Williams, now on that speculative and conjectural mode which is so important a characteristic of Valéry's style. *Une Conquête méthodique* naturally takes its place as one of the 'Essais *quasi* politiques' [my italics] of *Variété*. Yet it is engendered from a paradoxical concomitance of opposed responses: commissioned by Henley (Œ, II, pp. 982–6), the article responds unquestionably to an inner imperative of the writer; yet its economic and political subject matter is unfamiliar territory for the Valéry of the 1890s, which introduces a factor of arbitrariness into its dimension of external reference.

It is perhaps the dynamism of such singular questioning which invests the paradigmatic situation of Bismarck's Germany with its resonance in this text. The example proposed becomes a pretext for an investigation of the mind and of the organisation of reality. These two imperatives, integrated organically in Valéry's concept of a System and in the method on which the latter depends, stimulate writing which Valéry himself describes as 'research' (Œ, I, p. 975). On the level of reality we encounter ideas previously expressed in the model of Leonardo and the mythical virtues of Teste – the Testian proclivity to regard all objects, all resources or facts, however disparate, negative or apparently irrelevant, as potentially significant or applicable (pp. 976–77), the *tabula rasa* practised on all existing knowledge (p. 980), and the return to the ordinary, the *quelconque*, as the surest preliminary to the reappraisal in which 'methodical conduct' is rooted (p. 976). But Valéry pushes insistently further, adding other components as speculation delves more deeply into the hidden recesses of its field of enquiry. Arising from the primacy of reason, the methodical conquest realised by the Germans is 'organic', a line of argument which presupposes a corporeal conception of the economic, military and scientific potential of the country, working in unison to further the interests of the 'national body' (p. 982). (In 1919 the second letter of *La Crise de l'esprit* was to reaffirm this analogy, presenting Europe as the 'brain of a vast body' (p. 995).) In 1897 it would seem to have been Germany's role to demonstrate to the world what the methodical use of mind can achieve. Success is attributed to its capacity to reduce its competitors to 'objects of thought', 'workable quantities' (p. 979), to its ability to 'organise inequality' according to a 'general theorem' (p. 977), and hence to neutralise the intervention of chance (p. 981).

At this point speculation encounters an unexpected problem or paradox of far-reaching consequence; one which the model of Leonardo had implicitly identified without grasping its full importance. If genius is reduced to the totally methodical, chance-negating use of ordinary human characteristics and patterns of behaviour, the freedom to invent and to innovate is thereby severely restricted. The problem can be seen most clearly in Valéry's understanding and use of the notion of the *quelconque*. Emphasis on the banal and the commonplace is an essential prerequisite for the disjunctive, dislocatory power of refreshed forms of perception, yet the systematic elevation of the ordinary facilitates the institution of a lowest common denominator of banal response and intellectual distinctiveness. Moreover, the system envisaged on the basis of political fact turns, like the mind, on the thermodynamic principle of creation and expenditure of energy. The Germany of Bismarck, von Moltke and von Marshall is like a self-perpetuating machine, victorious in all its enterprises but necessarily negating all forms of individual initiative or creative difference, 'sans passion, sans génie, ... sans choix, sans enthousiasme' ('without passion, without genius, ... without choice, without enthusiasm') (*Œ*, I, p. 981). No inordinate personal expenditure of energy, however creative, can be accommodated, the 'extraordinary' (p. 986) being rigorously proscribed. To function properly, the text suggests, the machine of state, like the mind itself, cannot afford to found its actions on a principle of methodically employed equivalence if it is to avoid increased entropy.[13] Elements of disorder and of disjunction are necessary if the closed system presented is not to become etiolated, triumphant in its 'mediocrity' (p. 981).

Is the import of this 'strange idea' (*Œ*, I, p. 981) to suggest, then, that in Bismarck's Germany and beyond it, any systems organising thought and action are flawed? The concluding paragraphs wrestle with the paradox of a method which, by its very efficiency, seems self-negating and, in any case, severely restrictive of the individual's right to be differentiated, not to be enmeshed in the levelling necessities of a shared core of knowledge, albeit linked to the potential exercise of power, of a *Savoir* now universally equated to a *Pouvoir*. Teste's 'Que peut un homme?', with its open-ended interrogation which was to fuel the many fields of Valéry's thought, attracts a salutary qualification, rehabilitating with its very uncertainty a degree of individual difference in the context of its apparent eclipse, and reminding us of that readiness to think *beyond*, of a hesitation to conclude, on which alone ideas – and the creative energies of writing itself – can flourish: 'Mais — je ne sais pas. Je ne fais que dévider des conséquences' ('But — I don't know. I'm just spinning out consequences') (p. 987).

The exemplary models studied here are, in their own ways, deeply formative blueprints for the types of enquiry which Valéry pursued in his early writing. The significance of these fundamental points of reference, however, extends well beyond the problematics of source and influence. They are primarily a vital dynamic for creativity, a series of vibrant soundings of the self, whether expressed in the rethinking and recreation of the model afforded by Leonardo, in the constitution of the mythical paradigm which is Teste, or in meeting the challenge of cross-referencing fruitfully a projected 'Art of Thinking' and the method which Valéry sees at work in the powerfully assertive rise of Germany. These figures and paradigms people a theatre of the mind; they are leading *dramatis personæ*[14] in an emerging constellation of intellectual affinities and self-recognitions. But if the self-constructor finds his bearings in a personal pantheon of historical or mythical figures, and freely interprets the latter as a means of self-development rather than as an object for exegesis, the initial drive towards a larger-than-life inspiration does not disappear altogether. The range of references is vast, including heroes of the mind or of intellectual method (Descartes), models of mental agility and discipline (Loyola, Lord Kelvin, Henri Poincaré), masters in the literary exposition of the mind's imaginative potential (Poe, Rimbaud, Huysmans and, supremely, Mallarmé), great statesmen and politicians whose command of strategy and effective use of power place them in the forefront of the mind's search for the components of a totalising System (Bonaparte, Cecil Rhodes). Such figures (and many others) are certainly appropriated as the self's springboard to the universal, yet also retain the aura of their own singular specificity, their own deep fascination.

The pertinence of these exemplary instances of intellectual,

literary or strategic mastery is never really surpassed, never integrated so totally into self-identity that such figures can be laid
reverently aside. As late in his life as 1943 Valéry is still sufficiently
captivated by the exceptional vision of Leonardo, for instance, to be
quoting him (cf. *C*, XXVII, p. 111) on the interdependent relationship
of spider and web.

Perhaps most importantly: to inhabit the creative processes of a
great thinker and artist, to re-imagine the methodic genius of a great
people, or actually to create, in Teste, an embodiment of the power
of extreme intellection is to use these starting points as triggers for
innovation, as pointers towards the virtual and potential. In this
sense, the texts studied here are not just highly significant in terms of
Valéry's advancing thought and self-definition. By the window they
afford on inner and outer worlds, by the steps of speculation, analysis
and imaginative projection which they present and invite us to
follow, they encapsulate the activity which is, as Valéry writes in a
notebook of 1896, a fundamental definition of the mind: 'L'esprit
n'est que travail. Il n'existe qu'en mouvement' ('The mind is just
work. It exists only in motion') (*C*1, p. 869).

The same thing applies to writing itself. The attenuation of the
conceptual impetus which concludes *Une Conquête méthodique* highlights the shifting uncertainties of the writing process, and reaffirms
the unfinished, tentative accents which can occur even in the quest
for method and strategic supremacy. Composing, rethinking and
rereading are, as *Note et digression* makes clear, risky activities; but
they are the origin of the text, the stuff of its genesis. A major
function of Valéry's models and paradigms is to marry experimen-
tally the themes central to his thought and their personalised
expression. The complex creation for which such models provide a
necessary vehicle – Leonardo, like Teste, being situated on a critical
threshold relating the fictional to the autobiographical, the abstract
to the dramatic or the poetic[15] – engenders here writing of singular
density. The paradigmatic status of another's achievement spurs a
naturally transgressive inclination towards the 'demon' of 'purity' (*C*,
XXV, p. 617) and of possibility; yet a comment in a notebook of 1918
(*C*, VII, p. 226), taken up in 'Rhumbs' (*Tel Quel*), indicates clearly that
even the drive towards self-possession remains dependent on the
proliferating means to express : 'Ce n'est ni le *nouveau* ni le *génie* qui
me séduisent, — mais la possession de soi. — Et elle revient à se
douer du plus grand nombre de moyens d'expression, pour atteindre

et saisir ce Soi et n'en pas laisser perdre les puissances natives, faute
d'organes pour les servir' (*Œ*, II, p. 646).[16]

NOTES

1 'Mr Teste ... would be the type of a politics of thought ... The goal of
   that politics is to maintain and extend the idea one has of oneself. To
   prepare ceaselessly the advent of the favourable moment, to set aside
   any premature definition of oneself, to conquer by all weapons a
   legitimate scorn for others ... to use one's ideas and not be used by
   them'.
2 'To use one's self agilely, knowingly, methodically as universal origin of
   co-ordinates—such is the *ars magna*'
3 'I propose to imagine a man whose actions appeared so distinct that if I
   were to suppose a thought behind them, there will be none more
   extensive'
4 The importance of Valéry's 'marginal' writing is treated in a luminous
   article by Michel Lioure, 'Les marginalia de Valéry', in F. Marotin (ed.),
   *La Marge* (Clermont-Ferrand, Publications de la Faculté des Lettres et
   Sciences Humaines de l'Université Blaise-Pascal, 1988), fascicule 27, pp.
   51–9.
5 'I felt that this master of his means, this possessor of drawing, images,
   calculation, had found the central attitude from which the enterprises
   of knowledge and the operations of art are equally possible'
6 BN ms fo. 9 v, 'Je me propose de regarder cet esprit comme une chose
   quelconque, sans nom'.
7 For a definition of the preference for the 'inhuman', arising from the
   mistrust of 'humanity', see *C*, XVIII, p. 281.
8 'He makes..he passes on ... He brings alive ... he reconstructs ... He
   plays, becomes emboldened, translates'
9 '[this marvellous intellectual life] has surpassed all creations, all works'
10 The page (*JP* ms II, fo. 3 v) bearing a sketch of a ring, in a context
   defined by 'moi, le bizarre bijou', 'gardant dans ma chair la douleur
   comme un ordre', is reproduced and transcribed in S. Bourjea, J. Jallat
   and J. Levaillant (eds.), *Critique génétique* (Paris, L'Harmattan, 1991),
   Cahier no. 1 ('Pas'), pp. 84–7.
11 Jean Levaillant, 'Teste et l'impossible réel', in R. Pietra (ed.), *Valéry: la
   philosophie, les arts, le langage* (*Recherches sur la philosophie et le langage*, Cahier
   no. 11, Université de Grenoble II, 1989), p. 131.
12 Ernest Edwin Williams, *'Made in Germany'* (London, Heinemann, 1896).
13 For further investigation of this thermodynamic perspective, see Christine Crow's illuminating essay *Paul Valéry and Maxwell's Demon: Natural
   order and human possibility* (University of Hull, Occasional Papers in
   Modern Languages no. 8, 1972).
14 Analysing Leonardo and Teste, Michel Jarrety uses this term as the title

of one of the chapters of his interesting study *Paul Valéry* (Paris, Hachette Supérieur, 'Portraits littéraires', 1992).

15 Several texts in the *Cahiers* relating explicitly to Teste and Leonardo figure among the 'Poèmes et PPA' (see *C*2, pp. 1247ff., in particular the notes corresponding to *C*, I, p. 728; *C*, II, p. 332; *C*, III, p. 472).

16 'It is not the new or genius which attracts me, — but self-possession. — And it comes down to equipping oneself with the greatest number of expressions, to reach and grasp this Self and not let its native powers escape for lack of organs with which to grasp them'.

For further reading on the topic of this chapter, please see Bibliography, items 44, 54, 56, 57, 80, 93, 103, 121.

# CHAPTER 4

# The fascination of science

Judith Robinson-Valéry

'Mais la science est due ... à des imaginations de *poètes*'
(C2, p. 838)[1]

Valéry is undoubtedly one of the most striking examples in twentieth century literature of a writer more interested in science than in literature itself. He felt himself privileged to follow, as it were, over the shoulders of the creators of science, one of the greatest intellectual adventures of human history: the appearance in our mental firmament, from the last years of the nineteenth century to the end of our own, of a whole series of new scientific models, each one more surprising, more exciting and more philosophically suggestive than the one before.

The role of scientific modelling in the genesis and evolution of Valéry's own 'System' has been extensively studied.[2] What he seeks in science is not a loose analogy between the laws of mathematics, physics or chemistry and those of mental processes, but the fruitful lesson offered to us by what he calls 'leur rigueur, leur tension, leur difficulté pure, leurs bonnes manières de définir, leur recherche des opérations' (C2, p. 834).[3] What Valéry borrows from science is, he says, 'surtout des manières de voir et de raisonner'('above all, ways of seeing and reasoning') (p. 858). He also writes, significantly, of a case we shall have a chance to examine more closely: 'Ce que je cherche dans la physique (ex[emple]: p[rincipe] de la relativité) c'est de quoi aborder les problèmes du moi' (p. 845).[4]

It is usually for want of a sufficiently subtle or complete understanding of the relationship between his lifelong passion for science and the search for a 'science of the self' that Valéry's scientific enthusiasm was, for a long time, greeted by literary critics with a certain scepticism, occasionally mingled with condescension.[5] What is becoming ever clearer, however, as Valéry's much-annotated, personal scientific library comes to be methodically investigated, is the quality and range of a fascination that informs his whole mindset and underpins his entire work.

In this respect, Valéry is deeply attuned to his time. For better or for worse, science has left its powerful imprint; modern thought seeks the greatest possible number of links between science-in-the-making and new conceptions of the humanities in general, and philosophy and literature in particular. This latter characteristic of our century can be seen in many emblematic figures for whom the gap between the 'two cultures' did not exist. One need only mention Bertrand Russell, whose thinking straddled the philosophy of science, mathematical logic, and a deep concern with ethical values. His seminal work *Principles of Mathematics*, well-read and heavily annotated, is present in Valéry's personal library in both English and French. The case of Russell's favourite student, Wittgenstein is another case in point. In him as in Valéry, we note a search for an immediate contact with reality from which all ill-defined words and concepts have been eliminated. Between Wittgenstein's year spent in Norway meditating in an isolated hut built by his own hands, and Valéry's intense participation in the mysterious reconstitution of the world each day at dawn, there is a deep parallel, no doubt associated with modern man's need both to profit from all that science has to offer him, but also, periodically, to stand back from it, so as to maintain a balanced perspective on how it relates to other modes of human perception and feeling.

Accepting, then, that Valéry, like several of his great contemporaries, lived *astride* several cultures (but he would call them 'optiques' or 'points de vue' or 'manières de voir'), what did he know of science?

At school, his science teachers ranged from the mediocre to the disastrous, with no sense whatever, apparently, of the fundamental questions that have to be raised to explain why mathematics or physics or any other science exists in the first place. The result was that he was educated much more by the natural Mediterranean world of sea, sky, sun, stars, boats, fish, sea-shells, and in the dunes wild plants and flowers and insects (to observe which he bought himself a microscope, with a full range of samples, that he kept, and used from time to time, all his life). By this uncontaminated contact with the mystery of there being a sky, a sea or a sea-shell at all, he developed as a child the *habit of questioning*, the frustration but also the wonder of not-knowing, but needing-to-know. *L'homme et la coquille*, as I have indicated elsewhere,[6] puts to the test his full maturity in the art of asking oneself questions that are valid and precise. It is at one and the same time a great philosophical work, a piece of very structured writing, and a fine exercise in epistemological method.

Moving from the works of nature to the works of man, Valéry began as a very young adolescent to discover in the beautiful old municipal library in Montpellier a rich collection of books which, though pre-dating his encounter with science proper, prepared his understanding of its mode of thought.

The first was Viollet-le-Duc's *Dictionnaire raisonné d'architecture française*, a monumental ten-volume work which set out to demonstrate the necessity, if one was restoring a public edifice, of carrying out the restoration according to the architectonic principles used in the original building process. Even though Viollet-le-Duc did not always practise what he preached, he taught the young Valéry to imagine the invisible, inner-structures and forces concealed behind the visible outer-walls and roofs of great buildings such as Gothic cathedrals. 'Just like the human mind', we can imagine Valéry beginning to think.

Another book read in the same library at about the same time was the English aesthetician Owen Jones's *Grammar of Ornament*,[7] a fascinating introduction to the forms, both natural and artificial (that is, created by man), to be found in the art and everyday life of a large cross-section of civilisations, primitive and advanced, over an equally large span of time. This book, superbly organised and illustrated, analyses with an almost scientific precision the origins, nature and development of ornamentation throughout the world, stressing two initial points: firstly, that all ornamentation which is universally admired (such as Greek, Celtic and Arabic–Moorish) is in accordance with the laws governing the distribution of form in nature (for example in plants), and secondly, that however varied the manifestations of accordance with these laws may be, the main ideas on which they are based are very small in number.

This second notion is just as applicable to mathematics – both geometry and algebra. In both cases the many can be reduced to the few, just as the many can be drawn from the few. Just as Greek ornamentation derives directly from the acanthus leaf, the Celtic develops from a system of interlacings, and the Moorish from curved lines which develop gradually and harmoniously out of each other, without the slightest break. If two curves are separated by even a short space, they must be made to run parallel to an imaginary line at the point where the curves would become tangents to each other.

We notice from this last detail how profoundly ornamentation is related to mathematics. It is easy to imagine the delight with which Valéry must have made this discovery: that the laws of mathematics are far less difficult and abstruse than the novice – or the victim of a mediocre teacher – thinks. Perhaps mathematics was not such a dull and dreary subject, cut off from the living, breathing world, as a disappointed thirteen year-old had thought.

Valéry had to wait four years, until early 1889, for the seed sown by the *Grammar of Ornament* to begin to mature – when, having become a law student, he met in Montpellier Pierre Féline, a highly intelligent, very enthusiastic and slightly eccentric young man who was an unquestionable master of two arts: mathematics and music. In mathematics the gap between the two new friends could hardly have been wider: Valéry had failed to qualify for the Ecole Navale because of his inadequate (or insufficient) mathematics, whereas Féline was studying for the entrance examination to the École Polytechnique (in which he was to obtain the unheard-of mark of 20 / 20 in mathematics!). This new friendship was one of the important turning-points in Valéry's personal and intellectual life.

The notes and comments which have survived show that Féline was a remarkable teacher and interpreter of mathematics. He had the greatest gift necessary to initiate anyone into any field of science: the art of simplification, the ability to identify the basic concepts and relationships forged by scientists themselves to help us understand their attempts at structuring the functioning of the universe in meaningful and usable ways.

In *Paul Valéry vivant*,[8] Féline lists the aspects of mathematics in which, as we would now say, he 'tutored' Valéry. He pinpoints three areas which strongly attracted his young pupil: the theory of functions, set theory and the theory of groups of transformations. We note the great generality of these three theories, and, underlying them, Valéry's enthusiasm for what Féline calls 'une forme pure et precise'.[9] In addition, all of them are deeply relevant to Valéry's later analyses of mental functioning in the *Cahiers*, perhaps particularly group theory, as it is now commonly called, which deals with the invariants that groups of transformations permit. In other words, it enables a distinction to be made between those elements which are necessarily transformed by the dynamics of a given situation and those which are not. An obvious case is the question of which mental functions and potentialities remain invariant in the states of profound physiological change in the body-mind during sleeping and dreaming, and those which themselves change.[10]

Later, Valéry and Féline began to read the extremely abstract work by the great German mathematician Cantor on the theory of transfinite sets, comparing notes as they went along. Valéry was a little daunted, but quite as persevering as Féline. The annotations on all the major scientific works read during this period – such as the non-Euclidean geometers Riemann and Lobatchevsky – are a convincing proof that they were experienced by Valéry as a highly stimulating challenge to the mind, and an impetus to the working out of his 'System'.

One of the 'mysteries' of Valéry for Féline is the 'fascinating problem' of the influence of mathematics on his thought, on the fundamental way in which he 'sculpts' his thought.[11] He seems convinced that the pull of 'l'esprit de géométrie', as Pascal would say, is always present somewhere in Valéry's writing. We indeed see it when Valéry writes, for instance: 'Faire des mathémathiques — c'est-à-dire rendre visible et tangible tout le travail propre de l'esprit sur une question donnée — introduire éléments et opérations en pleine lumière — cela est tout à fait enivrant' ($C2$, p. 779).[12]

The next milestone was his initiation into physics, triggered, so he tells us ($Œ$, I, p. 856) by his reading in 1891–2 of Poe's *Eureka*. This exalted Romantic cosmogony – strangely prophetic of the model of cosmogenesis now known under the name of the 'Big Bang' – introduced him to Newton's law of universal gravitation on a cosmic scale, and indeed, more indirectly, to most of the names and problems of nineteenth century physics. In 1893, he read Lord Kelvin's *Scientific Lectures* (containing a section entitled *The Constitution of Matter*, and Maxwell's *Treatise on Electricity and Magnetism*). In addition, the importance given to Faraday (scholars have not sufficiently underlined that his name is the very first word in the very first *Notebook* ($C$, I, p. 2)), indicates that Valéry was familiar with his work, and full of admiration for it, before August 1894. He also includes Faraday in two of his very select imaginary 'societies' of great minds ($C1$, pp. 183, 395), in which, significantly, one or more scientists always figure.

Faraday, both a physicist and a chemist, is one of the prime examples in science of a completely self-made man. We owe him several fundamental discoveries in the area of electricity – including the principle of the electric motor, the theory of electrolysis, and the phenomenon of electromagnetic induction – which fired the imagination of the young Valéry because of the completely hidden power that electricity symbolised. Many terms still widely used, and familiar to the general public, such as 'electrode', 'cathode' and 'ionisation' are due to Faraday.

Faraday had both a remarkable experimental flair and an ability to draw from the results of his experiments the theoretical conclusions which they authorise, often completely novel. Valéry compares him in this respect to Leonardo da Vinci (*Œ*, I, p. 1194), attributing to both an '*imaginative logic*' that enables their minds to focus on and develop a completely new concept, for which they 'see' a group of inter-related phenomena providing them with conclusive evidence of a previously unsuspected principle. He thus brought to physics conceptions of an admirable daring, which were literally only the development, by his imagination, of the phenomena observed (cf. p. 1194). As Maxwell puts it: Faraday saw, with the eyes of his mind, lines of force crossing the whole of space where the mathematicians saw centres of force attracting each other from afar; Faraday saw a medium where they saw only distance ( cf. p. 1195).

How did Valéry approach Maxwell, whose treatise on electromagnetism had so excited him? He saw in him the great theoretician who had succeeded in translating Faraday's ideas into mathematical language, in such a vivid way that scientists' imaginations were filled with these 'dominant visions' (*Œ*, I, p. 1195). But Maxwell went even further, elucidating in his famous equations, still used today, the dynamic relationships within an electromagnetic field, showing how, for example, an electromagnetic current can produce a magnetic field and, conversely, a magnetic field an electric current. In addition he demonstrated in a remarkable insight that light is a kind of electromagnetic wave – which then suggested to him that the waves implied by his equations possessed a number of properties of light, and that they also made it possible to interpret many optical phenomena such as polarisation which had not up till then been understood. Valery called Maxwell's treatise (designed for professional research workers in physics) 'passionnant' and read it from cover to cover, with copious annotations, at a very young age.

He realised very early that there are many different *types* of

scientific mind, with varying degrees of abstraction and of attachment to *mathematical* proof. Lord Kelvin, our last example of classical
physics, belonged to the opposite camp: that of the scientists for
whom no new truth can be regarded as fully demonstrated without a
*mechanical* model (*Œ*, I, p. 1195). He was an extreme mechanist, given
to saying that he could understand nothing of which he could not
himself *make* a model.

Kelvin's very numerous and diverse inventions profited from this
mentality, and from the rare combination of an extremely concrete
mind (and hands to go with it) existing alongside a considerable
command of mathematics. Valéry was particularly interested by his
major synthetic contributions to thermodynamics, including a study
of heat engines, his definition of electric units and of thermometric
scales (he was the first physicist to define the absolute scale of
temperature) and his research on hydrodynamics, a science which
delighted Valéry throughout his life, always reminding him of the
changing face of the sea at Sète.

What interested him most, however, was the theoretical and then
strictly practical work Kelvin did on designing and laying the first
Atlantic underwater cable. This act – which was almost as symbolic
in its time as the landing of the first man on the moon – struck
Valéry (and most other people) as a veritable triumph of science: the
definition of a difficult problem, the work on the theoretical model,
its verification, the point-by-point design, of the most resistant cable
possible, the execution of the design, and finally the placing of the
cable on the ocean bed. To add to his delight, Valéry had a small
piece of this cable, spiral in form, of which he was very proud. He
once said to his son Claude, referring to Kelvin's achievement: 'Voilà
un homme qui savait *penser* les choses, puis les *faire*, en les faisant
réellement *marcher*'.[13]

The writings of Leonardo da Vinci in his *Notebooks* were of similar
significance to the young Valéry; he discovered them in the Montpellier Municipal Library, and they filled him immediately with a kind
of absolute intellectual passion, intermingled with aesthetic amaze-
ment. Their role in his inner life and in his literary production was so
fundamental that they gave him an almost overwhelming sense of the
universe as a process of perpetual becoming, as an infinite, endless
producer of forms, patterns, motions, tensions, but hardly ever static,
almost always in the dynamic *process* of becoming themselves, while
freely accepting their future, perhaps imminent, transformation into

something possibly quite different. The magnificent meditation on spiral forms in the *Introduction à la méthode de Léonard de Vinci* (*Œ*, I, p. 1167 ff.) is a remarkable example of Valéry as a budding specialist, years ahead of his time, in morphogenesis! It is therefore no coincidence that contemporary specialists in this field, from Thom to Petitot, have been attracted by his writings.[14]

This is not the place to pursue an exhaustive review of the mature Valéry's relations with twentieth century scientists.[15] Suffice it to say that he was astonishingly aware *at the time* of the importance of the period he was living through, just as he was when he was reading with such enthusiasm Faraday, Maxwell and Kelvin. He knew with great clarity that atomic, quantum and nuclear physics posed scientists with entirely new problems of theory, experiment, apparatus, interpretation and rethinking of epistemological presuppositions. It was no longer sufficient to read the key books as he had done in the 1890s: he needed as well to spend as much time as possible in the laboratories where equipment was being designed, then used, to observe elementary particles as they had never been observed before. But the laboratories had also taken on a new importance as 'think-tanks', where fresh ideas were thrashed out in common. It is significant that in and around the 1920s and 1930s, Valéry was quite often *invited* to participate in these gatherings.

Physics was a particularly striking example of an area in which a veritable explosion of theories and discoveries was occurring, and amongst his many personal friends in this field – many of them close, and most of whom he visited often – one could cite Jean Perrin (Nobel Prize in Physics, an atomic physicist, founding father of the French National Centre for Scientific Research); Paul Langevin (a brilliantly gifted child from a working-class background who shot to the top of the French educational hierarchy and became one of the great Professors of Physics of his time; he immediately seized on the crucial importance of Einstein's first theory of relativity and became its main populariser in France); Marie Curie (of whom it is not often enough said that she was, and I think remains, the only person to have received two Nobel Prizes – excluding the Peace Prize – in two different subjects, physics and chemistry); Louis de Broglie (Nobel Prize in Physics, author of the revolutionary theory of wave mechanics, which, in one of those extraordinary conceptual leaps which Valéry so admired in the history of science, posited a wave-particle dualism in matter as in light); Maurice de Broglie (a specialist in X-rays, who, like his brother, had a real attachment to Valéry, and asked him to sponsor his entry into the Académie française); Einstein (whose special and general theories of relativity powerfully stimulated Valéry's imagination, and with whom he had a very warm relationship); and several other distinguished non-French physicists such as the Dane Niels Bohr (Nobel Prize in Physics, author of the famous 'planetary' model of the atom, and who also did pioneering work on the theory of nuclear reactions – and other dangers to mankind); and the Englishman Patrick Blackett (Nobel Prize for Physics), who came to Paris to give a demonstration, attended by Valéry, of his development of the Wilson cloud chamber technique, enabling him to photograph and display nuclear collisions involving transmutations.

In the field of mathematics, Valéry was a complete devotee of Poincaré, regarded as the most illustrious of French mathematicians. He read and re-read throughout his life all of his epistemological reflections, books written in the most limpid style imaginable. Also known to him personally were three great mathematicians: Jacques Hadamard (who made major contributions to the theory of functions, the theory of numbers and the notion, one of the bases of Valéry's own thought, of a 'correctly posed problem'); Emile Picard (who applied to many types of equations the method of successive approximations); and Elie Cartan, famous for his innovative research on group theory, non-Euclidian (Riemannian) geometry, and notions of connection and invariance – all very close to Valéry's preoccupations.

Emile Borel, a specialist in many branches of mathematics, including notably the increased role of chance and probability in the new physics, was an intimate friend of Valéry's, whom he saw very frequently from about 1920 onwards. Valéry used him as a 'sounding-board' for his ideas on modern mathematics, or on the effect of mathematics on the fascinating but sometimes disconcertingly unfamiliar concepts in physics and cosmology which were developing on all sides. Borel, Perrin and Langevin in particular had reached with each other – and with Valéry – the special type of friendship characteristic of many scientists, in which the animated discussion of the latest theories is intermingled with the simple delight of being together, of exchanging views and hypotheses.

In what are now called the neuro-sciences, so close to the subject of his reflections in the *Cahiers*, Valéry was a close friend of Henri

Piéron, one of the key figures in early experimental psychology, in the areas of sensation and memory, and the neurologist, Théophile Alajouanine (an eminent specialist in language aphasia). He was an even closer friend of the Belgian Ludo van Bogaert, the founding President of the World Federation of Neurology, who, while teaching Valéry much, also regarded him as a master in his analyses of mental functioning.[16]

A central question, however remains. Why should distinguished scientists treat Valéry almost as one of their own? A fascinating 'reverse point of view' on this key question can be found in the proceedings of the first colloquium ever devoted to listening to eminent contemporary scientists talking about Valéry's thought in relation to theirs.[17]

Thus René Thom, having discussed the haunting effect on him of M. Teste's 'Que peut un homme?', goes on to say: 'j'ai découvert, avec surprise, sous la plume de Valéry, des idées, des métaphores qui jouent un grand rôle dans ma propre théorie des catastrophes'.[18] Ilya Prigogine, for his part, discovers in Valéry a mirror image of his own conviction that nothing is more scientifically dangerous than invoking the notion of a total determinism (which would require a god to see all the supposed links in the chain)![19] Far more precious, he declares, are Valéry's 'étonnement' and even his 'angoisse' in the face of the universe and of himself, feeling '*Pourquoi ainsi et pas autrement?*' ('Why thus and not otherwise?'), being aware that both the physical and the mental worlds are made up of 'nœuds' ('knots'), points of possible bifurcation, proofs of the 'possible à chaque instant' ('possible at each moment').[20]

These comments show that scientists, in the present as in the past, have admired Valéry's precise and strategic grasp of what is at stake in their own research. They value also his ability to go right to the heart of a complex question, but no less the challenge of his analogical creativity, never bounded by specialist conformities. They have also wanted, and no doubt needed, to see their own research in a philosophically broad and humanistic framework.

Critics sometimes regret that Valéry seems to have paid much more attention to physics and (to a lesser degree) chemistry than to biology. This was, of course, a characteristic of science in general during the first half of the twentieth century because of the dramatic knowledge-explosion in physics. But when Valéry does speak in detail of the dynamics of the growth of a plant, how incomparably he does it! Thom is *delighted* that an impending 'catastrophe' can be discerned in the detailed morphology of a plant, just at the point where the discontinuity is about to occur. 'Etonnant', he writes, 'capacités vraiment promonitoires de Valéry', 'fragment lumineux ... qui m'a énormement frappé', 'capacité d'intuition remarquable'.[21]

That these qualities extended also to the life-sciences appears strongly from a recent sister colloquium to *Fonctions de l'esprit* under the title *Quelle médecine demain? Sous le regard de Valéry.*[22] Here, it is Valéry's extraordinary sense of human physiology, and the interconnectedness of the mind and body, which are being explored, together with his keen sense of the questions that arise within the nexus Body-Mind-World. Valéry, it will be seen, plays Socrates as much to the doctor or the surgeon as to the physicist.

How can we summarise such a vast subject as Valéry's relations with science? If we take as established the example of rigour and the fruitfulness of borrowed models, procedures and viewpoints in representing the world of subject-consciousness (equivalent for Valéry to the triad 'Corps-Esprit-Monde'), the outstanding value of his scientific fascination lies perhaps in science as an exemplar of the passionate, imaginatively vital, truly creative acquisition and sharing of knowledge. Very often, in electromagnetism, and later in relativity, this knowledge is the expression of a *new unity*. What had been thought to be different turns out to be similar or identical *in another broader context*; and not only in comprehension, but in all the practical acts that comprehension makes possible.

Relativity epitomises just this fascination. It represented the second, and greatest, conceptual leap in which Valéry had the privilege and excitement of sharing – not only through his direct contacts with Einstein but through the intense intellectual activity which surrounded the birth of, first, the special theory of relativity, then of the general theory of relativity. His conversations with Langevin, in particular, gave him early and profound insight into Einstein's work.

Epistemologically, the special theory, incorporating mass into energy, and invoking imaginary 'observers', made an abiding impression on him which inflects the development of his own thought: 'Relativité – c'est comprendre que ce qui se passe est toujours relation entre le phén[omène] (que l'on tend à regarder comme en

soi et indépendant) et l'observateur' (*C*, VIII, p. 414);[23] the observer
must be introduced into the expression of the equation (cf. p. 443),
since 'rien n'est par soi ni en soi' (*C*, X, p. 646). It could be shown
that this conception, significantly different from his early, positivist,
emphasis on a single, absolute, 'protocol language' of thought,
underlies Valéry's mature theory of viewpoints, and influences his
more open, multivalent treatment of subjects as diverse as aesthetics,
love and religion.

No scientific discovery, it is safe to say, enchanted Valéry more
than Einstein's general theory. This colossal conquest of intelligibility
was won in part thanks to the aesthetic flair of the physicist (cf.*Œ*, II,
p. 264). Valéry is delighted by this 'grand artiste' – 'et c'est le seul
artiste au milieu de tous ces savants' ('and he is the only artist among
all these scientists') – with his 'FOI *fondée* sur l'architecture et la
beauté des formes' ('FAITH *founded* on architecture and the beauty of
forms') (*C2*, p. 875), which the physicist's imagination revealed to
him as inhabiting the whole universe. 'Ceci me touche intimement'
('this touches me intimately') (*ibid.*): Einstein was seeking his network
of relationships as Valéry felt he had been seeking his – through the
formal structures that bring together the most apparently disparate
objects and processes.

Certainly, this event reinforced his capacity, powerfully expressed
in the prose poetry of his 'Aubades', to see a given part of nature as
signifying a limited whole (cf. *C*, XII, p. 190). For, paradoxically, as he
realised, the dazzling richness and complexity of Einstein's thought
and visual imagination had as its main aim and effect the demonstration of the oneness of 'the universe', its coherence, its lack of
fundamental randomness, and in the midst of all forms of relativity,
the constants (like the velocity of light) which give it structure. He
told several friends that attending Einstein's two lectures in Paris in
1929, especially the second on the general theory, had given him a
powerful, even intoxicating, sense of the *unity* of nature.[24]

Yet, Valéry is also capable of writing, characteristically, that
Einstein has been as 'naive' as everyone – for instance Bergson –
who seeks to build a model of nature 'où tout doit figurer' ('in which
everything must figure'). 'C'est ce *tout* qui est leur naïveté. Je sais ce
que c'est' ('It's this everything that's their naivety. I know what this
is') (*C2*, pp. 874–5). Valéry's final pirouette here is to take upon
himself, as well as upon Einstein, the possible error in wanting to
include everything. This and many other inner debates, for example

on the growing importance of indeterminism, gave Valéry much food for thought, but also a certain feeling of unease in the last years of his life. A residue of the unanswered epistemological, philosophical and even metaphysical questions raised by modern science can certainly be read in the parable of Valéry's last work *L'Ange*, where the self-elucidating subject, who has sought to enfold himself in the light of a rationally and scientifically conceived 'connaître' recognises, in his equation of the self, the final pre-eminence of a tragically frustrated human 'comprendre'. The infinite question, the question that cannot answer itself, lies not only *without*; it lies especially *within* the universe of the mind, the universe proper to man.

Yet whatever may be posterity's judgment on the matter of unity and indeterminism, Valéry can only be admired for having clearly understood two basic truths. The first is expressed succinctly in the words: 'considérer le Corps comme l'instrument capital de la physique, et la physique comme ayant ce corps pour limite' (*C2*, p. 846).[25] The second lies in the extraordinarily rich affirmation (*C*, VIII, p. 153) which can be summarised thus: 'L'esprit [1] est un moment [2] de la réponse [3] du corps [4] au monde [5]' (*C2*, p. 1125).[26] If the earlier sentence quoted speaks of a limit and a possible relativity, the second, immensely admired since by biological and medical scientists, speaks of an interconnectedness which links [1] to [2], a specific point in time, and to [3], [4] and [5], the specific reaction here-and-now of the body.

The much quoted triad 'Corps-Esprit-Monde' indicates that Valéry considered the mind (and the brain and nervous system through which it functions) as part and parcel of the physical world. As such they cannot fail to be governed to a degree, which has to be fully determined, by its scientific laws – for example, physical, gravitational, electrical, chemical, biological, genetic and no doubt others.

The term CEM therefore in no way suggests a separation of any one of them from any other. Rather, they are a way of reminding us that in all we do, we are bringing both body and mind into an ever-new relationship with the world, and vice-versa. We need it, and it 'needs' us, to understand and to conceptualise it. Narcissus and the Angel need a pool to see themselves in, as the Jeune Parque needs the sea, the stars and the serpent. There is in this reciprocity something both profoundly scientific and profoundly human which comes close to the core of Valéry as both thinker and writer.[27]

NOTES

1 'But science is born of . . . poetic imaginations'.
2 See in particular J. Robinson, *L'Analyse de l'esprit dans les 'Cahiers' de Valéry* (Paris, Corti, 1963) and N. Celeyrette-Pietri, *Valéry et le Moi: Des 'Cahiers à l'œuvre'* (Paris, Klincksieck, 1979).
3 '. . . their rigour, their tension, their pure difficulty, their right ways of defining things, their search for operations'.
4 'What I look for in physics (example – principle of relativity – is the wherewithal to tackle the problems of the self'
5 Valéry has been variously called a 'super-dilettante' with a 'smattering' of modern mathematics and physics, an 'amateur' running to keep up with new discoveries, and criticised for the very eclecticism of his interests by such critics as Edmund Wilson, John Cocking, Jacques Duchesne-Guillemin and even Cioran. See my paper 'Valéry et la science: jugements et témoignages d'hier et d'aujourd'hui', *Œuvres et critiques*, 9 (Paris, J.-M. Place, 1984), pp. 9–46.
6 See my articles 'L'Homme et la coquille: l'apport de Valéry à la philosophie', *Nuovo Corrente* (Genova, Tilgher), special no. 'Cahiers di Valéry', 96, (1985), pp. 460–2 and 'L'Homme et la coquille – la forme en devenir', J. Hainault (ed.), *Valéry, le Partage de midi – 'Midi le juste'. Actes du Colloque international tenu au Collège de France le 18 novembre 1995* (Paris, Champion, 1997).
7 Standard reference work of Victorian aesthetics (original edition 1856).
8 Pierre Féline, 'A Montpellier, rue Urbain V en 1890 Paul Valéry vivant' *Cahiers du Sud* (Arles, 1946), pp. 45–8.
9 *Ibid.*, p. 46.
10 Valéry's detailed analyses of exactly what human capacities are reduced or even virtually eliminated in these two nocturnal phases are remarkable, especially in view of the fact that his observation preceded the dramatically new post-war techniques in neurology (such as the introduction of electrical measurement).
11 Féline, *Paul Valéry vivant*, p. 47.
12 'Doing mathematics — i.e. making visible and tangible the whole work proper to the mind on a given question — introducing elements and operations in full light of consciousness — that is absolutely intoxicating'
13 Oral testimony to the author.
14 See René Thom in J. Robinson-Valéry (éd.), *Fonctions de l'esprit: Treize savants redécouvrent Paul Valéry* (Paris, Hermann, 1983), pp. 198–200 and Jean Petiot on the development of the sea-shell ('La vie ne sépare pas sa géométrie de sa physique'). Remarques sur quelques réflexions morphologiques de Paul Valéry', in J. Hainault (éd.), *Valéry: Le Partage de midi*.
15 I have attempted such a review in 'Valéry et la science: jugements et témoignages d'hier et d'aujourd'hui', *Œuvres et critiques*, 19, 1 (1984), pp. 9–46.

16  See Robinson-Valéry, *Fonctions de l'Esprit*, pp. 159–180.

17  *Ibid.*

18  'What is a man capable of achieving? ... I discovered with surprise in Valéry ideas, metaphors, which play a major role in my own catastrophe theory' (*ibid.*, p. 193). Thom is an eminent mathematician, and the inventor of catastrophe theory.

19  *Ibid.*, p. 258. Prigogine is a Nobel prizewinner in Chemistry.

20  *Ibid.*, pp. 258–60.

21  'astonishing' ... 'truly premonitory capabilities of Valéry' ... 'a luminous fragment which struck me forcibly' ... 'remarkable intuitive capacity for divination' (*Ibid.*, pp. 200 – 6).

22  J. Robinson-Valéry (ed.), *Quelle médecine demain? Sous le regard de Paul Valéry* (Toulouse, Privat, in press).

23  'Relativity — means understanding that what happens is always a relation between the phenomenon (which one always tends to see in itself, as independent) and the observer ... nothing is in itself, by itself'

24  Oral testimony to the author by André Georg.

25  'to consider the body as the chief instrument of physics, and of physics as having the body as its limit'

26  'the mind [1] is a moment [2] of the response [3] of the body [4] to the world [5]'

27  For further reading on the topic of this chapter, please see Bibliography, items 56, 74, 80, 99, 101, 108, 111, 115.

CHAPTER 5

# An art of rethinking: Valéry's 'negative philosophy'

Régine Pietra

Traditionally, Valéry's reputation rests on his published work as poet and essayist. The era of the *Cahiers* has however brought to light another dimension already hinted at in *La Soirée avec M. Teste*, *Introduction à la méthode de Léonard de Vinci* and the Dialogues (*Eupalinos*, *L'Ame et la danse*, *L'Idée fixe*, *Dialogue de l'arbre*): Valéry is now seen as one of the major thinkers of the century.

To be sure, he himself wryly disclaimed any right to 'le beau titre de philosophe' ('the fine title of philosopher') (*Œ*, II, p. 1499), since he saw himself quite apart from the map of knowledge and specialist competence as drawn by the university establishment of his day. Unmistakably, however, the *Cahiers* show us an activity and practice of thought which, though it disdains the heavy apparatus of the systematic philosopher, nonetheless tackles many of the essential problems of philosophy. 'Fondateur de la Philosophie Négative' ('Founder of negative philosophy'), says Valéry, defining his originality with a self-ironic flourish. He adds significantly: 'La plus positive de toutes'('the most positive of all') (*C*1, p. 747).

Negative philosophy is critical philosophy. Valéry was, throughout his life, a consistent critic of his philosophic predecessors and their discipline as consecrated in traditional practice. His critical bent is best illustrated in the three favoured areas of language, metaphysics and ethics.

The philosopher is someone who, for the most part, does not know what he is saying. He uses words devoid of meaning, words he has insufficiently analysed and defined because of his prior failure to recognise their transitional status and the conventional character of language as such; thus words solidify into entities. The abstract terms philosophers deal in are viewed by Valéry as the naive products of primitive minds; greater analytical subtlety would show up their relativity (cf. *Œ*, I, p. 1248). Words such as: *reason, reality*,

85

*universe, cause, idea, origin, end*, etc. (cf. p. 874) are all defined only by context, and are thus variable in sense.

We may illustrate this from the notion of 'causality', seen by Valéry as essentially anthropomorphic: we see everything that happens around us in terms of human action; we seek to know who is the author, who is responsible. Hence the simplistic character of this concept, and its inability to account for the multiplicity of relationships between phenomena. If we are not to think in linear series, as we generally do, we would need to eliminate the concept of cause and replace it, for instance, with that of function – a substitution already suggested by Mach –[1] or else, when dealing with mind-made phenomena, by the notions of act, agent and motive.

What is true of causality is truer still of finality. We think that Nature acts like us, setting itself goals; we endow it with intentions, a past, a future. We project our categories onto it in order to catch it in the webs of our thinking, whereas we are in fact dealing with a blind, mindless process (cf. *C2*, p. 1438).

Valéry stands aside from such naivety. Characteristically, his procedure is to undertake what he calls a 'nettoyage de la situation verbale' ('cleaning-up of the verbal situation') (*Œ*, 1, p. 1316), an acid-like filtering of everything he deems not to be the object of rigorous empirical observation or of impeccable logical deduction. The philosophers whose language stands up to this test are few in number. Kant is certainly not one of them: 'On se passe aisément d'une *Critique de la Raison Pure* en observant que les mots sont des mots et que tous les résultats des raisonnements sont sans exception provisoires, c'est-à-dire impuissants, inopérants, si on ne les retrouve pas dans l'expérience' (*C1*, p. 608).[2] There is an entirely recognisable affinity between Valéry's position in these matters and that of the Vienna Circle and British analytical positivism (A. J. Ayer among others). The refusal of abstract notions elevated to the status of Ideas, linked to extreme methodological rigour, unites all these thinkers in a common suspicion of metaphysics.

Metaphysics claims to be a veridical discourse about Being. In fact, the reality of things ultimate lies outside our grasp, not because it refers to any form of transcendence, but because it is open to a multiplicity of interpretations and viewpoints.[3] It is, moreover, the epitome of empty discourse which substantifies and divinises words – such as the verb *être*, with its well-known history as cornerstone of an entire philosophical tradition, which in common speech is nothing more than a humble copula effecting predication ('this child *is* delightful'). 'Being' has contributed to imaginary creations, popular idols, veritable myths sustaining the wisdom of nations; and it is by no means alone in so doing. Consider Pascal's famous phrase, famously incriminated by Valéry: 'le silence éternel de ces espaces infinis m'effraye' ('the eternal silence of these infinite spaces appals me') (*Œ*, I, p. 1458). Is this not, asks Valéry, the very epitome of non-thought? Instead of thought, he sees pathos, impure exploitation of sensibility, the artificial search for theatrical effect, rhetorical eloquence as a means of tugging at nerves and heart-strings. Philosophy has become a brass band.[4] As to philosophy's pretention to Truth, this appears to Valéry totally vain, since truth lies in the order of belief and is nothing apart from the feeling one has for it (cf. *Œ*, II, p. 863). Philosophy, in consequence, has little to do with objectivity: it is partial, subjective, and expresses the particular viewpoint of its author. Like Nietzsche, Valéry considers philosophy to be the product of a temperament (cf. *C*I, p. 534), even of a particular hour of the day, or a particular mood: 'Sensualiste au réveil. / Criticiste à 11h. / Hobbiste sur les 4h.' ('Sensualist when I wake up, criticist at 11 o'clock, Hobbesian around tea-time') (*CII*, p. 29).

Idealism, which in continental tradition is virtually co-extensive with metaphysics, forgets simply that philosophy does not fall out of the intelligible heavens. Equally, it fails to recognise the primordial and founding role of the body: 'Tout système philosophique où le Corps de l'homme ne joue pas un rôle fondamental est inepte, inapte' (*C*I, p. 1124).[5] Few philosophers have understood this; and, in the *Cahiers* (where direct quotations are in general rare) it is noteworthy that Valéry should refer this view nominally to Lucretius and Epicurus. The point at issue is the importance of touch as a means of knowledge: '*Tangere enim et tangi nisi corpus nulla potest res*',[6] writes the author of *De Natura Rerum*. Epicurus, for his part, does not recognise incorporeity as the property of anything other than a void, since the soul, to the extent that it acts or is acted upon, is corporeal. One can also see from this double reference how Valéry could admire Thomism which does not really conceive the soul separate from the body, and how he might approve of the Catholic doctrine that the soul is reintegrated with the body in order to participate in the fullness of eternal life (cf. *Œ*, I, pp. 1214–5).

This latter reference illustrates his own approach well: Valéry will think as an empiricist, adhering as closely as may be to the material

conditions underlying our mental conceptions. Praising St Thomas
in the passage just mentioned does not by any means imply
acceptance of the entire Thomist system, which, like any system,
navigates amid abstractions. It simply means picking out from a
corpus of writing an idea which concords with his own thinking. All
the philosopher's '-isms' correspond to more-or-less crude cut-outs,
more-or-less facile and erroneous oppositions: spiritualism and
materialism, like realism and idealism, are merely 'points of view'.

We may thus summarise the charges he piles up in the course of a
life-long indictment of metaphysics, viewed as an 'astrologie de
mots' ('astrology with words') (cf. *CIII*, p. 337). Condemned in its
very definition (as a science of Being), metaphysics is refuted in its
pretensions to objectivity, universality and perennity. Preoccupied
solely with intelligible realities, the metaphysician fails to see that
there is more matter for philosophy in heaven and on earth than is
dreamed of in the whole canon of metaphysics. He is thus encaged
(cf. *Œ*, II, p. 871) and the questions which torment him are like the
comings-and-goings of animals in the zoo. Such thinkers, for Valéry
as for Wittgenstein, are comparable to 'cette chauve-souris qui se
prétend aveuglée par le soleil et qui se cogne simplement la tête
contre le murs du langage'.[7]

The futility of metaphysics brings about the ruin of ethics, which
generally relies upon it. The notion of the Good has no more
absolute validity than the notion of Truth. Good and evil are relative
to our sensibility; so are justice and happiness. The effort of moralists
consists of cloaking in abstract principles, which confer stable
authority, something that can only be understood piecemeal, in
strictly individual, concrete terms. Among these principles is duty,
which Kant makes into a categorical imperative, derived, according
to Valéry, from the argument 'If everyone were to do likewise ...';
and Valéry adds, somewhat unkindly – indeed, unjustly – that an
idea of this ilk could only have arisen in an envious mind who would
very much have liked to do likewise (cf. *CI*, p. 744).

It is helpful here to follow Valéry's very concrete handling of
moral notions. We may instance the notion of moral fault, closely
related to the notions of responsibility and punishment. The latter
two concepts presuppose an unchanging agent, the same yesterday,
today and tomorrow. But we know that nothing of the sort is true;
here is a patent absurdity, founded on an abstraction (i.e. 'Man'),
which bears no relation to the actual individual who was a scoundrel

yesterday, is repentant today and may tomorrow be a saint. All morality rests on the identity, past, present and future, of the moral agent; our common notions of commitment, promise, oath, suppose it. As to punishment, this belongs for Valéry to a commercial view of morality founded on exchange, the swapping of ill for ill (cf. *Œ*, II, p. 509). At bottom, Valéry sees all justice as a mercantile idea (cf. *ibid.*, p. 539) and a theatrical one (cf. pp. 839–40), as evidenced in the staging of the trial, the courtroom ritual, the accoutrement of judge and lawyers, etc. The thinker wishing to reflect on moral concepts should, like the metaphysician, go back to the concrete conditions which have allowed their formulation in language. Morality, on this view, is not independent of historico-economic circumstances.

If we now leave aside the abstract ethics of the philosopher, and question ourselves upon our own moral conscience and its strange deliberations, what do we discover in its depths? A magma of opposed impulses, now altruistic, now sordid, attempting self-regulation. If Valéry's reflections on the psyche proceed from a perspective different from Freud's, even at times opposed to it, many of his analyses of affectivity, of sensibility, like his interest in dreaming, reveal between the two thinkers as many affinities as incompatibilities. As concerns action properly so-called, reasoning has no control, and in most cases, it is the nervous system we are dealing with. Even in its most accomplished reaches, morality comes down to a certain number of automatisms.

Little is left, it will be seen, in the wake of Valéry's analytic rethinking, of the grandiose edifice of traditional speculative philosophy. Should we however conclude that this work of subversion is entirely negative and that this contemner of philosophic tradition has nothing to offer us but his disappointment? This would be to miss the point that behind every disappointment lies hidden a purer, more demanding idea. Am I perhaps pointing here to some unexpected Valéryan idealism? Not really; for Valéry, as we shall see, makes good his bid for something other, radically different, corresponding better to the essence glimpsed through traditional philosophy, but which traditional philosophy disfigures. This proposition seems as sure as does the philosophical spirit in Valéry. Indeed, for all his reticence, beyond his own denials, Valéry does accord himself a place, albeit a singular one, among the philosophers (cf. *LQ*, p. 245).

That Valéry is not of the same family within that community, is clear enough from the fierce and often summary disrespect he shows, from one end of the *Cahiers* to the other, to the great names of philosophy with whom he engages.[8] The dynamics of intellectual evaluation as pursued in these private writings (often implying also struggle and assimilation of one mind by another) are always instructive. The Presocratics are compared to intellectual griffons, whose 'fragments font rêver à des vestiges de taureaux ailés, à têtes de lion … accouplements extraordinaires de la profondeur et de l'absurde' (*C*i, 503).[9] Plato gets little of the credit we might think due to him for inaugurating Western philosophy. Instead he is said to draw 'de l'éclairage d'une grotte et des silhouettes qu'il engendre … des conséquences funestes' (*Œ*, ii, p. 1573)[10] and, while remaining within a mythic world, to transform myth into philosophy. The Socratic dialogues, apart from their beginnings, are dismissed as mere padding. Of Aristotle, Valéry retains only 'quelques formules' ('a few formulas'), judging that there is nothing in the *Rhetoric* (cf. *Œ*, ii, p. 1573). Plotinus' metaphysic is dismissed as 'ingénuissime' ('very simple-minded'), like that of Spinoza, for whom Valéry reserves his most scathing criticism (which might well scandalise more than the present reader).

Kant is frequently referred to: generally, he is taken to task for not having been radical enough in eradicating metaphysics; or else Valéry challenges his conception of space and time and overthrows his universal *a priori* judgments. Examining Kantian morality, Valéry concludes that Kant is an 'étourdi' ('scatterbrain') – the last epithet most people would have thought of to describe the author of the *Critique of Practical Reason*! Kant's definition of the beautiful reflects a 'curieux calvinisme' ('curious calvinism'), which is unsurprising, says Valéry, in someone who has a 'goût de chien' ('dog's taste') (*C*i, p. 636). While Valéry never read Hegel (cf. *LQ*, p. 242), he did read Schopenhauer, as indeed did many turn-of-the-century French writers for whom the German idealist philosopher was something of a fetish. The correspondence with Gide attests this declared influence, though it is difficult to detect its traces, at least outside the poetry.[11] We may suppose Valéry is won over by Schopenhauer's perspicacious remarks on stupidity, genius, or memory as a machine-like filter (as M. Teste has it) and on the word-chopping of those whom Schopenhauer calls the 'philosophastres'. Is Schopenhauer, then, a reassuring exception to Valéry's generalised negativity? We are soon undeceived: *The World as Will and Representation* is consigned (together with Plato's *Timæus* and all of Hegel) to the category of lyric poetry (cf. *C1*, p. 556). Valéry's most constant tendency, indeed, is to treat philosophy as a sub-branch of literature and the creative arts.

Nietzsche,[12] whom Valéry did read systematically in reviewing Henri Albert's French translation (1900–8) of the collected works, and to whom he owes a good deal more than he acknowledges, evokes in him ambivalent responses. Nietzsche is both stimulus and irritant. On the credit side, Valéry responds to the German philosopher's intellectual combativity, his fascination with human potential and its extremes; he appreciates the self-imposed demands of the dedicated mind, its ability to fuse the analytical and the lyrical, its concerted appeal to music, philology and physiology. On the debit side, he reacts with exasperated parody to the 'chef d'orchestre danubien furibond' ('a furious baton-wielder from the Danube') (*ibid.*, p. 534), and greets with incredulity or sarcasm his lack of rigour, his verbalism, his polemical overstatements, his protestant moralism, his mega-prophetism ('chrétien, trop chrétien' ('christian, all-too-christian')), and his failure to interest himself in science.

Valéry is severe, certainly, and readers of the *Cahiers* are likely to disown him when he attacks their favourite philosophers, just as they will react with glee to his audacious demolitions of less favoured thinkers. 'Il faut être *profondément* injuste. Sinon, ne vous en mêlez pas — Soyez juste!' ('One must be *profoundly* unjust. Otherwise, don't bother — be just!') (*C*, IV, p. 368), says Valéry, invoking the right of the powerful mind to take what he needs in the thought of others and to judge them self-referentially. Some famous heads do indeed escape the general massacre: generally, those whom Valéry identifies as having courageously traced out his own path. Among these, Zeno is the first, since his much-studied paradoxes on the way abstract thought immobilises life in order to know it encapsulate for Valéry the essence of philosophy. Achilles and the arrow take their place in the 'Le Cimetière marin', exhibiting the *impasse* of pure mind:

> Zénon! Cruel Zénon! Zénon d'Elée!
> M'as-tu percé de cette flèche ailée
> Qui vibre, vole, et qui ne vole pas!
> Le son m'enfante et la flèche me tue!
> Ah! le soleil ... Quelle ombre de tortue
> Pour l'âme, Achille immobile à grands pas![13]

Lulle and Leibniz are also spared: from them Valéry takes the idea

of a an alphabet of thoughts, hence of a formalised set of relationships between the products of the mind – very much the inspiration
of the early years of what he calls, with some irony, his own 'System':
the attempt, that is, to represent the relations discernable between
the imaginary and the real, and between body, mind and world.

His hero is of course Descartes, the only philosopher Valéry ever
consented to treat officially and publicly.[14] Valéry interprets the
celebrated *Cogito* ('I think, therefore I am') in his own way, not as a
valid epistemological proposition, but as a non-rational axiom,
positing existentially the omnipotence of the thinking mind in its
singularity and pride, and thereby founding its effort of rationality.
Throughout the *Cahiers*, he effects countless variations, too numerous
to be explored here, upon this ever-present formula, now denouncing its propositional weaknesses, now tempering his own courage
with its spirit of assertion.[15] Through these tireless variations, he
explores all the problems raised before and since by Descartes'
commentators, showing how an old formula can be revivified and
made profitable in the act of rethinking. To bring philosophy alive,
even at the price of radical disrespect, is the heart of his enterprise;
indeed, it is something taught by Descartes himself.

On closer inspection, Valéry's tribute is offered less to the *Cogito*,
than to the *Discours de la méthode:* Descartes represents for him the
inventor of a method borrowing its rigour from mathematics, 'le
premier constructeur d'un univers entièrement métrique' ('the first
constructor of an entirely metrical universe') (*Œ*, I, p. 802). More
centrally still: he is the only philosopher who, having destroyed
what seemed to him without foundation, attempted, as it were, to
remodel philosophy by integrating into it philosophic notions
rethought in the very unfolding of a new trajectory. Here is Valéry's
true model; or rather (all models being as dispensable to him as to
Descartes), here is the true brother mind. The trajectory of his
negative philosophy is that of a method, rather than a system, as
Valéry confides to a philosopher friend of his youth,[16] Gustave
Fourment, in informing the latter of his reflections concerning the
relations between mental phenomena viewed rigorously as such (cf.
*VF*, p. 141).

This intellectual proximity to Descartes illuminates Valéry's own
practice as philosopher: first destroy one's own earlier thinking or
that of others in order the better to rethink it (cf. *C*I, p. 721); strip
down the terminology, restoring the concrete origin of the abstract

words used ('hypothesis', 'substance', 'soul', 'spirit', 'idea', 'thought')(cf. *Œ*, I, p. 1094); entirely reconstitute the philosopher's lexicon,[17] polish its definitions so as to make language self-cognisant (cf. *C*I, p. 355) – thus M. Teste, thinking only in studied definitions (cf. *ibid.*, p. 359). Such mastery over language aims at exactness and precision; it makes thought operative and restores its true weight. 'Penseurs sont gens qui re-pensent, et qui pensent que ce qui fut pensé ne fut jamais assez pensé' (*Œ*, II, p. 767).[18] (In his preface to the French translation of Heidegger's *Principle of reason*, J. Beaufret quotes these words of Valéry's to show that thought, like the river, retains its memory of origin.) Philosophic meditation – always a difficult exercise if one is resolved to escape mental vacuity and stupor – can only happen on this basis: 'Méditer en philosophe, c'est revenir du familier à l'étrange, et dans l'étrange affronter le réel' (*Œ*, II, p. 501).[19]

This constant concern to retrace much-travelled paths so as to assure himself of their viability, and also to multiply available viewpoints, sometimes gives the reader of the *Cahiers* the impression of indefinite repetiton pursued over fifty years. Valéry compares himself shrewdly to a tethered cow grazing the same patch of grass (cf. *C*I, p. 11). His depth lies less in breaking new ground than in bringing fresh illumination to old ground – which thus ceases to be old. At bottom, the great philosophers are not those who have turned over a large number of ideas, but those who have delved with consistency into a central vision.

Renovation can only occur however if one manages to scrape away all the deposited clinker which encumbers the exercise of the intellect. Valéry's name for such encumbrances is *Fiducia*. By this latin word, Valéry designates everything which is in the order of belief, everything which feeds our myths, being purely verbal and without referential value: in other words, that pseudo-thought we pursue in the fields of history, law, politics and religion and which is in fact purely fictional. Humankind is spontaneously believing, inclined to adhere without examination to whatever offers itself. Such false knowledge is what Plato called *doxa*. Descartes referred it to the prejudices of childhood; Spinoza spoke of knowledge of the first type, knowledge by hearsay. Valéry wages a relentless war on such supposed knowledge, which is all the more dangerous in that it cannot justify itself, but may very well constitute virtually the whole

content of our so-called thinking. Philosophy can only begin when
the weeds stifling new shoots have been rooted out. Even then, the
good corn and the chaff must be distinguished. Yet the extent of the
fiduciary empire is such that this task is almost limitless.

Two points may be retained from Valéry's analysis: first, every
belief concerns an object outside our grasp, an entity which is purely
verbal in origin; second, consequently, the act of 'believing in',
having no true referent, returns boomerang-like to source and
reactivates belief. We are in a world of *values* which subsist only on
the credit we give to them. To believe, to trust, is to give independent
existence to figures of possibility in the mind; it is to transform what
we ask of reality into what reality supposedly grants us – a magical
operation. There is no encashment corresponding to the face value
of such paper money, on which we continue, however, to draw
hugely. Some examples may be offered here from History, Law,
Politics and Religion.

Valéry never *believed* in History. He has been criticised for this, but
had his good reasons. For History is not to be distinguished from the
discourse treating of it: the historian merely produces 'an effect of
reality', a referential illusion. To believe that a given historical
personage existed is to believe by hearsay. Historical fact is, as
Carlyle said, unique, non-reiterable, and, as such, outside verification.[20] 'According to the story I've been told . . .': such should be the
motto of the canny historian. One cannot restore the past, still less
relive it – hence the incongruity of a writer such as Michelet; one
can only re-invent or reconstruct it. No facts except facts-in-
representation (cf. *Œ*, I, p. 1133). The intentionality projected by
historical consciousness has no other depth than that of language:
people none the less believe in it, just as they believe in what they
themselves were, without really knowing what that signifies, nor
what can be drawn from it. That is why the 'lesson' to be learned
from History is the same as that which Jules Renard attributed to
personal experience: it allows us to make the same blunders over
again, albeit less blithely (cf. *Œ*, II, p. 313). Valéry, we observe,
accepts no knowledge – however well-established, whatever its
guarantors – without contesting its claims as knowledge. His scepticism is, indeed, proportional to the shared belief.

That we may be deluded in respect of the past we are perhaps
inclined to admit, but our critical sense hesitates to accept that the
power of language could invade our present, commanding us by

obligation and by sanction. Yet the world of Law[21] functions only within a régime of fiduciarity. It has no other foundation than an imaginary one, even if the imaginary is here instituted and guaranteed by consecrated forms. The origin of the Law is an act of Allegiance: the oath, the mysterious act by which words embed themselves in future time, sketching out the shape our liberty will take on. The language of the Law is essentially performative ('I declare', 'I decree') – that is to say, it has the singular property of being self-referential, referring to nothing outside itself. It is an act of authority, decked out in the costume of legality and presenting itself as the language of reason, whereas it is in fact the language of power. Society, when it emerges from barbarousness, sets up an order resting only on fictions (cf. *Œ*, I, p. 508): the magic of words pronounced by sooth-sayers (the Sacred, the Just), the deification of the law itself, ignorance of which will be no defence. Nor can we take refuge, as people from Antigone to Rousseau have sought to do, in Natural Law, which Valéry calls 'suprafiduciaire': Law is always artifice, artefact. Valéry does not deny the necessity for a social regulation; what he denounces is its camouflage beneath veils of rationality. Behind currency, marriage-contracts, wills, he detects the reign of this disincarnate and transcendent Word which lives only on our believing, and has no force except in our fascination with it.

Such trenchant views are thought-provoking. La Boétie, some centuries before, already warned us of our 'willing enslavement'; but no-one listened. It is always necessary to re-think and re-say that the Law, from which we expect justice and exact dealing, is arbitrary, word-bound, logic-chopping. Certainly, it assures social cohesion, but its coherence is a fiction, since language is both the condition of social being and its end, given that social cohesion finds its ideal realisation in language. Short of a – fictive – social cohesion, there is only confrontation and conflict. 'Le droit est l'intermède des forces' ('Law is the interval between brute forces') (*Œ*, II, p. 950).

Politics is treated elsewhere in this volume and we may pass lightly. It too comes in for Valéryan sarcasm directed at language. Politics is 'ventriloquie: *on fait parler l'Etat, le Peuple, la Justice etc*' ('ventriloquism: making the State, the People, Justice etc. speak') (*C*, XXIV, p. 588). Power rests purely on confidence accorded: like any credit-house, it reposes on the working assumption that not all clients will withdraw their savings on the same day (cf. *Œ*, I, p. 1034). The State is a myth; it makes greater demands in proportion as it confers fewer advantages. It functions by too many relay-mechanisms, too many heterogeneous systems, to be other than a mere abstraction, an entity requiring submission and veneration; so that it often appears as a sort of monster oppressing the healthy energies of the individual (cf. Œ, II, p. 966 ff.). The Leviathan is however a paper tiger who waxes strong only because we show lamentable faith in what makes the serpent's cunning – the force of words. The State, it will be seen, is for Valéry a fantastic book of animals.

The Nation fares no better: this is an artificial and outmoded notion, taking no account of our twentieth-century nomadism, founded still on the capital of territory. It is, according to Valéry, time we learned to think on a global scale, or at least a European one; Leonardo stands as founder of this view, Faust as representative embodiment of its spirit. But, as is well known, Valéry's Europe is in crisis; we are offered a diagnosis which bears re-reading (cf. Œ, I, p. 988 ff.).

Is Valéry a political philosopher? Certainly: a philosopher who, here as elsewhere, constructs no system (a system would be another abstraction), but seeks everywhere to flush out the idols of the tribe, which are the projections of our fears and which have no other reality than the belief we accord them.

As we might well suspect, it is in the religious sphere that *Fiducia* is seen to exercise its worst ravages. All faith is constituted, Valéry tells us, by an essential error multiplied by an energy. The error consists in founding belief upon words whose meaning invokes a signified which does double duty as both idea and referent – a semantic aberration. 'Credo quia absurdum', perceived by Valéry as the formula of all religious belief, becomes, in its very absurdity, something close to an argument for the non-existence of God (cf. C2, p. 687). In order to subsist despite the fragility of its conceptual underpinnings, religious faith finds strange resources in the desire for personal survival or immortality. Thus we can explain the will to believe which Valéry, in his time, saw as characteristic of Christianity. Valéry detests this 'Pascalian' aspect of faith, resulting from inculcated reflexes. 'La *race* d'un esprit se marque par son indocilité naturelle, une inaptitude à croire, à tenir la parole pour valeur autre que valeur de *parole* ... Rien de plus vulgaire que la crédulité' (C2, p. 716).[22]

That the theologian should be indicted in his intentions and in his attempt at systematisation seems fair enough. But what of the mystic? Is there not in him a power of certainty which owes nothing to the effort towards belief; are we not confronted here with a personal language anchored in experience? Valéry mistrusts this claim: the intrusion of sensibility operating now as request, now as answer, leads the mystic to accredit what he 'experiences', to construct a continuous account out of discontinuities, and to invest the future, the possible, with an emotive charge which the present, the real, denies him. 'God' lives only on credit. The religions are insolvent; and Valéry is not the man to wager. The idea of wagering implies a leap into the unknown in which, though we stand to gain everything, we also stand to lose essentials of emotion, sensuality and intellect which are not to be sacrificed. The leap of faith expresses a contempt for the here-and-now which is a form of renunciation, and an abdication of the will to intelligibility.

Of course, Valéry does not rest even in this protocol of religious scepticism, as his voluminous and developing attention to this originating zone reminds us. In important respects, religion marks the point of convergence of his critiques of history, the juridical spirit, politics, language and Fiducia. Indeed, all these cultural phenomena are viewed as products of the same self-mystifying, language-enhanced natural religiosity of the human psyche, as forms of that enigmatic and elusive phenomenon of Desire which Valéry's psychopoetics is centrally concerned to elucidate.

Many fruitful questions are raised by this approach. Is it the case that all religious believing is a form of common Fiducia writ large? Is all faith a form of idealism (e.g. is Christianity a popular Platonism?). Is it reducible to a self-mystifying product of 'complementary' sensibility? If faith had other sources, other guarantees, another meaning and status, how would we be able to distinguish these? What would 'le vrai Dieu' be like? Valéry's dynamic persistence in rethinking such questions relates to his determination, in an era of the crisis of idealist metaphysics, to sift all inherited responses – and to see what survives . . .

Whether in history, law, politics or religion, we are bamboozled by the very instrument we use to understand the world. How can we escape this plight, if indeed it can be escaped? What antidote can break the spell? The analysis of belief and its motivations is difficult and perilous. Our investment has been too great for objectivity to be entirely tolerable: hence various forms of conduct attempting to find a refuge. Yet *catharsis* is possible, at a high price: the price of rigorous analysis, hunting down the non-explicit, the prefabricated, the element of automatism in our thinking; the price of an appeal to experience, countering fictive ideas and scotching the dangerous flights of the idealist. We must demystify the words which come from above, which may be as laden with falsehood as those from the depths.

Valéryan philosophy is, we may say, a philosophy *en creux*. Like negative theology, it abstains from saying what being, reality, etc. are, but says instead what they cannot be. In this sense it offers striking parallels to Wittgenstein; the same mistrust of abstractions, the same appeal to experience, the same reiteration of thoughts, the same cavalier attitude to traditional philosophy, a comparably strenuous ethic of thought and, above all, a similar ambition, at once modest and overweening: to know what one is saying and to say it clearly. That is all. No longer does he seek for Truth, Nietzsche having allowed us to dispense with that philosophic deity. Thereafter, it is permitted to use language for any ends, providing one knows what they are: thus Valéry's praise of logicians, with their formal rigour, of Sophists and rhetors ('sel de la terre' ('salt of the earth')), all thinkers who have desolidarised language from any adequation to reality and restored its fruitful liberty (cf. *Œ*, II, p. 619). And if philosophy has abused its charter in aspiring to the True and the Good, perhaps it might legitimately lay claim to the Beautiful: philosophy would become, on this view an art of ideas, of their ordering and balance. It would be a sort of music of ideas allowing us to '*sauver les Noumènes* par le seul goût de leurs harmonies intrinsèques!' ('*save the Noumena* thanks to the taste for their intrinsic harmonies alone') (*Œ*, I, pp. 1249 ff.) and to consider that an *Ethics* and a *Monadology* are neither more nor less to be taken seriously than a *Suite in D minor* (*ibid.*, pp. 1236 ff.).

Philosopher, anti-philosopher, a-philosopher? In the end, it matters little. Valéry's ultimate disability in respect of the title is to have been too insolent with his predecessors, as we saw, but also too disrespectful of what has been in France – and remains – the sacrosanct history of philosophy: Valéry even dares to write of Cartesian metaphysics that it no longer has anything but historical significance, since, willy-nilly, it is linked to a time which is no longer ours in terms of religious and scientific awareness! His iconoclasm ensures that Valéry is unlikely to figure one day on the syllabus of the

*Agrégation de philosophie.* Territories must be respected; and, as everyone in the land of philosophy knows, Valéry is a *littérateur;* one, moreover, who had the misfortune to criticise the discipline for eliminating from its history such major cultural figures as Wagner and Leonardo so as to preserve a restrictively academic sense of the word 'philosophy'. How would he escape the same fate?[23]

We may legitimately wonder whether Valéry might not have felt more at home with analytical philosophers of the Anglo-American school, particularly those who are our contemporaries. Their logical bent and their distance from the history of philosophy would have encouraged him. Yet, eschewing polemics, he would have found their specialist quarrels of interpretation trying: too many arguments sent back to their authors for minute reformulation. He would have found all this wanting in . . . poetry.

Is Valéry, then, finally unclassifiable? Indeed he is; since for this profound sceptic, scepticism alone is salvational (*C*2, p. 409). He is too enclosed in the 'Moi', too devoted to Intellect – the one idol M. Teste consents to worship, having found no other (*Œ*, II, p. 37) – to seek to convince other people. His 'insularity' sets him as far from proselytism as can be imagined(*C*1, p. 77); this is a question of honesty, of decency (*ibid.*, pp. 78–9). Valéry transmits no message; he would have found that word unseemly, impure. 'Je ne veux ni être cru, ni être suivi' ('I do not wish to be either believed or followed') (p. 222). He leaves us to ourselves, face to face with the enigma murmured by Monsieur Teste: 'Méprise tes pensées, comme d'elles-mêmes elles passent – Et repassent! . . .'(*Œ*, II, p. 44).[24]

NOTES

1 Ernst Mach (1836–1916), German physicist and philosopher, whose theoretical work on mechanics and optics was acknowledged by Einstein, was particularly known in France through his translated work *La Connaissance et l'erreur* (Paris, Flammarion, 1908).

2 'One can well dispense with a *Critique of Pure Reason* by observing that words are words and that all the results of reasoning are, without exception, provisional, i.e. impotent, inoperative, if they are not found in experience'.

3 On the notion of 'point of view', which plays a key role in Valéry's thinking, see my article, 'De l'invention', *Lettres actuelles*, 10 (1996), pp. 71–5.

4 Valéry undoubtedly thought that Pascal intended the incriminated

sentence as a 'pensée' of exemplary philosophic weight pronounced in the author's own name. He may have been mistaken in this view: modern exegesis of the *Pensées* suggests that Pascal intended to attribute this thought to the *unbeliever* disorientated by the loss of the geocentric universe ushered in by the system of Copernicus. See, e.g. Jean Mesnard, *Les 'Pensées' de Pascal* (Paris, Société d'édition de l'enseignement supérieur, 1976), pp. 39–40.

5 'Any philosophic system in which the Body of man does not play a fundamental role is inept, inapt'

6 'Apart from the body, nothing has the gift of touching, or of being touched' (*De Natura Rerum*, 1, 304).

7 'the bat which claims to be blinded by sunlight but which is simply hitting its head against the walls of language' (J. Bouvresse, *La Parole malheureuse* (Paris: Minuit, 1971), p. 95 n.). See also my article 'Valéry, Wittgenstein et la philosophie', *Cahier du groupe de recherches sur la philosophie et le langage*, 1 (Grenoble, 1981), pp. 57–85.

8 For a fuller account, see my 'Valéry et les philosophes', *Nuova Corrente*, 32 (1989), pp. 371–400.

9 'fragments of which make us dream of vestiges of winged bulls, lions' heads ... extraordinary couplings, both deeply significant and absurd'

10 'fateful conclusions from the light in the cave and the shadows it generates'

11 The clearest Schopenhaurian trace is perhaps the passage in *La Jeune Parque* where the heroine rejects the life-urge, with its biological cycles, as too absurd to be endured or perpetuated (*JP,* ll. 258–78).

12 See M. Jarrety et al., *Valéry pour quoi? Précédé de Lettres et notes sur Nietzsche* (Paris, Les Impressions Nouvelles, 1987), pp. 15–52; M. Broc-Lapeyre, 'Le Chef d'orchestre danubien furibond et Monsir Fallerïe', *Cahier du groupe de recherches sur la philosophie et le langage* (Grenoble), 11 (1989), pp. 75–83.

13 'Zeno! Cruel Zeno! Zeno the Eleate! / You have sorely pierced me with that winged arrow / Which quivers, flies and yet flies not! / The sound alerts me and the arrow kills! / Ah! the sun ... What tortoise-like a shadow / Falling on the soul, Achilles motionless amid his mighty steps!'

14 Five texts are devoted to him: see *Œ* I, pp. 787–854.

15 See N. Celeyrette-Pietri, *Valéry et le Moi. Des 'Cahiers' à l'œuvre* (Paris, Klincksieck, 1979), ch. 2, 'Sous le signe de Descartes'.

16 See my article, 'Valéry et ses amis philosophes: G. Fourment and E. Kolbassine', *Remanences*, 4–5 (1995), pp. 61–9.

17 J. de Latour, *Examen de Valéry*, (Paris, Gallimard, 1935), p. 130, n.

18 'Thinkers are people who re-think, and who think that what was thought was never thought out enough'

19 'To meditate philosophically is to return from the familiar to the strange and in strangeness to confront the real'

20 For a fuller account of these criticisms, which risk appearing summary in the form given here, see my *Valéry, Directions spatiales et parcours verbal* (Paris, Minard, *Les Lettres Modernes*, 1981), pp. 284–90. One must add that contemporary historians have developed their own auto-critique which meets Valéry on several points. Note too that Valéry's condemnation strikes at general History and not at specific histories (architecture, navigation, political economy, etc.) which he valued (cf. *Œ* II, p. 1544).

21 We may recall that Valéry took a law degree and that as long-time secretary to A. Lebey, Director of the Agence Havas, he kept abreast of politico-economic problems. To-day, the analyses of P. Legendre, a specialist jurist and psychoanalyst, pursue Valéry's objections in greater depth: see *L'amour du censeur* (Paris, Seuil, 1974) and *Jouir du pouvoir* (Paris, Minuit, 1976).

22 'The pedigree of a mind is evidenced by its natural indocility, its inability to believe, to give words a value other than *purely verbal*' ... Nothing is more vulgar than credulity'.

23 See however the endorsement by F. Alquié: 'on le jugerait plus près des philosophes si l'on consentait à se souvenir que la philosophie est avant tout ce par quoi l'homme prend intellectuellement conscience de lui-même et des choses, transforme son rapport avec le monde en rapport pensé, et ne demande la force de vivre qu'aux puissances de la lucidité' ('Climat de Valéry', in *Paul Valéry vivant, Cahiers du Sud*, 1946, p. 330).

24 'Despise your thoughts, as of themselves they pass — And pass again!
...'

For further reading on the topic of this chapter, please see Bibliography, items 12, 18, 24, 26, 40, 64, 67, 74, 99, 101.

2

*Self-writings*

CHAPTER 6

# The Poetics of practice and theory

*Michel Jarrety*

Poetics, in its modern acceptance, is closely linked with the name of Valéry. He it was who refloated the ancient Aristotelian term and charged it with a new meaning reflecting the conception of poetry which, as the acclaimed poet of *La Jeune Parque* and *Charmes* – and very much against the prevailing aesthetic of the time – he was led on numerous public occasions to expound: a conception oriented towards the most rigorous exigencies of poetic form.

Poetics was, indeed, quickly perceived as the key notion defining Valéry's intellectual stance; all the more readily since, when the Collège de France created for him a chair, which he held from 1937 until his death in 1945, it was officially designated a 'Chair of Poetics'. Nothing however assures us that the same word has the same sense in its public and private usages; and many misunderstandings have arisen from this. It will be prudent to distinguish here, on the one hand, the theory of poetic composition which Valéry formulated essentially from his own poetic practice, and which the *Cahiers* have considerably enriched, and, on the other, the approach to analysing the functioning of literary works which is sketched out in the lectures at the Collège de France as a true discipline of the future. It is out of just such a semantic oscillation – despite Valéry's own attempt at rigorous definition – that the later career of the word has, to an extent, been made. In the discipline that Valéry sought to constitute, the Nouvelle Critique of the 1960s saw the elimination of history, biography, and, more broadly, of all circumstantial contingencies, in favour of a study which took cognisance only of autonomous and self-enclosed works; at which point, the term *poetics* itself was slowly watered down to the point where, today, it designates little more than a formalist approach to literary works.

To restore poetics to the first of the meanings distinguished above, as Valéry did, was to unbind it from the ancient tradition which envisaged only a set of prescriptions, and refer it instead simply to its etymological root in the Greek *poiein* (to make, 'le faire'): the notion that a poem is written, not in some state of passivity, but as a work of the mind – indeed, as a product of the mind at work. In this approach, some have been tempted to see a simple restatement of the commonplace opposition between a pure *vates* inspired of the gods and, antipodally, the poet who is so far the master of his means that he relegates creative writing to a merely technical function.[1] A less hasty inspection shows Valéry's position to be rather different: the real opposition is displaced, since he contrasts rather one practice whose end is the finished poem, and another practice – his own – whose object is first and foremost the writing of the poem, understood as an unfolding, ever more fully controlled, of all the acts supposed in that writing. For this reason, the true foundation of Valéryan poetics can be understood only in so far as it is explicitly related to the priority given to '*pouvoir*' and to the temptation of preferring pure potentiality to performance which asserted itself after the crisis of the 'Nuit de Gênes' in 1892; in fact, to the temptation, exemplified in the dream confided one evening in 1894 to Mallarmé, of 'un être qui eût les plus grands dons — pour n'en rien faire, — s'étant assuré de les avoir' (*C*, XXII, p. 600).[2]

Refounding his intellectual life, Valéry resolved to see in literature only *one* of the applications of the power of a mind whose task is none other than to constantly reinforce its means so as to ensure an ever-greater mastery over the self and over others. Conventional critical wisdom took from this the common view that, for Valéry, literature is to be approached as an *exercise*. Here indeed was one of the essential articles of Valéryan poetics, one which he himself was happy enough to stress, not without an element of teasing provocation. What is clear is that such an approach to literature privileges the act of making above the work made. As Valéry writes in 'Fragments des mémoires d'un poème': 'Il me souvient que l'idée seule de composition ou de construction m'enivrait, et que je ne m'imaginais pas d'œuvre plus admirable que *le drame de la génération d'une œuvre*, quand elle excite et déploie toutes les fonctions supérieures dont nous pouvons disposer' (*Œ*, I, p. 1483, my italics).[3] At the same time, the reader is set aside and herein lies Valéry's essential difference: in the shift, around 1892, from viewing writing as being directed towards others to a conception of writing as primarily self-directed, emphasising above all the journey that might bring a work to its perfect completion, rather than the completion itself. Of course, Valéry did write poems, and his poetics is also the corpus of rules by which he is concerned to define how prosodic constraints may be exploited as resources and which easy options are to be dismissed. In this perspective, the veto he largely places on inspiration is less a theoretical position of principle – like, say, Mallarmé's refusal of Chance – than the experienced sense of dispossession at the prompting breath of a word or act of speech which is submitted to rather than mastered: 'L'inspiration ... réduit l'auteur au rôle d'un observateur' ('inspiration ... reduces the author's role to that of an observer') (Œ, II, p. 484). It is another speaking within. Inspiration exists, no doubt, and Valéry concurs in its granting him a first line which is authoritative in its perfection, but which also calls for a sequel. To dwell further in this mode would however be to give himself up to a passive listening to something which passes through him but does not properly belong to him; but above all, it would be to condemn the poet to failure, given that the quality of the poem supposes a continuity which can only be secured by conscious effort and which rests largely on a steady 'charge' – in an electrical sense – which must run throughout; no line that is obviously better or worse than the rest can be allowed to disrupt the regular energy-flow. Moving from inspiration to a conscious working of the material is the shift from nature, which is not to be trusted for long – since nature merely lets things happen – to a craftsmanship which fashions a form, reworking the originally given model until a coherent whole is achieved.

This is the experience Valéry relates in 1928 to the Société de Philosophie:

Un certain *vers* initial se trouva non seulement tout fait, mais m'apparut comme impossible à modifier, comme l'effet d'une nécessité. Mais ce vers à son tour exigeait une suite musicale et logique. Le doigt était dans l'engrenage. Par malheur pour les poètes, l'heureuse coïncidence ne se poursuit pas continuement, et il faut en appeler au travail et aux artifices pour *imiter* celui qu'on fut pendant un instant.[4]

Work, artifice: the juxtaposition of these two terms is valuable providing we are willing to restore to the latter term, stripped of any negative connotation, its etymological force, and to preserve the link made by Valéry between nature and artifice. For the poem, like nature itself in its most beautiful objects (crystals, flowers), seeks a perfect conformity between matter (the words) and form (the line of verse); and Valéry, in the same public lecture, chooses explicitly to relate the unexpected and autonomous appearance of a first 'vers donné' to the development of a plant from a simple element, stem or leaf. What is conveyed by this vegetable metaphor is the quest for a mode of poetic composition which moves continuously from the part to the whole; in which the part *naturally* engenders the whole according to a process of which the outstanding example was the creation, between 1912 and 1917, of *La Jeune Parque*. Explaining the patiently won scale of this poem, originally intended to number forty lines only, Valéry spoke of the 'croissance naturelle d'une fleur artificielle' ('natural growth of an artificial flower') (*Œ*, I, p. 1632).

What is clear from this refusal of inspiration, taken together with this coveted harmony of form and sound, is that Valéry's practical poetics disqualifies any primary will to *expression* – the spontaneous effusion of feeling, but also the *intention of meaning* – and retains instead the *intention of doing* which is to be understood in the light of his central notion that '*la Littérature est, et ne peut être autre chose qu'une sorte d'extension et d'application de certaines propriétés du Langage*' ('*Literature is, and cannot be other than, a kind of extension or application of certain properties of Language*') (*Œ*, I, p. 1440). The first task of the poet is then to constitute the poem as an object which turns ordinary language inside out, like a glove: the function he assigns here to words is no longer to transmit a meaning, which, once transmitted, cancels out the verbal medium of its transmission; rather, it is the function of referring the reader back to that medium in a renewed act of reading. The quality he looks to in words is no longer that of abstract meaning-bearing signs, but that of a sonorous material to be worked up and enhanced in its evocative power. The poem does not give us back the world – it does not utter the world – but on the contrary sets us apart from it in constituting itself as another world. Poetic language is entirely without representational function, and the superiority of the poet is indeed that he does not seek to make us believe in any sort of 'outside'. The 'real' lies elsewhere, in the poem itself; and what makes poetry for Valéry 'le genre suprême' is that words *are* things and that consequently – this is to define its responsibility – 'elle doit payer argent comptant et n'user que de la *réalité* absolue des propriétés du langage' (*C*, VIII, p. 98).[5]

As soon as the poem escapes the orbit of what is not poetry – the meaning by which we might seek to summarise it, the external décor

it might evoke – the spell-binding continuity of its form alone should
be what charms the reader and causes us to pass durably from
reality to the intrinsic world of poetry; the ascendancy of poetic
voice guarantees the texture of the poem – which is also its tessitura
(characteristic vocal register). In *La Jeune Parque* and in *Charmes*, the
speaking subject maintains its exemplary presence, as if the poem
were always reborn from its first enunciation; as if, between the
inner voice-of-origin, which the poet seeks to capture, and the
externally heard voice of the text, there were no gap or interval.
When Valéry asserts that 'le problème d'*écrire* doit être assimilé à
celui de *mettre en musique* (écrire pour la voix)' (*C*, IX, p. 190),[6] he has
in mind something more than a musical parallel commonplace in
the symbolist order: the reference to music and the voice exceeds an
inherited contemporary reference and assumes the more challenging
task of defining the compositional principle of the poem. To take
over from music its ambition, if not quite its means, is to further
thwart representation, given that music itself expresses nothing
referential; and it is to allow the poem to constitute itself as an
autonomous totality. Not only does music set its own specific form of
temporal development, but its song also composes a certain type of
space. This two-fold resource allows it, no doubt uniquely, to
institute, in the poem, a veritable space-time: 'chanter, c'est instituer
un monde' ('to sing is to institute a world') (*C*, XV, p. 240).

For such a world to exist and hold the reader continuously in its
ambit, the writing, on which it of course depends, should discourage
as actively as possible the all-too-convenient translation of the poem
into a meaning which, substituting itself for the poem, would ruin it
as such. No doubt the nature of poetic language, necessarily woven
out of our common words, prevents any final predominance of
musical properties over meaning. Sense and musicality can however
combine in an essential 'music of meaning', a fundamental tenet of
Valéryan poetics and one of the most famous. It is one of the most
demanding, too, since it tends towards a unified poem in which the
work of composition has effaced the common-or-garden denotation
of words and replaced them with an ideal correlation between the
harmony of sense suggested by the text and the harmony of sound
engendered by its form. Hence the celebrated definition of *Tel Quel*:
'La puissance des vers tient à une harmonie *indéfinissable* entre ce
qu'ils *disent* et ce qu'ils *sont*' (*Œ*, II, p. 637).[7] But Valéry immediately
adds that ' "indéfinissable" entre dans la définition', which under-

lines in exemplary fashion that a correlation of this type is efficacious because the evocative power of sound associated with 'ce qu'ils sont' is always different, since it belongs to the emergence, variable within each reader, of 'ce qu'ils disent'. Between sound and sense is set up a kind of to-ing and fro-ing, a movement of pendular oscillation analysed in *Poésie et pensée abstraite* (*Œ*, I, p. 1332). As we advance in each reading, the sound evokes a meaning which is revoked and renewed in the proximity of another sound, in a continuous creation: that of a perceptible and separate universe. Each individual word of the poem is divested of its ordinary acceptance, but the contiguity of terms, re-inforced by the figurative aspect of poetry, creates a novel sense perpetually constructed in the very movement of the text.

However, to compose a poem is not to be concerned primarily with structure and ordering (with what traditional rhetoric calls *dispositio*) but more especially with the *legato* which unites matter and form in a work: as the manuscripts of his poems show, Valéry is only belatedly concerned with achieving overall thematic coherence, or with the accompanying emergence of 'meaning'. Rather, he is pre-eminently concerned to achieve, in all aspects of the work, a kind of harmonious inner balance. Unlike the discursive writer, composing, for Valéry, means cutting short any logical – or, even worse, any chronological – structure that might imply a preconceived plan (*La Jeune Parque* skilfully foils any such chrono-linearity). In this writer whose natural movement carries him towards beginnings, and whose measure remains the fragment, composition calls into play the different units written successively, but not actively interlocked as long as their unison is not asserted; *it enacts the work*. A taste for construction and for transformation no doubt appears in this activity, but in an aesthetic and architectural perspective. The multiplicity of solutions opens up almost infinite possibilities of reworking (as the manuscripts again testify) and it is clear that this search, having as its objective not primarily the production of the perfect (i.e. finished) work, is itself an endless labour for anyone who engages in it: '*A quoi peut-il connaître que son ouvrage est achevé? C'est une décision qu'il doit prendre ... Mais, en vérité, l'achèvement d'un ouvrage n'est qu'un abandon, un arrêt que l'on peut toujours regarder comme fortuit dans une évolution qui aurait pu toujours se prolonger*'.[8]

I have been speaking so far of a *particularised* or *restricted* poetics, entirely conditioned by the singular requirements of a writer with special interests within the literary game, rather than by the reader, on whom, often enough, he turns his back. There is a restriction in this sense that versified poetry remains for Valéry the central – we may say, solar – point within the literary domain, the only one he truly attempts to theorise in any very public way; this, despite the admirable prose poems making up a second, lesser-known aspect of his work and despite the 'alternative' prose-writing that he sought, which would be susceptible to rules and constraints as rigorous as those applied to poetry. Had Valéry developed them, his particularised poetics might have been inflected by them. It is thus not unimportant that the *Cahiers* record his unceasing attempts at experimental, self-theorising writing in these genres, since our progressive discovery of them over the past thirty years can only broaden the primary thrust of his poetics. Fragmentarily, no doubt, but with the coherence of a manner of thinking which remains faithful over half a century to certain central constants, an authentic theory of literature takes shape, which belongs strictly to the making of the work of art, and to the enhanced knowledge of the practitioner of such works. We may thus legitimately extend Valéryan poetics to all modes of Valéry's writing: not only versified poetry, but also *Monsieur Teste* and the *Histoires brisées*, which allow us to understand better his reflections on the novel, and the Dialogues or *Mon Faust*, which find their constant counterpoint in a veritable theory of theatre, as well as many reflections on the use of these very fragments which Valéry often transferred directly from his *Cahiers* into published collections of aphorisms (of which *Tel Quel* remains the best known).

What emerges is that Valéry's natural bent leads him to practise no form of writing which is not re-appropriated and re-thought according to his own most strenuous demands. Poetics, on this account, is not a general theory which the practice of creative writing might be held to illustrate by way of direct application. It is rather a discontinuous reflection which, in the *Cahiers*, precedes, accompanies or follows such a practice, and in many respects founds it. Yet this reflection remains at one remove from creative practice, since its primary thrust usually remains, first and foremost, that of autonomous speculation, and since, not infrequently, it is pitched beyond all possible creative realisation.

What is at issue and what immediately gives value to this broader poetics is a conception that not only takes the argument way beyond the field of verse poetry, but equally underlines Valéry's advance in relation to his own time. For if, as we have seen, those aspects that relate exclusively to his poetry-writing may, to some observers, appear to mark a return to an outdated literary aesthetic, conversely, a whole body of doctrine in the *Cahiers* anticipates in spectacular fashion, the preoccupations which surface with modern linguistics. They define the work of art, with decisive specificity, as a language-object bound up with the concern for a singular enunciation, but also with reading and with reception. And here, undoubtedly, Valéry sketches out a theory which, in many respects heralds the contemporary concern, exemplified in Jauss and Eco, to think out the place and role of the reader. This is still a matter of poetics, if only because it is the writing process which defines the place of the reader-to-be. One formula of Valéry's – significantly, dating back to 1910 – will give a clear idea of this orientation and perspective: ' "Faire de la littérature" — c'est écrire pour inconnus. La ligne que je trace est *littérature* ou non selon que je l'adresse à quelqu'un, ou à ce lecteur virtuel — moyen que je me donne. Une personne *imprévue* lisant une lettre à elle non destinée et dont les êtres lui sont inconnus change cette lettre en littérature' (*C*, IV, p. 387).[9] The relation between two subjects is immediately asserted, thanks to the allocutionary form, or 'address', yet also their separation. If the indistinctness of 'the public' means that one is writing *for* people unknown, it also means that one cannot speak or address oneself *to* them, since address is something personal. Linked to the requirement for a living enunciation, and therefore a reception which is also particularised on each occasion, it here operates according to distinct protocols: the address to someone known, a correspondence supposing interpersonal complicity, which seems to exclude letter-writing from the field of literature; an address to somebody who will be revealed as unknown, and who, as reader, is an active participant rather than a mere receiver. Because the reader is foreign to the work, the distance he maintains from it reinforces its *strangeness*, which thus appears constitutive of literary communication. Here is a radical disjunction, the benefit of which is to re-evaluate matters in the light of reader-function, to break any unequivocal relationship with the person of the author, and in a more complex way, to dissolve any simplistic link between the writer and his work.

Thus reading falls under the heading of writing, and prolongs its function. From this point, it is easy to see how Valéry, when he comes, in his lectures at the Collège de France, to lay the foundations of a poetics capable of constituting a new approach to literature, a new mode of knowledge of works of art, could put forward, under the same title of poetics, 'le dessein d'une théorie de la Littérature' ('the design of a theory of Literature') (*Œ*, I, p. 1441): in other words, a sort of *generalised poetics*, founded much more on the vast effort of analytical reflection of the *Cahiers* than on his own poetics of versified poetry. Simply, the difficulty of this public teaching role consisted of moving from a singular theory, designed to reinforce a specific mind and a particular *œuvre*, to a science that would be, if not universal, at least generalisable. Two texts, both published in 1937, sketch the outline: *De l'enseignement de la poétique au Collège de France*, a brief programmatic statement which is hastily written and somewhat disjointed, and the *Première leçon de poétique au Collège de France*, a piece which draws its greater solemnity from the occasion it records.[10] Apparently, at least, the definition given in the *Leçon* remains unchanged and publicises the ambition of the *Cours:* 'Le faire, le *poïein*, dont je veux m'occuper, est celui qui s'achève en quelque œuvre et que je viendrai à restreindre bientôt à ce genre d'œuvres qu'on est convenu d'appeler *œuvres de l'esprit*' (*Œ*, I, p. 1342).[11] In fact, however, it is about something very different, since the object of such an enquiry is no longer that of constructing a work – his own – but of analysing also the work of others: the first poetics aimed at writing (better), the second essentially at reading (better) – though perhaps still with some thought of enhanced writing; what remains constant is the interest in the process of creation rather than in the object created. At which point, poetics pulls together three questions: about the *nature* of this new discipline, about its *project* and about the *identity* – author or reader? – of the investigating subject.

A certain hesitation is perceptible when Valéry attempts to define this new approach to works of art and the place given to them in literary history – a discipline ascendant, we recall, from the beginning of the century. The novelty of the discipline indeed supposes that its difference be asserted: and certainly, Valéry, in referring to literary history, describes its results in laudatory terms. But we are not deceived: this is a conventional salute to the academic establishment and to the teaching long dispensed by his host institution of the Collège de France. For, if we grant that the real object of study is no longer the externals of the work of art but its inner functioning, poetics implies a radical dismissal of History; and this distancing is clear when Valéry asserts that '[s]a tâche doit se différencier néces-

sairement de celle qu'accomplit d'une part l'Histoire de la Littérature, d'autre part la critique des textes et celle des ouvrages' (*Œ*, I, p.
1343).[12] And the same prudence appears in the *Programme*, since
although Valéry, in concluding, refuses to oppose his own poetics to
literary history or consider it as giving literary history merely 'une
introduction, un sens et un but' ('an introduction, a direction, a goal')
(*Œ*, I, p. 1443), he nevertheless chooses once more to substitute for the
study of circumstances external to the work an '*Histoire de l'esprit en
tant qu'il produit ou consomme de la "littérature"* ' ('*the history of the mind
insofar as it produces or consumes "literature"* ') (p. 1439). This latter
formula is decisive: its stress, albeit indirectly expressed, on the
duration of the process, the primacy of the creating subject over the
object created, the reciprocal and equal status given to author and
reader, all these points essentially complete the definition offered in
the *Leçon*. A kind of logical impasse nonetheless comes into view, that
we may point to here by way of anticipating later thoughts: in
associating History – hence the written trace, the archive – with a
study of the mind of which History preserves only evidential testimony, regarding either readers or authors, Valéry opens up to view
vistas of difficulty surrounding poetics conceived as a *general* science.

A second uncertainty seems to me to surface concerning the
means of realising a vast discipline, one which

aurait pour objet de préciser et de développer la recherche des effets
proprement littéraires du langage, l'examen des inventions expressives et
suggestives qui ont été faites pour accroître le pouvoir et la pénétration de
la parole, et celui des restrictions que l'on a parfois imposées en vue de bien
distinguer la langue de la fiction de celle de l'usage, etc. (*Œ*, I, p. 1441).[13]

It is superfluous to underline here the spectacular novelty of this
perspective, in 1937, within the field of literary studies; in some
respects, Valéry seems already to recognise the notion of 'littérarité'
and to anticipate the very general analysis of literary forms which
today we call, precisely, 'Poetics'. Some of the terms of his formulation nevertheless seem to establish the enterprise as reader-
oriented, thus counterbalancing, as it were, the straightforwardly
etymological approach of a poetics resting tacitly upon the typically
Valéryan adage that '*Expliquer, c'est Faire*' ('To *Explain* is to *Effect*') (*C*,
XXIV, p. 479). We can see that for Valéry, the poetician aims to study
all works, but from an experience of creation – his own – which
separates him radically from the ordinary reader. True, a long
passage in the *Leçon* distinguishes, crucially and famously, the

producer of the work, the work itself, and the consumer who, in turn, produces the value of the work: a distinction which reinforces Valéry's assurance that the gap between author and reader produces, as we saw, an effect of literature, given that the person reading receives a text that was not nominally intended for him. Yet it is important, for our purposes, to stress that the poetics lectures are based on his experience as both author and reader.

Tacitly, the identity of the poetician is thus defined: he is a Janus-like subject who manages to engage in the analysis of works from two points of view and to witness a twofold process of creation. We may perhaps, from this, gain a clearer sense of what Valéry has in mind by 'l'Histoire d'un esprit'. In his lectures, introduced as 'le fruit d'une expérience individuelle, longue déjà de toute une vie' ('the fruit of an individual's experience, already a lifetime long') (*Œ*, I, p. 1340), the logical impasse I mentioned is resolved: the discipline advanced by Valéry can only be an *authorial poetics* since it consists of knowledge which is no doubt communicable – it is delivered in the form of a public lecture – but which bears the singular imprint of someone who has attempted to define a theory of *poiesis* as a process of creation by a given subject – someone who can only be the writer himself. Such is the profound ambiguity of the poetics defined at the Collège de France: it is advanced as a general practice, if not truly as a universal science, but it turns out to be a pure continuation of the author-related poetics pursued in the *Cahiers*.

The teaching of poetics in this sense can only be a public articulation of private reflexions, outside the concern to constitute, in any real sense, a doctrine separable from its author; in the end, it signifies a pursuit of pure research, as the *Programme* discreetly warns us: 'La *Poétique* se proposerait bien moins de résoudre les problèmes que d'en énoncer' ('Poetics would propose less to resolve the problems than to enunciate them') (*Œ*, I, p. 1442). This raises the question of what discourse is possible about literature. Valéry frequently displays, if not scorn, at least indifference for any form of criticism, whether it be of the journalistic type which incites us to read, or the academic type which sets itself to help us read better; for such forms of discourse stand between the book and the reader, a relationship which should be particularised, and free of foreign intrusion. It also disqualifies very openly any practice which considers the text independently from the writing-reading movement which alone gives it effect. Here is perhaps the founding assertion of the *Leçon*: '*L'œuvre de l'esprit n'existe qu'en acte*' ('*The work of the mind exists only in act*') (*Œ*, I, p. 1349).

The consequences of this view are considerable, and it is not clear that they have been fully assimilated. Valéry's critique of the inadequacy or the bankruptcy of any discourse which fails to insist upon the process of the work supposes that an authentic and useful commentary can only be either the account of a fruitful personal reading – rather as we speak of the account of a journey – or else an account of writing of the type suggested by a title of Raymond Roussel's – *Comment j'ai écrit certains de mes livres*. The latter indeed finds an echo in Valéry's own formula: 'Toute critique qui ne donne pas de recettes précises, ne sert de rien' ('Any criticism which establishes no recipes is worthless') (*C*, VII, p. 492). In fact, the *Leçon* suggests a condemnation of all discourses which consider the literary object separated from the subject (author, reader) who animates it, since it criticises any practice which 'consiste ... à traiter les poèmes comme des choses, à les découper comme si la composition n'était rien' (*Œ*, I, p. 1305).[14] In terms of the same ever-rehearsed motif, it involves forgetting, in short, that the poem exists only in act. The criticism made takes issue with a twofold separation: that between the text and a commentary intervening after the act of reading, which fixes the work, reducing it to the immobility of a statement without living enunciation; and that which, in the explicating process itself, isolates the component elements from the composition. This is a weighty objection which Valéry resurrects from time to time: for instance in *Questions de poésie*, where he stigmatises the possibility of an *optional form of speech* which breaks down into 'ornements, images, figures, épithètes, beaux "détails"' ('ornaments, images, figures, epithets, fine "details"') (pp. 1284 ff.), or in many a note in the *Cahiers*.[15] There is no point, as he sees it, in seeking within a mechanism at rest what may be the secret of its creative progression.

That Valéry, consequently, should at one point have figured as a tutelary presence of the Nouvelle critique and of structuralism could only have happened by a sort of misunderstanding, since these formalist approaches refused to take account of the essential role of the Subject. If we set aside the signs of superficial complicity evidenced, for instance, in the titles of the two reviews founded in 1960 and 1970 – *Tel Quel* and *Poétique* – Valéry's influence was felt essentially in two ways. There were tacit appropriations, as for instance in the case of Barthes' stress on the polysemic nature of literary works as linked to the singular reading of each person – a central affirmation of which Valéry was the originator. And, on the other hand, there was open recognition of the role of the father of poetics – the first to stress the study of the works themselves rather than all that surrounds them (sources, influence, historical context), the first to give primacy to the possibilities of form, and who never lost an opportunity to remind us that literature is, above all else, an application of the properties of language. However, the claim to filiation rested upon an assumed stability of the text-as-object and required the elimination of the dual – and each time unique – presence of an author and a reader.

In respect of the reader, the temptation of these two formalist decades was to consider that knowledge of literary works could lead to the definition of fundamental laws of functioning considered to be detachable from the works themselves. This is what Genette suggested in a still pioneering study, attributing to Valéry the merit 'de réclamer, et pour une part, d'établir quelque chose comme une *axiomatique*', given that 'la littérature ... repose sur des conventions que, sauf exception, elle ignore'.[16] This assertion is emblematic of the way Valéry was read; it was of course perfectly legitimate to stress his theorising lucidity and the Valéryan taste for *laws of functioning;* yet it was equally to forget that Valéry, for his part, never sought to separate such laws from the creation of the work itself, and that his poetics, precisely, consisted of observing these laws *in operation.* In a certain sense, the issue turned on a scientificity which Valéry implicitly condemned by maintaining the presence of the subject, and which the formalists, in their own different way, assigned to themselves as the foundation of their discipline. This was the case of Tzvetan Todorov, for instance, who, in a text precisely entitled *Poétique structurale* proposed that 'cette *science* [my italics] se préoccupe non plus de la littérature réelle, mais de la littérature possible, en d'autres mots: de cette propriété abstraite qui fait la singularité du fait littéraire, *la littérarité*'.[17] Such an ambition obviously constituted a radical hijacking of Valéryan poetics, which Todorov indeed invoked, but which was really concerned, for its part, with 'la création ou ... la composition d'ouvrages dont le langage est à la fois la substance et le moyen' (*Œ*, I, p. 1441).[18] There was a twofold breaking-point: on the one hand structuralism claimed to move from actual works to the abstract structure they manifest; on the other, it evaded the process of creation. A double disappearance of the Subject was involved, since the creating presence was dismissed as such and, equally, universal laws susceptible of scientific definition were supposed, which by definition were held to be independent of any enunciating subject.

This elimination of the author gave rise to a second misunderstanding. Taken together with Valéry's refusal of biography and his unrelenting rejection of any unequivocal relation between the author and the work, it was used to promote Valéry, more or less openly, to the role of theoretician of 'the death of the author'.[19] The *Cahiers* being still unknown, many of Valéry's formulations could indeed be read in this way: for instance, the one Genette quotes in 'La Littérature comme telle': 'Qu'est-ce donc qui nous fera concevoir le véritable ouvrier d'un bel ouvrage? Mais il n'est positivement *personne*' (*Œ*, I, p. 483).[20] Valéry does indeed sometimes desacralise the author (and correspondingly enhances the role of the reader); yet one cannot truly consider that he abolishes the author; merely that he divests him of demiurgic status and brings him back to his real condition as a struggling practitioner of writing, with his moments of brilliance, his weaknesses, his accidents, his advances and second thoughts. It remains true that a kind of pure subjectivity (just as there exists in Valéry a 'pure Self') is always maintained; this is particularly true, as we have seen, of the voice-of-origin, understood as source and sign of authenticity, that the text must never conceal. No doubt the empirical individual or 'person', disappears, together with his cortege of biographical contingencies, nevertheless the secret trace of a Subject is preserved; it is evoked, for instance, when Valéry writes 'l'art est l'action et l'affirmation de *quelqu'un*' ('art is the action and affirmation of *someone*').[21]

Despite the misunderstandings and the hijackings, there is an ultimate legitimacy in the structuralists having borrowed from Valéry whatever reinforced their own approach; this was, in the end, all that could be fully taken over. For the *authorial poetics* that I have tried to outline was not itself, of its very nature, transmissible; once its sole true practitioner had disappeared, it could only be, as it were, a certain 'spirit of research', the sustained awakening of self-cognisant creative thought which the poet had managed to carry to its highest point. His results might well provide a basis for subsequent work, yet he himself probably could not have any true descendency. This spirit was nonetheless crucial: it certainly survives today, although so totally infused throughout contemporary practices of literary research that its trace is hardly discernable as such; which is doubtless still a sign of influence. For the rest – I mean poetics as Valéry understood it – one has henceforth to return to him alone.[22]

1 See for instance *Entretiens de Francis Ponge avec Philippe Sollers* (Paris, Gallimard / Seuil, 1970), p. 162 ff.
2 'a being endowed with the greatest gifts – so as not to do anything with them — having once assured himself he had them'.
3 'I remember the very idea of composition or construction intoxicated me, and that I could imagine no work more admirable than the *drama of the generation of the work*, insofar as it excites and deploys all our higher functions'.
4 'La Création artistique', *Bulletin de la société francaise de Philosophie* (1928), p. 12. Reproduced in *Vues* (1948; Paris, La Table Ronde, 1993 edn), pp. 300–1. 'A certain initial line of verse was not only given, but appeared to me unmodifiable, like an effect of necessity. But this line in turn demanded a musical and logical sequel. My finger was in the machine. Unfortunately for poets, the happy coincidence does not happen the whole time, and appeal must be made to work and artifice so as to *imitate* the person one was for that inspired moment.'
5 'it must pay in cash and use only the absolute *reality* of the properties of language'.
6 'the problem of *writing* must be assimilated to that of *putting into music* (writing for the voice)'.
7 'The power of verse-poetry has to do with an indefinable harmony between what it *says* and what it *is*'.
8 'La Création artistique' in *Bulletin de la société francaise de Philosophie* (1928), p. 9. Reproduced in *Vues*, p. 296. '*How can he recognise that his work is finished?* That's a decision he has to take ... In fact, the completion of a work is only ever an abandonment, a halt that can always be regarded *as fortuitous* in an evolution that might have been continued.'
9 ' "To create literature" — is to write for people unknown. The line I write out is *literature* or not according as I address it to someone, or to that average, virtual reader — that I invent for myself. An *unforeseen* person, reading a letter not addressed to them and which mentions people unknown to them, changes that letter into literature.'
10 No proper transcription exists of this lecture course given between 1937 and 1945. The stenographic record established by the publisher Gallimard must by now be considered lost. It is however possible to consult the lecture notes, of uneven interest, taken by Georges Le Breton, in the review *Yggdrasill*, 9–34 (1937–9). Some fragmentary preparation notes by Valéry exist at the Bibliothèque nationale de France.
11 'Making, *poïein*, which is the subject I propose to speak of, is that form

of making which issues in some form of work, and which I shall shortly proceed to restrict to the type of works commonly called *works of the mind*.

12 'its task must necessarily be differentiated on the one hand from that accomplished by literary history, on the other from that of textual and literary criticism'.

13 'would have as its object to specify and develop the search for the properly literary effects of language, the examination of the expressive and suggestive inventions which have enhanced the power and penetration of words and that of the restrictions sometimes imposed to distinguish the language of fiction from that of common usage, etc.'

14 'consists . . . of treating poems as things, of cutting them up as though composition were nothing'.

15 See for instance a long passage of 1944 in which Valéry criticises disciplines such as phonetics, grammar, stylistics, linguistics for aiming to study literature and thinking that their object is divisible (*C*, XXVIII, p. 426).

16 Gérard Genette, 'La Littérature comme telle' in *Figures 1*, (Paris, Seuil, 1966), p. 258; 'of laying claim to, and to an extent, establishing, something approaching an axiomatics' given that 'literature . . . rests upon conventions of which, it is only occasionally aware'.

17 'La poétique structurale', first part of the chapter entitled 'Poétique' in François Wahl (ed.), *Qu'est-ce que le structuralisme?* (Paris, Seuil, 1968), p. 102 ff.; 'this *science* is concerned not with actual literature, but with possible literature, in other words: with that abstract property which makes for the singularity of the literary phenomenon, *literarity*'.

18 'the creation . . . or the composition of works of which language is both the means and the substance'

19 In 1968 Barthes theorised this 'disappearance', a concept later to be abandoned: see 'La Mort de l'auteur', in *Le Bruissement de la langue* (Paris, Seuil, 1984). The following year, Michel Foucault, from a different perspective, came to similar conclusions: see 'Qu'est-ce qu'un auteur?' in *Bulletin de la société de philosophie* 63 (1969), p. 3.

20 'who can get us to imagine the true workman responsible for a fine piece of work? But he is positively *no-one!*'

21 'La Création artistique' in *Bulletin de la Société française de Philosophie* (1928), p. 6. Reproduced in *Vues*, p. 290.

22 For further reading on this topic please see Bibliography, items 4, 8, 29, 37, 52, 53, 55, 58, 59, 63, 105.

CHAPTER 7

# 'Esprit, Attente pure, éternel suspens …':
## Valéry's Prose Poetry

*Stephen Romer*

When Valéry came to classify his *Cahiers* into different thematic chapters, he devoted one to 'Poèmes et PPA', or 'Petits poèmes abstraits', with the sub-heading 'Impressions — Sensibilia — Fragments / Ciels — Mers / Attitudes, croquis et Ciels-mer'. One might imagine from this description a writer's loose ends or occasional 'sketches', rather than what they are, the startlingly original, high-voltage prose poetry of a consummate artist.

The impression is strengthened if one turns to the titles Valéry gave to the prose poetry which he published during his lifetime. It forms a considerable bulk: we find 'Mélange', 'Petites Etudes', 'Poésie brute', 'Colloques', 'Instants'; and in 'Rhumbs', itself a sub-heading of 'Tel Quel', we find, among other titles, 'Au hasard et au crayon', 'Croquis' and 'Poésie perdue'. Valéry's curious mixture of deference and defiance in his various prefatory notes to these collections, suggests that the *classification* of these pieces was a source of anxiety, as for example the collection 'Cahier B 1910', which is offered up to the 'monstrueux désirs des amateurs du spontané et des idées à l'état brut' (*Œ*, II, p. 571).[1]

The source of his anxiety is not far to seek: Valéry, the author of an acknowledged formal masterpiece like *La Jeune Parque*, is presenting his public with what appear to be disordered fragments in a bewildering variety of genres – poems in free verse, prose poems, Socratic dialogues, aphorisms, 'Moralités', ideas for stories … how would they be received? He is defiant because what he is in part unveiling is the work of his *Cahiers*, that minute description of his 'fonctionnement mental' carried out in the early morning hours throughout his life, with no foreseeable end in publication, and which he considered to be his major contribution. Spontaneity, and the multitude of ideas that press upon him in those moments – and which he so often apostrophizes – are of the very essence. His whole

'System' was in fact, as he well knew, an 'anti-system' also, being so dependent on what he calls 'le hasard', and composed of an infinite modulation that proscribed closure: this flux and uncertainty was as authentically *himself* as any of the more polished, reformulated thoughts (*LQ*, p. 244). The problem of classification was in fact, for Valéry (if not for his public), a false one, for his centre of interest was always in those 'événements de l'esprit qui s'éveille' ('events within the awakening mind', *ibid.*) that *precede* any recognisable 'genre'. His formal poems are the prolongation, or the 'éternelle élaboration' of an impulse that springs from the same source as the briefest 'Petit poème abstrait'. But as I have suggested, nothing could prepare the reader for the sheer intensity, exactitude and diamantine compactness of the latter.

Contemporary Valéry scholarship has foregrounded the achievement of the 'Poèmes et PPA';[2] in doing so, it has presented a very different image of Valéry to the classicizing formalist of popular misconception. The prose poetry, as we shall see, represents a body of work of astonishing modernity and freshness; by remaining so close to his initial impulse, Valéry can offer us a reflexive second-by-second report on experience:

> Sous ma fenêtre
> Et aux reflets et aux reflets des reflets
> Du soleil et des soleils sur la mer
> Dans les glaces,
> Après le bain, le café, les idées,
> Nu au soleil sur mon lit tout illuminé
> Nu—seul——fou—
> Moi!                                    (*C*2, p. 1297)[3]

This kind of euphoric writing, *à l'état pur*, can surely never date, or 'wrinkle', to adapt the evocative French expression.

Valéry, as much as Rilke, is the poet of beginnings. 'La mer, la mer, toujours recommencée!' of 'Le Cimetière marin' remains the apt analogue of this relentlessly inquiring spirit. The scope of the *Cahiers* may put us in mind of Leonardo's *Quaderni*, but in their remarkable fusion of analytic and affective aspects of the self they are equally comparable to Coleridge's *Notebooks*. It is this fusion, achieved at a high level of intensity, that is the salient feature not only of the 'Poèmes et PPA' but also of several passages in the chapters 'Ego', 'Eros' and 'Thêta' which equally concern us here. At its best, each notation is an arrow-shot, starting from zero, gaining maximum velocity in the minimum time, and accumulating *en route* a richness of suggestion that brushes as many of the perceiving senses and tickles as many intellectual nerve-ends as possible. Hence, Valéry can present us with a 'Poème Complet' which consists of two lines:

> Le ciel est nu. La fumée flotte. Le mur brille.
> Oh! que je voudrais penser clairement!  (*C*2, p. 1250)[4]

It is worth pausing over the audacity of that title – 'Poème Complet' – when it comes from the man who preached that a poem was never completed, only abandoned ... And yet, as readers, we are beguiled by the analogical richness Valéry manages to set up in these two lines, suggesting the obscure relations between thought process and the surrounding virtualities of sky, floating cigarette smoke and shining wall: by creating a décor, a set of physical circumstances that predisposes the mind for analytic thought, Valéry creates in miniature that network he termed 'CEM' – Corps-Esprit-Monde – and sets a current running through it. What he called his *'sensibilité intellectuelle'*, his genius for the 'Divinisation du possible psychique' and his 'Reconnaissance du réel psychique' is seen in action here ('Divinisation of the mentally possible ... Recognition of the mentally real') (*C*1, p. 131). 'Poème Complet' surely justifies its title. Under the rubric 'Ego', Valéry identifies and anatomizes his obsession with 'beginnings' and his 'terrible desire' to treat everything 'from zero' (p. 155). As a poet, however, he realized this was a natural state of affairs: 'Toute poésie gît dans le commencement, ou plutôt est tout le temps *un commencement*' ('All poetry resides in beginnings, or rather is continually a beginning') (*C*, XXIV, p. 862).

Valéry never tired of celebrating a natural 'beginning': the dawn. Not surprisingly, for this poet, it is the privileged moment, and the theme, of course, of his formal poem 'Aurore', which prolongs, and organizes many of the perceptions noted *à vif* in the prose poetry (though at the price of a notable diminution of immediacy). Whole studies have been devoted to the thematics of light in Valéry's work,[5] and his celebrated 'Aubades' compose the largest group in the 'Poèmes et PPA'; several of them were published, often in slightly revised form, during his lifetime, in the 'Poésie brute' section of 'Mélange' for example, or in 'Rhumbs', collected in *Tel Quel*. They also figure under the opening letters of his magnificent lyrical prose sequence 'Alphabet', which was not, unfortunately, included in the original Pléiade edition of the *Œuvres*. The letter 'C' contains this striking, almost heroic image of Valéry at the prow of his window – 'gladiator' and pioneer – confronting the start of day:

Comme le temps est calme, et la jeune fin de la nuit délicatement colorée! Les volets repoussés à droite et à gauche par un acte vif de nageur, je pénètre dans l'extase de l'espace. Il fait pur, il fait vierge, il fait doux et divin. Je vous salue, grandeur offerte à tous les actes d'un regard, commencement de la parfaite transparence! Quel événement pour l'esprit qu'une telle étendue! Je voudrais bien vous bénir, toutes choses, si je savais![6]

By evoking the swimmer's breaststroke action, throwing open the shutters, Valéry deftly fuses his two elements of predilection, sky and sea, and sets up a metaphoric modulation between them. It is a vividly physical apprehension, which serves, as always with this poet, as a springboard for an essentially meta-physical discourse. The vigour is typically Valéryan. In another of the 'Poèmes et PPA', entitled 'Nage' – one of several devoted to the sea – the poet wrestles with the element as he might with a mistress in the act of love. The analogy is worked out in erotic terms:

Je saisis l'eau à pleins bras, je l'aime, je la possède, j'enfante avec elle milles étranges idées. Alors / En elle, / je suis l'homme que je veux être. Par elle mon corps devient l'instrument direct de l'esprit et fait mon esprit. Je m'éclaire par là. Je comprends à merveille ce que l'amour aurait pu devenir avec moi, si les dieux l'eussent voulu … (*C*2, pp. 1273–4).[7]

A similarly 'masculine' approach to the experience of dawn, and the poet's coming to full consciousness with it, occurs in a kind of 'Aubade' in 'Ego': 'Il est des instants (vers l'aube) où "mon esprit" (ce personnage très important et capricieux) se sent cet appétit essentiel et universel qui l'oppose au Tout comme un tigre à un troupeau' (*C*1, pp. 140–1).[8] One of the dialectics at work in these 'Aubades' is undoubtedly 'gender-based'; in a late entry in 'Ego', Valéry recognizes this: 'Ma pensée est, je crois, toute — — mâle, ma sensibilité — des féminines' (p. 163) ('My thought is, I think, wholly — — male, my sensibility — feminine in type'). Analogically, we can talk about active and passive attitudes, of 'engendering' ideas or 'receiving' them in a more meditative mode, and this in turn might lead to a more general consideration of Western and Eastern philosophical approaches: certainly they co-exist in Valéry, and nowhere more explicitly than in the 'Poèmes et PPA'. Other dialectics abound in the 'Aubades' – Being / Non-Being, Being /

Knowing, Fullness / Emptiness, Presence / Absence, the Subject / Object divide in cognitive perception, the Conceptual / Non-conceptual nature of language. An interesting sidelight on these major concerns is how the affective aspect, the sensibility (notably in the 'Eros' rubric), can affect and 'distort' consciousness with the tyranny of an 'idée fixe'. Since, as I have suggested, the 'Aubades' form the heart of Valéry's project in the 'Poèmes et PPA', I want to take a closer look at how the dialectics mentioned above find expression. The questions they raise reach far into matters of contemporary philosophical concern.

For Valéry, famously, 'Un poème doit être une fête de l'Intellect' ('A poem should be a festival of the intellect') (C2, p. 1079); André Breton, equally famously riposted that it should be 'la débâcle de l'intellect'.[9] It is a crucial distinction. Valéry had a horror of the arbitrary – witness his perennial scepticism in regard to systematic philosophy or theology as merely 'un usage particulier des mots' (C1, p. 479), a juggling of terms lacking rigorous definition. A right understanding of mental functions, a minute recording of cognitive processes, a serious engagement with Kant or Descartes in respect of forms of knowing – all this is carried out under the aegis of Reason. His work has nothing to do with the automatic writing experiments of Surrealism, or the exploitation *for its own sake* of dreams or secondary, drug-induced states.[10] Breton came to castigate Valéry for clinging to what we might call the Apollonian principle, above all for exhibiting a *controlling consciousness* over his formal work that is a hallmark of classicism. The 'Aubades', and the 'Poèmes et PPA' in general are also 'classical' in the sense that they are celebrations of consciousness – or of that faculty which enables us to organize experience – and of coming-to-consciousness, like a swimmer surfacing, and *only* in that sense; otherwise, their compact, disjunctive character, their fusion of widely divergent fields of knowlege and experience, their very existence as 'fragments' or 'crystals' or 'instants' are of the utmost modernity.

Given Valéry's foregrounding of consciousness, and of a perceiving subject, a 'Moi', that predicates *self*-consciousness (though these remain uncertainties and variables in his work) it comes as no surprise that the 'somatic' or 'existential' 'Aubades' describe the physical act of waking (and simply getting out of bed!) in terms of a struggle. 'Colloque dans un Etre' dramatizes this struggle in the form of a Socratic dialogue. In psychological terms, voice 'A' might represent the superego exhorting voice 'B', the befuddled ego, to consciousness, much as a first ray of light pierces the darkness at dawn:

> A
> Allons ... Sors de l'instant ... Compose tes puissances ... Dégage qui tu es, de cette boue vivante qui gît, en forme d'homme abattu et abandonné, dans le désordre du linge de ta couche ... Renais! Il est temps. ...
> B
> Pitié! Je ne puis pas. Tu ne demandes rien de moins que l'impossible! Le poids de mon corps est celui de toute la terre qui est sous moi. Comment veux-tu que je me dresse, que je soulève à la fois tout l'être et tout le non-être qui sont intimement confondus en moi? (*Œ*, I, p. 360)[11]

Part of the distress for 'B' is in having to take on the same identity as that of the previous day ('Pourquoi me rendre au soleil connu, et au *Même* trop connu?' ('Why deliver me up to the familiar sun, and to that *Same* I know too well?') (p. 364). In other 'Aubades', as we shall see, this question of 'naming', and of the classifying function of language when applied to external reality, is of paramount importance. While dreams, with their mysterious deformations of the familiar, exercise him as much as any other domain in the *Cahiers*, Valéry seems more interested in the *restoration* of the world effected by waking consciousness: the dream-state, or more exactly the intermediate state between sleep and waking is described in derogatory terms. One of the 'Poèmes et PPA', entitled 'La Toilette', is a memorable example:

> Au matin, secouer les songes, les crasses, les choses qui ont profité de l'absence et de la négligence nocturne pour croître et encombrer; les produits naturels, saletés, erreurs, sottises, terreurs, hantises —
> Les bêtes rentrent dans leurs trous.
> Le Maître rentre du voyage. Le sabbat est déconcerté.
> Absence et présence.                              (*C*2, p. 1268)[12]

In the free verse 'Poème. Je suis l'idée maîtresse' (later somewhat revised and published in 'Mélange' under the rubric 'Poésie brute' as 'Chant de l'Idée-maîtresse'), the poet is apostrophised, and exhorted by his 'idée maîtresse' in similar vein to voice 'A' in the 'Colloque dans un Etre', with the difference that here the interlocutor has no '*droit de réponse*'. The conception is uniquely Valéryan in spirit; only he, one suspects, could give speech to a *potential* idea – for the idea, as such, is never realized, and cannot be, until the interlocutor is disposed to receive it. Valéry calls it a 'poème' or 'chant', but it is very much a 'Petit poème abstrait' in tendency, that is, without a defined physical décor or circumstance, something like an insistent 'monologue within a being'. This is the Valéry able to divine the possibilities of the mind, his 'idée maîtresse' an example of what he calls elsewhere his 'étranges personnages ... Toi, Présent, — et vous Formes, et vous Significations, Fonctions et Phases et Trames'; he poses the question 'pourquoi ne seriez-vous pas une poésie?' (*C*2, p. 1258),[13] his novel ambition being to write a poem that might consist, for example, of nothing but Kant's transcendental categories, remaining, if such were possible, *unapplied*.

So far the prose poems we have looked at have been, in the main, written in the rapid, staccato, disjunctive prose characteristic of the *Cahiers;* 'Chant de l'idée-maîtresse' is a kind of hybrid, written in the familiar exclamatory spurts and dashes but here aspiring to a more organized existence in verse, which is nevertheless very different in nature from the highly elaborated orchestration of a poem from *Charmes.* 'Poésie brute' is, on the face of it, an apt expression; equally telling is a section of 'Tel Quel' entitled 'Poésie perdue' and, like 'Poésie brute' containing slightly revised versions of the originals, to be found in the 'Poèmes et PPA' dossier of the Pléiade *Cahiers.* 'Poésie perdue', however, carries with it a sense of regret, or of deference; Valéry seems to imply these *could* have been worked up into formal verse. As I suggested at the outset, this is an implicit genuflection by Valéry to public expectation, and as such not to be taken too seriously. The 'Chant de l'idée-maîtresse' forms a significant subgroup with several other pieces, scattered throughout various rubrics of the *Cahiers,* often entitled 'Psaumes'. These are usually highly exclamatory, antiphonal and anaphoric pieces, written with energy, and of considerable originality. It may be that Valéry simply lost his appetite for the painstaking toil of formal composition, after the effort of *La Jeune Parque* and *Charmes.* What is clear, however, from the evidence of these 'Psaumes', and of the 'PPA' dossier as a whole, is that his poetic impulse never flagged, but was rather channelled into novel directions.

The 'somatic' 'Aubades' are singularly concerned with the biological human organism at the moment of waking, and with a description of accompanying mental states. There is one prose poem of surpassing beauty that escapes the egocentric parameters of the

'Colloque dans un être'. Here, the poet on waking turns to contemplate the sleeping woman at his side:

S'éveillant au côté de la femme endormie, à demi éclairée, chaude et odorante, dans le silence respirant, exhalant; ... Elle dort, et en elle comme une graine dans un hypogée, repose et dure la vie du jour précédent dans l'attente du jour suivant. Celui-ci héritera du précédent et en lui tous les autres antérieurs. Ainsi se transporte le Même. —
Quel chant l'esprit de nuit s'éveillant ainsi jette à soi-même et ... (*C*2, p. 1282)[14]

The passage breaks off unfinished, but Valéry has expressed the essential thing. By means of a wonderfully discreet ambiguity, he raises once again the question of the unified subject, much contested in contemporary thought, and finds *organic* grounds for a continuity in the seed of extraordinary potential, that lies in the woman, like grain in a hypogeum, after love. This prose poem is as completely achieved, in its way, as the poems in formal verse like 'La Dormeuse', 'Les Grenades' or 'Le Vin perdu', to which it is thematically linked. It is a *lyrical* elaboration, and celebration, of his wonder, many times expressed, in the dossier 'Bios' of the *Cahiers*: 'Un spermatozoïde, un rien, emporte l'effigie morale et physique de son auteur — ! C'est confondant — Quelle monade!' (*C*2, p. 721),[15] or 'La graine contient de grands secrets — Car elle vit et ne vit pas. Ressort bandé' (*C*2, p. 737).[16] It is a further indication of how the 'Poèmes et PPA' themselves arise as it were organically out of the homogeneity of the *Cahiers*.

How does the mind, on waking, re-encounter the world? How do our cognitive processes work? What is the nature of perception, and how far is our experience of the world dependent on *a priori* categories? What is the role of conceptual language and how far does it dull our sensory antennae, and seal up the 'doors of perception'? These are the perennial preoccupations of philosophy, and they are all present in the next, major group of 'Aubades' I want to look at, the 'metaphysical' or 'phenomenological' 'Aubades', as we might call them. The related chapters in the *Cahiers* are chiefly 'Philosophie' and 'Langage', but also the theological speculations gathered under 'Thêta'. In 'Philosophie', Valéry refers extensively to Kant, but also to Descartes and Pascal – the latter being treated with scant respect. Valéry's interrogation of perception, of the obscure relations between perceiver and perceived, subject and object, parallel similar investigations by more modern philosophers like Husserl and Merleau-Ponty, and even Heidegger in the latter's descriptions of 'Being-in-the-world'. There are also insights into the two-way process of perception that remind one forcibly of the nature doctrine of the English Romantics, Wordsworth in particular.

'Réveil', a prose poem dated 1913, and published with revisions in 'Poésie perdue' (*Œ*, II, pp. 658–9) raises these questions eloquently:

> Au réveil, si douce la lumière—et ce bleu—Le mot 'Pur' ouvre mes lèvres.
> Le jour qui jamais encore ne fut, les pensées, le *tout en germe* considéré sans obstacle—le Tout qui s'ébauche dans l'or et que nulle chose particulière ne corrompt encore.
> Le Tout est commencement. En germe le plus haut degré universel ...
> Je suis un effet de la lumière. Ma fonction est entièrement sous mes yeux.
> J'équilibre le total du jour nouveau.
> Ah! retarder d'être moi — Pourquoi, ce matin, me choisirais-je?
> — Si je laissais mon nom, mes maux, mes chaînes, mes vérités, comme rêves de la nuit?                                          (*C2*, p. 1261)[17]

With an 'intensité de pureté' (p. 955) such as he identifies in the music of Bach, the word 'Pur', here, 'opens his lips'. It is essentially the same impersonality he finds in Bach that Valéry admired in Mallarmé, and the latter's attempt to 'Donner un sens plus pur aux mots de la tribu' ('To give a purer sense to the words of the tribe'); that impersonality which is born of language itself, among the 'reflets réciproques', set up between words, and within words, phonemes.[18] In 'Réveil', impersonality is desired in the sense that 'personality' – with its 'name', 'troubles', 'chains' and 'truths' – is seen as *restrictive*, and 'purity' here is also the purity of full potential, which exists before choice. Such a moment, he writes in another passage, is a triumph of suspense and possibility (p. 1296). The dawn is an apogee, a zenith of purity 'que nulle chose particulière ne corrompt encore'; even here, however, the poet is as it were 'used' by 'parasitic' conceptual language – 'Le mot "Pur" ouvre mes lèvres' – though Valéry chooses to sidestep that particular impasse this time. He is less a perceiving subject than a perceiving function, the impersonal 'analogue of what is'; and as such *equivalent* to the sum of visible, audible, olfactory phenomena he perceives simultaneously. This is perception *à l'état pur*, a state of passive, non-conceptual receptiveness, something equivalent to Merleau-Ponty's 'Etre sauvage' or 'brut'.[19]

Valéry worries away at the threshold of perception, and describes, in a very late passage, 'Modulation de l'aube', an apprehension of the biblical 'Fiat Lux':

> Il y a un moment où la lumière commence à s'en prendre aux choses, à leur faire *balbutier* leurs formes, et puis leurs noms successifs, à partir de celui-ci même de 'choses' qui est le commencement. Il y a d'abord *quelque chose;* puis, *des choses.* Et c'est exactement comme dans la *Genèse.* (*C*2, pp. 1305–6)[20]

It is frequently this pre-nominal – almost prelapsarian – state that Valéry seems to yearn for, this obscure *'quelque chose'* that importunes him (the vagueness of the term is symptomatic of its inexpressibility). Sometimes it takes the form of the dialectic Absence / Presence, and though Valéry always protested wryly when a commentator tried to see in him an unconscious Buddhist (*C*1, p. 188), this apprehension of emptiness comes close to the doctrine of dependent origination, or *Sunyatta*, the emptiness of all phenomena when considered in terms of their strict contingency upon one another. It is combined here with an insight common to many visual artists:

> Le vide de tout ce plein. Ce bâillement, le Jour et le Monde. — Cette impression non pas de voir ce que je vois, mais d'être *vu* par ces objets, ce ciel — ou encore d'un échange sans résultat possible entre mes yeux et ces choses — échange sans issue – qui cache je ne sais quoi, sous couleur de montrer. (*C*2, 1259)[21]

It is extreme states of perception like these, that led to Valéry's interest in mystical writers like St John of the Cross and to his self-description as a mystic without God. God's absence, for Valéry, and in this he recalls Heidegger and even Derrida, becomes in the end as 'telling', as rich in implication, as His presence.[22] But Valéry would have baulked, I suspect, at Heidegger's poetico-ontological descriptions of *Dasein*, at his 'poeticisation' of philosophical thought just as much as he does at Pascal's rhetoric of eternal silence; he would have been wary, too, of Husserl's attempt to construct a systematic 'eidetic' science.[23] As Merleau-Ponty has well said (and he shows a shrewd understanding of Valéry here) in the concluding passage of *Le Visible et l'invisible*:

> En un sens, comme dit Husserl, toute la philosophie consiste à restituer une puissance de signifier, une naissance du sens ou un sens sauvage, une

expression de l'expérience par l'expérience qui éclaire notamment le domaine spécial du langage. Et en un sens, comme dit Valéry, le langage est tout, puisqu'il n'est la voix de personne, qu'il est la voix même des choses, des ondes et des bois. Et ce qu'il faut comprendre, c'est que, de l'une à l'autre de ces vues, il n'y a pas renversement dialectique, nous n'avons pas à les rassembler dans une synthèse: elles sont deux aspects de la réversibilité qui est vérité ultime.[24]

Valéry the poet is also Valéry *agonistes*, whose very medium, language, is an eternal temptation and a snare. In his assault on a logocentric philosophy of presence, Derrida has recruited Valéry as a 'witness' who noted that 'la philosophie s'écrit' ('philosophy writes itself'); that the intimate 'entendre-parler' ('hear-say') of the philosopher that would keep him safe within the 'cercle logocentrique' ('logocentric circle') is already eroded by 'la discontinuité, le délai, l'hétérogénéité' ('discontinuity, delay, and heterogeneity').[25] With Derrida, of course, there is no escape. And yet, he cannot recruit Valéry entirely, for the latter returns constantly in his 'Aubades' to that obscure, pre-nominal '*quelque chose*'. He is also intrigued by apparently *non-conceptual* uses of language, utterances provoked by extremes of physical pain or pleasure for instance. He explores this in 'Thêta', in the 'Psaume — (L'onomastique)':

> Où est encore le *nom* de Celui qui s'éveille?
> Qu'est devenu le *nom* de celui qui est saisi par l'extrême douleur?
> Comment s'appelle celui qui, cramponné et saisi dans les charpentes de la femme, se foudroie en soi-même et subit son éclair?
>
> Au dela, en deça des *noms*
> Sont les *pronoms*, qui sont plus — *vrais* déjà, et plus près de la Source ...
>
> (*C*2, p. 673)[26]

In predicating an intimate, subjective 'Source', anterior to the conceptualizing noun, Valéry comes close to the position of a contemporary poet like Yves Bonnefoy, otherwise hostile to him, for whom the task of poetry is, precisely, to escape the conceptual, and manifest the immediacy of what he defines in his own terms as 'Présence'. It is in that sense that both Valéry and Bonnefoy oppose 'poetry' to 'literature'.[27] The further language ventures from this kind of 'Source', the more liable it is to corrupt and betray it. And the 'Psaume' continues with an ultimate 'source':

> Avec le nom, commence l'Homme.
> Avant le nom n'est que le Souffle,
> La rumeur

> Qui doucement consume le dormeur,
> Le râle du jouir, du mourir,
> Dans tous ces temps qui sont sans connaissance.
> Ecoute le son de la Voix, Vierge ou Veuve de mots.
>
> (pp. 673–4)[28]

This experience of aporia, when language is exceeded – and breaks down – is frequently a stylistic hallmark of the 'Poèmes et PPA'. The connection between aporia and the sensibility is noted by Valéry in 1943, in a brilliantly sketched analysis of Rimbaud's method in the *Illuminations*, his work of prose poetry that is clearly an influence on Valéry:

> 'Le système 'Illuminations' — ne donne évidemment que des oeuvres 'courtes'. — Peut-être, même pas plus longues que deux lignes …
> D'ailleurs, les éléments ou germes psychiques de ce genre de travail sont eux-mêmes, *par essence, instantanés* — c'est-à-dire que leur 'existence' et leur 'effet' (d'autre part, chez le patient) sont de *sensibilité pure* = non développables, et non reconstituables à loisir — exactement *comme une sensation de douleur vive* et *toute* dans un minimum de 'temps' (*C*2, p. 1139).[29]

The dossier 'Eros', which contains some of Valéry's most poignantly personal texts, abounds with examples of this 'sensibilité pure'. Here is a wonderful passage, written under considerable emotional pressure, which is almost an exercise in aporia; and with its constant interchange between internal and external worlds reminds one forcibly of some of the great passages in Coleridge's *Notebooks*:

> Grand vent d'été — violence du pur, du d'or dans un été qui n'a pas été et ne fut que pluie. Mais tout à coup ce jour terrible de beauté. Déjà automne — Grand tourment des grands arbres — Accès de détresse personnelle — Souvenirs de forêts perdues — Déchirante bêtise — Je te connais, morsure — visage perdu — Lever de lune, coucher de lune — Terrasse — Grand arbre — Pavillon.
> Là appris à percevoir à travers la distance — J'ai appris … (*C*2, p.499)[30]

Symptomatically, the passage breaks off unfinished. One of the aspects of love which Valéry most feared, was the threat it posed to his reason, in particular the *slant* or *bias* it gave to the virgin potentialities of his consciousness, as he reveals them especially in the 'Aubades'. One remarkable passage, written during the great crisis of 1921, is a description of despair, written in despair:

> A 4 heures, je regardais le palmier orné d'une étoile.
> Ce calme infiniment doux, source immobile de la journée,

Était infiniment voisin de la source des larmes,
Et le jour est venu lentement éclairer
Bien des ruines. ... (*C2*, p. 455)[31]

In Valéry's lyric imagination, there is a rich thematic nexus, relating to the concept of 'purity', between the tear, or its mysterious source, the diamond and the crystal. One thinks of the opening of *La Jeune Parque*, but also of that limpid text *L'Ange*, which Valéry returned to at the very end of his life and which, in a sense, composes a parable of that life, dramatising as it does the paradox of an angelic reason fused with a suffering sensibility that is the human condition:

— Ce que je suis de pur, *disait-il*, Intelligence qui consume sans effort toute chose créée, sans qu'aucune en retour ne l'affecte ni ne l'altère, ne peut point se reconnaître dans ce visage porteur de pleurs, dans ces yeux dont la lumière qui les compose est comme attendrie par l'humide imminence de leurs larmes. (*Œ*, I, p. 206)[32]

With extreme, one might say Faustian lucidity, Valéry describes the finally tragic outcome of his 'programme', which was to answer the question 'Que peut un homme?': '*Et pendant une éternité, il ne cessa de connaître et de ne pas comprendre*' ('And for all eternity, he did not cease to know and not understand') (p. 206).

In similar vein, in a famous late entry in 'Thêta' entitled 'Station sur la terrasse', which must count as among the most moving of his prose poems, he attempts a 'résumé' of his life's achievement. Looking at the night sky, he sees it constellated as it were with the poetic masterpieces, mostly by Mallarmé, but autonomous and impersonal now in their arctic purity. Contemplating the ambition, and the achievement of his one-time Master, and his own by comparison, he reaches a crowning paradox:

Et surtout je connus toute la valeur et la beauté, toute l'excellence de *tout ce que je n'ai pas fait* — —
Voilà ton oeuvre — me dit une voix.
Et je vis tout ce que je n'avais pas fait.                    (*C2*, p. 689)[33]

It is both a grand, and I think entirely sincere, act of humility and at the same time Valéry realises with pride that 'Ce que je n'avais pas fait était donc parfaitement beau, parfaitement conforme à l'impossibilité de le faire' *Ibid.*)[34] – the supreme masterpiece only realisable as an essence, or a hypothesis, like God or a Platonic Form, and discoverable by a process of refusal and negation and discontent with what *has* been realised.

Yet these grand, even grandiloquent, retrospective acts are aty-
pical of Valéry. The poet of the prose 'Aubades' and the other
'Poèmes et PPA' is a more austere figure, with the nobility of Rilke's
poet, that 'eternal beginner', whose icons are 'Matin noir — Lampe
— Éveil — ' ('dark morning – lamp – awakening') (*C2*, p. 1296). We
can read him on the way to the formal poetry, or on the return
journey from it; but not without seeing Valéry in a fresher, dawn
light.[35]

NOTES

1  'monstrous desires of lovers of the spontaneous and of ideas in their
   pure state'.
2  See in particular Judith Robinson-Valéry's 'Préface' to *Ego Scriptor et Petits
   poèmes abstraits* (Paris, Gallimard, Coll. 'Poésie', 1992), pp. vii–xxxi. For
   an in-depth analysis of the lyrical prose in the *Cahiers*, and an exhaustive
   inventory, see Robert Pickering, *Paul Valéry: Poète en prose*, Coll. 'Archives
   des lettres modernes' (Paul Valéry no 5), (Paris: Minard, 1983).
3  'Under my window / And in the reflections and the reflections of the
   reflections / Of the sun and the suns on the sea / In the mirrors, /
   After the bathe, the coffee, the ideas, / Naked in the sun on my light-
   flooded bed / Naked — alone — mad — / Me!'
4  'The sky is bare. The smoke floats. The wall shines. / Oh! How I.
   should like to think clearly!'
5  See Jean-Marc Houpert, *Paul Valéry: Lumière, Ecriture et Tragique*, (Paris:
   Méridiens Klincksieck, 1986).
6  *Alphabet* (Lettre C), (Paris, Blaizot, 1976). 'How calm this time is, and
   how delicately coloured the young ending of the night! The shutters
   thrown open left and right with the brisk action of the swimmer, I enter
   the ecstasy of space. It is pure, pristine, tender and divine. I greet you,
   grandeur offered up to all the acts of scrutiny, beginning of perfect
   transparency! What an occasion for the mind, an expanse like this! I
   should like to bless you, each and every thing, if I knew how!'
7  'I grasp the water in my arms, I love it, I possess it, I conceive a
   thousand strange ideas within it. And so / Within it, / I am the man I
   want to be. Through it my body becomes the unmediated instrument of
   my mind and fashions my mind. Through it I become clear to myself. I
   understand to perfection what love might have become with me, had
   the gods willed it so ... '
8  'There are moments (towards dawn) when "my mind" (that grand and
   capricious personage) feels that essential and universal appetite which
   opposes it to Everything, like a tiger preying on a flock'.
9  André Breton and Paul Eluard in 'Notes sur la poésie', *La Révolution
   surréaliste*, no. 12, December 1929.

10  See also the text by Roland Barthes on *Monsieur Teste* in Michel Jarrety, *Paul Valéry*, (Paris, Hachette Supérieur, Coll. 'Portraits littéraires', 1992), p. 190.

11  'A / Come … Leave the instant … Compose your powers … Detach who you are from this living slime that lies, in the form of a man crushed and abandoned, in the disordered sheets of your bed … Be reborn! It is time … B / Have mercy! I can't. You are asking nothing less than the impossible! The weight of my body is that of the whole earth beneath me. How can you ask me to arise, and shift both all of the being and the non-being that are intimately fused within me?'

12  'In the morning, shake off the dreams, the deposits, the things which have profited from the absence and neglectfulness of the night to grow and encumber; the natural products, deposits, errors, stupidities, terrors, hauntings — The beasts withdraw into their holes. The Master has returned from abroad. The sabbath is disconcerted. Absence and presence'.

13  'Mistress Idea … strange personages … You, Present, — and you Forms, and you Meanings, Functions and Phases and Frames … why would you not be a poetry?'

14  'Waking next to the sleeping woman, in the half-light, warm and fragrant, breathing in and out in the silence; … She sleeps, and within her, like a grain in a hypogeum, rests and perdures the life of the previous day, awaiting the day to come. The latter will inherit from its precedent, and from all the others preceding that. Thus the Same is carried over. —
      What a song the spirit of night awakening transmits to itself and … '

15  'A spermatozoa, a nothing, contains the moral and physical effigy of its author — ! It is bewildering — What a monad!'

16  'The seed contains great secrets — For it lives and does not live. A coiled spring'.

17  'On waking, the light is so tender — and this blue — the word "Pure" opens my lips. The day which never yet was, the thoughts, the *everything in embryo* considered without restriction — the All sketched out in the gold and which nothing in particular corrupts yet. The All is a beginning. The highest universal degree in embryo. … — I am an effect of the light. My function is entirely under my scrutiny. I am in balance with the entirety of the new day. Oh! to delay being me — why should I choose myself, this morning? — What if I were to leave behind my name, my torments, my chains, my truths, like nocturnal dreams?'

18  'Crise de vers', in Mallarmé, *Oeuvres complètes*, ed. Henri Mondor and G. Jean Aubry, 'Bibliothèque de la Pléiade' (Paris, Gallimard, 1979), pp. 360–8.

19  For a general discussion of Being and Perception, of pertinence to Valéry's 'Aubades', see Maurice Merleau-Ponty, *Le visible et l'invisible* (Paris, Gallimard, Coll. 'Tel Quel', 1995), pp. 142–204.

20  'There comes a moment when the light begins to get to grips with things, and makes them *stammer out* their forms, and then their successive names, starting from that which in those "things" signals commencement. First there is *something*; then, *things*. And that is exactly what happens in *Genesis*.'

21  'The emptiness in all this fullness. This yawning, the Day and the World. — This impression not of seeing what I see, but of being *seen* by these objects, this sky — or else of an exchange that can never reach any possible conclusion between my eyes and these things — an exchange without issue — which conceals I know not what, while pretending to show.'

22  On Valéry's 'negative theology' see Paul Gifford, *Paul Valéry: Le Dialogue des choses divines* (Paris, José Corti, 1989).

23  For a synthesis of these and related questions, see Iris Murdoch, *Metaphysics as a Guide to Morals* (Harmondsworth, Penguin, 1993), pp. 188–269.

24  Merleau-Ponty, *Le Visible et l'invisible*, ed. Claude Lefort (Paris, Gallimard, 1979), pp. 203–4. 'In one sense, as Husserl says, the whole of philosophy consists in restoring the potential for meaning, for the birth of meaning or of unmediated meaning, for an expression of experience by experience which casts light notably on the special domain of language. And in one sense, as Valéry says, language is everything, since it is the voice of no one, since it is the voice itself of things, of waves, of woods. And what has to be understood is that these two viewpoints do not cancel each other out dialectically, nor do we have to gather them into a synthesis: they are two aspects of that reversibility which is ultimate truth.'

25  Jacques Derrida, 'Qual Quelle' (1971) in *Marges de la philosophie* (Paris, Editions de Minuit, 1972), p. 346.

26  'Where is the *name* of Him who awakes? / What happened to the *name* of him who is convulsed by extreme pain? / What is he called who, fixed and gripped in the body of woman, blasts himself with his own lightning? / Beyond, before *names* / Come *pronouns*, which are — *truer* at least, and closer to the Source ... '

27  See Yves Bonnefoy, 'La Présence et l'image' and 'Poésie et liberté' in *Entretiens sur la poésie* (Paris, Mercure de France, 1990), pp. 179–202 and 308–31.

28  'With the name, comes Man. / Before the name there is only Breath, / The murmur / That gently consumes the sleeper, / The groan of love, of dying, / In all of these moments of unknowing / Listen to the sound of the Voice, Virgin or Widow of words.'

29  'The method of the "Illuminations" — obviously only produces works that are "short". — Perhaps no more than two lines in length ...

What's more, the elements or psychic seeds in this kind of work are themselves *essentially instantaneous* — which means that their "existence" and their "effect" (elsewhere, on the patient) are of the order of *pure sensibility* = they cannot be developed, or reconstituted at leisure — exactly *like a sensation of piercing pain* and the *whole thing* experienced in the shortest possible "time".'

30 'Great summer wind — violence of the pure, of gold in a summer that has been nothing but rain. But suddenly this day terrible in its beauty. Autumn already — Great torment in the big trees — Access of personal distress — Memories of lost forests — Lacerating stupidity — I know you, wound — lost face — Moonrise, moonset — Terrace — Great tree — Pavilion.

There I learned to see through the distance — I learned . . .'

31 'At 4 o'clock, I looked at the palm tree decorated with a star. / That infinitely gentle calm, motionless source of the day, / Was infinitely close to the source of tears. / And slowly the day came to light up / Any amount of ruins.'

32 ' — That of me which is pure, *he said,* Intelligence which effortlessly consumes all created things, and which nothing can affect or alter in return, cannot begin to recognize itself in that careworn face, in those eyes where the light which composes them seems to be softened by the moist imminence of their tears.'

33 'And above all I recognized the full value and beauty, the excellence of *all I have not done —* — / There is your life's work — said a voice. / And I saw all that I had not done'.

34 'What I had not done was perfectly beautiful, perfectly consonant with the impossibility of doing it'

35 For further reading on the topic of this chapter please see Bibliography, items 5, 18, 27, 33, 34, 40, 65, 79, 90, 94, 96, 117.

# CHAPTER 8

# Counter-fiction

### Brian Stimpson

Valéry's aversion to the novel is legendary, from his mocking of the paradigmatic arbitrariness of narrative in 'la marquise sortit à 5h' ('the marchioness went out at 5 o'clock'), his reservations on Flaubert and Proust, his sometimes acerbic remarks on Gide's work, to the manifest absence of the genre in an *œuvre* which nevertheless encompasses effortlessly and unproblematically poetry, drama, dialogue, essay, prose poetry, aphorism and libretto. Yet, from the *Conte vraisemblable* of 1888 and the prose narratives of the Teste cycle right up to to the posthumous publication of the *Histoires brisées*,[1] he displays a continuous interest in experimental forms of prose fiction that quite belies this public stance. Throughout the *Cahiers*, too, Valéry delights in sketching out micro-stories, or 'sujets': accounts of dreams, fragments of dialogue, computations of relationships between $X$, $Y$ and $Z$, mini-scenarios which play out one moment of an 'abstract tale', one set of variations in the continually evolving dialogue between mind and body.[2] There emerges a fascination with exploring the different possibilities of fictional prose from the earliest moments of the *Cahiers* through the next fifty years; so much so that the voice of the writing 'I' which finds expression in various forms of counter-fiction is as persistent – and arguably both more continuous and more subversive – than the poetic voice.

It is in this context that Valéry's indictment of the novel must be considered. The critique is consistently sustained and flows directly from his analysis of the problematic relationship between language and the world; it derives ultimately from his determination to establish the epistemological basis of knowledge in the reflexive sensibility of the writing subject rather than in any mimesis or other form of *a priori* values. Language, he argues, is both the writer's tool of discovery and his most potent source of self-deception. Semantically, prose fiction carries the intrinsic danger that it will generate a reductive comprehension, abolishing its own form: 'l'objet du roman est de faire oublier le langage' ('the objective of the novel is to make one forget its language') (*C*, XVIII, p. 736). But Valéry mistrusts the attempt to confer formal, aesthetic qualities on fiction by elaborating complex stylistic and descriptive effects; ornate verbal structures, he claims, may be employed to designate the most ordinary of objects (*Œ*, II, p. 802).

His polemical approach would thus appear to condemn the novel on both counts: for paying too little attention to formal qualities of composition and style and for being too artificial when it does. The characteristics of the novel which he challenges – the fixed narrative system, the claim to a mimetic representation of reality, the biographical presentation of character, the organisation of events into plot, the omniscient narration which effaces the narrator, and 'le dernier des genres ... le descriptif' ('the lowest of genres ... description') (*C*, XVII, p. 551) – are those, most particularly, of nineteenth-century fiction.[3] Such conventions of genre founder, for Valéry, upon their claim to be absolute when they are in fact quite arbitrary; they render fixed and coherent, what is unstable and singular.[4]

Above all, fiction for Valéry is open to the charge of fashioning out of a discrete and discontinuous tissue of experience a coherence that is illusory and purely verbal; it constructs an entire spatio-temporal universe which acquires the autonomous status of apparently objective reality, though it is in fact totally spurious. The words of a fictional text function as signs pointing to a universe beyond, which comes into existence simply by being named: the word is a seemingly transparent progenitor of meaning and reality, which turns back upon the subject in full autarchic splendour, imposing its message while eluding all reference to the medium of its transmission. The form of writing prized by Valéry must, on the other hand, find its own *inner* authority, in the singularity of voice and in a discourse that admits rather than masks its arbitrariness and its particularity.

The construction of reality which Valéry attributes to fiction is thus antipodal to the subjective phenomenology which he himself practises. For him, reality can only be perceived as something singular and fundamentally separate: 'Toute vue des choses qui n'est pas étrange est fausse' ('any view of things which is not strange is false') (*Œ*, II, p. 501). Language masks this strangeness in familiar discourse and habits of mind, operating as a kind of shorthand or lowest common denominator of the signified; but by the same token, the meaning which this language makes available is commonplace and pre-established: as a reservoir of ready-made ideas, it can only express what is already known; it can neither say anything new nor point to the manner of its saying. Its neutrality is specious, being founded upon implicit assumptions, existing ideologies and recognisable cultural references. But above all it denies the Subject any role, cowing the intellect and imposing a passive mode of apprehension. For Valéry, the perceiving consciousness of the subject is an integrating factor in the triadic equation of 'Corps-Esprit-Monde', constantly responding to the exigencies and stimuli of the body and the world, while simultaneously projecting its own modes of perception. This is central to an understanding of Valéry's counter-fiction and is one of the keys to the *Histoires brisées*, as indeed one of the stories hints: 'Il y avait un homme qui s'appelait Assem, Azem, ou Acem . . .' (p. 451); or perhaps, we might add, A – C.E.M.

Linguistic theory recognises that definition is a process of discrimination and categorisation of items into classes or sub-sets. Valéry's celebrated poetic pendulum, oscillating endlessly between sound and sense, is based on just such a process. The published essays of *Variétés* tended to establish a binary polarity between the transitive, instrumental function of ordinary language and the formal aesthetic features of poetic language: the one is a communicative sign, its transactional function readily exhausted once translated into action, meaning, gesture or commonplace exchange, to all of which it remains subservient; the other is valued for its non-reducible polysemy and its 'forme sensible' indissolubly linked to the content. However, the *Cahiers* reveal not only considerable refinements but also an undermining of the whole distinction.

Valéry had originally sought a language uncoupled from its arbitrary association with reality and capable of expressing pure analytical functions, his Arithmetica Universalis or algebra of the mind. The practice of writing involved in the daily act of self-discovering thought reveals an inner complexity of subject–object encounter such that both the poetry and the prose counter-fiction – despite the differences of form and purpose – may be seen as extensions of the same confrontation which forms the basis, the spur and the goal of the Valéryan enterprise.

Both poetry and prose counter-fiction are founded upon a poetics of enunciation; the articulation of a speaking subject is the sole source of authentification of reality, but in making its utterance the subject recognises itself as fundamentally and irremediably 'other'; the writing is a transcription exteriorising and transforming the silent cries proferred within, the tears of the mind which alone declare the full otherness of the subject. In the prose fiction, the only continuity is that of a singular present moment, or rather, a consecutive series of present moments linked by and in the mind of the perceiving subject, but varied and even unconnected in respect of the objects of its attention: this is the 'self-variance' of the phases of consciousness. In 1943 he envisages *Alphabet* as a 'novel', 'le journal d'une journée de quelqu'un', linked only through 'un *certain regard*' which would trace 'cet enchaînement incohérent et pourtant enchaînement de substitutions de moments et phases bien différents (*C*, XXVII, p. 364).[5] The phrase curiously recalls the description in a letter to Fourment in 1901 of the project *Agathe*: it would, he said, introduce 'de la suite, dans le moment de l'incohérence et de l'inattention' ('succession into a time lacking coherence or attention') (*Œ*, II, p. 1388). Here the possibilities are taken to an extreme point, exploring the inner transformations of a subject cut off in extended sleep from all external stimuli: how does thought react when its only sensation is its own thinking and dreams? As the project evolves (though never completed to his satisfaction), the sleeping woman becomes the mind itself, the dream narration replaced by a manuscript, the text retitled 'Manuscrit trouvé dans une cervelle' ('Manuscript found in a brain').

Such a conception suggests a kind of writing which inscribes the genetic process into its own form: the manuscripts of the *Histoires brisées* show very few corrections as though a spirit of permutation and improvisation were more significant than any polished final form; events are repeated within the stories, replayed in different form, rewritten with modifications (in 'L'Esclave' and in 'Robinson' for example) like musical variations upon a theme. Valéry even envisages the *absence* of subject-matter as itself a form of stimulus: 'pas d'envie, de sujet etc. Le conte est celui de cette recherche ... Chercher des noms et commencer par là — A tâtons' (*C*, XI, p. 299).[6] But the stories are not only 'inachevés' ('incomplete,'), they are, to use Jean Levaillant's expression 'inachevables' '(not completable').[7]

In this way, Valéry's literary production calls for reassessment, for there is in fact a surprising recuperation of fiction – albeit in a redefined and subversive manner. Not only can we now see the poetry as intimately informed by the intense abstract preoccupations of the *Cahiers*, we can recognise a prolonged exploration of the different possibilities of prose that locates these experimental fictions as a direct tributary of the most searching quests of the inquiring mind, offering a different angle of approach to these issues. The hesitations, the almost obsessive refusal of closure, the disruptive shifts of focus and time, the lack of sequence, the repetitions, the fragmentation, the lacunae and ellipses – all these features characterise the *Cahiers* as much as the 'contes'. Where the poetry builds up layers of harmonic resonance and metaphoric richness, the 'contes' are metonymic, partial, indicative, unconstructed, disjointed, all symptomatic features of a refusal to construct a narrative system that is other than singular and subjective. At one end of the spectrum the counter-fiction merges with the poetry, the prose poem and the 'récit de rêve'; at the other end of the spectrum it merges with the most abstract writing and the attempt to forge 'une prose tout autre' which would be capable of articulating directly the movements of the mind in a language free of 'fiduciary' constraint; it would be an 'artificial language' based upon 'le réel de la pensée, langue pure, système de signes — explicitant tous les modes de représentation ... *excluant* la *croyance aux significations des termes* en soi' (*C*, XII, p. 280).[8]

Where the *Cahiers*, for the most part, confront the difficulties inherent in realising the System, fiction allows Valéry to envisage their hypothetical resolution. This is already true of M. Teste who is born out of the very impossibility of his real existence, and recounted as a self-announcing fiction, yet with all the markers of an authentic first-person narrative. But it is equally the case in Valéry's prospective 'Sujets' which propose, for example, the story of the 'Vieillard ... qui a *tout* vu' ('old man ... who has seen *everything*') (*C2*, p. 1332) or the 'Conte de l'homme trop intelligent ... Le surmonté, le dépassé, le prévu. Le possible' (p. 1327).[9]

But the tales are also those of the sensibility and the passions: 'Pour un conte—Moment où un visage soudainement prend une valeur, un aspect nouveau, inconnu' (p. 1326);[10] the story of a repeating pattern of tragic love affairs (*Ibid.*); or of physical passion overcoming deep antipathy to the 'other' (pp. 1342–3). From the period of 'Tabulae meae *Tentationum*' (1897–9) dates a project for a 'psychological novel' based upon 'a mathematical law' (*CII*, p. 251): a woman who loved a man when they were together, while he loved her when they were apart. In other cases, the stories are of the purely physiological: 'Quel livre il y aurait à faire sous ce titre: *Journal de mon Corps* !'[11] (*C2*, p. 1323); the 'Story of a hand' (p. 1338); the 'Poem of the body' (p. 1341). As in the *Histoires brisées*, the stories portray characters at the very margins of society, those who have gone to extremes or 'to the last point': 'Conte — / Il y eut une fois un homme qui devint sage. / Il apprit à ne plus faire de geste ni de pas ... qui ne fussent ... *utiles*. / Peu après on l'enferma' (p. 1324);[12] or the sufferer from vertigo made for life on another planet (p. 1336). Equally, issues explored more seriously under the heading of 'Thêta' are here dramatised as lively discussions on death and divinity or as amusing dialogues between the atheist and the believer.

Although the *Cahiers* never cease to question the ability of language to translate the experience of the dream, the 'récits de rêve' feature prominently; it is not only a matter of dream accounts augmented by theoretical reflections, but clearly the boundaries between dreams and the narrative are porous, such that the passage between them might also be reversed: thus, for example, after proposing a dialogue of love in terms of two serpents devouring each other, absorbing each other's consciousness, he adds significantly: 'On pourrait en faire un rêve' ('It could make a dream') (pp. 1326–7). On another occasion a recurrent dream of poetic endeavour is associated with what seems to be the beginning of an account of his attempted suicide in 1896 (which will itself acquire a certain mythic status for him): '«Tel matin — à Londres un dimanche, la lampe et le jour noir jaune ... »' (*CIV*, p. 41).[13]

We see here, as in a previous account of his life in Paris, likewise distanced by speech marks and past tense ('«J'étais en ce temps inutilisé dans cette grande ville, dans une chambre extrêmement petite ... »' ('At the time I was unutilised in that great city, living in a tiny room') (*CII*, p. 128), the early signs of perhaps one of the most striking features of the fiction. For, accustomed as we are to the relative impersonality of the *Cahiers* and the elimination of personal anecdotes, we find that the prose fiction offers a singular opportunity for recounting the self, in a form of quasi-anonymous (auto)-biography. The self becomes fictionalised and all those aspects of the personality that are systematically depreciated in the notes of 'Ego', resurface with a new name, age or even gender, transposed into a world that is 'elsewhere' or 'nowhere' or which, when it is identifiable, is also clearly fictitious. 'Robinson' permits a deep identification with and appropriation of the fictional hero, learning everything through his own resources: 'EGO — = Robinson' (C1, p. 158). How can one fail to sense the personal resonance of a suggested novel of 'modern life': 'Un homme et sa femme. La femme, pieuse. L'homme absolument pur (ou épuré) de toute religion' (C2, p. 1323).[14] Yet there is no question of direct portraits of Valéry and his entourage in the figures of Gozon, Hera, Elizabeth or Rachel found in the *Histoires brisées*: they are not 'characters' in the traditional sense of rounded figures with their own 'carte d'identité'; features are shared across characters and perspectives and identities are intriguingly fluid, each note enacting one moment, one function of the self in a set of possible parameters of relationships. Acem appears androgynous, while 'la tête' on L'Ile Xiphos is otherwise without body at all. Gozon may take on the narrative voice in one manuscript draft, only to be the object of discussion between 'Elizabeth' and 'Rachel' in another, as they discuss the impossibility of coming to any consensus about this man 'qui dans une heure était mille personnages' ('who within an hour was a multitude of different people') (N.a.f. ms 19085, fo. 20). Or he may be a construction of the mind of an equally uncertain female identity variously called Rachel-Emma-Sophie-Agar: a most precisely imagined lover: 'Il s'appelait peut-être *Gozon*. Mais il y avait aussi un vrai *Gozon*' ('His name, perhaps, was *Gozon*. But there was a real *Gozon* too') (fo. 32v). The texts of the Carnet 'Agar-Rachel' on which Valéry has inscribed Gaston Gallimard's request 'Faites-moi un roman cérébral et sensuel. Et je vous couvrirai d'or' ('Write me a cerebral and sensual novel and I will deck you with gold') is intensely charged with eroticism, with love, and deep tenderness ('Nous ne pouvions nous détacher ni nos yeux tout proches entre eux se détourner de leurs échanges ... Que de plus près de toi? Quoi de plus près de moi? (fo. 28));[15] but it also offers anecdote, irony and a rigorously lucid and sometimes acerbic analysis of love, of the physiological process, the intellectual challenge, the possibility of raising the act of love to the power of 'un mode ... de connaissance' ('a mode ... of knowledge') (fo. 29v).

An example in a different vein of this mode of self-writing may be seen in the brief manuscript notes for a projected 'Album de Moi / Histoire de Boris' ('Album of Myself / Story of Boris'). It was to present 'Moi — en tant que personnage fantastique, — incroyable — *jeune* '('Myself — as an imaginary character — unbelievable — *young*'), a recreation of the preoccupations of his youth, now perceived as 'strange' (N.a.f. 19084, ff. 20–6). Boris, alternatively called 'Ambroise', enters a restaurant variously peopled by future politicians and doctors, prostitutes, as well as Verlaine, Poincaré and Teste. He envisages the reactions of each to the milieu and a conversation of almost geometric formality between those representing different 'ideas of "purity"'. Seemingly realistic local detail and personal anecdotes are introduced, but remain subservient to an overall formal construction.

It is apparent that the boundaries of genre are shifting and unstable. If *L'Ange* veers towards the prose poem, *Agathe* is envisaged rather as a 'conte' written in the simplest and most abstract language (*Œ*, II, p. 1388). Indeed it was to this project that his thoughts turned when approached by Gide in 1912 with a request for the republication of earlier material; the 'ex-commencement d'*Agathe*' might, he responded, feature as 'l'intérieur de la nuit de M. Teste' ('inside the night of M. Teste') in a volume which would be 'très rompu — prose, vers assez mêlés — comme un cahier très artificiel de travaux' ('very broken — prose, a mixture of poetry — a sort of artificial workbook') (*GV*, pp. 426–7). *Alphabet*, though composed of a series of prose poems, is envisaged as the narrative of a day. The tale of the 'Raccommodeur de fayence' ('The porcelaine repairer') is labelled 'conte "philosophique" ou poème en prose' (*C*, VI, p. 317), while the 'tale' of the man who has isolated the emotion of Beauty is also a 'sorte de Poème abstrait' (*C*2, p. 1337).

The *Histoires brisées* display the same intense alliance of the physical and the mental that characterises the poetry, but the notion of aesthetic closure is constantly subverted as the stories articulate the very impossibility of resolving the tensions between mind and body, between self and other, order and disorder: 'Les *Histoires brisées* se brisent sur l'indicible, au moment où elles diraient la réponse aux questions qui commencent les poèmes ... le moi est fendu et refendu, et l'autre de moi ne pourra jamais se dire'.[16]

The inner divisions between self-as-subject and self-as-object are encapsulated in the counter-fiction both in the subject-matter and the form of the writing, as the 'abstract Tale' 'La Révélation anagogique' makes clear. The subject is confronted by two terrible angels *Noûs* and *Erôs;* these twin adversaries – who figure both the external forces of Intellect and Love and the internal manifestations of 'Celui qui est Soi' ('He who is Oneself') – drive him to the extreme limit of knowledge and the enclosing wall of selfhood. However much the subject might try to think beyond the limit, the wall is effectively a mirror which offers neither the solace of another's gaze nor the comfort of self-recognition; it can only reflect back his ultimate, searing solitude (*Œ*, II, p. 467).

This too is the situation of Robinson on his island, self-sufficient, self-creating, constructing his own rules of operation and controlling his own environment. 'Le "Robinson pensif" — système isolé' ('The "pensive Robinson" is a closed system') (*Œ*, II, p. 415).[17] But the total freedom from material and temporal constraints that have arisen from his accumulation of provisions and freedom from economic necessity leave him uncoupled from time in a suspended present, able to confront pure existence, totally reliant upon his own mental ressources. The self-sufficiency of his island becomes a metaphor for the autonomy of the mind, appropriating, discarding, fashioning its own intellectual tools (*CI*, p. 41). If this is his strength, it also leaves him disconnected from all that surrounds him, subject to fears, fantasies and liable to experience a kind of existential anguish. No Other can consecrate his sense of identity; the solitude is so absolute that he is obliged to *imagine* 'un Autre. Scrait-ce un homme ou une femme? / Robinson divisé — poème' ('Another. Man or woman? / Robinson divided — poem') (*Œ*, II, p. 415). In the manuscript version he dresses to create an imaginary Other: 'Quoique son île fut déserte il mit une plume à son chapeau. Il lui semblait qu'il créait par là quelqu'un qui regardât cette plume.'[18]

But if the self is an island, the island is at the same time a creation of the self, with all the uncertainty of person that is entailed: 'Robinson finit par avoir fait son île ... C'est la mémoire qui m'a fourni mon île' (*Œ*, II, p. 418).[19] The text reveals a constant and inevitable tension which is that of consciousness itself, articulating the desire to be both on the island and offshore, within and without, all-encompassing yet self-recognising: 'Je pourrais dessiner cette île sur la mer. / Note que cette île où *tu serais*, tu l'imagines vue du large, conique, dorée, blonde ...' (*ibid*.).[20] But one cannot at the same time be part of a whole and perceive the whole as one: the story of Robinson is impossible.

This is one of the principal tensions underlying the effort to develop 'une prose tout autre'. For the prose work should be written in an absolute, non-arbitrary language which would make it a rigorous instrument of discovery, observation and exposition (*CV*,

63), an intimate language capable of articulating the inner dialogue of self with self, an exploratory, open, unformed language which passes from the act of inwardly directed listening through silent enunciation, verbalisation and ultimately scriptural encoding while maintaining as much as possible of its initial authenticity and sacrificing as little as possible to 'the language of the tribe'.

The texts articulate a theory of language and of the activity of thinking that addresses the dynamic interaction between continuity of mental activity and the discontinuity of reality. The question arises in the earliest *Cahiers* and in the notes for the projected *Essai sur Stéphane Mallarmé*, where Valéry envisages a form of writing that is 'an extension of the properties of language' and that explicitly acknowledges the arbitrary link between words and objects in the world (*CII*, pp. 275–87). Reading is a process of transforming the discontinuous images designated by words into a continuous mental construction, whether by substituting an act of understanding in the case of everyday language or by creating a continuous web of verbal semes and sounds in the case of poetry. But the goal of 'l'œuvre en prose' is quite different from either of these forms. For Valéry sought a language founded in the reality of the individual thinking-sentient being, a language which unites sensation and abstraction and is constructed according to a new discipline based upon 'rules of intellectual metrics' (*C*, VI, pp. 552–3). It is an intimate language of the subject and the senses, a prose exploring the possible, while fashioned into a form that articulates its impossibility.

It is, moreover, a prose that maintains its discontinuity, while translating the continuous variation of the mind: not by describing or telling, but by positively inciting its operation; the reductive and, for Valéry fundamentally entropic, tendencies of language cannot convey the full scope of the variations, the phases, the inconsistencies and incoherences of mental states. Language must be both exploited and outwitted if it is to be brought to say the unsayable.

It would be misleading to speak of any narrative system in the *Histoires brisées*. What emerges, rather, is the mobility of perspective, the temporal uncertainty, the absence of structure and sequence and a full sense of the arbitrary positioning of language. Events appear as singular and disconnected, divorced from any chain of causality. Characters and situations operate within their own sphere of reference in a strange, seemingly continuous present.

The stories do give an indication of character, of situation and of place, yet there is little in the way of plot, the spatio-temporal co-ordinates are ambiguous, contradictory even, while details have a random and seemingly arbitrary characteristic; above all the stories remain intriguingly elusive, constantly on the point of revealing their secret, of opening on to another dimension that will pull all the disparate information together into a single revealed sense, when they are interrupted, broken. Sentences end in suspension marks, with an expectation that is constantly incited but can never be satisfied, as though any solution were equally valid or superfluous: 'Mais la vérité est celle-ci, qui est plus profonde ...' ('But the deeper truth is this ...') (L'Ile Xiphos', Œ, II, p. 440); 'Les auteurs sont ...' ('Authors are ...') ('Voyage au pays de la forme', p. 466) And of course, there is Calypso, who, though enticing, 'jamais n'allait si avant dans l'empire de la pleine lumière que tout son être se détachât du mystère des ombres d'où elle émanait' and who escapes all attempts at embrace by retiring into 'le manteau vivant de sa conque' (pp. 409–10).[21] Or L'Esclave, the shipwrecked philosopher made slave who, having been commanded by the queen to recount everything he knows, eventually finds that he has exhausted his store of knowledge and memories; his mind becomes an empty desert, 'Mais tout à coup une lumière se fit en moi. Que les voies de l'esprit sont ...' ('But suddenly it came to me: the ways of the mind are ...') (p. 426) And there the passage ends. The answer is left in suspense, unless it is precisely the discursive act of the following fragment: 'Je chanterai les sens ... Ne pense point.' ('I will sing of the senses ... Think no more.') Henceforth the senses are the only source of truth, reality and purity: 'Promène-les, ces yeux, je te dis qu'ils sont le plus profond de nous' ('Let your eyes wander, they are what is deepest in us') (ibid.).

These are indeed the tales of 'mon corps' and 'mon esprit' in a world which is not that of external reality: a world apprehended by the self as a series of mental and physiological phenomena, and one that is created by, formed by the observer, and represented by the lucid vision of the pure self ('L'Ile Xiphos') or by the precisely located physiological voice ('Journal d'Emma'), a voice trapped in the specificity of its physiological function, as though from a Beckettian drama. But at the same time, the very distance from the everyday world permits a reflective ironic gaze upon contemporary society and an implicit critique of fiduciary myths, while many fragments posit alternative values and different social mores.

The stories do not present a biographical persona with recognisable features, a set of relationships and a past, present and future – in short, an identity – but rather a distillation of all these things that points up their arbitrary nature, here reduced to a pure and almost archetypal simplicity: dependence in 'L'Esclave'; solitude in 'Robinson'. Calypso embodies promise, possibility, desire in the fullest sense: the intellectual promise of a sexually desirable body, or is it the sexual promise of the ever-elusive idea, a visual equivalent of the siren voice of the Idée-maîtresse, the whole embodied in a text that constantly advances and retreats, starts and stops (as indeed the original typographic form of the title 'C.A.L.Y.P.S.O.').

The prose fiction remains at once direct and strangely remote, because unmediated by any consistent narrative presence. Voices emerge directly, as if spontaneously, without the filter of narrative position; Valéry makes no attempt to justify the source or identify the 'situation d'énonciation', even though the text is, precisely, personalised and demonstrates numerous marks of deixis. Although many of the pieces employ a first-person form ('L'Esclave', 'Journal d'Emma', 'D'Elizabeth à Rachel', 'Rachel', 'L'Ile Xiphos', 'Acem' as well as *La Soirée* and *Agathe*) they do not so much record the narrator's participation in any sequence of events as record his / her observation and mental perception. For the voice is not that of a social being located in an identifiable time and space: it is that of the writing 'I', finding identity in partial, exploratory expression, an impersonal voice enunciating in an indeterminate space-time, hesitating between the personal and the impersonal. As Valéry wrote in the 'Avertissement' to the *Histoires brisées*, 'il se fait des contes en moi' ('stories are written in me') (Œ, II, p. 407).

In many instances the story is based upon an initial act of utterance, in a striking phrase which establishes a speaking 'I' as founding source of verification: first person pronoun, present tense or a past that implies continuity with the present: 'La bêtise n'est pas mon fort. J'ai vu beacoup d'individus; j'ai visité quelques nations' (*La Soirée*, Œ, II, p. 15); 'Plus je pense, plus je pense' (*Agathe*, p. 1388); 'J'étais esclave, et le plus heureux des philosophes' ('L'Esclave', p 423); 'Mes yeux, mes cheveux sont châtains. J'ai un faible pour mon épaule droite, je la baise parfois, je lui parle' ('Journal d'Emma', p. 428); 'Je suis née au lieu même où j'étais née pour vivre' ('Rachel', p. 431); 'Je suis à présent dans Firgô' ('L'Ile Xiphos', p. 436).[22] While 'Acem' seems to adopt for the most part the

anonymous third person narrative system and subsequently employs
past historic tenses, it relies nevertheless upon a founding first-
person present, both in the opening preface: '*Ceci est un conte qui vient
toutes les fois que je passe dans le quartier où est ...*' (*ibid.*) and in the
sudden interjections which punctuate the text: 'Il ne riait jamais; il
ne marchait jamais ... J'ai dit qu'il ne riait jamais..' (pp. 452–3).[23]
One of the 'Fragments' even locates its narrative in the subjective
hypothesis of the first-person conditional: 'Je ferais une ville modèle
...' ('I would make a model town') ('Voyage au pays de la forme', p.
463).

Yet, while the enunciating voice is the source of authenticity by
the very fact of its utterance, nevertheless this subject remains vague
and mysterious, devoid of specificity within the paradoxically
authentifying present. It is as though, refusing all diegetic reality in
the content of the narration – because the subject matter is either
mythic, 'impossible' or avowedly fictional – Valéry is equally determined not to let it in by the back door: nothing permits the reader to
identify the time, the place, the identity or even the wherefore of the
enunciative present. The narrator of *La Soirée* writes: 'Ce soir, il y a
précisément deux ans et trois mois que j'étais avec lui au théâtre ...
J'y ai songé tout aujourd'hui' (p. 20).[24] Here, as in many cases, the
deictic markers seem provocatively present but non-specific. Where
Gide's *L'Immoraliste*, for example, offers layers of authentification to
corroborate the narrative, Valéry's counter-fiction presents layers of
indeterminacy which studiously elude the confirmation of reality at
the point where it is most anticipated. What is distant both in time
and space is brought to the immediacy – and the indeterminacy – of
the present: 'Je reviens d'un pays qui est assez éloigné du nôtre ...'
('I have returned from a land far from our own ...') (p. 466).
Moreover, even though a speaking 'I' necessarily implies a 'You',
there is no interlocutor, either internally within the narrative or
externally, in the shape of an addressed reader; for the discourse is
essentially private, a verbalisation that is directed towards the self:
the articulation of the writing 'I' is a means of recounting self to self,
of externalising an inner monologue, of taking cognisance of the
different facets of the subject, as internally apprehended – something
which language can only express through difference and disjunction.

A complex set of relationships between narrator, event and time is
thus found. Past events and habitual actions are often recounted in
the imperfect tense, so that it is the aspectual quality rather than the

repetition and the way they impinge upon the present state of mind that is emphasised: the past recurs within the present. If the first-person narrative denies what it might be supposed to affirm, by transforming into an abstract, de-personalised presence, the third person provides no more secure a reference-point. For while, in isolated fragments, it seems to offer the certainty of retrospection or the privileged insight of internal focalisation ('Robinson humait avec l'ennui de son passé la certitude de son avenir' (p. 412), 'Robinson commençait d'oublier ses commencements' (p. 419)),[25] it becomes rapidly apparent that there is neither any filtering narrator behind the statements, nor any consistent location of the fragments of text in relation to each other. In fact the text shifts from past to imperfect to present, from third to first and even second person, sometimes within a single fragment. The only sequence of events relates to Robinson's assurance of his survival and these are relegated to the pluperfect tense ('Il s'était bâti un bon toit; il s'était fait des habits de palmes et de plumes ...' (p. 411))[26] putting them at an even greater distance from his present state of mind.

The most distinctive, consistent and ultimately enigmatic quality of the fiction is, then, the very lack of consistency: shifts of person and of time, lack of sequence, connection and consequence. Whole periods of life seem to open up in vast array, but may just as readily be encapsulated within the closure of the past and consigned to history, enfolded in uncertainty. Forms are mixed, even within stories, and may include diaries, monologue, direct speech, poetry, correspondence and psalms, as well as narrative. Each fragment stands autonomously against the others, sometimes complementing, sometimes contradicting, but no voice assumes overall authority, no linkages are made. There is no opening or closure, no construction; rather than linking and composing the different elements together, the writing decomposes – the provisional and the hypothetical remain dominant, for such is precisely the movement of the mind and the reaction of the senses.

The quest for 'une prose tout autre' is not unproblematic and indeed, rather than a single type of prose, we should recognise the diversity of forms in Valéry's prose writing, each a partial response to an intractable problem. We might glimpse in *Agathe* one manifestation of the pure language based upon 'le réel de la pensée' and fashioned into a prose *'non arbitraire'* (C, XXVI, p. 319); but the

*Histoires brisées* and the 'Sujets', in a different way, portray too the interaction of abstraction and sensibility in a language of pure virtuality, a new form of literature in which the text and the interstices between become 'un curieux tableau de *signes des possibles*' ('a strange table of *signs of the possible*') (*C*, XIX, p. 511). It is as though Valéry employs the formula of myth and fairy-tale 'Once upon a time ...' not to launch a sequence of events but to explore a singular state of the self, a moment in the continuing dynamic of 'Corps-Esprit-Monde'; each traces an instant of pure potential – tantalisingly elusive as a figure of the mind itself – which merges with the present in a form of unresolved stasis or questioning possibility: 'Que vais-je faire de cet immense temps que je me suis mis de côté?' ('What am I going to do with this boundless time I have stored up for myself?') asks Robinson (*Œ*, II, p. 420); or as Rachel comes to realise after the revelation of love, 'On a dès lors un commerce tout nouveau avec soi-même, et ceci est toujours possible' (p. 433).[27]

NOTES

1  The *Histoires brisées* were published in 1950 on the basis of a dossier essentially prepared by Valéry himself, including the 'Avertissement'; the stories were written between 1916 and 1943, though principally in 1923 in response to a request from Gaston Gallimard. The manuscripts in the Bibliothèque nationale de France contain variants and additional texts not published in the 1950 edition.

2  It is perhaps less well known that he was at times an avid (and very rapid) reader of novels, as well as, on the insistence of his children, an inventor of fairy-tales.

3  In the nineteenth century, only Stendhal partially escapes his strictures. There is, on the other hand, an admiration for the eighteenth-century novel, founded on the naturalness of tone, the presence of singular voice in the writing, the ironic distance from mimetic reality and the experiments with form. See Michel Jarrety, 'Le Roman et le refus de la représentation' in *Valéry devant la littérature* (Paris, PUF, 1991), pp. 299–349.

4  The tales of fantasy which Valéry invented for his children proved to him that fiction can be an almost mechanical pursuit of the arbitrary, a system of variation, suspense, development and resolution (*C2*, 1234–5); it is a question, 'simply', of taking metaphors to an extreme. One of the manuscript dossiers of the *Histoires brisées* contains several pages devoted to fairy-tales, sometimes plotted out with formal developments and variations.

5 'the diary of someone's day ... a *certain way of looking at things* ... the incoherent sequence made up of substitutions of moments and quite distinct phases'.

6 'no desire, no subject etc. The tale is about this search ... Find some names and begin from there – feeling your way'.

7 Jean Levaillant, 'Préface', *Paul Valéry, 'La Jeune Parque' et poèmes en prose* (Paris, Gallimard, 1995), p. 7.

8 'the reality of thought, a pure language, a sign-system — avowing its modes of representation ... *excluding* any *belief in the inherent meaning of terms*'.

9 'Tale of the over-intelligent man ... What is overcome, overtaken, foreseen. The possible'.

10 'For a story —The moment when a face suddenly acquires a new value and look, previously unknown'.

11 'What a book might be written entitled: *Diary of my Body*'. This will become 'Journal d'Emma' in *Histoires brisées*.

12 'Story — / Once upon a time there was a man who became wise. He learned henceforth to make no gesture or step ... which were not ... *useful*. Shortly afterwards he was locked up'.

13 'On such a morning — a Sunday in London, the lamp on, a blackish-yellow light outside'.

14 'A man and his wife. She, very pious. He absolutely free (or purified) from all religion'.

15 'We could not separate, nor could our eyes turn away from their close proximity ... What could be closer to you? What could be closer to me?'

16 Levaillant, 'Préface', p. 12; 'The *Broken Stories* break up at the point of the unsayable, just as they might offer answers to the questions that launch the poems ... the self is split asunder and its other side can never be expressed'.

17 See Brian Stimpson, '«Insulaire que tu es, Ile – » : Valéry, the Robinson Crusoe of the mind', in *Robinson Crusoe: Myths and Metamorphoses*, eds. L. Spaas and B. Stimpson (London, Macmillan, 1996), pp. 294–315.

18 'Although his island was deserted, he put a feather in his hat. It seemed to him that by doing so, he was creating someone to look at the feather.'

19 'Robinson ends by having created his own island ... Memory has supplied it to me'. Cf. *C*1, p. 440: 'Le moi se dit *moi* ou *toi* ou *il*. Il y a les 3 personnes en moi'.

20 'I could draw this island on the sea. Note that this island where *you would be*, you imagine seeing it from the open sea, conical, gilded, fair'.

21 'never advanced so far into the realm of the daylight that her whole body emerged from the mysterious shadows whence she came' 'the living cloak of her shell'.

22 'Stupidity is not my strong point. I have seen many people; visited many countries'; 'The more I think, the more I think'; 'I was a slave

and the happiest of philosophers'; 'My eyes and hair are brown. I am fond of my right shoulder; I kiss it from time to time, and speak to it'; 'I was born in the very place I was born to live'; 'I am now in Firgô'.

23 *This is a tale which arises everytime I go through the quarter where . . .*'; 'He never laughed; he never walked . . . As I say, he never laughed . . .'

24 'This evening, exactly two years and three months ago I was with him at the theatre . . . I have been thinking about it all today'.

25 'Robinson inhaled both the tedium of his past and the certainty of his future'; 'Robinson was beginning to forget his beginnings'.

26 'He had built a good roof over his head; he had made clothes for himself from palm leaves and feathers . . .'

27 'And then one enters into a new relationship with oneself, and this is always possible'.

For further reading on the topic of this chapter, please see Bibliography, items 4, 19, 57, 59, 80, 101, 121, 125, 128, 137.

CHAPTER 9

# The Dialogues and 'Mon Faust':
# the inner politics of thought

*William Marx*

Consideration of the place of the Dialogues in relation to the rest of Valéry's work is at once a literary and an historical issue; which is not to confine it, merely, to literary history. Evidence for the importance of the genre is certainly compelling: from 1921 onwards the dialogue form is the major public genre adopted by Valéry, apart, that is, from the essay. The Dialogues form an extensive corpus: *Eupalinos ou l'architecte* and *L'Ame et la danse* were published in 1921 and were followed by *L'Idée fixe ou deux hommes à la mer* (1932) and *Dialogue de l'arbre* (1943); to these must be added the *Colloques* 'Socrate et son médecin' (1936), 'Orgueil pour orgueil' (1939) and 'Colloque dans un être' (1939), collectively re-published in *Mélange* (1939); the libretti for the two operatic melodramas *Amphion* (1931) and *Sémiramis* (1934); and finally the dramatic sketches for *'Mon Faust'* (1941). In addition there were many unpublished or unfinished texts such as the 'Dialogue des choses divines' ('Peri tôn toû theoû') begun in 1921 and pursued throughout the rest of the *Cahiers*.

This list is all the more remarkable when one considers that there was little explicit use of the dialogue form prior to 1921; from this perspective, it would appear that Valéry the poet gives way to the writer of dialogues. But this over-simple division requires more complex shading: for there is a sense in which the intimate dialogue with self is at the very heart of the Valéryan project, whatever the expressive modality. Indeed from the earliest stages, the use of dialogue is to be found, as in the unpublished project 'Le Yalou' (1895) or *La Soirée avec Monsieur Teste* (1896).

Such is the diversity – and even self-contradictory nature – of the Dialogues that they must be considered from three distinct, but complementary perspectives: the manifestations of the dialogic voice prominent throughout his work; the problematics of dialogue within

155

the Dialogues themselves; and finally, the manner in which the works engage in dialogue with their times.

In theory, dialogue is the least personal of all literary forms, since intentionality and meaning may not be directly attributed to any agent whom we may conventionally identify as the *author*. Paradoxically, although dialogue attaches great importance to the presence and sounds of voices and is indeed constituted by their alternation, it is precisely when they are multiplied that *the* Voice disappears. Or so, at least, it seems, for if the authorial voice is no longer perceptible as such, it may nevertheless be present by implication, in the links and gaps between the multiple voices of the dialogue. *La Jeune Parque* opens with an invocation, uttered by a voice that is both her own and that of another. The Parque emerges, alert and forewarned, from the interval separating two inner *personæ*. The nascent Voice is multiform, adopting in turn the multiple masks of consciousness in response to its own questions.

The Valéryan dialogue arises in fact from two significant absences. From the point of view of the reader – or the listener – the multiplicity of enunciative agents adds considerably to the difficulty and complexity of interpreting the whole. The absence of any single source that might be identified as the prime enunciator[1] makes the dialogues appear to have no parentage and so it is up to the reader to construct the meaning of the dialogue. In this respect the Valéryan dialogue does not differ significantly from any other in the genre. This form has always, from its origins, been presented as a play of meaning to be constructed, rather like a game of hide-and-seek: the platonic dialogue encapsulates an epistemological process in literary form.

What is different about the Valéryan dialogue, however, is that the absence of given meaning – of meaning given by a single voice – is not integrated into a reflection upon the origins of knowledge, but into a critical theory, a theory of literature itself. The erasure of any single authoritative source of meaning is in harmony with Valéry's consistently practised desacralisation of the authorial role.[2] If not entirely absent from the dialogues, the author is located in a space beyond the texts, which remains to be constructed. Speech is never attributed explicitly to the self, but is put into the mouth of one or more fictional *alter ego*, and thus from this perspective the dialogue form lies at the heart of Valéry's work and symbolises the impersonality often considered as typifying his art.

If the first absence upon which the dialogues are based is that of Valéry as author, the second relates to a psychological dimension. Literary dialogue for Valéry is above all 'inner dialogue', that is 'l'*opération qui transforme* des données par voie d'échanges (DR) (demande-réponse)' (*C*1, p. 300).[3] The alternation of responses may thus be considered as the play of ever-renewed contact of the self with its own constitutive otherness: 'Cette étrange, essentielle propriété d'être *deux* en *un* — en contraste avec quoi le désir d'amour — d'être *un* par *deux* apparaît complémentaire de la connaissance consciente ... Tout monologue est un dialogue' (*C*2, p. 519).[4] For Valéry the inner division on which consciousness is constructed may be assimilated to that which separates two speakers, or two lovers, and he will consistently argue that inner discourse is related to dialogue, as for example in the Lectures on Poetics at the Collège de France.

Such a conception is clearly mirrored in – if it is not modelled upon – the myth of Narcissus, whose amorous monologue is in fact dialogue:

PIRE.
    Pire? ...
              Quelqu'un redit *Pire* ... O moqueur! (*FN*, l. 93)

The pitiful death of Narcissus abandoning himself to the depths of the water may in many respects represent another, more abstract, but no less real death: that of a sharply delimited, opaque, reified self. As an allegory of consciousness, Narcissus announces the end of belief in the Homunculus, the reductive concept of a person which some psychological theories would imagine to lie at the centre of each individual, and which Valéry persistently denounced as illusory. For him, on the contrary, the self is nothing more than 'l'invariant' among a set of relations which are themselves variable (*C*2, p. 294). About 1907–8, he envisaged writing a dialogue that would be consciously based on the model of a shifting and fragmented subjectivity.

Que j'aimerais écrire — — ou plutôt avoir écrit! — un dialogue qui s'appellerait *Protée* — et chaque interlocuteur aurait sa voix, son *style* — et sa voix mentale. Plusieurs modes de voir, et leur alternance ferait dialogue.

N'ai-je pas vu de plusieurs façons et n'aurais-je pu me rencontrer moi-même? — Et cela n'est-il pas arrivé, n'arrive-t-il pas?
N'ai-je pas vécu plus d'un personnage? (C2, p. 1314)[5]

Valéry's conception of dialogue is quite strikingly drawn from inner experience, that of the plurality, or perhaps rather the disjunction, of the self. This is a founding motif of his thought, as of his poetry, even if it may be defined in different ways: at times the self is considered as the point of intersection between varying functions, a zero point of no autonomous substance; at others, it is seen in opposition to the personality (p. 292), while at still others, as here, personality itself breaks down, collapsing in on itself in apparently schizoid fashion. But whatever the definition, it is clear that the reality of intrasubjectivity is transposed into fictional intersubjectivity.

Thus the second absence which generates the dialogues is again that of Valéry, but this time as subject rather than as author. The dialogues are products of the fragmentation of the self and bring together two fundamental aspects of Valéry's critical and psychological reflection: the withdrawal of the author from his work and the 'centrifugation du Moi' ('centrifugation of the Self') (C2, p. 295).

A predilection for the spoken voice is manifest not only in the Dialogues, but is a prominent feature of the poetry too, where its importance is related to the emergence of consciousness: it can be represented through the figure of 'Bouchoreille' ('Mouth-ear'), an allegory of the division of the self into a presence that speaks and one that listens.[6] In the short poem *Chanson à part* (published in *Pièces diverses*, 1942) an inner voice of Augustan tone is heard; in an alternating series of questions and answers, the tragic basis of thought is constantly lightened by a knowing irony. The dialogue form is accompanied by a play of rhythm and tone, clearly perceptible in the final stanza:

> Où vas-tu? A mort.
> Qu'y faire? Finir,
> Ne plus revenir
> Au coquin de sort.
> Où vas-tu? Finir.
> Que faire? Le mort. (Œ, 1, p. 163)[7]

The predilection for spoken dialogue lies, then, at the source of the poetic voice in Valéry.

Thus one can perceive the principal characteristics of the Valéryan dialogue. Several works offer a suggestive image: his poetry, the fragmentary *Cahiers*, the texts with attached commentaries displaying a renewed dialogue with the self (for example the annotation of the *Marginalia* of Poe (1927),[8] the 1930 edition of 'Variations sur une «Pensée»' or the 1931 edition of *Introduction à la Méthode de Léonard de Vinci* and *Note et digression*).[9] But to what extent do the Dialogues themselves conform in practice to the model which, though never explicitly elaborated as a theory, is imprinted implicitly in so much of the writing?

## DIALOGUES WITHOUT DIALOGUE?

Are Valéry's dialogues typically Valéryan dialogues? In order to address this question, we shall concentrate upon the major works, *Eupalinos*, *L'Ame et la danse*, *L'Idée fixe*, *'Mon Faust'* and the *Dialogue de l'arbre*.

The first three were commissioned works and, though this may initially seem incidental to their composition, it is particularly significant that from the outset they are conceived as fundamentally 'other': since the works originate not with Valéry but with a third party, they signal directly the writer's alienation, an alienation which is as much financial as poetic. The author is dispossessed of his work from its inception.

The choice of the dialogue form was dictated by practical considerations; as 'la plus souple des formes d'expression' ('the supplest of expressive forms') (*Œ*, I, p. 448) it facilitates the task of meeting the most detailed typographical requirements of the commission. Valéry liked to recall that for *Eupalinos* 'la commande déterminait le nombre de lettres que l'écrivain devait donner à composer: 115.800 *signes*' as well as 'l'ordonnance des pages' (*Œ*, II, p. 1401).[10] Elsewhere he describes the commission literally as an algebraic equation to be solved (*C2*, p. 1014), thereby once again enabling the author to hide behind externally imposed requirements.

The flexibility of the form which arises from the possibility of arranging the text as a series of responses has implications for the structure and meaning of the dialogue: 'Une réplique insignifiante, introduite ou supprimée, permet, par quelques tâtonnements, de remplir des conditions métriques fixées' (*Œ*, II, p. 1402).[11] Dialogue is above all a virtual form, the ultimate 'œuvre ouverte' ('open work')[12] in which nothing is predetermined or necessary. But while the gratuitousness of the constituent parts is entirely consistent with

Valéry's notion of the contingency of a work in relation to its author, it undermines any sense of the Dialogues as the product of a dialectical process. The structure and progression of the dialogue according to Platonic or Hegelian dialectics is based upon an inner logic which determines the place of each element, whereas there cannot be a Valéryan dialectic because, for him, the dialogue is not governed by any inner necessity, either in its whole or in its parts: everything – from the beginning, through the choice of form, to the submission of the manuscript – is determined by the commission and the resulting contingency of discourse.

Even the apparently platonic inspiration of the first two dialogues (*Eupalinos* and *L'Ame et la danse*) is less to do with the underlying logical framework than with a patronage that relieves the author of his responsibility. *L'Ame et la danse*, with its classical décor and the discussion over dinner of Socrate, Phèdre and Eryximaque, might well seem a follow-up to the *Symposium*. Valéry, however, was fond of reminding those only too readily convinced of its platonic style, that he knew very little of Plato and even theorised his own lack of knowledge: 'le peu que l'on sait, parfois est plus actif et fécond que le beaucoup' ('knowing a little can be more activating and fruitful than knowing a lot') (*C1*, p. 283).

At the same time, a quite original structure underpins and counterbalances the somewhat florid and even predictable dimensions of this aesthetic: 'Mon dialogue sur la danse est une danse dans laquelle tantôt le brillant des images, tantôt le profond des idées sont coryphées, pour s'achever en union' (*C1*, p. 268).[13] Valéry establishes a dynamic counterpoint between the discussions of the guests and the movements of the dancers, as, through their dialogue, the speakers seek to capture in words the essence of Athikté, the principal dancer, and to capture in thought the essential qualities of dance and movement.[14] In vain; for Athikté, etymologically, means 'the untouchable one', the saint, the unattainable holy woman. Their dialogue ends on a note of aporia, vanquished by the very object it was seeking to grasp. The momentous effect of the intermingling of mystical and physical Eros, awakened in Valéry by the encounter with Catherine Pozzi in 1920, is quite in evidence here, as it is also in the projected – and precisely contemporary – *Dialogue des choses divines*; the latter was intended to complete the trilogy of dialogues with an extended reflection upon the 'divine' objects and aspiration of the soul.[15] The inability to complete the work secretly mirrors the failure of spoken dialogue to capture the upward, transcending flight of Athikté in *L'Ame et la Danse*.

A similar subversive irony is at work in *Eupalinos ou l'Architecte*. The imaginary figure of *Eupalinos* is used as a pretext for a conversation between Socrate and Phèdre, in which questions about the relationship between thought and action and the definition of art are explored via the examples of music and architecture. Yet, in the end this skilfully constructed edifice with its pyramid-like hierarchy of themes[16] turns in upon itself and collapses in ruins: Socrate repudiates his own thoughts and paints the picture of an 'Anti-Socrate' as if he were himself a platonic myth (*Œ*, II, 139–47). The reference to Plato negates itself in the moment of its affirmation, thereby signalling that it should not be read too literally.

Some twenty years later further literary tributes are paid in *Dialogue de l'arbre*, a poetic meditation in blank verse: the Lucrèce of *De Rerum Natura* converses with a Tityre who is straight out of the *Bucoliques* which Valéry was translating at the time. This pastiche of Virgil, written in the middle of the Second World War, serves as a pretext for returning to the origins of Western culture and for writing in praise of a pacifying, mythical Nature and of the tree as an inexhaustible source of metaphors. More than in any of the preceding dialogues, thoughts, taking on feminine forms, proceed in lyrical, poetic bounds as the two characters of the philosopher and the shepherd seem two inextricable parts of the same writer. All three of these dialogues may thus be characterised as brilliant intellectual and artistic constructions in which the powerful stimulus of ideas is married to the pleasure of a refined language drawn from ancient sources.

The approach is, however, quite different with *L'Idée fixe*. Here, Valéry abandons the classical model for a more original, more baroque one. There is, in fact, no single 'fixed idea': the whole dialogue is built upon the Valéryan notion of the 'implex' – a pure virtuality which paradoxically itself becomes an 'idée fixe'. The conceptual challenge underpinning the dialogue is rooted in the attempt to replace a psychology of substance and hypostasis with one based on probability, just as the epistemological revolution which substituted quantum mechanics for Newtonian physics. The singular modernity of the dialogue lies in the successful match of thesis and form: the two characters – the narrator and a doctor he meets by chance – seem almost interchangeable, especially as a shift of speaker is indicated simply by a dash in the text. But above all, the sense of unreality which pervades them is reinforced by the way in which the eristic dialogue[17] proceeds through play of words and wit, sometimes quite trivial, as though language itself were functioning automatically. The flow in the association of ideas proves the existence of the implex, just as Diogenes demonstrated movement by walking. The style of writing, with its excessive use of exclamation marks and suspension points, may irk the reader, seem facile or appear to be stretching the point. Valéry excuses himself at the outset, presenting the book in a preface to the reader as an 'enfant de la hâte' ('a child of haste') (Œ, II, p. 195); but it is precisely the undisguised spontaneity, the pure working of unfettered and unembellished language displayed which makes this perhaps the most Valéryan of Valéry's dialogues.

While, in many respects, 'Mon Faust' is written in similar stylistic vein, the purpose is quite the opposite: rather than offering an outlet for the inexhaustible resources of the 'implex', 'Mon Faust' presents the search for 'la Dernière Pensée' ('the ultimate thought'), which will cancel out everything and bring existence to an end.[18] This seemingly mythical quest for the absolute, which echoes the mysticism of L'Ame et la danse and runs throughout the Cahiers, is most visible in the fictional writing, just as the pure potentiality of Monsieur Teste could only be portrayed as a figure of the imagination. But the dialogue form compensates for the negative qualities of fiction; drama, for Valéry, is not subject to the same criticisms as the novel, as dramatic speech may become a truly autonomous act rather than a mere imitation of reality.[19] In this sense, dialogue is thought transformed into action, an energised act of thinking.

The choice of the Faust figure as incarnation of the intellectual hero locates Valéry's dialogue in the context of Western literature, alongside Marlowe's version and Goethe's two versions. The attraction for Valéry is dual: as myth, Faust is a creation without author, like Narcissus; but it inscribes too a sense of reworking and renewal into the very concept of the character. It is not surprising that 'Mon Faust' is incomplete; for it is also without beginning. A work of pure virtuality, it is in this respect Valéry's most innovative, deliberately offered as 'work in progress' and evoking a plurality of other drafts, as the sub-title 'Ebauches' suggests.[20]

The desire to leave open the possible developments of the character is evident in the work itself. 'Mon Faust' is made up of two parts, the three Acts of 'Lust' and the two Acts of 'Le Solitaire', which complement each other, like the two theatrical archetypes Valéry identifies in 'Mes théâtres':[21] 'Lust' represents 'Le Guignol', 'Le Solitaire' represents 'Le Temple'; the former, vaudeville, the latter, symbolist theatre. In the first part, Faust is confronted by the enigma of amorous desire in the form of Lust, his secretary, and the Goethean figures of Mephistopheles and the Disciple are presented, largely in comic mode. In the second part, the role of Faust is reversed: instead of dominating Lust, he is dominated by 'Le Solitaire', his own double representing the pure, or 'zero' self.[22] And just as the dialogue between Faust and Lust seemed driven towards a culminating point of erotic fusion, especially in the unpublished fourth Act, so the encounter between Faust and 'Le Solitaire' evolves relentlessly towards an ultimate breaking point, ending with the collapse and disappearance of the characters: it dramatises the extreme case of a dialogue without communication between two irreconcilable forces: the person and the self.[23]

'*Mon Faust*' thus represents for Valéry an exploration in writing of the virtualities of the mind and a presentation of certain strategic themes of the *Cahiers*: this is effected through a systematic exploitation of all the resources of the stage, from the witty bourgeois comedy of the nineteenth century to the dramatic spectacle of magical enchantment inherited from *A Midsummer Night's Dream* and Wagnerian total theatre. The fact that the play is incomplete perhaps inevitably means that it cannot be totally satisfying: but certain projects, by definition, cannot be fully realised. It is not possible to embody the total negation of the pure self in concrete terms; thus, 'Le Solitaire' never quite seems the measure of the abstraction he is supposed to incarnate and, on the contrary, seems strangely marked with a hint of ridicule. Only the negating irony of the character undermines the mediating role of his portrayal and points to the reality behind. The Brechtian theory of alienation is clearly not far off.

Nevertheless, the relative failure of 'Le Solitaire' is symptomatic of the overall impression which Valéry's Dialogues give. For though, in theory, the author is absent from a dialogue, in practice his presence is constantly evoked by one of the characters: in *Eupalinos*, Socrates relates as his own a recollection of walking on the seashore that is in fact recounted in the *Cahiers*; the narrator of *L'Idée fixe* is a writer and offers his name as 'Edmond T.'; Faust is described as an official intellectual. The identification between character and author may be less precise in the detail of the texts and touches of irony may set the portrait at a distance from the real model; at the same time, certain secondary characters may also take on aspects of Valéry or his theories (e.g., Eupalinos himself, the doctor in *L'Idée fixe*, Lust even). Nevertheless, with the exception of *Dialogue de l'Arbre*, the characters are not equally weighted: one of them is always prominent and seems to be the favoured spokesman for Paul Valéry.

Two features in particular set Valéry's dialogues apart from others in the genre. Firstly, this strong presence of one of the characters who seems to bear a concentrated investment of attention; secondly, the sense in which each character has his or her own coherence and functions independently of all others. The different roles are not separated yet complementary fragments of a single Voice; rather, they are an almost arbitrary grouping of distinct, autonomous voices. Whatever Valéry might say in theory, 'le Solitaire' can never be perceived as Faust's double, and it is this gap between theory and practice, between the Valéryan dialogue and the Dialogues of Valéry that must be now addressed.

## THE REPUBLIC OF THE MIND

'Le dialogue est la forme la mieux adaptée aux perplexités d'une conscience mouvante':[24] this statement, referring perhaps surprisingly not to Valéry but to *Le Rêve d'Alembert*, alerts us to the wider context and function of the genre, and to the position of Valéry's Dialogues in relation to the literary and social climate of the period.

The dialogue became a fashionable mode of writing during the 1920s and 30s, utilised, among others, by Alain and by Claudel.[25] But it had had an even more major impact at the time of the transition from the Second Empire to the Third Republic with the *Dialogue aux Enfers entre Machiavel et Montesquieu ou la politique de Machiavel au XIXe siècle* (1864) by Maurice Joly and the *Dialogues et Fragments philosophiques* (1876) by Renan, the former denouncing the absolutism of Napoleon III, the latter dramatising a positivist set of principles.[26] The revival of the dialogue as literary genre reflects then the aspirations for a more democratic and modernised society: it draws upon two principal models – the picture of an ideal, democratic Athens that emerges from Socrates and Plato, and the

Enlightenment *philosophes*, who often used dialogue as a weapon against the rigid social structure of the *ancien régime*.

Valéry's dialogues are part of this historic continuum. He elects this form, which closely matches the functioning of his mind, at the same time as he is accorded the status of official writer of the Republic. Dialogue is the parliamentary genre *par excellence*, and represents the literature of the Third Republic both from a formal and a thematic point of view (we may recall the doctor of *L'Idée fixe* recounting an election campaign in a Parisian constituency (*Œ*, II, p. 249)). Perhaps much of the contemporary success of the Dialogues is due to the way that they were so fully in accord with public aspirations – the desire for a return to normal democratic life and freedom of expression after the harrowing years of war.

At the same time the Dialogues may be sited within a wider socio-economic dialogue of commission and provision, of contractual engagement and of financial necessity. The Dialogues had an exchange-value, both for the professional architects and doctors who commissioned *Eupalinos* and *L'Idée fixe* as well as for Valéry who, after the death of Edouard Lebey in 1922, found himself having to write for a living. From a Marxist and sociological point of view, they might be looked on as an alliance between the official intellectual and the corporate bodies which constitute the Republic. But they cannot be reduced to this dimension, for not only did Valéry participate freely, if sometimes reluctantly, in this exchange, the form moreover corresponds closely to the inner mechanism of his mind: republican democracy finds itself in resonance with his inner 'democracy' of the mind. However, although this democracy of mind may appear to be in temporary harmony with the republican climate of the 1920s and 30s, it will be surpassed in *Mon Faust* by a mental autocracy that radically questions all comfortable assumptions.

For we should not suggest that Valéry is simply a spokesman, willing or otherwise, for the political system. The Dialogues are much more ambivalent on this point. In the first place, they cannot be identified with the rationalist idealism that so frequently characterises the Third Republic (however unfairly, as in the case of Bergson); rather, they tend to affirm the importance of a certain mysticism of the mind. Secondly, it is evident that other contemporary writers, including Alain and Claudel, are much more prolific users of the genre. The *Entretiens au bord de la mer*, which uses the same décor as *L'Idée fixe*, or the *Conversations dans le Loir-et-Cher*, demonstrate a much more balanced, polyphonic, and indeed 'democratic' kind of dialogue: each character assumes one facet of the author, without becoming pre-eminent for any significant period of time, as in Valéry.

Perhaps the truly Valéryan quality of Valéry's Dialogues lies precisely in the unresolved tension between a plurality of voices and the pre-eminence of a single one. For this is the contradiction that lies at the core of his reflections on the mind: the mind is at once potential and action, implex and method, open-ended possibility and disciplined implementation. However much he may wish to reconcile these conflicting tendencies by fully exploiting the constantly seductive possibilities of the method while maintaining the pure potential of the implex, their opposition remains fundamental. From this perspective, Teste is the opposite of Léonard. These same tensions and dynamics of the mind may also be projected to the level of the State, as the ironic formula '*L'Etat, ce Moi*' ('*the State, this Self*') (*Œ*, II, p. 760) indicates; and when, in the early 1930s, Valéry defines the mind as both cause and remedy of the evil afflicting Europe, a similar discord is revealed.[27] The links between the theory of the mind, an art of thinking and the machine of politics had been explored by Valéry since the early essay *Une Conquête méthodique*. But where the early essay tentatively examines the implications of an over-rigorous application of the method – at the risk of controlling and suppressing all the forces of disorder and pure potential which can alone assure renewal of the system[28] – the situation in Europe in the 1930s and 40s is such that the tensions between implex and method are differently orientated for Valéry: the forces of disorder must be brought under control.

'*Mon Faust*' elaborates the response of the mind to the issues raised by its own dynamic system: the search for the supreme thought which will encompass, but as a result also cancel out all thought. '*Mon Faust*' seeks to close off those potentially disruptive forces of the implex which were celebrated in *L'Idée fixe*. Faust, the 'Prince des Idées' ('Prince of Ideas') (*Œ*, II, p. 285), embodies the triumph of the autocratic mind over the democratic – or the demagogic – mind: no longer is Faust the intellectual corporate mediator, product of a self-satisfied and chattering Third Republic; instead, he is the intellectual who rises above all parties, who visibly dominates the dialogue, indeed *all* dialogue. This, then, is Valéry's 'pouvoir de l'esprit', the powerful mind which is the sole legitimate and effective force that the Republic can set against the fascist threat. Published in 1941 when the Government of Collaboration was still getting underway, Valéry's *'Mon Faust'* is a powerful yet ambiguous political proposal.

Thus it may be seen that Valéry's Dialogues reflect the dynamic tensions within the mind, oscillating perpetually between a determined affirmation of inner democracy and the avowed fascination with mental autocracy. They reveal too the different historical patterns of equilibrium and disequilibrium affecting the world in which he lived. And we should not be surprised by this mediating role, for a literary genre which is based on the encounter with the Other will by definition explore the relationship between the inner and outer worlds of the writer and be especially concerned with the frontier between the two domains: this is the space occupied by the Dialogues, a space in which Valéry's writing traces the encounter with these inner and outer voices, creating from the form a strange object that is both mental structure and political ideal.[29]

## NOTES

1 Michael Issacharoff refers to this function as the 'archi-énonciateur' (*Le Spectacle du discours* (Paris, Corti, 1985), p. 9).

2 See Michel Jarrety, *Valéry devant la littérature: Mesure de la limite* (Paris, Presses universitaires de France, 1991), pp. 155–200.

3 'the *operation which transforms* data by means of exchanges (DR) (demand-response)'. Cf. Alexandre Lazaridès, *Valéry: Pour une poétique du dialogue* (Presses de l'Université de Montréal, 1978), pp. 11–14.

4 'This strange, essential property of being *two-in-one* — in contrast to amorous desire — to be *one* through *two* — appears complementary to conscious knowledge ... Every monologue is a dialogue'.

5 'How I should wish to write — or rather to have written! — a dialogue which would be called *Proteus* — and each interlocutor would have his voice, his *style* — and his mental voice. Many modes of seeing. The alternation would make the dialogue.

  Haven't I seen in several ways and might I not have met myself? — And hasn't that happened, doesn't it happen?

  Haven't I lived as more than one person?'

6 See Jarrety, *Valéry*, pp. 127–31.

7 'Where go you? To death. / Why so? To end, / Come back no more, / To rascally fate. / Where go you? To end. / What for? To be dead.'

8 *Quelques fragments des Marginalia*, tr. and notes Paul Valéry, *Commerce*, 14 (Winter 1927), pp. 11–41. Brief extracts are given in *Œ*, I, p. 1801.

9 Lazaridès, *Valéry*, pp. 113–22.

10 'the commission determined the number of letters that the writer had to supply to the compositor: 115,800 signs ... the ordering of the pages'

11 'An insignificant line, introduced or cut out, allows you, with some trial and error, to fulfil fixed metric conditions'

12 Lazaridès, *Valéry*, pp. 101–2.

13 'My dialogue on dance is a dance, in which now the brilliance of the images, now the depth of the ideas are leading dancers, before ending in union'.

14 Cf. the discussion of the text as staging and choreography: 'une représentation à la fois sensible et intellectuelle du regard de l'esprit, manifestation dans l'espace théâtral de l'espace intérieur du moi, de tous ses mouvements et échanges, la danse des parfaites pensées' in Brian Stimpson, 'L'Espace théâtral dans *L'Ame et la danse* de Paul Valéry' in S. Bourjea (ed.) *Mélange c'est L'Esprit* (Paris, Minard, 1989).

15 Paul Gifford, 'Le dialogue *Des choses divines:* une genèse résorbée', in *Paul Valéry* (Paris, Champion, 1991), pp. 29–41.

16 Lazaridès, *Valéry*, pp. 180–184.

17 *Ibid.*, p. 48; Suzanne Guellouz, *Le Dialogue* (Paris, Presses universitaires de France, 1992), pp. 90–1.

18 Ned Bastet, 'Apocalypte Teste', *Micromégas*, 27–8 (1983), p. 90.

19 Jarrety, *Valéry*, p. 295.

20 Bastet, '*Mon Faust* de Valéry comme "work in progress"', *Littératures*, 20 (1989), pp. 89–105.

21 The manuscripts of Act 4 of 'Lust' and the Act 3 of 'Le Solitaire', partially published in 'Mes théâtres', *Cahiers Paul Valéry 2* (Paris: Gallimard, 1977), pp. 51–88, are held at the Bibliothèque nationale de France.

22 Nicole Celeyrette-Pietri, 'Deux font un', *Cahiers Paul Valéry 2*, pp. 148–52.

23 Jarrety, 'Faust écrit', *Europe*, 813–14 (1997), p. 123.

24 Jean Terrasse, *Rhétorique de l'essai littéraire* (Presses de l'Université du Québec, 1977), p. 51; 'the dialogue is the form best adapted to the perplexities of a moving mind'.

25 Cf. *La Visite au musicien* (1927), *Entretiens au bord de la mer* (1931) and *Entretiens chez le sculpteur* (1937) by Alain and *Conversations dans le Loir-et-Cher* (1925–28), *Le Poète et le shamisen* (1926), *Le Poète et le vase d'encens* (1926), *Jules, ou l'homme aux deux cravates* (1926), *Richard Wagner: Rêverie d'un poète français* (1927) and *Ægri Somnia* (1937) by Claudel.

26 Marieluise Blessing, *Der philosophische Dialog als literarische Kunstform von Renan bis Valéry* (Tübingen, Präzis, 1965); Guellouz, *Le Dialogue*, pp. 241–3.

27 Jarrety, 'Réflexions sur une politique de l'esprit', *Secolul*, 20 (1995), pp. 7–12.

28 R. Pickering, *Genèse du concept valéryen – 'pouvoir' et 'conquête méthodique' de*

*l'écriture* Paris (Lettres Modernes, Archives des Lettres Modernes 243, 'Archives Paul Valéry', no 8, 1990).

29 For further reading on this topic, please see Bibliography, items 1, 6, 7, 11, 13, 18, 31, 32, 41, 72, 82, 110.

CHAPTER 10

# Major poems: the voice of the subject

Jean-Michel Maulpoix

In relation to his nineteenth-century predecessors, Valéry inaugu-
rates a newly critical relationship to poetry, its illusions, its glamorous
pretensions, its powers of magic spell-binding or *'charmes'*. His
violent inner crisis of 1891–2 led him, abidingly, to relativise 'la
chose littéraire'. He stood aside at that point from the prevailing
symbolist mysticism,[1] opting resolutely instead for the Intellect. He
ceased to treat Art as an absolute and undertook to limit the status of
writing to that of one mind-generated activity among others.

This withdrawal, this renunciation or this denial, was, however,
such as to lend itself to over-simple and stereotyping interpretations,
which have, for half a century and more, distorted the appreciation
of his poetry. Referred predominantly to this intellectualist stance,
Valéry's poems have often been read simply as exercises of style
excluding any inner authenticity or expressive virtue. Yet Intellect is
no more to be considered the defining element in Valéry's practice of
poetry than it is to be viewed as a secondary contributor. If, as poet,
he indeed subjects the creative process to a wide-awake critical
scrutiny of high technicity, maximising its action and effect, such
scrutiny functions in the service of a complex process of composition
which aims essentially at what Valéry terms 'l'obtention de la voix'
('obtaining the voice') (*C2*, p. 1077): an aim which, in his view, defines
the characteristic quality of 'pure' poetry (a poetry, that is, purged of
non-poetry, raised to the power of its own poetic essence) and which
he sees as compatible with, indeed complementary to, the enunciation of a subject voice. This important modern perspective, generated by the availability of manuscripts and the insights of the *Cahiers*,
offers new opportunities for re-examining some of Valéry's major
poetic texts.[2]

Genetically speaking, the first poet in Valéry is not a major poet.
Written for the most part between 1889 and 1891, before the crisis of

170

the mind dramatised as the 'nuit de Gênes' of 4–5 October, 1892, the poems revised and brought together in the *Album des vers anciens* of 1920 display their original symbolist inspiration. They are mostly precious tableaux, legendary or mythological in theme, which seek effects of diaphanous enchantement looking back to a Mallarméan *sorcellerie évocatoire*. A young girl bathing, a young girl spinning, or sleeping, or dancing: the poetic *personæ* we encounter in these pages are highly feminised incarnations of the poet's own rêverie. As the sub-title of 'Profusion du soir' (*Œ*, I, p. 86) suggests,[3] a mood of surrender, and a danger of *fin-de-siècle* enervation, preside over this languid verse. Here is an aestheticism captive to its play of mirrors, in which neither forms nor affective substance manage any real incarnation. It is, for all the reworking of former material, a post-Mallarméan poetic manner at odds with the conditions and possibilities of genuine creativity; a manner lacking an original voice.[4]

Valéry needs to experience the awakening bite of conscious intellect and to quit the realm of ambient poetic discourse by developing his own critique of it. In time, at the end of a twenty-year detour of pure thought, he is led to re-discover his own dynamic *raison d'être* as poet. *La Jeune Parque* emerges from and reflects upon just such a drama of identity transformed; a drama centrally involving the notion of poetic voice.

Reworking his adolescent verse at the request of André Gide and the publisher Gallimard, Valéry found himself confronted with a buried and separated part of himself mediated through the voice that spoke to him out of his own manuscripts, disturbingly, across the interval of his twenty-year silence. 'Miroir formé par cette voix' ('Mirror formed by this voice') (*JP* ms III, fo. 30), we read in the earliest manuscript stammerings in 1913 of his most famous poem. The voice, his own and yet strangely other, reflects back at its author the unsuspected enigma of the writing self: of its troubled depths, of its secret continuity through time, of its conflictual vocation as a being of desire refusing the world in which it exists – in short, a prescient divination of the 'mystérieuse Moi' who will speak in the great poem of 1917.

What we may call the proto-drama of the Young Fate is already attributed to a mysteriously feminine persona, speaking subject of a monologue of voice. This drama demands adequate poetic enunciation: 'Et je ne trouvais pas une autre voix pour me répondre' ('And found no other voice to answer me') (fo. 33). The five-year labour of composition expended on Valéry's most central work has no other goal than to 'obtain', in enacted fullness, just such an answering voice. *La Jeune Parque* emerged from this remarkable acoustic self-confrontation of 1913, thanks to an epic labour of poetic writing, deciphering the 'figure voilée' of the protagonist's drama, discerning its shape and import, organising it compositionally in the very effort of articulating the voice and following its successive shifts of tone.

'J'ai essayé de mon mieux, et au prix d'un travail incroyable, d'exprimer cette modulation d'une vie' (*Œ*, I, p. 1622),[5] says the poet, significantly invoking the musical term[6] that best captures the perceptible key-shifts by which is articulated the obscure, inner continuity of a human existence *modulating* in time; he will speak, in the same sense, of a labour pursued 'sur la *corde* de la *voix*' ('on the *cord* of the *voice*') (*C*, XXII, pp. 435–6).

Rather than looking to any imitative return to his symbolist origins, or espousing the iconoclastic but superficial dislocations of 'l'esprit nouveau', Valéry's singular posture is that of the pure poet; for him, the transparency of a language at once gratuitous and essential favours the exercise of a reflexively faithful enunciation. Having made himself the assiduous observer of mental phenomena, Valéry concentrates his attention on the combinatory-expressive possibilities of language and on the art of 'making', understood in a sense at once enunciatory and compositional, musical and philosophic.

Such a posture does not betray the rigorous demands of the thinker; it relays and develops in the mode of poetic self-utterance the morning labour of the *Cahiers*. Indeed, the poetic voice is in many ways the subject-voice *of* the *Cahiers*: the voice implied and even, fragmentarily and fleetingly, assumed within M. Teste's laboratory; a voice not absent, but sacrificed, strictly contained, to the point of abnegation or of denegation, within the circuits of self-intimacy and objectifying self-attention. Poetry, on this account, tends to constitute a testing of the mind's powers (*Œ*, I, p. 1504); yet in this very role, it shows itself finally the only language capable of expressing 'ce qui est inexprimable en fonctions finies de mots' ('what is inexpressible in finite functions of words') (*Œ*, I, p. 1450). Poetic activity takes over from the labour of intellect precisely at the point where the latter declares its inadequacy before the unsayable. In so doing, it enables the writing subject to accede to the idea of a unity or fruitful form, 'composing' its own inner diversity.

Harnessing technical intelligence to self-listening sensibility, without sacrifice of either, Valéry can thus develop a work rich in rhetorical and symbolic 'figures', which sensuality enfolds and unfolds. No neo-classical marble here; rather, a concerted and subtle poetry displaying the perpetual reflexivity of a hall of mirrors. The mind, finely scrutinised, is staged at once lyrically and critically; while, on the horizon of its poetic representation, appears an ethics and a poetics of patience.

*La Jeune Parque* sets to a music of voice a crisis of the mind. It is a complex, polyphonic work of introspection, enunciating the different moments which animate the life of our consciousness: it is, in Hartmut Köhler's words 'une description de l'essence de la fonction de la conscience dans ses phases caractéristiques'.[7] Yet these phases are now explored on the home ground of poetry, according to the rules of poetry; they may even be said to present or stage dramatically the return of the mind to poetry.

What is at stake in the poem is nothing less than a new form of expression. Composed as 'un petit tombeau sans date – sur les bords menaçants de l'Océan du Charabia' (*Œ*, I, p. 1630),[8] while the guns of the Great War were still thundering, set over against the scorched, abstract desert of M. Teste's making, this poem is the locus of an inner debate re-apprehending the 'self'. As poet, Valéry appeals once more to the all-too-human subjectivity upon which he had cast his anathemas of 1892; he dramatises it, handles it roughly and makes it speak somewhat beneath and beyond itself, at the point where it questions itself, anxiously seeking identity in a conscious doubling back upon its own traces. Lyricism, normally understood as an 'uttering of central emotion', is here replaced by a lyricism of quest, an enunciating subjectivity, challenging, seeking in disarray and giving distraught expression to a sense of lost selfhood:

> Qui pleure là, sinon le vent simple, à cette heure
> Seule, avec diamants extrêmes? . . . Mais qui pleure,
> Si proche de moi-même au moment de pleurer?     (*JP*, ll. 1–3)[9]

The poem opens with this twice repeated question, enacting the startled awakening, in radical uncertainty, of a feminine protagonist seeking to reconstruct her own situation and being in the world. An enunciative modality is established: the question *who weeps?* situates the subject in the interval between immediate feeling and self-recognition. What is expressed is not yet any defining sense of identity, but rather doubt and anxiety at being without such a sense. It is a *who weeps in me when I weep?*; hence, in indirect form, a *who am I?* Self-cognisance passes necessarily through just such an inner scission: it means ceasing to be joined unreflectingly to oneself; it involves a break with what is closest, what is inwardly 'si proche', and is, in fact, oneself.

Valéry writes in his *Cahiers*: 'dès que le cerveau est le moindrement éveillé, il est le siège d'une variation, d'un changement psychique incessant : *il est habité par l'instabilité même.* Il est livré à une sorte de désordre qui ne lui est pas généralement sensible, il ne perçoit que les éléments de ce désordre, qui est le changement en soi, sans repères' (*C*, 1, p. 963).[10] It is this disorder of awakening that is presented, with dramatic immediacy and mythic universality, in the prelude of *La Jeune Parque*. In an obscurity favoured by the withdrawal of all human presence and by the uncertainty of any intrinsic sense of identity, a being rises up and asks questions of her existence under an awesome night sky, which gives cosmic extension to her own inner mystery, and alongside bitter, turbulent seas that speak indistinctly for her own inner grief and tumult. When the world is disengaged from explanatory prose, the simple fact of being alive is restored to its primary status as formidable enigma . . .

The monologue is dramatically modelled on the Racinian *huis-clo*s, albeit confined to a single, insular, consciousness. Yet it does admit into the poem the sentient, embodied presence of the protagonist and the natural décor in which she exists. The speaking subject is projected as 'Corps-Esprit-Monde', mirroring an interiority which includes the external world. The monologue is semantically dense, just as our own consciousness is, since it is saturated with the mutiplicity of states which it registers in addition to direct perceptions of the natural world – physiological, sensual, affective, intellectual. Incorporating also the non-actual dimensions of consciousness – memory and anticipation – it will seek to formulate the entire relation of the self to the possible and the impossible, so that the voice articulating consciousness transports with it the articulated totality of an individual experience.

Throughout the poem there is an inner modulation. The poetic voice maps out vocally, in the perceptible terms of tonal register, a complex process of psychological change registered in an experiencing present time. The Young Fate changes perpetually, moving through a complete cycle of inner states: from the awakening disarray in the prelude, temporally marked by the last stars ('diamants extrêmes' (l. 2)), to the near-terminal anguish of her temptation to suicide in the 'nuit noire' (l. 303) immediately preceding dawn, at the end of the first 'Act'; and again, inversely, from the rising curtain of dawn (l. 325) at the beginning of the second 'Act' to the crescendo of light and life in the joyous finale anticipating midday.

Yet her inner modulation traversing this cycle is anything but a linear progress. In her lived present, the past and future intervene, giving a sinuous movement to the succession of inner states vocalised. Thus in the heart of the nocturnal first 'Act', globally devoted to the crescendo of her disarray, a sunlit hymn of joyous assurance bursts forth, recalling the distant time of original harmony-in-Being and her 'noces' with the world (episode V). Symmetrically, in the luminous second 'Act', the inverse crescendo of existential assurance is punctuated, antithetically, by a vibrant rememoration of her immediately previous 'noces' with the Absolute, reliving the mystic temptation of the soul's 'dark Night' (episodes XIII and XIV). Thus is established a sinuous play of minor and major tonalities, structurally patterned as a series of antithetical symmetries: Min. (*MAJ.*) Min. : Maj. (*MIN.*) Maj.[11] The total figure, representing the dual polarisation of the protagonist, displays the secret architecture of the 'mystérieuse Moi' herself.

The monologue of voice itself appears as the golden thread of a desire for self-understanding. Visibly, it allows the Young Fate of the finished poem to decipher the drama of her dark night of the mind, and, accepting her own inner mystery as irreducible, to find her way back nevertheless from the precipice of despair and suicide to the world of sunlight, incarnate being and existential affirmation:

> Cherche, du moins, dis-toi, par quelle sourde suite
> La nuit, d'entre les morts, au jour t'a reconduite?
> Souviens-toi de toi-même, et retire à l'instinct
> Ce fil (ton doigt doré le dispute au matin),
>
> Ce fil, dont la finesse aveuglément suivie
> Jusque sur cette rive a ramené ta vie ...      (*JP*, ll. 413–18)[12]

The break in the text – all Valéry's textual punctuations are significant – marks precisely one of the poem's many 'moments of modulation'. The Parque here undergoes a key-shift: from her ardently nostalgic rememoration of an ultimate awakening of pure mind, striving towards disincarnation and a mystic fusion with the

Absolute, she moves to the tender evocation of her own sleeping form, of her consent to bodily weakness, and of her descent into sleep. This evocation (made in reverse order of lived time) corresponds to episode XV, the penultimate in the sequence of sixteen 'episodes' making up the poem.[13] The new tonality is a lyric air 'left to the voice'. Compositionally, it balances the hymn to springtime (ll. 222–42) in the first 'Act' of the poem, since it marks a yielding to that same temptation to live which the earlier passage had evoked only by way of exorcism and rejection.

By sustaining just such a highly-calculated play of balanced symmetries within the modulating song of the Young Fate, the poem as a whole comes to represent a dialectics of selfhood; it displays a quest for identity oscillating between the attractive polarities of pure mind and sensuous embodiment, torn between the vocations of Essence (symbolically associated with the dark Night) and of Existence (placed under the sign of Light). Architecturally, the poem exhibits the speaking subject as a dialogue of contrary tensions, each of which is secretly present in the heart of the inverse postulation.

We perhaps glimpse here that Valéry's mature practice of poetic voice is a revealer of the deeper psyche. The contralto register he designates belongs to a veiled, 'feminine' sensibility – the poem indeed speaks of a 'secrète soeur' (l. 48); it is the essential mediator between a poetry of precision-engineered, linguistic effect and the inner authenticity perennially associated with lyricism. Certainly, there emerges in this poem a whole pathology of voice, a minor-mode exploration of the sigh, the shiver, of tears, of the wound, of burning desire: all bodily manifestations linking the articulated to something underlying and inarticulate, associating thought with the body. Setting out in quest of the self, following the sinuous modulation of the voice, the mysterious self does not accede to any knowledge lifting the fundamental enigma; it reaches no pure term of gnosis or essentialist self-seizure. Yet it does travel a certain way in the recognition of its own depth and serpentine complexity. Relative self-cognisance is to be had in following the vocal thread, in articulating its pattern and the total figure of its modulation. We might say that it is to be had within the labour of writing.

For the poet, self-comprehension is, indeed, inseparable from self-writing. To seek to comprehend oneself, is to seek to enunciate one's own voice. As this leading thread is followed throughout the poem, the questing voice passes – not without sinuous returns to the minor key – from anxiety to a more major tonality, acquiring a fullness and, indeed a splendour of assured invocation, as though the self-articulating voice could confer upon itself an authority and a substance at first lacking.

True, the lost paradise of the 'Harmonieuse MOI', evoked in a memorable hymn of love (episode V), is indeed lost; yet it is multiply refracted in the series of luminous memory-flashes that haunt the first 'Act', leading logically, in the very moment of the most violent despair, to the anticipated evocation of springtime:

> Demain, sur un soupir des Bontés constellées,
> Le printemps vient briser les fontaines scellées:
> L'étonnant printemps rit, viole ... On ne sait d'où
> Venu? Mais la candeur ruisselle à mots si doux
> Qu'une tendresse prend la terre à ses entrailles ...     (ll. 225–29)[14]

And, as we have suggested, these refractions of the major tonality already prefigure the crescendo of Light in the second 'Act', a crescendo rising towards a finale of exultation which exorcises the regrets of the ascetic Night in a splendour of surging waves and the appetitive bite of refreshing sea-spray.

In reading the poem by which Valéry returns to poetry, we thus witness, in the strictest sense, a renaissance of the voice: a voice born in a plaintive moan and rising towards assured song. It is, in this sense, the renaissance of poetry itself which we are given to hear; and this voice is not distinct from the unfolding in time of the subject-identity of the Young Fate. Valéry's 'jeune pensive' – one of the many projected titles of the poem – is the doubly representative figure of thought captivated by poetry, and of poetry capturing thought: not to transport ideas, nor to ensure any transitive function, but to endow consciousness of the centrally mysterious human subject with a pure, non-anecdotal voice of essential resonance.

'*Charmes* naquit ou naquirent de la *Parque*' (*LQ*, p. 184). Whereas the latter poem welcomed diversity within the unity of a single speaking consciousness, the immediately succeeding collection of 1922 expresses the unity of the life of the mind by a range of vocalisations which embody its aspects and moments diversely. Singular or plural, the new collection retraces in song the inner modulation of the mysterious self, with its play of light and shadow, major and minor tonalities, reflecting in the second degree on the voice of poetry, embodied and delectable sign of the potential of human creativity as such.

It is of course not inaccurate to speak here of Valéry's 'classicism': this volume is classic in its elegant sobriety of writing, its alliance of distinction and subtlety. It presents an architecturally developed set of rationally measured poetic forms, explicitly referred to Apollonian Greece. It brings to fruition the reign of the golden number, harmony, technical virtuosity: a whole manner of valorising the French language and of exploiting the resources of traditional prosody. It exemplifies and exalts an integration of antagonistic natural forces within the second-order reality of consciously elaborated form.

Yet the word 'neo-classic' often used of this collection ignores what we are now able to see as most characteristic of it: namely, a lyricism attached as much to the authentic places of personal subjectivity as it is to purity of formal expression. *Charmes* too is composed on the acoustic thread of a subject-voice: a voice reaching down into the uncharted recesses of existential / ontological sensibility, and raising up from those depths, in a transparent language, a 'transcendent' idea or ideal of the self which the act of poetic creation exemplifies.

'Aurore' gives the keynote. The poet dialogues with ideas, with the world, with himself, in a newly joyous freedom. Self-interlocution is an opportunity for the creative mind to discover and greet the alterity within. 'Les prémisses de sa voix' stir the webs of naive or mythic ideation woven by the – again, feminine – spinners of forms ('maîtresses de l'âme, Idées') who inhabit the preconscious psyche. Deeper still lie the 'oracles de mon chant' situated at the sources of perceptual or sensorial sensibility. Here the subject is pure receptivity to the impinging world, the whole of being, and Being itself:

> Etre! Universelle oreille!
> Toute l'âme s'appareille
> A l'extrême du désir...
> Elle s'écoute qui tremble
> Et parfois ma lèvre semble
> Son frémissement saisir. (ll. 55–60)[15]

Close by are the concrete images held by the unconscious, compared to a rustling of leaves or a tinkling wellspring, a source to be apprehended acoustically, in a thirst of desire:

> Toute feuille me présente
> Une source complaisante
> Où je bois ce frêle bruit ... (ll. 65–7)[16]

Throughout the whole of *Charmes* poetic utterance is thus referred to an intimate self-hearing. To sing with the spellbinding song of poetry is first to listen inwardly, within the circuit of reflexive apperception and auto-enunciation that Valéry terms 'Bouche-oreille'. The resonant interiority of the sentient self – the lyric subject which (or perhaps whom) Valéry, at least in his poetic texts, never ceases to call 'l'âme' – listens to itself throughout *Charmes*. From witty banter to fervent prayer, and from trembling impatience to serene and patient assurance, it speaks in all the modulating tonalities and key shifts which *La Jeune Parque* has taught us to recognise. At the heart of the poetics which the collection illustrates *in actu* is thus enshrined the new, acoustic modality of Valéry's perpetual reflexivity (the same form Narcissus exemplifies in the mode of visual contemplation).

Among the major poems of *Charmes*, 'La Pythie' gives perhaps most fully the measure of the lyric voice in which poetry originates. The depths of the creative psyche are archaic and savage; they are intimately linked to the primitive sense of the sacred. The prophetess of Apollo, possessed by the invasive 'dieu dans la chair égaré', and struggling with this 'inspiration', as with some monstrous rape occurring in the deep caverns of herself, is an exact and powerful mythic representation of these beginnings:

> La Pythie exhalant la flamme
> De naseaux durcis par l'encens,
> Haletante, ivre, hurle! ... l'âme
> Affreuse, et les flancs mugissants! (*P*, ll. 1–4)[17]

At the birth of language, prior to any articulate speech, there is violence, violation. The primitive psyche, illuminated and alienated by the inner god, gasps in spasmodic pulses of Dionysian terror:

> Qui me parle, à ma place même?
> Quel écho me répond: Tu mens!
> Qui m'illumine? ... Qui blasphème?
> Et qui, de ces mots écumants,
> Dont les éclats hachent ma langue,
> La fait brandir une harangue
> Brisant la bave et les cheveux
> Que mâche et trame le désordre

> D'une bouche qui veut se mordre
> Et se reprendre ses aveux?                    $(P, \text{ll. } 41-50)^{18}$

We recall the Young Fate, gasping and chilled with horror, amid violently surging seas, uncertain, in its first emergence, of the identity signified by her own voice; she too spoke of an initiatic possession which had awakened her. Here, as there, the speaking voice changes by a process of modulation in time ('toute lyre / Contient la modulation'). Thus we will hear successively: the phonetic and rhythmic jaggedness of her awakening in horror (st. 1–7), tender nostalgia for the springtime of pre-sexual and pre-conscious innocence (st. 8–10); ringing metaphysical revolt (st. 11–18); exultant, orgasmic release as the upsurging waters of metaphysical fear and grief, are felt, in their very articulation, to replace knotted dread with self-understanding and to offer the promise of fabulous creativity (st. 19–21); pure, classical serenity in a final oracular deliverance, which is also a delivery from prophecy (st. 22–3).

As P. Gifford has suggested:

> Valéry is here meditating on his own experience of the liberating voice of poetry: on his discovery within himself of a psychic underworld of violence and primitive horror which resounds inwardly like a vociferation or suicidal scream; on the way in which that original cry from the depths modulates as it becomes taken up by the conscious intelligence in language; on how the shaping act of articulate poetic discourse reacts upon the uttering 'I' of the poet, transforming both voice and self; so that the poetic song emerging from the travail of creation is indeed a form of oracular wisdom, capable of declaring to the poet and to all men higher possibilities of metamorphosis.[19]

The oracle indeed celebrates the advent of 'une voix nouvelle et blanche', by which the inarticulate is articulated, the shapeless given form, and impure, confessional emotion transmuted into mythic universality. The 'pure' voice is, as we have seen, secretly continuous with the animal vociferation of the Pythia's pre-articulate beginnings; yet it is also antipodally different from them. What is celebrated is the 'Discours prophétique et paré' (P, ll. 222) itself: the lyric utterance of the poem, in so far as it *integrates and yet transcends* the primitive and 'inspired' prophetism of its own origins:

> Voici parler une Sagesse
> Et sonner cette auguste Voix
> Qui se connaît quand elle sonne
> N'être plus la voix de personne
> Tant que des ondes et des bois!           $(\text{ll. } 226-30)^{20}$

The oracle, in short, salutes the human metamorphosis which, in measured and musicalised modulation, has been represented to us in this poem; it is to this transforming action of form that our attention is drawn.

The celebration of 'Saint LANGAGE' valorises this 'language within a language' (as Valéry elsewhere calls poetic song) as the sacred locus of man's relation to a 'divine' Wisdom as the Greeks might have conceived it. It is the place where the potent god encountered in the flesh is sublimated (in a near-Freudian sense), by a process of elevation and de-realisation. This is very different from the Romantic sublime, which directly exalts what exceeds human measure: the frightening, the grotesque, the daemonic. The sublime is here properly human, the measure of man. Like Freud, Valéry envisages a modification of aim, or a substitution of object, which are characteristic of feeling-drives that cannot succeed in meeting the psychic needs from which they arise. The Valéryan thematics of delay, patience, suspended fulfilment, is linked to a poetics of sublimated desire.

The second Word of poetry thus eliminates the spontaneous and given, just as it filters out the immediate past (of war and crisis); it links up with an ancient melody remembered and enacts a reconquest of beauty. Poetic de-realisation, whereby memory retains only the beautiful trace of experienced reality, inscribes the ephemeral into the eternal, delivers it from contingency, and musicalises appearances. The labour of obtained voice thus idealises as it de-realises: it creates a 'ravissement sans référence'.

The higher lyricism, composed on the thread of voice, attests the passage from individuality to an ideal and representative subjectivity: this formula still holds good of the best-known and perhaps the greatest of the poems of *Charmes*. 'Le Cimetière marin' is distinctive perhaps only in its almost algebraic power of recapitulation: the vibrantly meditative voice of this poem is closest to the intellectual sensibility of the poet himself; it reflects within and upon an archetypal Valéryan setting of sunlit Mediterranean sea-and-landscape that both measures the protagonist's human situation in the world and is measured by it; it modulates through an affective and tonal spectrum that is an epitome of Valéry's range, from ardent aspiration towards a pure spirituality of Light, through bitter-sweet elegy on finitude and mortality, to a courageous and revivifying affirmation of the human condition, chasing away the philosophic impasses discovered by an over-consequent uttering and writing of the self:

> Le vent se lève! . . . Il faut tenter de vivre!
> L'air immense ouvre et referme mon livre,
> La vague en poudre ose jaillir des rocs!
> Envolez-vous, pages tout éblouies!          (*CM*, ll. 139–42)[21]

Above all, this poem arises in self-hearing from the central void Valéry knows so well and here designates so memorably:

> O pour moi seul, à moi seul, en moi-même,
> Auprès d'un coeur, aux sources du poème,
> Entre le vide et l'événement pur,
> J'attends l'écho de ma grandeur interne,
> Amère, sombre, et sonore citerne,
> Sonnant dans l'âme un creux toujours futur!          (ll. 43–8)[22]

These lines directly recall the Pythia's re-echoing inner caverns of metaphysical dread and of the wound of original loss discovered by the Young Fate. They show the same subtle brilliance in the acoustic transcription of the inner experience of the creative mind: in the metaphor of the cistern; in the triple insistence on the self-enclosure of individual human consciousness; in the sense of bitter waiting between void and the mental event of that longed-for creative spark which is the sole, fragile guarantor of a self-generated grandeur; in the recognition that this expectancy will always re-echo with intrinsic unfulfilment. This stanza might perhaps stand for Valéry's entire poetic sensibility and art. It defines the fundamental note of poetic sensibility to which all harmonic keys are related.

We know that, genetically, 'Le Cimetière marin' took shape out of an 'empty rhythmic pattern', apparently without necessity in the personal sensibility of the poet.[23] Yet the acoustic experience voiced indubitably supplies a deeper logic of connection. A certain rhythmic and prosodic form – the 'deficient' ten-syllable line, which Valéry set himself to raise to the metric power of the alexandrine, and, algebraically, in the poem as a whole, to twenty-four six-line stanzas (i.e. 144 lines, or $12^2$) – presents, we may well suspect, a cogent correspondence with the existential key-signature which this form awakens in the deepest subjectivity of the poet. As 'Les Pas' reminds us, rhythm engenders form, and poetry itself is the daughter of memory. . .

Remembering its 'site originel', the mind contemplates its own being and condition in the natural elements. The Mediterranean sunlight becomes the model and mirror of the supreme power of the conscious mind, while the protagonist's gaze resting on the sea discovers there its own effulgent surface, its own infinite aspiration, but also its own hidden depths and its secret mutability (*Œ*, I, p. 1093). The natural world is thus a theatre of articulated self-awareness. The monologue of voice enunciates, recapitulatively, a drama of finitude and infinite aspiration, the essential drama of human desire. Recalling the secret architecture of *La Jeune Parque*, 'Le Cimetière marin' is distinctive, finally, in that it pursues the search for a balance or poise, for a 'just' spiritual form. Stanza 13 defines this point in situating the human presence between the twin absences represented by the noumenal light of Midday above and the entombed dead here below:

> Les morts cachés sont bien dans cette terre
> Qui les réchauffe et sèche leur mystère.
> Midi là-haut, Midi sans mouvement
> En soi se pense et convient à soi-même ...
> Tête complète et parfait diadème,
> Je suis en toi le secret changement. (ll. 73–78)[24]

Two antipodal absolutes are here paradoxically linked, closed self-sufficiencies both; between these extremes, human consciousness occupies a median and intermediary position. The poet-protagonist is at once radiant and earth-bound; he too is noumenal effulgence, yet subject also to variability and secret change; thus, he is spirit written in time-conditioned flesh. If, in the Icarus flight of desire, he approaches the 'Tête complète et parfait diadème', it is as a flaw contained in the perfect diamond of that Thought which thinks the being of all things. Yet his true status and dignity in nature are also thereby defined. He is the self-speaking consciousness, who is both '*la mesure des choses*' (*Œ*, I, p. 1092) and the lonely voice, which can, amid the pulsing silence of midday, render a communicable account of itself.

If human consciousness is for Valéry, like the created world itself, a 'défaut / Dans la pureté du Non-Etre' ('a fault in the purity of Non-Being') (*ES*, st. 3), then human voice – the fact, the labour and, singularly, the poetic delight of it – rewards the defect. In poetry, the subject, dispersed or diffracted in the numerous psychic personae, shimmering reflections and echoes (everything speaks the self, the whole world utters it) has the advantage of being delivered from the visquous clutch of repetition. It is rewarded, too, in the pure form of the poem itself which weaves these heterogeneous emanations and effects together, projecting the idea, the possibility, the energetic charge, of 'un moi merveilleusement supérieur à moi' ('a self marvellously transcending myself') (*Œ*, I, p. 1339).

Poetic voice constitutes the space in which the individual subject, henceforth deprived of substantial reality, seeks an ideal form in song; and in which its obscure depths surface in a fascinating play of reflections. It is also that ideal fusion of sound and sense which formulates, yet also sets at a distance, an act of presence to the world.

*La Jeune Parque* dramatises Valéry's return to poetry; *Charmes* contemplates and celebrates it, rather as one might reconstitute a religion after the death of faith. It reworks the ideal virtue of the poet figure, yet very differently from the great public celebrations of Romanticism and Symbolism: for here, the ideal engages shifting, essentially private, values, a lyricism of disbelief, an aesthetics of scepticism. The lyrical number is performed gratuitously, by classical torch-light, as in the 'Cimetière marin' ('Fermé, sacré, plein d'un feu sans matière / … Ce lieu me plaît, dominé de flambeaux' (ll. 55, 57)[25]). Valéry's higher lyricism of voice no longer opens onto the Beyond and ultra-mundane mysteries; instead, it plays out its part in the perennial drama of human aspiration towards the Absolute, while composing skilful harmonies, insatiably desired.

Voice, as it emerges, is a pacifying force. As its melodic contours acquire substance and architectural shape, the subject recognises the vanity of its deep, despairing thirst for the absolute, and acquiesces in the reflected glory of the world of the senses, of the elements, of consciousness itself. This is the human measure.

A poet despite himself, *à son esprit défendant*; yet in the pure, essentialist lyricism of voice, and through the merits of form, Valéry is essentially a poet. He stands uniquely at the quick of a paradox, which is neither that of lyric poetry alone, nor of analytical intelligence alone, but of their painful disjunction – and their accomplished embrace – in a supremely conscious poetic writing of the unknown or subject or self.[26]

NOTES

1 See *C*2, p. 1152: 'Entre 1800 et 1900, l'art eut un caractère religieux – le symbolisme était une sorte de religion'. (Cf. also p. 1180.)

2 I am indebted to the following colleagues who have explored this approach: Ned Bastet, 'Valéry et la voix poétique', *Annales de la Faculté des lettres et sciences humaines de Nice*, 15 (1971), pp. 42–9; Nicole Celeyrette-Pietri, 'L'écriture et la voix' in K. Blüher, J. Schmidt-Radefeldt, eds., *Poétique et Communication, Cahiers du XXe siècle*, *11*, (Paris, Klincksieck, 1979); and Christine Crow, *Valéry and the Poetry of Voice* (Cambridge University Press, 1982).

3 'Profusion du soir' is sub-titled 'poème abandonné'.

4 'Cette perfection parnassienne, toute postiche, me donne de grandes nausées quand j'y pense, et pourtant, c'est la seule qui satisfasse. / Certaines heures, je trouve risibles ces efforts pour tâcher de redonner du mystère à des choses qui n'en ont plus. Nous sommes comme des refaiseurs de virginités mortes' (*GV*, p. 121).

5 'I tried my best, at the expense of an unbelievable amount of work, to express this modulation of a life'.

6 Cf. *Œ*, 1, p. 1629: 'je voyais quelque récitatif d'opéra à la Gluck; presque une seule phrase, longue et pour contralto' (letter to A. Mockel, 1917).

7 Hartmut Köhler, *Paul Valéry, Poesie et Connaissance. L'œuvre lyrique à la lumière des Cahiers* (Paris, Klincksieck, 1985), p.190; 'a description of the essence of the function of consciousness in its characteristic phases'.

8 'a small undated tombstone—erected on the menacing shores of the Ocean of Gibberish'.

9 'Who weeps there, save just the wind, at this hour / Alone, with diamonds extreme ? ... But who weeps, / So close to myself at the moment of weeping?'

10 'as soon as the brain is even slightly awake, it is the seat of variation and unceasing psychic change: *it is inhabited by instability itself*. It is delivered up to a sort of disorder, which is not generally perceptible, it perceives only elements of this disorder, which is change in its essence, continuous, unsignposted change'.

11 An admirable account of the secret architecture of *La Jeune Parque* is given by R. Fromilhague, '*La Jeune Parque* et l'autobiographie dans la forme', *Paul Valéry contemporain* (Paris, Klincksieck, 1974), pp. 209–35.

12 'Seek, at least, and know by what sequence unperceived / Night from among the dead has led you back to day? / Remember but yourself, and withdraw from instinct / This thread (your gilded finger wrests it from the morning) / This thread, whose blindly followed slender trace / Unto this shore has safely now delivered you ...'

13 These divisions are not numbered in Valéry's text. The reader is advised to number them as an exercise in discerning and interpreting the 'modulation' presented. It will be found that a major interval of

structural importance separates episode X ('Terre trouble, et mêlée à l'algue, porte-moi', l. 324) and episode XI ('Mystérieuse Moi, pourtant tu vis encore!', l. 325); this marks what are here called the two 'Acts' of the poem.

14 'Tomorrow, upon a sigh from gracious Constellations, / In steals spring-time, breaking sealed fountains: / Spring astonishing, laughing, violating ... Sprung from who-knows-where? / Yet soft luminosity falls with words so sweet / That tenderness assails the very womb of earth ...'

15 'Being! Universal ear! / The soul entire sets sail / To extreme limits of desire ... / She listens tremblingly within / And sometimes my lips seem / To seize her quivering.'

16 'Every leaf offers / An obliging source / From which I drink this frail sound ...'

17 'The Pythia exhaling her flame / From incense-flared nostrils / Panting, drunken, vociferates! ... Her soul in terror, / Flanks heaving to the voice roared forth!'

18 'Who speaks in place of me? / What echo answers me: you lie! / Who illumines me? ... Who within blasphemes? / And who, with these foaming words / Whose jagged edges cut my tongue / Makes her brandish a harangue / Breaking through the slaver and the hair / Which disorder tresses, ruminates / From a mouth that would bite itself / And snatch its own avowals back?'

19 Paul Gifford, *Valéry. Charmes* (Glasgow Introductory Guides to French Literature 30, 1995), p. 20.

20 'Here speaks a Wisdom / Here sounds an august Voice / Which knows itself, when it sings / No more as the voice of anyone / But of the woods and trees!'

21 The wind is rising! ... Let us try to live! / The air immense shuts up again the opened pages of my book / The wave in powdered plume dares dash up from the rocks / Fly off, my pages dazzled by the light!'

22 'O just for me, for me alone, within myself / Where feeling springs, at poem's source / Between the void, and pure event / I wait upon the echo of a greatness within / Bitter, sombre, sounding cistern / Ever-future hollow in the soul!'

23 See 'Au sujet du "Cimetière marin"' (*Œ*, I, p. 1503).

24 'The hidden dead are well off in this earth / Which warms them through and dries their mystery up. / Midday above, midday above and motionless / Within itself reflects and with itself agrees ... / Intelligence accomplished, perfect diadem, / In you I am the secret spring of change.'

25 'Closed, sacred, filled with immaterial fire / ... This spot delights me, under presiding torch-light'.

26 For further reading on the topic of this chapter, please see Bibliography, items 5, 23, 35, 40, 43, 65, 73, 76, 78, 86, 87, 91, 109, 112, 117, 123, 126.

# CHAPTER 11

# Other voices: intertextuality and the art of pure poetry

## Suzanne Nash

If the presence of other poets' voices in the work of Paul Valéry has gone largely unheard or unacknowledged, it may be because his poems are composed in such a way as to seem the embodiment of what Valéry occasionally referred to as 'pure poetry': resistant forms bound by a law of internal necessity so strong that they appear to be 'absolute objets'. Mallarmé's poems represented for Valéry the supreme example of such 'purity' (Œ, I, p. 639).

The determination to ward off any attempt to read his work from a perspective outside of itself is reflected in Valéry's metaphor of poetry as dance, in the importance he attaches to voice as the origin and essential vehicle for lyric expression,[1] and in his strong redefinition of influence as a radical modification of the mind, one that guarantees the singularity of the creator. In 'Lettre sur Mallarmé' he writes: 'Le développement séparé d'une qualité de l'un par toute la puissance de l'autre manque rarement d'engendrer des effets d'*extrême originalité*'(Œ, I, p. 635).[2] One of his most celebrated images for the 'originality' that emerges from genuine influence implies the destruction and reconstitution of the predecessor work: 'Rien de plus original, rien de plus *soi* que de se nourrir des autres. Mais il faut les digérer. Le lion est fait de mouton assimilé' (Œ, II, p. 478).[3]

Each new poem is conceived as an ongoing transformative process, a substantiation of agency essential for the life of a culture. This preoccupation with the freedom of creative expression is central to Valéry's concept of an 'ethics of style' and accounts for the transfigurative use of intertexts which, I believe, lies at the generative core of his poetic works.

Valéry returns throughout his life to his concept of influence as a source for originality: in his idea of the 'classical', for example; in his essays on other writers; and, most interestingly perhaps, in his poetic representations of Narcissus, Echo, and the Fountain.[4] The praise he bestows upon writers he admires, such as Racine, Hugo, Poe, Baudelaire, and Mallarmé, includes their ability to forge a voice of their own by way of a critical understanding of a poetic tradition; and the word 'classique', which he applies to these writers, is defined by the same terms he uses to describe his own poetics of immanence – words such as 'forme', 'exigence', 'contrainte', 'rigueur', 'composition', 'mesure', 'idée de perfection', 'système de conventions', 'universalité', 'tournure critique', 'profondeur'. The connections that Valéry, as a classical modernist, establishes between originality, purity, universality, and the tradition would suggest that an understanding of the function of intertextuality is crucial for a properly critical appreciation of his work.

In a striking reconfiguration of the Echo / Narcissus scheme, Valéry suggests that the already-said of the past gains new life and even originality through a reflective exchange with the present. As the lucid poet / reader gazes into the fountain, the voices of the dead themselves become revivified: 'Les morts n'ont plus que les vivants pour ressource ... il est juste et digne de nous qu'ils soient pieusement accueillis dans nos mémoires et qu'ils boivent un peu de vie dans nos paroles' (*Œ*, I, p. 715).[5] The act of orchestrating these other voices that together comprise the lyric tradition will take on a special urgency for Valéry in the aftermath of the first World War. As the creative individual becomes increasingly alienated from the so-called 'progress' of a mechanistic culture, one that seems to preclude and even require a collective forgetting, the process of exchange between the artist and the past becomes more complex and more ambiguous – a measure, one might say, of an epoch's literacy. At the same time, the ever-deepening and darkening waters of the source make the desire for the image of a unique and originary self more compelling. Metaphors of self-reflection and murmurings from the past abound in Valéry's writing as he considers the crisis of modern times.[6] Indeed, Valéry's 'originality', vis-à-vis the poetic predecessors whom he most admires and whose voices we find transformed within his writing can only be grasped if one understands the commitments and paradoxes at work in this reconceptualisation of the classical from within an historically embattled and determinedly self-problematising art.

Although less obviously parodic and satirical than in avant-gardist writing, Valéry's use of intertextuality (as opposed to imitation or mere borrowing) has the important critical function of what Laurent

Jenny has aptly called 'cultural re-appropriation' or 'turning aside' ('détournement culturel'). The perturbation caused by the reworking of other texts opens the way for a new language born out of the fissures of the old. Wherever there is a genuine poetic odyssey, there is, according to Jenny, a plurality of subjects and a multiplicity of writings.[7] To see the image of one's 'charming' self in the fountain means for Valéry (if not for the self-enthralled Narcissus within the poem), to 'reveal the cultural mythologies of the past' (*ibid.*) and to include their presence as a condition of a unique critical identity within one's own creation. This may be why the voice of the Nymph becomes more intrusive and the figure of Narcissus more tentative with each new version of Valéry's self-ironising story of the beautiful ideal. Narcissus' bedazzlement with his own image, his wish for an *end* to the quest,[8] is a symptom of the potential loss of critical distance which could render lyric expression irrelevant in an age already threatened by collective amnesia.[9] The question for Valéry was how to accept the growing estrangement of the self without being destroyed by it, how to re-establish a connection to the past without losing one's unique power of inventiveness.

Having studied the laws governing linguistic expression for many years, Valéry was aware that without the 'already said', language would be incomprehensible and unwritable. The sea of the 'Cimetière marin' or the moonlit pool of the Narcissus poems, as metaphors for the source on, within, or out of which the body of poetic figuration is drawn, contain and subsume all the other poetic voyages, shipwrecks, 'brises marines', and mirroring ponds that preceded them. Valéry's Narcissus figures do not discover their reflection in the water for the first time – the poems in which they appear begin with a *return* to the source. Even the self-enthralled Narcissus recognizes that his wish for an originary condition requires an inaugural gesture of denial, a stilling of a past clamorous with other claims:

> Nymphes! si vous m'aimez, il faut toujours dormir!
> La moindre âme dans l'air vous fait toutes frémir; (*FN*, ll. 7–8)[10]

The poet writes in his *Cahiers* that every work is a synthesis of different 'minds', ancestors, accidents, earlier writers etc., orchestrated, he would have it, under the direction of the Author (*C*, VII, p. 483). To speak, as Narcissus does in 'Narcisse parle', is to pick up this instrument from the hands of others in the way the Musician creates a symphonic score out of notes already played:

On peut considérer les types de notre poésie, Racine, Hugo, Baudelaire, etc. comme des instruments chacun plus approprié à tels effets et plus adapté par sa langue *choisie*, ses rhythmes, ses images à telles ou telles nécessités. Il n'est pas impossible de conjuguer ces violons, ces 'cuivres et ces bois' pour posséder un orchestre ... il suffit de rappeler que chacun de ces poètes est dans la langue, que leurs effets sont distincts, incomparables, non contradictoires dans la suite. Il faut, naturellement, savoir orchestrer (*C2*, p. 1080).[11]

In 1912 when, at Gide's urging, Valéry turned back to his early poetry written under the influence of a host of nineteenth-century poetic fathers with differing poetic ideals, many of whom had set new terms for a definition of the lyric, the issue of the status of these other voices for his own concept of *poiesis* must have seemed particularly acute. Everywhere in the revised versions of these early poems published in the *Album de vers anciens* of 1920 Valéry calls attention to the presence of other voices and the dynamics of their critical transfiguration by indicating that he is writing in the style of his poetic fathers: Mallarmé ('Vue', 'Valvins'), Baudelaire ('Anne'), Heredia ('La Fileuse', 'César'), Vielé-Griffin ('Eté'), amongst others. It is from within this 'sea' of voices that Narcissus 'speaks', bringing the rhetoric of a *fin de siècle* symbolism out of the dictionary of dated poetic effects to naturalise it and infuse it with a contemporary voice of his own.[12]

What is involved in the *Album* and elsewhere in Valéry's use of intertextuality is not only an appropriation and rewriting of the language of his poetic predecessors, but, implicitly and most significantly, a subversion of the poet's own claims for an originary project. Valéry's poetic personae are multiple (César, Sémiramis, Narcisse, the Parque, amongst others) and their status within his texts profoundly ambiguous. By writing and rewriting his many 'Narcisse', the poet can be seen to be seeking new forms for the expression of the problematical nature of lyric subjectivity. The discovery of himself as another, a former 'Narcisse', as an 'il' to be quoted, indeed echoed, and even parodied, for example, in 'Fragments du Narcisse', beclouds the adolescent dream of 'pure' self-representation. Rather than a means of transcendence, as in Mallarmé's work, the reflecting surface is figured in the later poem as a knife forever separating the gazer from his image in the water:

> Et que la nuit déjà nous divise, ô Narcisse,
> Et glisse entre nous deux le fer qui coupe un fruit!
>
> (*FN*, ll. 126–7)[13]

Every poetic word the desiring Narcissus utters disturbs the image, makes the water ripple, and awakens the nymphs sleeping in its depths (cf. *FN*, ll. 9–11). Every utterance betrays the vision, and yet it is from within the utterance that the illusion of unity, of a 'pure source', must be re-invented. In fact, the paradoxical nature of the utterance, its destructive and transformative potential, lends the mouth of this modernist Narcissus its unique, seductive beauty:

> Mais que ta bouche est belle en ce muet blasphème!
>
> ...
>
> Voir, ô merveille, voir! ma bouche nuancée
> Trahir... peindre sur l'onde une fleur de pensée,
> Et quels événements étinceler dans l'oeil!     (*FN*, ll. 121; 141–3)[14]

The story of seduction and betrayal is not only a metaphor for the story of influence, but for the relationship of the poet to his craft and for the process by which a poem is produced out of the language of the tradition. As the Nymph of the fountain says to Narcissus at the end of the self-parodying *Cantate du Narcisse*:

> Songe qu'il n'est plus temps pour toi de me haïr,
> Narcisse, et laisse-toi séduire à te trahir...     (*Œ*, I, p. 419)[15]

The occulted intrusion of Hugolian intertexts into Valéry's exchange with Mallarmé in the Narcissus poems can be seen as one such betrayal. If, in 'Narcisse parle ...', Valéry opposes Hérodiade's sacrifice of the natural world by re-animating the potent but delusional adolescent Faun from Mallarmé's 'summer poem', 'L'Après-midi d'un faune', he may have done so because the Faun is evocative for both Mallarmé and Valéry, of the hubristic, self-divinising pans and satyrs which stand in for the poet in Hugo's work. The Faun's hyperbolic claim: 'Ces nymphes, je les veux perpétuer' ('These nymphs, I mean to perpetuate them'), can, for example be read as Mallarmé's parody of Hugo's claim, in 'Pan' from *Les Feuilles d'automne*,[16] to transcendent creativity. Ironical references to Hugo appear here and there throughout Mallarmé's work. Several commentators have identified Hugo as the parenthetical 'Maître [qui] est allé puiser des pleurs au Styx' ('Master [who] has gone to draw tears from the Styx') in the late sonnet, 'Ses purs ongles ...', for example. One might say the same for the absent father of the 'Ouverture ancienne d'Hérodiade', who is oblivious to the fact that the ancient source has dried up. His progeny can only wonder if he will ever return:

> Depuis longtemps la gorge ancienne est tarie.
> Son père ne sait pas cela ...
> Reviendra-t-il un jour des pays cisalpins!
> Assez tôt? Car tout est présage et mauvais rêve!
>
> (ll. 74–5; 80–81)[17]

Valéry responds playfully to Mallarmé's question by transforming the self-reflective Narcissus back into a pan-like piper at the end of 'Narcisse parle ... ', to awaken, as we have seen, the sensuous nymph of 'Episode'.

One might pause here to ask why Valéry invokes Mallarmé's Hugo in this ironical way. Perhaps in exposing the historical dimension of the idealisms underlying the evolution of the lyric, he is suggesting that the genre depends upon persistently self-deluding myths for its definition, that behind the Symbolist ideal of a self-reflexive language lies the Romantic belief in a transcendental creative subject capable of safeguarding the uniqueness of lived experience through memory, and behind them both the myth of the lyric as pure expressivity and the origin of all language.

The subversive Hugolian tropes of potent lover and falling tresses seen in 'Episode', reappear in Part 2 of 'Fragments du Narcisse', this time in the language of the romantic story of love betrayed, reminiscent of Hugo's well known 'Tristesse d'Olympio'.[18] Valéry crystallises Olympio's long lament (thirty stanzas, in Hugo's poem), beginning 'O douleur ...' and ending 'O sacré souvenir', into three drastically condensed lines, represented as three separate voices or echoes quoted from the past. He borrows a distinctly Romantic vocabulary to introduce them, yet the topos of the poet's return to the sacred site of a unique experience only to discover its effacement by time also uncannily resembles the anxiety that surrounds the Valéryan paradigm of Narcissus's return to the fountain in 'Fragments du Narcisse' (cf. *FN*, ll. 198; 205–08).

But if Valéry quotes Hugo to undercut Mallarmé's claim to originality, he has done so in a way that undercuts both Hugo's gesture of self-divination and Valéry's own claim to purity. The repetition of 'd'autres' echoes Olympio's dread of being rendered redundant by other poetic voices in a self-ironising way:

> D'autres vont maintenant passer où nous passâmes.
> Nous y sommes venus, d'autres vont y venir;
> Et le songe qu'avaient ébauchés nos deux âmes,
> Ils le continueront sans pouvoir le finir![19]

The ironic use of a Hugolian intertext to reveal the loss of the privileged, originary experience is evidence that Valéry understood that his own Narcissistic ideal of a pure poetry was one more 'détournement culturel' erected to resist the contemporary loss of individual expression. If 'Fragments du Narcisse' begins with Narcissus's plea for a clear source in which to re-discover an image faithful to himself, it does so in the knowledge that the lyric voice is inscribing itself within a long tradition of similar pleas: first the poet's own in 'Narcisse parle ...', itself a story of punishment by repetition, told and retold by Ovid, Hugo and Mallarmé, amongst others. In fact, the lyric has traditionally defined itself as a distinctive form of identity in love with its own reflections, deaf to any response. By conflating the figures of Narcissus and Echo, Valéry is recognising the inevitable disjunction between image and voice, the impossibility of a truly correspondent language. One might say that when Valéry chooses to separate himself in this way from the Symbolist ideal of an internally cohesive system of signs, he opens a self-questioning gap which becomes abyssal, never-ending, the very opposite of unifying. Even a tightly structured sonnet like 'Les Grenades' (*Charmes*) is built out of such a gap. The violence of its vocabulary ('entr'ouvertes', 'entre-baillées', 'crève', 'rupture') and of its initial metaphor force open the jewelled doors of the Symbolist temple. The poem risks implosion by the sheer energy of its generative potential, very like Western civilisation itself, as Valéry describes it in his beautiful, apocalyptic lecture, 'La Crise de l'esprit', of 1918.

'Fragments du Narcisse' reflects the same kind of 'breaking of form' in every feature of its construction, from its title, to the graphic irregularity of its lines, to its ironical use of self-citation. From the outset Valéry's poetic persona in the 'Fragments' seems to recognise the futility of his claim for uniqueness:

> Je suis seul! ... Si les Dieux, les échos et les ondes
> [...] ... permettent qu'on le soit!     (*FN*, ll. 30–31)[20]

The first direct quotation from 'Narcisse parle' occurs simultaneously with the appearance of the image of Narcissus in the water:

> La voix des sources change, et me parle du soir;     (*FN*, ll. 35)[21]

thus making the illusion of sameness between poetic voice and the subject of its enunciation dependent upon a changing temporal condition.

The second use of self-citation, this time slightly altered, comes after an expression of dismay at discovering that the image of himself is a form of enslavement containing a premonition of death in its reflected gaze:

> Que je déplore ton éclat fatal et pur,
> Si mollement de moi, fontaine environnée,
> Où puisèrent mes yeux dans un mortel azur,
> Les yeux mêmes et noirs de leur âme étonnée!   (*FN*, ll. 72–5)[22]

The third citation:

> Une tendre lueur d'heure ambiguë existe . . .
> Là, d'un reste du jour, se forme un fiancé,
> Nu, sur la place pâle où m'attire l'eau triste,
> Délicieux démon désirable et glacé!          (*FN*, ll. 111–14)[23]

emerges after a romantically coloured evocation of nature's betrayal and indifference to human experience reminiscent of Lamartine's 'Le Lac' or Hugo's 'Tristesse d'Olympio' (*FN*, ll. 100; 107–10). The fourth citation, following immediately after the third, is a clear distortion of the 'original', as if in recognition that every repetition is necessarily a perturbation and an alteration:

> Te voici, mon doux corps de lune et de rosée,
> O forme obéissante à mes vœux opposée!
> Qu'ils sont beaux, de mes bras les dons vastes et vains!
> Mes lentes mains, dans l'or adorable se lassent
> D'appeler ce captif que les feuilles enlacent;
> Mon cœur jette aux échos l'éclat des noms divins! (*FN*, ll. 115–20)[24]

Part II of 'Fragments du Narcisse', as I have shown, is filled with the voices of Romantic poets who have sung of love discovered and love betrayed, of nature's indifference to the wish for a unique experience of communication and presence. In the final section of Part III Narcissus repeats the age-old lyric call for an eternalisation of the moment, the wish to stop nature's diurnal course (most famously rendered in French by Lamartine's 'O temps suspends ton vol!'):

> Formons, toi sur ma lèvre, et moi, dans mon silence,
> Une prière aux dieux qu'émus de tant d'amour
> Sur sa pente de pourpre ils arrêtent le jour!   (*FN*, ll. 277–79)[25]

The poem ends with the futility of that wish expressed in a magnificent image of the disappearance of all things, including that of perception itself:

> L'arbre aveugle vers l'arbre étend ses membres sombres,
> Et cherche affreusement l'arbre qui disparaît ...    (*FN*, ll. 301–02)[26]

The sound of Narcissus's own name is brought back, Echo-like, to leave a final trace as he utters one last, decoupled sound:

> L'insaisissable amour que tu me vins promettre
> Passe, et dans un frisson, brise Narcisse, et fuit ...    (ll. 313–4)[27]

In 1942, near the end of his life, Valéry wrote in his notebook (*C*, XXV, p. 571), that Hugo had composed 'le plus beau vers *possible*', 'aucun moyen ni espoir de faire mieux' ('the most beautiful line *possible*', 'no way or hope of doing better'):

> L'ombre est noire toujours même tombant des cygnes.[28]

The great 'engenderer'[29] had found a way to harmonise the light ('cygnes') and dark ('ombre') sounds of language in such a way as to figure its own temporal condition. In the finale of 'Fragments du Narcisse', one line in particular, composed from the echoing '-*isse* 'seems to want to imitate that inscription of temporality so perfectly rendered by Hugo:

> Bientôt va frissonner le désordre des ombres![30]

This line in turn suggests the larger play of intertextual echoes that traverse this remarkable and still little-known Valéryan 'chantier'. The onset of night, eclipsing his own idolised and now broken reflection, delivers Narcisse up to a fundamental cosmic vulnerability:

> Ma fontaine n'est plus qu'une splendide nuit
> Qui représente aux cieux leur merveille fermée
> Par les mêmes clartés dont toute elle est formée.
> Où fut Narcisse, hélas! Narcisse que j'aimais
> Ce précieux silence étincelle à jamais !
> O quelle profondeur, sage et transformée,
> A la place de l'onde occupe la durée!
> Elle brille des dieux qui m'ont abandonné!
> Seul au milieu des temps, d'étoiles étonné
> Je m'afflige, effacé par ces filles de l'ombre ...
> ...
> Rien ne manque à l'orgueil de ce monstre divers.
> Je ne suis rien, Narcisse, il n'est que l'univers:
> Lui seul trouve en soi-même à se perdre sans crainte[31]

This stellar confrontation is an inhabited space of cultural memory, alive with a murmur of intertextual voices. As Paul Gifford points out, the 'closed marvel' is that of the Kantian *En-soi*, evoked in *Note et Digression* (Œ, I, p. 1223). The eternal 'silence' is that of Pascal's famously indicted – but, it seems, strangely resonant – thought about infinite space (cf. pp. 458–73). The 'gods who have abandoned me' are, allusively, all the Absolutes of nineteenth-century transcendent-alism. The cosmic space-time that astonishes and appals the human mind is a direct echo of Poe's *Eureka*, while the sense of grievous exclusion from complicity in the Poem of the divine Artist refers both to Poe and to the dice-throw of an esoteric and 'absolute' poetry attempted by Mallarmé. Significantly, however, creative transformation here declares an *impasse*. These fragments of a finale, despite writing of remarkable power, remain tentative and unfin-ished, the cosmic 'text' providing a limit case.[32]

Short of this 'absolute' limit, Valéry's metaphor of poetic language as 'source' works well. If the pool gathers all of the stories of the past:

> O présence pensive, eau calme qui recueilles
> Tout un sombre trésor de fables et de feuilles, (*FN*, ll. 165–6)[33]

it also produces their dissolution and recomposition into new, unfinished 'chants fluides'. This process that includes continuity and renewal, fidelity and betrayal, repetition and differentiation, is the very definition of literary language. If it is condemned to repeat itself, however, in Valéry's work it does so with insight into its own condition.

The 'détournements culturels' that Valéry enacts through his use of intertextuality define his position as a classical modernist. Origin-ality is understood as something to be re-created, re-made, through a mastery of the techniques of creative expression. Richard Shiff has convincingly argued that Cézanne's awkward and sketchy renderings of bathers are examples of purposeful 'gaucherie', stylistic *signs* of naivety or primitivism, guarantees of sincerity, placed there by the artist to signal his commitment to the regeneration of art by bringing nature back into the equation – a way to disassociate himself from the fallen classicism of dead academic representation.[34] Through his 'misappropriation' of other voices, I would argue, Valéry introduces similar gestures of rupture or disturbance into the composition and smooth functioning of his verse – as signs of his modernist 'facture'. Narcissus's return to the source is not naive and direct as for the animal who comes to drink at the beginning of 'Fragments du Narcisse'. The return to nature is accomplished by way of a detour through a critical, even ironical apprehension and recomposition of the poetic stories or myths that man has invented to assure himself a place within nature's permanence. But, if Valéry's ideal of 'pure poetry' is revealed to be only one more myth amongst many, the beauty of its enchantments and self-disclosures remains as eloquent testimony to the restorative force of its creative refashionings.[35]

NOTES

1 'Le lyrisme est la voix du *moi*, porté au ton le plus pur, sinon le plus haut' (*Œ*, I, p. 429). See Jean-Michel Maulpoix, 'La voix du moi', *Secolul 20* (Bucharest, 1995), p. 121.

2 'The separate development of a quality of one mind by the whole force of another rarely fails to engender effects of *extreme originality*'.

3 'Nothing could be more original, nothing more characteristic of *oneself* than to nourish oneself on others. But one must digest them. The lion is made up of assimilated sheep'.

4 Valéry's many recreations of the myth include: the two versions of 'Narcisse parle ...' (*La Conque*, 1891 and *Album de vers anciens*, 1920), 'Fragments du Narcisse' (*Charmes*, 1922), *Etudes pour un Narcisse* (1927), the Narcissus of *Paraboles* (1935), *Le Cantate du Narcisse* (1939) and *L'Ange* (1921–45).

5 'The only resource of the dead is the living ... it is just and worthy of us that they should be piously welcomed into our memories and that they should drink a little life in our words'.

6 See *Discours de réception à l'Académie française*: 'Le monde au sein duquel nous nous sommes formés à la vie et à la pensée est un monde foudroyé ... On commençait de saisir dans l'air intellectuel la rumeur d'une diversité de voix surprenantes et des chansons encore inouïes, le murmure d'une forêt très mystérieuse dont les frémissements, les échos, et parfois les ricanements pleins de présages et de menaces, inquiétaient vaguement ...' (*Œ*, I, pp. 716, 718).

7 Laurent Jenny, 'La stratégie de la forme', *Poétique* 27 (1976), pp. 279, 280.

8 See the expectant energy of the poem's opening line invoking '[le] terme pur de ma course' (*FN*, p. 1). David Elder points out that the unpublished manuscripts of the 'Finale' figure, on the contrary, a 'Narcisse sans reflet, dans le plus noir de lui-même'. See 'Le finale fragmenté des "Narcisse" de Valéry', *Cahiers Paul Valéry I* (Paris, Gallimard, 1975), pp. 187–206.

9 Valéry's sensitivity to the ideological implications of a 'pure' poetry can be heard in his often confided sense of having written *La Jeune Parque* at the time of Verdun, like a monk of the fifth century composing hexameters while the Barbarians were overrunning the Empire. 'Je me

disais que j'élevais un monument funéraire à la tradition de la poésie française' (unpublished ms quoted in *Secolul 20* (1995), pp. 40; 42).

10  'Nymphs, if you love me, you must still sleep on! / The slightest breath of air makes you all to quiver'.

11  'One may consider the types of our poetry, Racine, Hugo, Baudelaire, etc. as instruments, each more appropriate to certain effects and more adapted by its *chosen* language, its rhythms, its images, to such or such a requirement. It is not impossible to join together these 'violins', these 'brass', and these 'woodwinds' so as to get an orchestra ... It is enough to recall that each of these poets is in the language, that their effects are distinct, incomparable, non contradictory in their succession. Of course, one must know how to orchestrate'.

12  For a detailed analysis of the 'naturalising' effects of diction in 'Narcisse parle ...' see my study of intertextual transformation in *Paul Valéry's 'Album de vers anciens': A Past Transfigured*, (Princeton University Press, 1983), pp. 180–97.

13  'And that the night already divides us, oh Narcissus / And slips between us the knife that cuts the fruit!'

14  'But how beautiful thy mouth in this silent blasphemy! ... To see, oh marvel, see! my finely shaded mouth / Betray ... and paint upon the water a flower of thought / And what events sparkle in the eye!'

15  'Dream that time is no more for thee to hate me / Narcissus, and be enticed thyself to betray'

16  Victor Hugo, *Œuvres complètes*, ed. P. Albouy, 'Bibliothèque de la Pléiade', vol. 1 (Paris, Gallimard, 1964), pp. 803–5. Early unpublished versions of Mallarmé's *Après-midi d'un faune* (see *Œuvres* (eds.) Henri Mondor and G. Jean-Aubry (Paris, Gallimard (Pléiade), 1945), pp. 1448–66) bear striking resemblance to this poem.

17  'Long since the antique throat is dried up / His father knows that not ... / Will he return one day from lands beyond the Alps! / Soon enough? For all is presage and bad dream!' (*Ibid.*, pp. 41–3)

18  Hugo, *Œuvres*, vol. 1, pp. 1093–98.

19  *Ibid.*, 1096; 'Others will now pass where we did pass. / We came here, others here will come; / And the dream our two souls had sketched / They will continue it, without being able to finish it!'

20  'I am alone! ... If the gods, the echoes and the waves / ... allow it so!'

21  'The voice of the springs changes and speaks to me of evening'

22  'How I deplore your pure and fateful brightness, / Fountain loosely by my arms embraced / In whom my eyes found 'mid mortal azure / The eyes, dark eyes, astonished, of their soul'

23  'A tender glow of doubtful light subsists ... / There, of dying day's remainder, is formed a fiancé, / Naked, on the pale strip where sad waters draw me / Delicious demon, desirable and chill!'

24  'Saluted be, sweet body made of moon and dew, / Obedient form contrary to my longing! / How fine the vast and vain gifts of my arms!

/ My supple hands grow weary in the golden adoration / Of calling to
the captive held by leaves; / My heart throws out to the echoes the
glory of names divine!' Cf. 'Narcisse parle ...' (*Œ*, I, p. 82):

> Voici dans l'eau ma chair de lune et de rosée,
> O forme obéissante à mes yeux opposée!
> Voici mes bras d'argent dont les gestes sont purs! . .
> Mes lentes mains dans l'or adorable se lassent
> D'appeler ce captif que les feuilles enlacent,
> Et je crie aux échos les noms des dieux obscurs! ...

25 'Let us form, you upon my lips, and I within my silent heart / A prayer
   that the gods, moved by so much love / Should halt upon its purple
   slope the dying day!'
26 'The blind tree stretches out its dark limbs, / And seeks in horror the
   disappearing tree ...'
27 'The love unseizable you came to bring / Passes, in a shiver, breaks
   Narcissus, flees ...'
28 'The shadow still is black e'en though it fall from cygnet plumes'
29 See 'Victor Hugo, créateur par la forme' (*Œ*, I, p. 583).
30 'Soon will shiver here the disorder of the shadows'. This line is also
   rendered 'Je m'afflige, effacé par ces filles de l'ombre' and 'Leur univers
   m'efface, à peine il sort de l'ombre'. See Elder, 'Le finale fragmenté
   ... ', pp. 189, 191.
31 I reproduce here, lightened of variants, an extract of the manuscripts
   cited by Elder. 'My fountain is no longer but the spendid night / Which
   mirrors to the heavens a marvel closed / By all the gleamings that
   compose it. / Where Narcissus was, alas, he whom I loved / This
   precious silence glitters on eternally! / Oh, what sage, transfigured
   depth / Within the water occupies the space of time! / It shines from all
   the gods who have abandoned me! / Alone, amid all times, by stars
   amazed / My grief acute, effaced by daughters of the shadow ... /
   Nothing lacking to its diverse and monstrous Pride, / I am nothing,
   Narcissus, there only is the universe: / Alone it finds itself within itself
   and has no fear'
32 I am grateful for these editorial suggestions derived from an unpublished article to appear in a Festschrift volume for Simon Lantieri:
   'Autour d'un livre stellaire: Paul Valéry et l'*Eureka* d'E. Poe'.
33 'O pensive presence, water calm which gathers to itself / A whole, dark,
   treasure of fables and of leaves'.
34 Richard Shiff, *Cézanne and the End of Impressionism* (University of Chicago
   Press, 1984), p. 230.
35 For further reading on the topic of this chapter, please see Bibliography,
   items 5, 28, 61, 65, 76, 77, 78, 84, 86, 87.

# CHAPTER 12

# Manuscript steps: 'Les Pas'

## Florence de Lussy

Access to an author's manuscripts has long been considered to offer a valuable means of renewing our vision of his writing. It is well known that Goethe, for example, built up a substantial collection of manuscripts by his contemporaries. But the extension of critical study from an author's published text to his rough drafts and the whole range of sketches and notes that are generically known as the *avant-texte* (or 'prior text') is a more recent phenomenon. While James Lawler was one of the first to venture into this field,[1] genetic study as such only really began to develop in the early 1970s with the creation, within the Centre National de la Recherche Scientifique, of the Institut des Textes et Manuscrits modernes (ITEM); this Institute was dedicated to establishing the basis of a new discipline called genetic criticism or textual genetics. From the very beginning, the team of scholars working on Valéry's manuscripts has played a prominent and pioneering role.

Valéry's manuscripts constitute a remarkable corpus of raw material for this new type of exploration:[2] for here is a poet who always valued the process of fabricating a poem more than the published work itself – which is considered almost as a 'cast-off' – and who dreamed of a form of criticism that might recompose the poem of the poem, and thereby mirror the genetic process itself. Moreover, Valéry serves in exemplary fashion the essentially modern perspectives which have given rise to these new forms of critical enquiry: they answer a desire, on the one hand, to uncover the process of creation marking all the stages of the writing from first trace to last (which itself may merely signal suspension, incompletion, failure or even regression ...); and at the same time, they meet our desire to penetrate the mystery of the writer's creative personality.[3]

The poem 'Les Pas' offers a near-ideal configuration for this type of study. It is a miniature piece, subject to a minimum of prosodic constraints: the octosyllabic quatrain is a supple, easily manipulated frame which comes close to spontaneous utterance. The very simplicity of form seems to stimulate and invite the dynamic forces of the poet's creative psyche. 'Content' is no longer subject to the overriding pressures of 'form' as is so often the case in traditionally versified French poetry, particularly so in Valéry whose principal concern is usually to accentuate the demands of prosody.

In October 1918, with five years of continuous poetic creation behind him, Valéry is at a high point of lyric expectation as he listens attentively to the inner forces seeking form and expression. The first traces in the manuscripts are like 'seeds' or 'embryos' – in this case, of exceptional promise; they were noted down in a very private, even secret, notebook ('PV 1918', classified as 'cahier *Ch* II'), containing some of the most valuable pointers to the heart of the poet's creative domain.[4] The spidery handwriting, the way that words, incomplete phrases and poetic fragments are scattered across the surface of the manuscript, the constant to-ing and fro-ing between one page and another – refuting any illusion of linear, chronological progression in the writing – all these things speak of an intimate inner dialogue.

Moreover, this short poem is seen to possess a thematic richness that is perhaps unexpected on reading the published version: the manuscripts reveal the operation of an intricate, tightly-woven web of symbols and a variety of accumulated tonal registers that belie the smooth, unified surface of its final form. In particular we observe two themes, interweaving and overlaying one another: the expectancy of creative invention in the silent depths of the soul; and the capacity of the mind to generate its own images or of desire to create its own object, a theme which is to be read in the frame provided by Valéry's own re-invented 'psychology', tirelessly pursued in the *Cahiers* since the turn of the century.[5] The line 'Tes pas, enfants de mon silence' ('Your steps, children of my silence') resembles the thirst which, in *Note et Digression*, 's'illustre d'elle-même de ruisselantes visions' ('spontaneously engenders radiant visions') (*Œ*, I, p. 1204); this is closely linked to the theme of introspection, as it already had been in the hybrid text *Agathe*.[6] Parallel to this speculative, somewhat abstract, thematic is the theme of amorous desire which is foregrounded and colours all. The latter, though obviously attractive, indeed inevitable, nevertheless bears within the metaphoric framing of the poem a 'true' second meaning for the writer:

both amorous desire for a woman *and* – paradoxically – a love which
is self-directed. Psyche, the heroine of this brief poem, stands for the
feminine part of our being made up of body and flesh, hopes and
fears, heartbeats and tremors of voice; desire for the feminine Other
here figures the desire for self-possession, thus giving an added,
Valéryan depth to the conventional theme. There is, finally, the
theme of mystical love which the poem enacts, a night-ascent
towards a fusional encounter in Being.

The unified yet multiple theme of the writing – expectancy in the
night – goes back to the earliest Valéryan texts and raises the
question of sources. There are throughout the work of a great writer,
and especially in a poet, certain currents of sensibility, particular
lodestars, and a characteristic curvature of mind, such that a
number of intertextual resonances emerge from one work to
another. On a diachronic axis, we can identify the immediate
antecedence of *La Jeune Parque*, the first sketches of which, in 1913,
show a graphic of a naked female torso 'proceeding' (*JP* ms III,
fo. 31), while the finished poem counts her steps in desire and self-
understanding, towards the extremes of pure consciousness, and,
ultimately, towards death ('Hélas! De mes pieds nus, qui trouvera la
trace ...' (*JP*, l. 322)). *Agathe* is a more remote, though equally
evident source, with its register of abstract emotion ('ab intimo — il
ne reste que la place de l'espace, son culot mobile — la base
mouvante de la vue. L'espace — Silence où se déploie l'ange
intérieur').[7]

On a synchronic axis we may consider a range of associated
contemporaneous texts, in the ambit of what may be called – Valéry
notwithstanding – his overflowing 'inspiration' of that moment in
time.[8] 'Les Pas' resonates intertextually with other poems: with the
unattainable mystery of 'Fragments du Narcisse'; with the 'bouche
d'ombre' and the 'temps lacté' of 'Poésie';[9] with the abyss of
'Equinoxe' into which 'l'âme de mon âme ose à peine descendre'
(Cah. *Ch* I, fo. 22). 'Le Cimetière marin' presents a draft third stanza
– split in two at this early stage, though later brought together into
one six-line stanza (like a secret folded upon itself) – in which the
same murmured confidence springs forth, a heart beating at the
sources of the poem; 'Auprès d'un cœur et non loin du poème', we
read on the reverse side of a folio of notebook 3 of *Charmes*[10] (the
verso being frequently used as an extended margin for the following
recto, or as a large reserve space for a freer type of writing).

The external matrix of the genesis consists of events which may have triggered the act of writing, or else fed its inspiration: in the present case, a re-reading of La Fontaine undertaken by Valéry during a leisurely stay in a country house near the northern French coast, where he accompanied his employer Edouard Lebey during the last months of the War. Valéry was particularly struck in the work of the seventeenth-century *conteur* by the delightfully delicate prose blossoming into verse-interludes. One of these gives us the direct origin of 'Les Pas', a short sequence of octosyllabic lines following the exquisite description of Psyche approaching the bed in which sleeps her husband Eros: 'A pas tremblants et suspendus / Elle arrive enfin où repose / Son époux aux bras étendus'.[11] This visually striking scene is clearly present in Valéry's imagination throughout the successive stages of the poem.

It would be difficult to find a more intrinsically 'genetic' theme than this measured advance, which is both physical approach and mental process. A poem is a measured thing and the step or footfall is the measure of its writing. We shall follow here, step by step through the earliest manuscripts traces, the advent of this 'écriture de pieds nus' of which the poem is at once the product and the sign. The primary approach will be linguistic, incorporating analysis of the graphic, lexical, semantic, syntactic and enunciative features of the writing, since such an approach remains closest to the text; yet we shall also see how genetic study opens onto thematic and psycho-analytical dimensions.

The first trace or inscription (*Ch* II, p. 30) reveals from the outset two quatrains placed side-by-side, the first of which emerges fully formed, apparently out of nothing. In fact, as we have seen, the theme, the tonality and the verbal music are those of La Fontaine's *Psyché:*

Tes pas, fille de mon silence,

Saintement, lentement ~~posés~~ placés,
     ma vigilance
Vers le lit de ~~mon indolence~~
    Procèdent
~~Comptent~~ muets et glacés

It is commonly thought that words lead the creative dance; yet it often happens in poetry that even before the words take shape, there is a rhythm or beat in the musical sense. This perceptible inner

Narcissus – c'est un dialogue entre lui et son image, roulant sur
la passion de soi-même, qui est la seule —

    Il n'y a jamais satisfaction de cette passion-là, qui met aux prises
le stable et l'instable, —

    Le quis invisible se voit et ne peut se reconnaître, etc. —

Echange et impossibilité —

——

    Retard –

Tu me fais comme si je vivais au-dessus de moi – comme si j'étais
~~plus~~ une partie de moi-même.    (infini continu)      Comment dire ceci?

                      découvre l'ombre   entr'ouvre
      Et si dans ce regard toute une     s'ouvre

    Non ce n'est pas tendresse, hélas, que j'y découvre,
             amour Vénus
                Eros
   L'amour —     éclair ennemi   désir plaisir              4 4
   Mais de cruels ⌊*dégoûts*⌋ dédain     choisir         3 3.2 … 0
         qu'on                         2.6  … 00
   Il n'aime pas celui qui se puisse saisir
     Je           que je puisse          *[abri]*  . . 0 …
                                    *écrit*

*Psykhé*    **PSYKÉ**               *[retentisse]*

                                   qu'ils sont frais, |*l* + c| es pas
                           *aise*              là-bas
                         pure,  ombre
Tes pas, fille de mon silence,      Personne ~~d'ombre~~, –         divine
                          ~~dans~~ (mon) esprit
Saintement, |lentement| ~~posés~~ places,  Qu'ils sont beaux ~~dans l'ombre ici bas~~
      ma vigilance           *Où Ces pas*   *l'*     *seul*   *dans une attente*
Vers le lit de ~~mon indolence~~     ~~Tes pieds que mon~~ âme  sent  devine
     Procèdent                Ces pieds nus
~~Comptent~~ muets et glacés      C'est mon cœur ~~même qui les bat~~
                          qui compte tes pas
                    Baisant le sol      qu'elle surprit
                    Dans le néant     que
J'attends de la nuit

                    Ces pieds qui viennent
    *frais*                *une phrase qui s'*
*Qu'ils sont doux ces pieds [divins]*  *Comme [ … ]*   *d'un [ … ] écrit*
*[Pieds insensibles]*               *Pas à pas*
                    ~~Ils ne~~
                    Silencieux, ils retentissent

Cah. *Ch* II, fo. 30, transcription

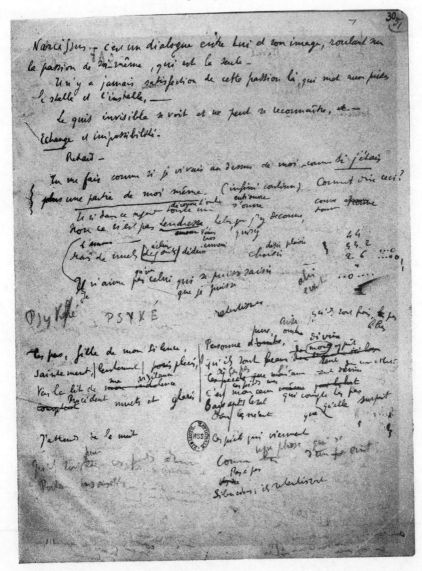

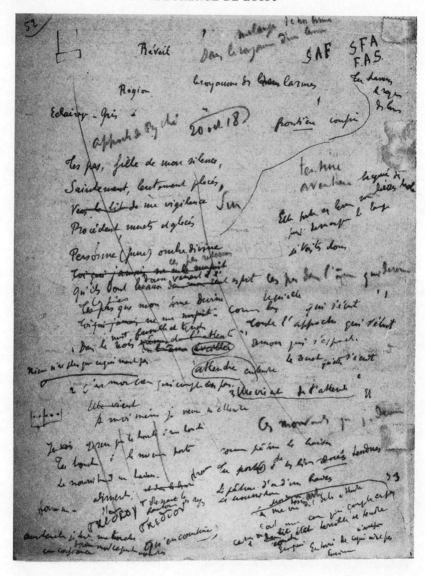

Cah. *Ch* II, fo. 30v.
Courtesy of Bibliotheque nationale de France

*mélange de nos larmes*

Réveil      *Dans le royaume d'[une larme]*

SAF    SFA

F.A.S.

*le royaume des larmes*

Tu traverses

le royaume

Région      des larmes

Eclairage – Gris

*Approche de Pyché*      *20 oct. 18*      *frontière*    *confins*

Tes pas, fille de mon silence,

Saintement, lentement placés,      *tenture*

*aventure*    becquée de

~~Vers de lit~~ de ma vigilance    *Sur*      lèvres [. . .]

Procèdent, muets et glacés      Elle porte ses lèvres son

[que] démasque la lampe

Personne (pure) ombre divine

*ces pas retenus*      je vois tes dons

~~Toi qui jamais ne me surprit~~

doux venant à l'

Qu'ils sont ~~beaux dans mon seul~~ esprit    *Ces pas dans l'âme qui devine*

Ces pieds

~~Tes pas~~ que mon âme devine      Et qu'elle

Comme ~~les~~    qui s'écrit

~~Toi qui jamais~~ me ~~surprit~~ –

nuit favorable et tendre      Tout l'approche qui s'écrit

1 Dans le noir ~~même, de l'attente~~

[de] ~~l'âme~~ (éveillée)    Amour qui s'approche

Rien n'est plus pur que ce qui ment pas (attendre    Le secret    s'écrit

entendre)      qu'elle

2 C'est mon cœur qui compte ces pas.

3 Ma vie est de $|l+t|$' attendre      Et

|..|...|    ~~Elle vient~~

A moi-même je veux m'attendre

~~Je vois~~   Je sens que ta bouche à ma bouche      *Ces mouvements que je devine*

Ta bouche à la mienne porte      comme pâture de baiser

de

La nourriture d'un baiser –      drame      Tu portes à tes lèvres dorées tendues

~~et dans le drame~~

aliment      La pâture d'or d'un baiser

[forme] un      dressant le      La nourriture

fantôme des [repas]

σχεδιον      Mon devoir *art*

σχεδιον      désir

Car ma vie est de les attendre

C'est mon cœur qui compte ces pas

aux ténèbres je tends ma bouche    qu'en courtine   [Ce m'est] *Dans* ^lit^ état terrible et tendre

donne-moi ce que tu voudras      couche

en confiance      ~~En qui~~   ~~n'est pas~~

Entouré de ce qui n'est pas

Cah. *Ch* II, fo. 30v, transcription      Envir[onné]

drumming, which is the marvellous trace of an inner phenomenon which does not ordinarily appear outside the mental laboratory, is noted by Valéry above the quatrains, indicating the possible divisions of the octosyllable: '4.4 / 3.3.2 / 2.6'. The first line embodies the rhythm 2.6, the second 3.3.2, as the vertical lines placed by Valéry after 'Saintement' and after 'lentement' indicate. The strong evocation of line 1 – the silence engendering a form and its coming – will not vary; or rather, it will oscillate marginally, as Valéry hesitates between the near-synonyms 'fille' and 'enfant', playing with the phonetic values of these words, weighing the sexual ambiguity of the word 'enfant' and exploring the subtle shifts of rhythm.[12]

Poets who cultivate classical prosody often derive inspiration from the play of rhymes, from the homophonic possibilities of language. Thus 'silence' at first calls up 'indolence', with its suggestion of rêverie; the syntagm 'le lit de mon indolence' is in fact a close echo of La Fontaine. The borrowed 'indolence' is however quickly, if not immediately, replaced by the eminently Valéryan 'vigilance' with its suggestions of wakefulness, acuity and attention.[13] The original vision, which is soft and sensual, undergoes a decisive modification, introducing a new register which enters into an oscillatory dialogue with the first. The alternation of masculine and feminine rhymes is traditional and predictable. The footfalls are 'posés', a word soon replaced by 'placés', with its greater precision and more elevated register. The accompanying rhyme seems to emerge unfalteringly: the footsteps are said to be 'muets et glacés'.[14] They are imperceptible to the ear straining to catch sound of them in the darkness, but their silence is resounding in the amplified mental space of expectation ('Silencieux, ils retentissent'), just as the sounding sibilants insistently mark this first quatrain. The 'fille' / 'enfant' is given as 'personne': an admirable latinate word which suggests the collocation 'personne d'ombre' (an approaching figure 'masked in shadow'). These two words are soon dissociated, but in a way which continues to suggest their close proximity.

Both 'personne' and 'ombre' are part of the semantic 'halo' or 'aura' of the Greek word *phantasma* which seems to control the play of inventive variation at this point. Etymology too is a directing inspiration for Valéry, multiplying the strata of meaning latent in a word with centuries of philosophic resonance behind it: *phantasma* is an apparition, a vision, a dream, a fantasm or a phantom (the latter sense engendering the 'spectre' of a later stanza which the poet will not retain). French also hears in this word the diminished sense of 'fantaisie', and even 'fantasmagories'. All these senses are part of the suggestive resonance explored in the four stanzas of the poem. Most probably, there is a reminiscence of Plato: the *phantasmata theia, skiai ton onton*, the 'divine images', the 'shadows of real objects' evoked in the *Republic*, seem to have prompted Valéry's expression 'ombre divine', with its atmosphere of transparency and purity, which recalls the devotional tonality of the beginning of *Palme*. Here too, Valéry dares to write 'saintement', not a word common in his personal everyday lexicon! He will, indeed, attempt on several occasions to tone this word down, but without ever resolving to be rid of it. Perhaps we may detect here a sort of poetic instinct counterbalancing excessive intellectual lucidity...

The change of verb from steps which 'comptent' into steps which 'procèdent' – a further word of solemn, religious resonance – consolidates this atmosphere, while maintaining contact with the sense of a writing process which proceeds 'step by step' (the expression 'pas à pas' figures in the first manuscript draft)[15] and which engenders its own progress in conformity with measured steps or metric feet. The word 'pied' in its literal sense is considered too banal and inappropriate at the opening of the poem and calls for an accompanying adjective: hence 'ces pieds nus ... Baisant le sol', highlighting both the lover's vigil and the implicit sensuality of the birth of poetry. The manuscript shows that these fragments of the second stanza are written in close contiguity to the adjectives 'muets et glacés' of the first stanza alongside. The rhythmic beat of the steps in turn summons up the key line 'C'est mon cœur même qui les bat' (replaced by 'qui compte tes pas'), which is perhaps an acoustic transposition of a visual fantasm.[16] The reciprocity of heartbeat and footfalls is in any case central to the ambiguity of the poem: do the steps cause the heartbeat, or does the heartbeat engender the steps?

Implicitly, the 'love-scenario' that is sketched here is self-directed: I am the object of my own hearing, my own waiting. Within the same flow of imaginative anticipation, 'Le Cimetière marin' speaks of waiting upon 'l'écho de ma grandeur interne'. Both instances of Psyché's self-directed quest recall the funereal and anguished night of Mallarmé's *Igitur* and also the sequence from *Agathe* in which hearing is unbound 'à la limite du suspens de moi-même, — jusqu'au timbre de mon sang et à l'animation de ma propre durée' (*Œ*, II, p. 1391).[17] Amorous waiting thus connotes self-approach and

self-apprehension. This second sense introduces into these manuscript drafts, as into the finished poem, an exquisite ambiguity.
Psyché, certainly, may be a woman, a feminine Other, if we wish to
see her so: the straightforward 'sentimental' reading of the poem
remains entirely possible ...[18] Perhaps inevitably, the love-register in
the end predominates, casting its tonality of tenderness over the
whole piece. Indeed, the mythical figure of the love-struck soul,
inherited from the world of Greek mythology gives the first proposed
title to the murmured promise of the poem, as the dual inscription
'Psykhé' and 'PSYKE' on the manuscript fo. 30 clearly demonstrates. The use of pencil shows that this is added in a second phase
of writing, just as the words 'Approche de Psyché' in the following
version, explicitly linking the poem's action to the mythical scenario.

This second manuscript draft (*Ch* II, fo. 30v) casts some light on
the central ambiguity, in a surprising way. Here, in the margin of the
page, as a sort of *hors-texte*, outside the main corpus of writing, Valéry
sketches the setting for a drama of the mind played out within the
deepest regions of the self. The milieu or 'field' is a zone of 'ténèbres
éveillées' in which a cold, grey, indistinct light is associated with a
'royaume des larmes'. It marks the critical moment of awakening, a
bleak, dawn moment, when defences are at their weakest and the
soul lies naked and vulnerable, abandoned 'sur le pôle de ses
trésors'.[19] Valéry appears to touch here the very depths of his own
being, the ontological bedrock of his existence, just as, in *Agathe* he
writes: 'C'est mon fond que je touche' ('I touch the very ground of
my self') (*Œ*, II, p. 1389).

The manuscript page takes on a particular beauty as a result of
this intimate and confiding emotion. Its graphic appearance resembles a scattering of stars against a dark background, or else a series
of islands emerging from an inner sea. The marks of the writing in
lead pencil, with their diffusive and evanescent halo, add to the
emotional charge: here are confidential, fading glimpses, entrusted
to the manuscripts, attesting the value and fragility of these unique
documents which are the only witnesses to the most intimate
resonance of the poet's act of creation ... It is suggestive of this very
personal dimension that Valéry, who never dates his manuscripts,
should have felt the need to write on this one, in the upper centre of
the page: '20 oct. 18'.

What is particularly striking in the first two drafts is the manner in
which the core of the poem progressively destabilises and fragments

on the page as the writing tantalisingly 'comes and goes', eluding the grasp of the writer while holding out the promise of its gift. One of the fragments explicitly enacts the mystery of scriptural expectancy with the rhyme 'esprit / s'écrit' and the dynamic interplay between 'attendre — entendre — écrire'. The use of the pronominal verb accords an impersonality or a self-referentiality to the process from which the poet is somehow excluded: 'Comme l̶e̶s̶ [. . .] qui s'écrit', 'Toute l'approche qui s'écrit', 'Amour qui s'approche', 'Le secret [qu'elle] s'écrit' (fo. 30v). The expectant desire of the subject is here portrayed as a figure in secretive communication with herself, approaching but withholding, full of promise but as yet autonomous and impenetrable.

Two apparently distinct visions confront each other on the same page. 'Amour qui s'approche', we read, in a notation which evokes amorous Psyche in her traditional role. At the same time, the self-love of the reflexive Narcissus is clear in the expression: 'A moi-même je veux m'attendre'; this in turn is replaced, or rather, absorbed into 'Ma vie est de t'attendre', which re-establishes the amorous scenario, while perhaps simultaneously signalling an alterity within the self. A similar oscillation is pursued on fo. 29, which is a continuation of the previous sketch: the mythical Psyche is here drawn in the margins, like a shadowgraph figure with her lamp and dagger (the lamp already added in the margin of fo. 30v). The vision is eroticised, her naked shadow suggesting 'le venir même d'un frisson'. Yet while Valéry at one point cuts short this 'temptation' of his writing and goes on to draft a stanza beginning: 'O soyeuse, je te refuse', in the margin of the facing manuscript folio (which seems to offer a convention-free zone, a hypermargin, as it were), he asks the crucial, if apparently crude, question: 'Eros [corrected to read: 'Sexual'] / Psyché vient / pour quel amour' (fo. 28v).

But what is the nature of this psychosexual eros ? What, indeed, is sought in all forms of desire, whether reflexive or externally directed, amorous or creative, by the mind's perceptible tension towards an ecstatic limit or threshold? The enigma echoes throughout the manuscripts, is evident in the imagery of anticipated encounter and consumation. Folio 30v gives us the image of lips straining towards a kiss which embraces an essential – metaphysical – darkness ('Aux ténèbres je tends ma bouche') and of the nourishment there promised ('La nourriture d'un baiser', 'La pâture d'or d'un baiser'). For the poet of *La Jeune Parque* darkness is, consistently, the symbolic colour of the unknowable, while the 'golden' pasture refers us, in the same poem, to a paradise of being now lost ('Souvenir, ô bùcher dont le vent d'or m'affronte' (*JP*, l. 190). Further intertextual echoes are provided by 'Anne' ('La dormeuse ... / Tette dans la ténèbre un souffle amer de fleur'), and by 'Poésie' ('je touchais à la nuit pure'). Closest perhaps to 'Les Pas' is the aspiration of Narcisse to an infinite 'douceur d'être et de n'être pas', the ambiguous fusion of sexual drive and transgressive yearning for transcendence evidenced in the vain and tragic attempt, also nocturnal, to embrace his wondrous double ('Et bientôt je briserais, baiser, / Ce peu qui nous défend de l'extrême existence' (*FN*, ll. 295–6)).

If the poem in its final form subsumes all the multi-layered possibilities into a wiser, more reflective postponing of the moment of satisfaction, here in the early stages the manuscripts seem to demonstrate an almost headlong exploration of the different routes, accompanied by an almost immediate self-correction and change of direction. Scanning these virtualities of desire, with their activated circulation of dynamic images, Valéry seems intent on exhausting all the possibilities of a nexus of themes, which leads the writing into a zone of paroxystic torment, suggested in some instances by verbal association. In the first full version of the poem (*Ch* I, fo. 30), for example, the awakening is portrayed as a moment of terror: 'Surgi des drames [corrected to 'terreurs', 'fureurs'] de ma couche', which, in a subsequent version, becomes 'Spectre surgi jetant ses draps' (VRY ms, 19$^5$ in-4° v), the fantasm shifting through phantom to spectre. This tumultuous scenario, exploring the imaginative logic of Eros, is however effaced from the poem, like a bad dream. (It reappears in the manuscript drafts of *Air de Sémiramis:* the genetician knows that nothing is wasted in the economy of poetic creation.)

The containment of these images of violence and the inscription of desire within the realm of a purely ideal virtuality may be ascribed to various reasons. A psychoanalytical reading might see it in terms of a censuring response to the threat of the Other, and a resistance to the potential loss of self-control that is represented by giving way to the Other within the self. The forms of erasure, both scriptural and emotional, offer revealing insights, for the delicate restraint of 'l'écrit', the refined control of the finished work is betrayed by the passionate uncertainty of 'l'écriture'. A diachronic approach to the manuscripts might examine the way in which fragments are developed, incorporated into other more broad-reaching fragments or, simply, excised in favour of achieving a coherent pattern of form and content within the versified mould. Aesthetic criteria of coherence here interface with a taste that rejects the intrusion of too private or intimate an emotion in a work, while composition, as Valéry often states, is as much about elimination as addition. A thematic approach might point to underlying figures of the Valéryan psyche, in relation to the finished poem as well as to other texts and life-events that this writing both echoes and anticipates. From this perspective the poem offers a deferral of realisation in favour of prolonged anticipation. The desired figure emerging from shadows, both real object of love and projected idealisation of an 'other' within, can only retain its essential mystery insofar as it remains ungrasped. The 'ombre' will only remain 'divine' if its promise is confined within the realm of pure virtuality. The deepest philosophic sense of the poem will lie in a mistrust of the very excess of the heart's desiring.

Each of these approaches is complementary and would require detailed study of the succeeding manuscripts. But we have sought to focus upon the earliest stages in order to foreground the dynamic forces at work in the writing, the sense of intensity, excitement and anticipation so strong as to present a threat. And thus already the manuscripts point to the need for restraint: 'Ne hâte pas cet acte tendre', we read in a trace at first faint, but soon to be repeated with firmer echoes. The act of writing thus returns to a first inspiration already noted on a page begun under the auspices of 'Narcisse': 'Je n'aime pas celui qui se puisse saisir' (*Ch* II, fo. 30). It is telling that both 'Narcisse' and 'Les Pas' share the same manuscript, overlapping in their occupation of the page and seemingly one, were it not for the title 'PSYKE' pencilled into the middle: the latter poem, indeed, seems born of the failed embrace of Narcissus.[20] There is a circularity in Valéry's manuscript steps; leafing through the inscribed traces of one's memory is an act which often refreshes and renews the creative life of the mind, as clearly happened here following a re-reading of the notes on 'Narcisse'. The first fair-copy of the poem bears eloquent witness to such a reaction: 'Proche et pourtant non saisissable', the poet notes by way of marginal addition. The crucial exhortation is insistently re-echoed: 'Ne te hâte pas', 'Ne hâte pas', 'approche, mais n'arrive pas' (*Ch* I, fo. 30). Perhaps something of the essence of poetry lies in this delight in immobilising sensibility at its limit-point of expectancy.

214      FLORENCE DE LUSSY

The version of the poem given for publication presents a smooth, even surface, the multiplicity of potential developments having been contained or rather enfolded upon each other. A point of balance, an essential poise, is superbly struck, absence and presence held in perfect equilibrium. The desire which animates the substance of the poem never attains its object, yet the pulse of desire is thereby renewed indefinitely – the very epitome of the 'phoenix effect' Valéry attributed to poetry. The polished verbal surface, product of many simplifications, holds in its depths inexhaustible virtualities of meaning and symbolic interpretation that may be glimpsed in the manuscripts. But above all the marvel of ambiguous multivalency realised in the poem may stir the reader to experience something of the essence of creative desire, with its musical awakening, and its need for restraint, as we allow our own heartbeat to follow the rhythm of these softly measured footfalls.

Genetic analysis can reveal this buried treasure, so that the poem becomes resonant with the virtualities from which it has emerged. As Paul Klee wrote in 1920: 'L'oeuvre d'art est au premier chef genèse; on ne la saisit jamais simplement comme produit'.[21]

NOTES

1 James R. Lawler, *Lecture de Valéry: Une Étude de 'Charmes'* (Paris, PUF, 1963).
2 The voluminous collection of Valéry's manuscripts is kept mainly at the Bibliothèque nationale de France, Paris. Fortunately for researchers, he is among those authors who preserve all their manuscripts, including jottings and rough notes.
3 This concern goes back to Wilhelm Dilthey, father of the *Geistesgeschichte*. See A. Grésillon, *Eléments de critique génétique* (Paris, PUF, 1995), p. 182.
4 The first stages of the writing of 'Les Pas' occurred in concentrated and intense form within the month of October 1918. The first manuscript draft is in cahier *Charmes* II, 30r, followed by 30v and 29r. Towards the end of October a first draft of the poem comprising five stanzas but untitled is copied into cahier *Charmes* I, 30; two intermediary sketches follow (*Ch* III, 15 and ms John Polak Foundation, Utrecht); the second draft, from March 1919 is titled 'Nocturne' (VRY ms, $19^5$ in-$4^\circ$ Bibliothèque littéraire Jacques Doucet). But the poem is left incomplete until a preliminary published version appeared in *Feuillets d'art*, November 1921, and the definitive manuscript was not completed until February–March 1922 (Doucet ms 1128, fo. 50).

5 The first fair-copy of 'Les Pas' bears the marginal comment 'Quaerere figuras in Psyche' (*Ch* I, fo. 30), a clear reference to Valéry's own concerns as analyst around 1900.

6 This text was long known only through a bibliophile's edition published by Agathe Rouart-Valéry in 1956. It is now published among the annexes of the Pléiade *Œuvres* (*Œ*, II, pp. 1388–93).

7 *Agathe* ms fo. 94 v.

8 See my study *Charmes, d'après les manuscrits de Paul Valéry. Histoire d'une métamorphose* (Paris, Lettres Modernes, 1990) vol. I, ch. 4, pp. 279–326.

9 Valéry refers explicitly to 'Poésie' – at this stage entitled 'Nourrice' – in the margin of one ms folio of 'Les Pas' (VAL ms, $19^5$ in-$4°$).

10 Cf. also the very precise notation: 'J'écoute un cœur battre un secret poème.'

11 'With trembling and hesitant steps / She reaches the place where / Her husband rests his arms outstretched'.

12 Successive versions explore different resonances and rhythmic divisions (2.6 / 2.2.4 / 4.4) with the substitution of 'enfant', 'épris', 'les fils', 'enfants' for 'fille' and the omission of the comma after 'Tes pas'.

13 Valéry may also have in mind the Biblical *Song of Songs*, from which he elsewhere quotes in Latin: 'Dormio, cor meum vigilat' (*C*, VIII, p. 496). The nocturnal vigil of the Biblical poem is a feminine one, but is adapted to a masculine viewpoint in 'La Dormeuse' – '... ta forme veille, et mes yeux sont ouverts'.

14 A metonymic transfer: the floor underfoot is icy to the touch (one thinks of the floor-tiling of a French country cottage). But also felt as icy in the intensely imagined perspective of body-contact? A palette of possible adjectives unfolds: 'nus', 'frais', 'doux', 'beaux'.

15 Folio 29 specifically bears the notation 'une écriture de pieds nus' (marginal variant: 'un songe écrit par tes pieds nus'), cf. also 'comme une phrase qui s'écrit' (fo. 30).

16 Valéry also attempted an olfactive transposition, evoking roses and perfumes: this is one of the *impasses* of the writing process.

17 'at the limit of my suspended reach, — even to the very tone of my blood and the life-pulse of my inner time'.

18 Curiously, Valéry himself at a later period, reverted to this reading by referring to 'Les Pas' as a 'petit poème purement sentimental' into which intellectual meanings ('un symbole de l'«inspiration»!') had been projected (*C2*, p. 1054).

19 Cf. *Note et Digression, Œ*, I, p. 1230. This prose text written very shortly after 'Les Pas' (in March 1919) continues to recirculate its themes.

20 The page begins: 'Narcissus — c'est un dialogue entre lui et son image, roulant sur la passion de soi-même, qui est la seule — / Il n'y a jamais satisfaction de cette passion-là, qui met aux prises le stable et l'instable.'

21 Paul Klee, *Théorie de l'art moderne* (Paris, Denoël / Gonthier, 1971, 'Bibliothèque Médiations'), p. 38.

For further reading on the topic of this chapter, please see Bibliography, items 40, 45, 76, 77, 84, 85, 86, 87.

PART 3

*Body, Mind, World*

# CHAPTER 13

# An aesthetics of the subject: music and the visual arts

## Brian Stimpson

At the time of his death in 1945, the view of Valéry as a writer whose predominant interests lay in the arts was incontrovertible: of the twelve-volume *Œuvres Complètes* published by the *NRF*, the vast majority comprised the essays and lectures on literature, painting, architecture, dance and poetics. This work undoubtedly founded his reputation during his lifetime and in the decade or two thereafter; but former success has also played a part in its more recent eclipse, tending to identify his aesthetics as of a period and even of a certain taste, characterised, if not caricatured, by the preference for Wagner in music, and for Mallarmé and Racine within the literary canon.

His writings on art too have tended to consecrate the view of Valéry as a formalist, a classicist, of conservative and anti-modernist taste: a Valéry who appears to hark back to certain early Impressionists or else to the Italian masters; a Valéry attentive to earlier periods when aesthetic criteria were defined in terms of anatomy, perspective, composition, verisimilitude and when form and content were united in harmonious structure; who either ignores or takes issue with the major artistic movements in the twentieth century and who mocks the reductionism of modern subject-matter ('deux prunes sur une assiette *valent* une Descente de Croix' ('two plums on a plate *are worth* a Descent from the Cross') (*Œ*, II, p. 1206)); a Valéry in whom the absence of reference to Picasso or Braque, as to Stravinsky or Schoenberg, only echoes a resounding silence with regard to contemporary writers.[1]

However a number of factors indicate that these perceptions should be viewed with caution and suggest, indeed, a much more radical stance underlying Valéry's approach to aesthetics. There is no doubt that Valéry saw the writing of his commissioned pieces as a necessary diversion from the 'real work' of the *Cahiers*, but when read alongside them, common threads emerge and it becomes clear that the striking originality of his approach lies not so much in offering a critique of particular works of art, as a series of insights into the practice, the modes of operation and the particular artistic vision that motivates the works. Valéry does not set out to be either an art historian or a music critic; eschewing all interpretative judgement and subjective appreciation, he offers instead a reflexive praxis of creativity, an analysis of the mental forces underlying artistic production; hence also an insight into the very act of seeing and an exploration of the deeper meaning of music in the human psyche.

The issue has been further blurred by the professions of ignorance and the disavowal of any authority on the subjects that seemed to be a necessary preface to any statement of his on art or music, whether in private or in public. Writing to Pierre Louÿs in 1890 he confesses the pleasure to be found in listening to Beethoven 'même aux épouvantables ignares qui ne savent pas les notes comme P. Val.' ('even to extraordinary ignoramuses who can't read a note like P. Val.') (*LQ*, p. 36). The same reticence is to be found when introducing a concert given by Nadia Boulanger in the 1930s:

Rien de plus intimidant, de plus périlleux, de plus indiscret, en somme, que de s'insinuer entre la Musique et ses amants légitimes, pour faire entendre une voix qui ne chante point, qui vient énoncer sur un art auquel le discoureur est étranger des propos essentiellement impertinents. (N.a.f. 19072, fo. 186).[2]

We should read here, not the diplomatic precaution of a deficient but determined music critic, but rather a pointer to Valéry's authentic radicalism. Among his published works, music is the least well-represented, and the most obliquely treated, of the arts. 'Au Concert Lamoureux en 1893', 'Histoire d'Amphion' and 'Avant-propos à la connaissance de la déesse' are concerned with the relationship between music and literature; 'La Conquête de l'ubiquité' discusses the phenomenon of the more widespread availability of music beyond the concert hall, while the fascinating though less well-known 'Esquisse d'un éloge de la virtuosité' focuses upon the role of the virtuoso as the person giving reality to a work in the act of performance.

The essays on art are much more numerous, including pieces on da Vinci, Degas, Manet, Corot, Véronèse, Morisot, and references to Monet, Renoir, Delacroix, Raphaël, Michael-Angelo, Rembrandt, Daumier. Yet there are only a few brief passages on specific paintings: two short texts, written when he was 20 years old, 'Tête d'un page' by Cristoforo Allori and Zurburán's 'Sainte Alexandrine', references to 'Lola de Valence', 'Olympia' and 'Berthe Morisot au bouquet de violettes' in 'Triomphe de Manet', and to Raphaël's 'Vénus couchée' in 'Choses Tues'. Of course, Valéry's expertise in art was of a quite different nature from that in music and the amount of graphic work that he produced during his lifetime was quite considerable, including drawings, water-colours, paintings and engravings, as well as the large number of sketches and drawings that are part of the *Cahiers*. Expressing himself in the visual medium was not simply a recreation, but an inner necessity.[3] Nevertheless, the same hesitations occur in the writing: 'Mais comment parler peinture?' (*Œ*, II, p. 1179); 'je ne me risquerai dans la critique d'art dont je n'ai nulle expérience' (p. 1302).[4] An ironic portrait of the dangers of discoursing on art, significantly titled '*Jugements*', suggests the profound reason for this:

> Une Exposition de peinture. Un tableau et deux hommes devant lui.
> L'un, à demi penché sur la barre, parle, explique, avec éclat. L'autre est muet. On devine à sa courtoisie qu'il est absent. Il tend l'oreille et refuse l'esprit ...
> Une manière d'artiste, à deux pas derrière eux, me regarde; son œil m'adresse tout le mépris de ces explications sonores qui s'entendent d'assez loin. (pp. 476–7)[5]

The scene effectively dramatises the play of different gazes, establishing a hierarchy of vision as each in turn encompasses a wider perspective; the apparently objective becomes subjective, the absolute becomes relative, knowledge becomes more complex, multi-faceted and disinterested. But even the superior all-embracing gaze of the protagonist will ultimately collapse into a recognition of its own contingency. There can be no 'art criticism' in an authorised, traditional sense, only the confrontation of a number of subjective viewpoints.

Although 'on doit toujours s'excuser de parler peinture' ('one must always apologise for talking about painting'), Valéry's presentation of a collection of Corot prints articulates the importance of the dialogue between the observer and the work: 'Toute œuvre exige qu'on lui réponde, et une "littérature", écrite ou non, immédiate ou méditée, est indivisible de ce qui pousse l'homme à produire, et des productions qui sont les effets de ce bizarre instinct' (*Œ*, II, p. 1307).[6] Here we glimpse the paradox founding Valéry's singular approach:

the act of seeing and listening is, for Valéry, inseparable from that of producing, and the medium through which this 'bizarre instinct' most naturally finds its expression for him is in the act of writing; but the suspicion of language is such and the relationship between words and things, between mental constructs and external reality, so necessarily and fundamentally problematic, that a different kind of expression is sought, a form of discourse that permits him to re-enact the creative process of the artist without attempting to elaborate a discourse that can be substituted for it. The work of art demands a response, seeks to enter into a dialogue, but one which will prompt the inner dialogue of self with self, one which places the observer as closely as possible in the position of mimicking the creative act.

From the earliest moments of Valéry's project to explore the potential and functioning of the human mind, the arts are a model, a lodestone, for the deepest forms of self-discovery; the project to rationalise the sensibility and to mathematise the mind and all its productions encounters in the artistic domain forms of experience that are 'non-reducible' and that represent more effectively than any philosophy or metaphysics, the ideal goal he is seeking. Abstract mental models generate a new aesthetics; but only when tested against artistic production, and reconverted into his self-language. This is an aesthetics of the subject, rather than of the artistic object, rooted in the subject's modes of perceiving itself in relation to the image or musical performance; its starting point is the effect rather than the cause; its reality lies not in the mimetic quality of the representation nor in the illusory reality of the work, but in the enunciative present, in the moment of performance or the phenom-enology of perception.

A singular example of the way in which music and art are inter-connected with the attempt to realise a pure vision of mental operations may be found in the notes preceding the *Cahiers* proper, made on the occasion of his visit to London in June and July 1894. The 'Pré-Cahier' and the unpublished 'Carnet 1894' are full of drawings, sketches, annotations, graphic use of the space of the page: Valéry seems to be putting into practice the lessons drawn from the notebooks of da Vinci he had been studying before leaving France. Thus, we find terms such as 'Modèle mécanique d'un cerveau, d'un individu (*for* Lionardo)', 'énergie', 'analogie', 'le corps et la sensation';[7] notes on dynamics are accompanied by sketches charting the movements of people in the City of London as though they were currents in a fluid; art, music and electro-magnetism are conjured up in relation to da Vinci's studies of the vortex; a reference to William Thomson (subsequently Lord Kelvin) adds a scientific dimension; while music seems to encompass all: 'musique en lignes de force / induction du centre / Bach ... Bach / travail imaginaire sur ces ornements / rapidités, intrications / étudier suivant la commune mesure / Oui, il n'y a rien qui ne soit un langage pour l'esprit – il n'est que langage et tout le peint' (fo. 23v); 'petit tourbillon d'ouïr' (fo. 24).[8]

Whereas the published writing on music is not extensive, the *Cahiers* reveal a surprising range of references both to music in general and to specific features such as melody, rhythm and harmony which bear witness to a sustained reflection on the subject. Music is an aspect of his 'self-system' that Valéry cannot overlook and which – because of its immediacy, its non-verbal character, its relation to temporal duration and its unique capacity to combine formal compositional structure, emotional impact and an absence of referential specificity – is both a language of the emotions and a language of the mind. Music is the means of understanding the formal, its fundamental non-specificity infusing it with an 'âme abstraite' ('abstract soul') (N.a.f. 19121, fo. 86). It is both abstraction (*C*, XIV, p. 268) and sensation (*C*, XXI, p. 456).

At times, it seems to have reduced him to near-despair. The sense that music, and Wagner in particular, had already achieved what he was seeking is invoked among the reasons for his turning away from poetry in 1892: 'Rien ne m'a plus désespéré que la musique de Wagner. (Et je suis loin d'être le seul)' (*C2*, p. 979; cf. *C*, XV, p. 505).[9] The view persists, to such an extent that even the achievement of *La Jeune Parque* is seen as a kind of compensatory acrobatics, while music, he says, might have provided the ideal means of expressing the 'system' (*C*, XVI, p. 18).

Valéry shared the Symbolist desire to 'reprendre à la Musique [son] bien' ('to retrieve from Music what was rightly its own') (*Œ*, I, p. 1272); but what was an act of imitation for some, an act of self-defence for others, became for him a more radical reappropriation, a musical poetics framed within – and against – the terms of language. In this kind of writing the music is not so much an external model, nor a technical device applied to poetry, nor even an overt reference point within the text: the approach is characterised by the kind of writing where the musical process is so fundamental, has been so internalised, that the very struggle for expression itself articulates the foundations of music in human consciousness.[10] Indeed, Valéry repeatedly affirms the central and defining rôle of music: 'Concevoir en poète, c'est concevoir musicalement' (C, XI, p. 618); 'Le problème d'*écrire* doit être assimilé à celui de *mettre en musique* — (écrire pour la voix)' (C, IX, p. 190).[11]

The *Cahiers* reveal a profound reflection on music, envisaged as opening up forms of experience that cannot be readily expressed within language in such a pure and intense manner – the domain of dream, emotion, love, spirituality but also that of form, space, geometry, construction, and the harmonic marriage of the two. There are many notes which are concerned with the effects that music generates, both personal and generalised, as well as the mechanisms by which they occur. The starting point is without doubt Valéry's own sensitivity to music which provokes extremes of response, so that it is described in a gamut of expressions from 'divine', 'mystical' and 'pure' to 'intoxicating', 'irritating' and 'boring', even an 'art des spasmes ... des mensonges ... [qui] n'est pas très éloigné de l'insupportable toute-puissance du doigt mouillé sur la vitre' (C2, pp. 936–7).[12] His response is determined both by a sense of rivalry and self-protection (p. 938). The supreme master is, again, Wagner who occupied the strategic point of being (p. 956) and organised the means of acting at will upon the general nervous system (p. 930). At times the effect is expressed in scientific metaphors (neurobiological, electrical, chemical ... ); but above all Valéry admires music's ability to operate in the domain of 'effects without cause':

> [La musique] compose un système comme celui de tes sentiments que tu ne t'expliques pas à toi-même. Une terreur sans monstre, des effets sans machine, des machines sans masse, des êtres sans corps, des lumières sans formes ...
> ... Tout volonté sans but; — tout souvenir sans souvenirs; tout lucidité sans idées; — tout mouvement sans mobile; — tout effet sans cause; — tout pressentiment sans acte; — tout vivant sans corps; tout figures sans matière; — tout présence sans personne; tout tons et inflexions et propos sans parole, ...
> jusqu'au besoin de parler final. (N.a.f. 19121, fo. 91)[13]

He acknowledges too the capacity of music to construct its own pure world of sound, the musician being able to create shape and space, structure and development through composition, orchestration and modulation in a medium devoid of specific reference or meaning; Bach, Mozart and Ravel are cited as examples of 'pure musicians' whom he distinguishes from the atmospheric, and almost programmatic, Wagner, Beethoven or Berlioz. If the latter are experienced as a threat, requiring temporary submission of the emotions which nevertheless leaves the intellect intact, the former are a greater challenge, for their ability to simulate flux of the mind – 'toutes les feintes et les démarches réelles du penser, retours, symétries, tendances vers — durées nulles, absences, spontanéité, attentes, surprises, niaiserie, éclairs' (*C2*, p. 929)[14] – occupies the very space of the intellect itself and imposes itself in the mind of the listener.

The search for an analogical method leads him to pursue a far-reaching analysis of some of the principal features such as melody, harmony, rhythm, sound, form, song, recitative, modulation, continuity. What is melody and how are we able to recognise it? How does it relate to memory? How is it that our expectation of what will come next is progressively determined as one note follows another? How does this succession of points come to form a single unit which functions not as a series but as a whole? And how can this function which operates in a particular way in the medium of pure sound be realised within the different context of verbal language? In such a manner we see that melody for Valéry can be created in poetry, not by the linear succession of sounds, but as units of meaning, as themes, as images, as lines or pairs of lines, which set off counter-melodies, parallels, reversals that build up to give shape and movement to the piece. Analysis of the functioning of harmonics leads him to see a parallel between the successive layers of harmonic overtones that resonate in a note and that define its timbre and the different resonances and connotations that may be added to the single denotative meaning of words. Thus melody and harmonics can function as linear and vertical axes in a piece of writing, both constructing the music of meaning.

Finally, and perhaps most importantly, music articulates a writing of desire, rejoining the point of inner song that declares itself as source of creative energy. In this deeper sense there is, perhaps, no significant difference between the medium of sounds in music and that of words in language; however different their constraints, their logic and their possibilities, both may be seen as exteriorisations of the same inner process. At its furthest point, the purest, most

226 BRIAN STIMPSON

absolute form of music is the inner music of the self. Music in this sense is a form of experience deep within the pysche; it expresses the whole being as a living organism with thoughts, feelings and physiological reactions, with responses, energies and aspirations to suspend or transcend time itself. It is a domain where the self perceives itself as subject, emerging from silence, creating interludes which allay the silence yet which seem as they are produced to be strange, like the voice of an 'other'.

For Valéry the voice of poetry is identified with the attainment of song born out of the pure inner silence: 'La musique qui est en moi, / La musique qui est dans le silence, en puissance / qu'elle vienne et m'étonne' (C2, p. 1267).[15] At the core of the self, in the depths of being, Valéry encounters a highly charged 'obscurité-silence' ('obscurity-silence') (C, XXII, p. 699), a point of inner turmoil, of soundless cry, the source of tears from which the voice emerges. At once singular and universal, private and generalised, this music of the inner life gives form and expression to everything which escapes everyday language. It is the language of the unsayable, the unnameable, giving access to the obscure and insuperable power of the dream as well as the modulations and transformations of the mind. From the tensions and desire of this inner music emerges, like Orpheus from the underworld, an impersonal voice, the subject both singular and universal: 'La plus belle poésie a la voix d'une femme idéale, Mlle Ame ... la voix intérieure ne supporte que les paroles dont le sens est secrètement d'accord avec l'être *vrai*; dont la musique est le graphique même des mouvements et arrêts de cet être' (C, VI, p. 170).[16]

Study of the manuscripts of the poems reveal a practice of writing that is in the fullest sense akin to musical composition – that proffers itself to an inner and an outer ear, that has its source in the cries, murmurs and exclamations of inner speech and seeks to harness language to the purpose of articulating the modulations of the formal and emotional shapes of the music of being: 'J'écoute quelqu'un qui parle ... Et quand il parle bien, — j'écris' (C, X, p. 308); 'que mon ouïe intime écoute avec ravissement ma voix intime' (C, XXIV, p. 283).[17] The writer wants to make his own music, not by borrowing models but by internalising and applying the compositional process both as writing and as an unfolding structure. The poet must write like a composer at the piano, as though the instrument were himself:

Se considérer, s'assembler, s'accorder, s'attaquer, s'attendre et s'écouter comme un instrument; — comme résonateur d'un désir, comme présence, imminence de choses désirables (C, VI, p. 824).[18]

It can thus be appreciated that the music of greatest import for Valéry is neither the art of combining sounds, nor the verbal music of poetry, but rather a music of the innermost subjectivity which precedes all sound, verbal and musical.

While the ear, and particularly the inner ear, remains attentive to a cadence of inner song, the eye and the inner eye of the mind play an equally crucial role in relation to painterly production. For recognition of the visual in human experience leads not to a contemplation of reality, an acceptance of the 'natural', nor even to a study of the culture and traditions of art, but rather to consideration of the productive act of the artist, to issues of colour and composition and above all to the process of looking itself. M. Teste's 'certain way of looking at things' was his most distinct and irreducible feature, and the artist's gaze must be the starting point of any analysis of art. Certainly the example of Berthe Morisot suggests that the conditions of painting lie in the vision and eyes of the painter (Œ, II, p. 1303).

It is understandable, given the circumstances of his artistic environment, that Valéry should acknowledge the importance of light and colour, but what emerges from both the published writings and the *Cahiers* is an attachment to a certain approach towards art rather than any particular style – an approach identified as much in the Impressionists as in his formative study of Leonardo da Vinci, indeed a 'lesson' learnt from art that resonates throughout the entire enterprise: 'Une œuvre d'art devrait toujours nous apprendre que nous n'avions pas vu ce que nous voyons' (Œ, I, p. 1165).[19]

The supreme example of multiple viewpoints was da Vinci who was able to combine the analytical gazes of the painter, the scientist and the thinker and move without contradiction between each of them. As Valéry writes in his preface to the notebooks of Leonardo da Vinci:

Il y eut une fois quelqu'un qui pouvait regarder le même spectacle ou le même objet, tantôt comme l'eût regardé un peintre, et tantôt en naturaliste; tantôt comme un physicien, et d'autres fois comme un poète; et aucun de ces regards n'était superficiel.[20]

All too often, argues Valéry, perception is not an act of looking but a projection of prior meaning onto an object, an attachment of a previously defined 'signified' onto the visual 'signifier'. Memory, habit, utilitarian purpose or our individual perspective as scientist, engineer, naturalist, poet etc., each directed through language, will filter our vision; mental constructions will obscure the image and predispose us to see it in a particular way. Non-artistic vision hastens to transform what is seen into *signs*, to attach meanings and names; indeed, just as the prose paraphrase destroys the poem, just as the creative flow of mental activity is halted by 'understanding', so the naming of the image effaces the object. The artist teaches us to see things differently, to 'revoi[r] les choses déjà vues avec des yeux nouveaux' ('to renew our vision of what we have already seen') (*C*, III, p. 67). Rather than reading the image in terms of past connections or future possibilities, the artist's vision eliminates time-linked associations, allows perception to give way to visual sensation, to 'l'impression-sans-signification' ('the impression-without-meaning') (*C*, XIII, p. 350) and sees only the coloured forms of the present: 'les taches de l'instant pur ... la présence chromatique' ('the marks of the pure moment ... chromatic presence') (*Œ*, II, p. 1303). 'L'œil pur efface les noms qui sont sur les choses' ('The pure eye effaces the names attached to things') (*C*, XIX, p. 302; cf. *Œ*, II, p. 1240). The nature and quality of the gaze remains the only constant and is, for Valéry, his own most distinctive feature.

This of course raises questions about the resemblance of the painting to reality, a matter over which Valéry takes issue with Pascal, who is taken as construing painting as the laborious attempt to create visual likenessess. A view such as this overlooks the aesthetic pleasure of the visual, which is neither a substitute for, nor a simulacrum of reality, but a composition of elements which constitute a different set of relationships between the observing subject, the visual image and what is represented – a shifting and dynamic interaction between mind, eye and object.

If Valéry mocks the 'distortions' of cubism and the non-representativity of abstractionism – 'L'univers du peintre devient exprimable en polyèdres et en corps ronds. Il n'est de seins, de cuisses, de joues, de chevaux, ni de vaches que l'on ne puisse bâtir de ces durs éléments. Il en résulte des nus terribles' (*Œ*, II, p. 1222)[21] – nevertheless the purpose of painting is neither to slavishly copy reality nor to endlessly copy itself by reproducing the styles of the past. The artistic vision is unique and consists in constituting its own autonomous world as a response to what is observed and in dialogue with it:

mimesis is creative, the transposition of object into image is based upon close and detailed observation of its inner form. The act of drawing or painting something re-plays its genesis and growth, re-creates it as living form: 'Lionardo ... l'ange de la morphologie ... perçoit en dessinant les forces formatives' (C2, p. 949).[22]

The point is well-made in discussion of Corot's relationship to the natural world. Nature was for him neither a dictionary of images as for Delacroix, nor a scene to be copied with realistic accuracy, it was, on several counts, a model which enabled him to 'se peindre en la peignant' ('portray himself as he painted [nature]'): it requires extreme attention to the representation of light, so that beneath the evanescent forms of mist-draped scenes the definite but shrouded forms may be suggested, the structure implicit beneath the veil 'non absente, mais différée' ('not absent, but deferred') (*Œ*, II, p. 1312); it requires acute visual attention (Valéry cites Corot's close observation of the land); and it is an example of the poetic value achieved by certain arrangements of visual forms. Corot is one of those artists who are less concerned with reproducing the model than with producing in the observer the impression it creates, combining optical truth and the real presence of feeling, adding or subtracting from what is seen; sometimes they enrich the scene and sometimes '[ils] poussent leur désir jusqu'à l'abstraction, et n'épargnent même les formes' (p. 1312).[23] There is in fact a necessary and dynamic tension between the mental image, the act of seeing and the object of the gaze:

cet homme a vécu dans la vue des choses de nature comme vit un méditatif dans sa pensée. L'observation de l'artiste peut atteindre une profondeur presque mystique. Les objets éclairés perdent leurs noms: ombres et clartés forment des systèmes et des problèmes tout particuliers, qui ne relèvent d'aucune science, qui ne se rapportent à aucune pratique, mais qui reçoivent toute leur existence et leur valeur de certains accords singuliers entre l'âme, l'œil et la main de quelqu'un, né pour les surprendre en soi-même et se les produire (pp. 1318–9).[24]

Painting thus seeks to achieve a reciprocal equilibrium between the visual likeness of something, the aesthetic pleasure of looking and the resonances generated in the mind. Generally, either self and gaze merge in contemplation of the object, as experienced by Valéry on London Bridge: 'tout à coup saisi d'absence ... *je suis ce que je suis, je suis ce que je vois*' ('suddenly gripped by absence ... *I am what I am, I am what I see*') (p. 514); or else the object loses its identity and the self is defined by its gaze (*C1*, p. 97). The art which Valéry prizes above all is that which is able to create a permanent dynamic harmony between all three elements, each influencing the other and each feature of the painting in resonance with each other. He identifies this harmonic unity in which all elements radiate upon each other as the extreme poetry of vision, creating a state of tension and hesitation, as in the work of Monet: 'ce point où la rose et le rose, la forme et la couleur sont en échanges dans la perception ... où ce ne sont pas les *objets*, c'est-à-dire les idées, qui enivrent, transportent, ravissent mais / mystique des couleurs' (*C2*, p. 948).[25]

Vision is not purely a matter of physiological perception: the gaze is both receptive and projective, it is filtered through the intelligence, such that the canvas is the meeting place of the inner gaze of the artist and the object of vision, the act of painting an externalisation of the mental image. Two artists in particular achieve this supremely for Valéry: da Vinci[26] and Degas. Art is an 'art savant', a painting the result of a series of mental operations, an 'action de l'esprit' (*Œ*, II, pp. 1163; 1196). Drawing especially depends upon the close interaction of eye and intellect. And it is a two-way process, for the gaze and the mind act in reciprocity, as Berthe Morisot demonstrates (p. 1304); the artist gazes both outwards and inwards, in dialogue with the objects that observe him: 'Les choses nous regardent. Le monde visible est un excitant perpétuel: tout réveille ou nourrit l'instinct de s'approprier la figure ou le modelé de la chose *que construit le regard*' (p. 1212).[27] While Valéry retains his admiration for the expansive composition of scenes in Italian classical painting, there is too a recognition of the value of simplicity and of the greater challenge that, in many respects, it offers; his insights into the originality of Degas's drawings are profound, and confirm certain of his own preoccupations:[28] the preference for black and white, the mastery of one's means that is an essential prerequisite for any freedom and improvisation, the physical freedom of the hand, the close interaction between mechanical features of draughtsmanship and mental activity: drawing for Degas is a way of looking at form, and leads both to the possession of the object and the possession of the self. The source of art is thus, ultimately, the inward gaze of the subject contemplating the space of selfhood. Painting is an act of self-discovery which shifts the gaze between the object in the world, the forms on the canvas, the response of the sensibility and the inner image in the mind – which becomes, as it were, the image *of* the mind: 'Beau. S'asseoir, non devant *la chose* mais devant soi ... *Infini sous forme finie*' (*C*2, p. 982).[29]

Just as music creates form and shape from sounds that are themselves in a constant state of flux and evolution, so the gaze articulates a process of decomposition and recomposition, operating within a dialectic of the continuous and the discontinuous, the successive and the formed, the incomplete and the fixed. Degas's exploration of 'l'informe' is specifically related to Valéry's reflections on da Vinci: the haphazard forms that are composed into a work are not without substance or contour, but retain their unexpected, irreducible, even unidentifiable shapes as the boundaries of the image are transgressed, perspectives of foreground and background merged, viewpoints multiplied, identity challenged, the whole resonant with possibility (*C*2, p. 1194). Music in its purest form is likewise 'le plus puissant engin ... à exciter le possible pur' ('the most powerful vehicle ... for arousing pure possibility') (p. 974), Bach's music in particular is 'intrinsèque', his *Suite in D Major* suggesting 'l'exploitation totale formelle fermée d'un Possible tout commensurable' (p. 968).[30]

Clearly, there are differences in what music and art represent for Valéry. The former is more of a rival, a threat to the intellect or a supreme model that is all too effective; the latter is welcomed as a complementary adjunct, images and words seeming each to compensate for the inadequacies of the other. But beyond these differences, there is perhaps a common point of visual and aural perception which is 'inner' rather than 'outer', active rather than passive, projective rather than receptive and intimately associated with the creative act. While it is true that one encounters a certain circular play of metaphor between art, music and poetry, each serving to characterise ideal features of the other, when suggesting that all arts aspire to capture 'la Poésie', Valéry defines this as 'un état d'attente — Résonance — chantant' ('a song-like state of expectation — Resonance') (p. 944), a highly-charged, self-replicating state in which the work touches the energy system of the observer and the energy is directed to the work. The gaze of the artist and the inner ear of the musician are closely related, each creating a moving geometry in space that gives shape to their own inner sensitivities.

Two principal features are at the heart of Valéry's aesthetics: firstly an affirmation of 'le possible pur' ('pure possibility'), a recognition of 'la puissance multiple de tout objet réel' ('the multiple potential of all real objects') (Œ, II, p. 475); secondly, a poïetics of action shared by creator, performer, listener, observer, which determines the creative process and in turn predominates its reception: 'Je conçois les arts en tant qu'actes. *Chacun des arts conserve une partie des actes générateurs.* ... Une œuvre est résidu d'un travail' (C2, p. 970, cf. p. 957).[31] Unlike the natural entropy of the physical world where dynamic processes tend towards stasis, the world of artistic sensibility is one which mobilises the instability that lies within stability, as stimulus and satisfaction, desire and repetition are eternally renewed in the 'infini esthétique': 'Le parfait impose l'inachèvement ... Il n'y a donc que l'acte et cet acte n'est rien' (p. 975).[32]

Valéry suggests here an aesthetics of the *incomplete*, based on the act, the possible and the capacity for renewal. The work of art is not fixed in a marmoreal perfection of classical, formal purity, at least not in any traditional sense: the terms themselves are radically redefined, such that its purity is pure possibility and absence of reductive specificity, its classicism lies in the studiously composed relation of all elements to each other, its perfection lies in the capacity to create a self-referential completeness which opens onto a world of autonomous otherness in which 'le formel = le sensible pur' ('the formal = the purely sensory'); its rock-like quality the mark of the crystalline irreducibility which inscribes the multiple resonances of the self – 'le possible du réel. Et c'est tout MOI' ('the possibilities of what is real. And that is entirely ME') (C1, p. 201).

Valéry thus proposes an aesthetics of the subject which recognises the multiplicity and singularity of perspectives, which locates the creative event within the inner perception of the subject rather than in the work itself, and which affirms a reciprocity in the act of looking and listening that marks a truly subjective phenomenology. Despite the cultural relativism of some of Valéry's specific comments on the arts, such an approach in fact represents a fundamental challenge to orthodoxy, as so many major artistic innovators of the twentieth century have subsequently demonstrated in their actual practice.[33]

NOTES

1 Stravinsky nevertheless says that in the 1920s and 30s he saw Valéry so regularly they might be thought to have formed a 'circle'. In 1939,

when Stravinsky was staying at Le Mesnil with Nadia Boulanger, he read excerpts of his *Poetics of Music* to Valéry, who notes the close similarities to his own 'Cours de Poétique' (see B. Stimpson, *Paul Valéry and Music*, pp. 33, 39).

2  'Nothing could be more intimidating, dangerous or, indeed, indiscreet, than to insinuate oneself between Music and its legitimate admirers, speaking to you in an unmelodious voice and making basically impertinent remarks about an art which is foreign to the speaker.'

3  See François Valéry, 'Paul Valéry, dessinateur, graveur et peintre' in *Paul Valéry et les arts* (Arles, Actes du Sud, 1995), pp. 25–36 and Robert Pickering, *Paul Valéry, la page, l'écriture* (Clermont-Ferrand: Publications de la Faculté des Lettres et Sciences Humaines, 1996), pp. 227–80.

4  'But how can one talk about painting?'; 'I won't venture into art criticism of which I have no experience'.

5  'An art exhibition. A painting and two men standing in front of it. / One, half leaning over the rail, is animatedly talking, explaining. The other is silent. You can tell from his courteousness that he is thinking of something else. He lends his ear and refuses his mind ... / An artistic type, two steps behind them, looks towards me; his expression conveys his total scorn for these ringing explanations which can be heard from afar.'

6  'Every work demands a response, and any "literature", whether written or not, spontaneous or studied, is inseparable from the strange instinct to produce and the productions which result from it'.

7  'Mechanical model of a brain, an individual (for Lionardo)', 'energy', 'analogy', 'body and sensation'.

8  'music as force lines / induction from the centre / Bach ... Bach / ornaments worked in the imagination / fast, intricate passages / to study according to the common measure / Indeed, everything is a language for the mind – it is nothing but language and everything illustrates it; little vortex of hearing'.

9  'Nothing caused me as much despair as Wagner's music (and I am far from being alone)'.

10  See E. Ansermet, *Les Fondements de la musique dans la conscience humaine* (Neuchâtel, La Baconnière, 1961) and Anthony Storr, *Music and mind* (London, Harper Collins, 1992).

11  'To think poetically is to think musically'; 'The problem of *writing* must be assimilated to that of *setting to music* — (writing for the voice)'.

12  'art of spasms ... of lies ... which is not very different from the unbearable omnipotence of a wet finger on glass'.

13  'Music composes a system like that of the feelings you can't explain to yourself. Terror without a monster, effects without a mechanism, machinery without mass, beings without body, lights without shapes ...
    ... It is all will without a goal — all memory without memories; lucidity without ideas; — movement without motive; — effect without

cause; — foreboding without action; — living being without body; — figure without substance; — presence without person; – tones, inflexions and statements without speech . . .
  even to the ultimate need to speak.'

14 'all the ducking and weaving and forward progress of thought, reversions, symmetrical movements, predilections — absence of time, emptiness, spontaneity, expectations, surprises, idiocies, flashes of understanding'.

15 'The music which is within me, the music which is latent, in silence, may it come and surprise me'.

16 'The most beautiful poetry has the voice of an ideal woman, Mlle Soul . . . the inner voice will only bear those words whose meaning secretly accords with the *true* being; whose music traces the curve of the movements and suspensions of this being'.

17 'I listen to someone who speaks — And when he speaks well — I write'; 'let my inner ear listen with delight to my inner voice'.

18 'Look at yourself, gather yourself, tune, attack, await yourself, listen to yourself as an instrument; — as the resonator of a desire, as presence, imminence of desirable things'.

19 'A work of art should always teach us that we have not seen what we see'.

20 'Préface aux 'Carnets' de Léonard de Vinci' (1942), in *Vues* (Paris, La Table Ronde, 1948), p. 217; 'There was once a man who could view the same sight or the same object, sometimes in the way that a painter would, sometimes as a naturalist; sometimes as a physicist, and at others as a poet; and none of those gazes was superficial.'

21 'The painter's universe can be expressed in polyhedrons and rounded forms. There are no breasts, no thighs, no cheeks, no horses or cows that cannot be constructed from these severe elements. It produces some terrible nudes'.

22 'Lionardo . . . the angel of morphology . . . perceives as he draws the forces of formation'.

23 'push their desire into abstraction, not even sparing the forms'. Even more explicitly, Valéry says in the 'Petit Discours aux Peintres Graveurs' that the artist is *against* Nature, for the power of abstraction and composition that make the work belong to the artist (*Œ*, II, p. 1300).

24 'this man has lived in the sight of natural things as one who meditates lives within his thought. The artist's observation can attain an almost mystical depth. The objects illuminated in his gaze lose their names: areas of shadow and light form quite specific systems and problems, which are not related to any knowledge or any practice, but draw their existence and their value from certain particular harmonies between the soul, the eye and the hand of someone born to surprise them in himself and produce them for himself.'

25 'the point where rose and rose-coloured, form and hue, become

transposed in one's perception ... where it is no longer the *objects*, i.e. the ideas, which intoxicate, transport, delight but / mysticism of colours'.

26  Da Vinci was able to 'développer ses curiosités illimitées, pour revenir tout à coup de son temps universel de méditation et d'analytique rêveries, à la Peinture bien-aimée' (*Œ*, II, p. 1347). To this extent, the vision of the artist and the scientist do not differ, since both see 'par les yeux de l'esprit' (*Œ*, I, p. 1195): the imaginative logic of da Vinci's meditative, analytical gaze is associated for Valéry with Faraday's mental image of the lines of force created by electro-magnetism.

27  'Things observe us. The visible world is a perpetual stimulus: everything wakens or feeds the instinct to appropriate for oneself the figure or outline of the thing *which is constructed by the gaze*'.

28  See R. Kendall, *Degas: Beyond Impressionism* (London, National Gallery Publications, 1996).

29  'Beauty. Sit down, not before the *thing* but before oneself ... *Infinite in finite form*'.

30  'the complete formal closed exploitation of an entirely commensurable Possible'.

31  'I think of the arts as acts. *Each art retains something of the acts of its creation* ... A work of art is what is left over from creative labour'.

32  'aesthetic infinite': 'Perfectness imposes incompletion ... There is only the act and that is nothing'.

33  For further reading on the topic of this chapter, please see Bibliography, items 25, 42, 75, 101, 107, 123, 124, 127, 133, 135, 136.

# CHAPTER 14

# Politics, history and the modern world

*Nicole Celeyrette-Pietri*

Although a key aspect of his thinking, Valéry's political writings have been studied less than the rest of his work. No doubt this is partly because their more public appearance came relatively late in his career, when he was called on to respond to particular events. Valéry's project was in essence philosophic and psychological; yet it could not but encounter the real world. The little-known notes in the *Cahiers* on the topic, which Valéry grouped under the heading H[istoire] P[olitique],[1] taken together with the writings published between the wars as *Essais quasi politiques* and *Regards sur le monde actuel*, may however be seen to tackle important questions and to establish his reputation as a major political thinker.

These studies, it is true, are not always fully developed and certainly no single overall political doctrine emerges. The writings are fragmentary, conditioned by circumstance and date from different periods; yet they fully reflect both the upheavals of half a century and Valéry's own characteristic approach. While his starting point may be a particular situation, Valéry deliberately seeks a generalising and more theoretical view of politics which is often linked to abstract, and, especially, scientific models.[2] His intention is less to predict the future of nations, than to reflect upon issues such as equality, the organisation of power, economic warfare, the growth of industrialisation, the development of communications, the crisis of values, nationalism, and so on.

Let us from the outset clarify a question which still has a contentious edge in France. Our own century, having been sorely afflicted by racism, often judges the end of the nineteenth in relation to the Dreyfus Affair. A young employee at the Ministry of War at the time, Valéry, like his friend Degas, did not support Dreyfus. A number of factors came into play: his natural loathing of petitions and 'doing the right thing', his identification with the honour of the service, as well as his probable under-estimation of the symbolic importance of the Affair. All these things led to a position that was no doubt regrettable, but for which he was unjustly condemned when he subsequently became a celebrated writer and major thinker. Valéry was not a racist. In 1940 he wrote of 'la grande commodité du bouc émissaire' ('the great convenience of the scapegoat'):

On dit qu'il y a une question des Juifs. On le dit, on le redit. ... Toute minorité dont on soupçonne la Puissance excite ou permet d'exciter la majorité, dans un pays où l'opinion est d'autant plus facile à exciter qu'elle se croit virtuellement plus forte. Mais l'opinion se fait. L'argent et le pouvoir d'une part s'y emploient; les instinct s'y prêtent. Le principe est envie (*C*, XXIII, p. 570).[3]

Under the Occupation he delivered a funeral oration for Bergson who had worn the yellow star. He denounces the myth of 'racial purity' and argues that, if such a thing exists, it can only lead to uniformity, passivity and submissiveness on a grand scale, and thence to '[la] conséquence fatale, la crédulité qui est, à mon avis, le fondement nécessaire des calculs et des entreprises les plus détestables'.[4] On the other hand, he saw the mixing of races as necessary for progress and a guarantee of development and cultural enrichment:

En fait d'excitation à l'intelligence, l'impureté est plus féconde que la pureté, le mélange et la dissemblance créent de la richesse. On constate que les races pures sont intellectuellement inférieures, ou du moins, incomplètes.[5]

The history of the European people and in particular the French, who are descended from an extremely diverse mixture of races, corroborates this notion to which he often returns and which he projects into the future. This is perhaps one of the most modern, and, I would venture, most important of his ideas.

The key notion underpinning Valéry's analysis of politics is that of 'le pouvoir', an essential and very early feature of his System, encompassing both 'power' and 'potential'. Beyond the closed world of M. Teste, he becomes interested in figures exercising power in the world, whether political, economic or military: Tiberius who acquired for him the status of myth; Napoleon in whom, like Nietzsche, he identifies a European vocation but who made the mistake of seeking to 'faire ... Charlemagne' ('play ... Charlemagne') (*C*, XV, p. 110); Cecil Rhodes and the affair of the Chartered

Company; and even von Moltke who symbolised 'the German conquest'. In 1931, the speech for the reception of Marshal Pétain to the Académie française offers an opportunity for studying the actions of a military leader and the art of winning battles. In 1934, in a preface to a book on Salazar, he constructs the imaginary portrait of an 'intelligent tyrant' and examines the idea of dictatorship, though without any specific historical detail (Œ, II, pp. 970–6). In such a régime one person takes on 'les fonctions supérieures de l'esprit' ('higher functions of the mind') while the rest of the populace is a 'matériel humain' responsible for all the automatic functions (p. 980). Valéry's concern, always more with the interaction of forces within a political system than with ideology, leads him to note that all political thinking is inclined to view those who are governed as 'matter': dictatorship offers an extreme and most revealing case for this type of abstract analysis.

Valéry's approach to political thinking is closely related to the critique of history, the severity of the judgements reflecting the rebellious nature of his critical mind. He calls 'history' a 'catch-all' notion and the most dangerous product ever produced by the chemistry of the intellect (Œ, II, p. 935). Valéry views with dread the dead weight of outdated structures and the inherited hatreds, the uneasy truces that beset the world. He establishes the epistemological basis for an approach that sees history as an art rather than a science, but one that can offer no lessons. History speculates on causality while ignoring the multivalence of things; it perpetuates tensions and conflicts between 'enemy' nations and it corrupts politics. The historian cannot claim to be objective because he fails to make explicit his point of view, his prejudices and his adopted conventions: he stresses *major events* and '*great men*', while Valéry is more concerned with *functional* events which have an impact far beyond their time: the discoveries of Pasteur and Volta are much more important than treaties and battles. Valéry warns against the political use of history: a political method for the future cannot be built by looking backwards and copying the past, especially in the modern period when political events have undergone such a massive 'change of scale'. It is essential to invent what will be, not to gaze at what was. A nation should be 'muette sur sa gloire et sur ses avantages' ('silent about its glories and advantages') and have 'la politique de son avenir probable et non de son passé' ('the politics of its probable future, not of its past') (C, XII, p. 133).

Though he does not seek to learn lessons from history, Valéry does find favourable examples of the organisation of power: the Venetian Republic with its Council of Ten, for example, or France before Louis XIV. He charges absolutism with having weakened the aristocracy and thereby its essential role in the state. Valéry has reservations about democracy and, borrowing the notion of hierarchy from Nietzsche, prefers an oligarchy, or 'aristarchy'. Democracy is based upon 'la parole et les effets de parole' ('speech and the effects of speech') and is governed by 'les lois du théâtre' ... 'tout pour l'effet' ('the laws of theatre' ... 'everything for effect') (*C*2, p. 1454). Its principle of advancement followed by stabilisation makes it a fundamentally bourgeois idea, founded upon a *statistical* notion of the *average*. But Valéry also enjoys the word-play of certain formulae: 'La démocratie est de dire: l'ensemble des non chefs est un chef' ('democracy is like saying: the collection of non-leaders is a leader') (*C*2, p. 1470); 'c'est penser que la moyenne sera la *meilleure* (quel que soit le *meilleur*)' ('is believing that the average will be *best* (whatever *the best* might be)') (HP ms VIII, fo. 207); and more bluntly, it is 'couper le caféier pour avoir son fruit' ('cutting down the coffee-tree for its fruit') (*C*2, p. 1452). His critical attitude extends to egalitarianism as the basis of a system, because he believes that in the political or economic sphere equality obstructs operations. He would like people to be stronger, not more 'equal' and he finds it unjust that equality of rights coexists with inequality of risk and responsibility.

He judges, too, that democracy leads to 'une machine bureaucratique et à une autre machine, qui concasse et trie les volontés individuelles'(*C*2, p. 1463).[6] Indeed, the role of the State in relation to the individual is a fundamental question: should the State have limited or unlimited power? (*C*, XXIII, p. 11) Just as he sets oligarchy against democracy, so too he values elites above States, provided that elites emerge naturally and are not selected by paper qualification. He criticises most strongly the centralised administrative system which, in France, makes no attempt to relate the services offered by the State to the burdens put on the individual (*C*2, p. 1513). Should the State assume a greater or lesser role? Valéry raises, but offers no answer to, this topical, and still divisive, question. In point of fact, he has reservations about state control, favouring rather what is known, in the French acceptance of this term, as 'liberalism'.

Valéry's attention focuses more upon the means by which power is acquired in the world than upon its exercise. He shows little concern for political parties, for which his critical mind has little time: '[ils] ne représentent que des désirs' ('[they] represent merely desires') (*C*, XII, p. 136). He does not value their role in political life and feels himself to be neither of the right nor the left. The role of money, the power of capital, the increasing importance of financial questions in political affairs, these are the matters that interest him. 'Il y eut des contrats de placement d'emprunts qui eurent plus de conséquences que le traité de Westphalie' (*C*, XXIII, p. 724).[7] He had been fascinated by the City when in London in the 1890s and notes that democracy became established at the same time as large-scale capitalism. 'Le monde moderne est gouverné par Travail et Capital, c'est-à-dire par absence d'idées — ou du moins — de toutes idées qui ne se rapportent pas à ces deux facteurs alliés et ennemis' (*C*, XIII, p. 431).[8] He is astonished that the history of the nineteenth century could have been written without mention of the Stock Exchange, the Bank or even of the 'penny press'. Next to the flow of financial investments, it is the large-scale manipulation of public opinion that controls the social fabric. 'La politique aligne nos multitudes, leur fait lever la main ou dresser le poing, les fait marcher au pas, voter' (*Œ*, II, p. 1062).[9] Indeed, the press may so inhibit freedom of thought that democracy is at the mercy of advertising (*C*, XVIII, p. 400). We can recognise here the powerful influence of 'Fiducia' – i.e. 'Mythologie' or 'Sémeiotique dynamique' ('Mythology' or 'Dynamic Semiotics') (*C*, XXIV, p. 479) – which, Valéry stresses, is the basis of the customs and institutions necessary for the social organisation of a country, but also of the false values which may generate formidable political movements.

Real power seems to lie with financiers and industrialists rather than political leaders, even the best, who often disappoint Valéry: 'Faiblesse d'esprit de ces politiques ... J'ai vu les conducteurs et je n'ai pas été édifié. Idées vulgaires et élémentaires' (*C*, XII, p. 361).[10] As a *moraliste*, he considers that they do not have 'une idée très élevée [de l'homme]. Le contraire leur sied plutôt' ('a very elevated idea [of man]. Rather the opposite') (HP ms I, fo. 24), while their public office itself leads them to adopt the opinion of the greatest number. For the modern era is subjected less to the tyranny of men than the *tyranny of things* and the 'industrial ideal'.

Valéry in fact shows less interest in the internal politics of his country than in the organisation and equilibrium of the world, and the role that Europe might play within it. The idea of Europe as a distinct entity came to him as the result of two conflicts at the end of the nineteenth century – the Sino-Japanese war and the Spanish–American war – and demonstrated the strength of countries henceforth Europeanised.[11] Along with the knowledge he gained working for the Chartered Company in London and preparing 'La conquête méthodique' (where his interest in political strategy was developed), this was the beginning of his lifelong interest in the European idea.

From his broad historical perspective, Europe began with the crusades, when the aristocracy fought against Islam (*C2*, p. 1463). But it was already rich from its Mediterranean heritage which had provided it with values, rational structures and a set of reference points: Rome and the notion of citizenship, Judeo-Christianity with its respect for the individual, Greece laying down the foundations of positive science. Valéry underscores 'le contraste de l'Europe — à partir du XV$^e$ siècle — avec le reste du monde, auquel elle s'oppose par sa volonté de connaissance précise et objective, et par la puissance qui en est résultée' (*Œ*, II, p. 1558).[12] Mediterranean Europe was able to assimilate what came from elsewhere, the diversity of races and favourable position offering outstanding opportunities for its future (*C*, XXIII, p. 588). Its hegemony was assured by the successful operation of trading and the growth of the sciences. But, argues Valéry, conditions in the twentieth century are no longer the same and, as in the sciences, different laws are at work: this is 'l'ère du monde fini' ('the era of the finite world') (*C*, XV, p. 131). Conquests are impossible, the entire Earth has been explored and divided up, as though space itself had diminished as time has accelerated. Any action provokes 'un désordre de résonances: les *effets des effets* ... reviennent aussitôt vers leurs causes' ('unpredictably resonating shockwaves: the *effects of effects* ... rebound straight back upon their causes') (*Œ*, II, p. 924).

Politics exists within a universe of ever-increasing complexity and almost immediate communication; the countless interconnections between things produce unprecedented consequences of potentially catastrophic import for the dependent populations. Everything is interdependent, tensions, risks of war, industrial and commercial situations and so on, while science has given man a powerful means that he cannot control, a single invention being capable of turning the whole world upside down. Valéry is, then, acutely aware of the unpredictability of the modern world.

The importance of economic questions in contemporary society is frequently stressed in Valéry's writing, his sense of the primacy of economics perhaps a trace of 'marxist' affinity (having 're-read' *Das Kapital* he notes that it is 'splendid'). The mechanism of production and consumption is considered one of the essential processes. The industrial and commercial developments of Germany made him aware, as early as 1896, of the presence and danger of economic warfare. 'Une conquête méthodique' is a powerful text – even if its construction is rhetorical and based upon the parallel with military war, even if Germany is described, without any study of the political and social structure, as a race of disciplined beings. Valéry uncovers the close proximity between discipline and method, the efficient study of the market and the division of labour which requires only low-qualified workers. The 'methodic conquest' has prevented the co-operation between Western nations he judges to be essential. The strategy entitled 'Made in Germany' has upset the balance of trade: having organised inequality to its own advantage, Germany has thereby threatened neighbouring markets. She has revealed the dangers of worshipping productivity and 'financial return', based upon price-cutting, cheap goods, low-cost luxury ('apple champagne'), the imitation product calculated to succeed – in short, the triumph of quantity over quality. The manner in which this analysis prefigures subsequent developments in the world market-place is only too clear.

Valéry senses with great lucidity the globalisation of the economy and the 'delocalisation' of labour with its massive implications for social organisation. 'Considérez ce qu'il adviendra de l'Europe quand il existera par ses soins, en Asie, deux douzaines de Creusot ou d'Essen' (*Œ*, II, p. 927).[13] China, as the draft of *Le Yalou* makes clear, has an industrious and undemanding workforce (which eliminates social problems) and demographic strength: 'Il nous suffit de caresser une femme pour vous engloutir' ('We only have to touch a woman to bury you') says the Chinese man in *Le Yalou* (*Yalou*, ms fo. 64 v).

By 1897, Valéry had succeeded in defining the major risk faced by the West: competition with other continents and the end of unequal trading relationships which had long operated to Europe's advantage. In a letter to the deputy d'Estournelles de Constant he sets out his 'Théorème du nivellement' (*C*I, p. 474). 'Le globe s'égalise ... Donc au bout d'un certain temps, les nations physiquement peu favorisées seront les inférieures' (p. 298).[14] In 1919, recapitulating his 'fundamental theory', he affirms that the levelling is complete: the Western world has been weakened by spreading the science and technology that were the source of its power to larger, more populated countries (*Œ*, I, p. 1038). The relative order of importance of the inhabited regions of the globe is now determined purely by *'la grandeur matérielle brute, les éléments de statistique ... Nous avons étourdiment rendu les forces proportionnelles aux masses!'* (p. 998),[15] and as a result the political equilibrium of the world, which is as dependent on inequality as any thermal machine, has been disturbed.[16]

How can the former 'fluid balance' be re-established? Having analysed the conquering efficiency of Germanic method, Valéry turned his attention to the old world of the Mediterranean, which constituted 'a kind of harmonious pre-Europe'. It operated as a kind of huge system in which the diversity of countries and of wealth, like the mixture of cultures, excluded the risk of excessive uniformity, hence also of entropy. But ever since Xerxes, an unparalleled air of crisis has ruled over Europe, a key notion which he defines as 'le passage d'un certain régime de fonctionnement à quelque autre'.[17] Economic rivalries, wars and the colonial problem continue to weaken Europe and undermine its economic and cultural specificity. In the absence of any 'politique de sa pensée' ('politics equal to its thinking'), it remains in a state of 'désordre insensé' ('senseless disorder'). The admixture of contrary principles of knowledge and life have brought it to the limits of 'modernism' in 1914.[18]

The reflections on Europe are varied, sometimes based upon the rhetorical antithesis of *grandeur* and *decadence*: the crises and ills of the continent have been engendered not only through its vices, but also through its own virtues (such as the generous diffusion of knowledge to other countries). Eulogy of the richness of its past is matched by a sombre view of its present and future: decline and loss of identity are apprehended. If Europe has previously been a prosperous market-place and an industrial and intellectual factory, in 1919, when Valéry wrote *La Crise de l'Esprit*, it seemed that the situation could only deteriorate. The abuse of mechanical power, 'l'exigence d'intensité, d'instantanéité, de nouveauté' ('the demand for intensity, instanta-neity and novelty') had weakened the influence of Europe (*Œ*, I, p. 1037). The rule of speed and urgency had accelerated the Western world's decline into maximum entropy. Its dominant position and its prestige were being wrecked by insoluble internal conflicts: 'La malheureuse Europe est en proie à une crise de bêtise, de crédulité et de bestialité trop évidente' (Œ, II, p. 989).[19]

At the time of the Great War, the anxiety provoked in Valéry was so intense that it played a significant part in driving him into the inner refuge of poetry. However, later in 1931, his speech at the Académie française offered the opportunity to develop a political analysis of its significance. He evokes the period from 1875 to 1914 when Europe lived in expectation and dread of the cataclysm (Œ, I, p. 1108). He recalls having been aware of the superior strength of neighbouring Germany since 1889–90 and – evoking his scorn for the so-called 'science' of political history – reminds his audience that French politicians had spent seventy years denying this. He foresees Western civilisation being torn apart by 'une mêlée de nations furieuses' ('a mêlée of enraged nations') in a second world war. He identifies the 'system of nations' as responsible for fostering deep antagonisms rooted in historical enmity and he denounces nationalism, which is only aggravated by economic competition. His subsequent visit to Munich when a Nazi rally was in progress prompted forebodings of the tragedy to come. Convinced that the future of Western nations lay in a united Europe, he saw instead that possibility receding, while another threat appeared: religion. 'Cinq religions au moins en Europe: catholiques, protestants, orthodoxes, philosophique, et disons aussi la religion communiste' (C, XXIII, p. 462).[20]

Unlike Gide, Valéry did not visit either colonial Africa or Soviet Russia. He did nevertheless express concern about the colonial situation, albeit in the attitudes and words of the period. In his 'Introduction' to Pierre Féline's Dialogue sur l'Art, he identifies the most pressing problem facing the contemporary world as the relationship between Europeans and the rest of the world, 'et singulièrement avec ceux qui, sujets ou protégés d'une puissance européenne, se trouvent ... posséder une culture et des traditions artistiques ou intellectuelles' (Œ, II, pp. 1036–7).[21] Yet, argues Valéry, Europeans have ignored indigenous values and seen themselves as educators and transmitters of European culture. Even if he believes in the inherent superiority of the latter in respect of everything that can be taught, he recognises many spheres of art, spirituality and life-style where 'ceux dont nous sommes chargés peuvent nous offrir quelques exemples' ('those of whom we have charge can give us a few lessons') and he advocates 'une réciprocité de relations' ('reciprocity in relationships') (p. 1038). Moreover, the colonial problem feeds tensions between nations and upsets their normal functioning. Thus, France had benefited from the rivalry of more powerful nations and acquired an Empire that its demography did not call for. However, Valéry does not envisage decolonisation, but a rather unusual solution: 'Toutes les colonies dans lesquelles la main d'œuvre n'est pas en grande majorité européenne (c'est-à-dire qui pourraient passer d'une nation à l'autre) – sont déclarées européennes et communes à l'Europe' (*C*, XV, p. 131).[22]

Valéry does not foresee (prior to his death in 1945), the importance of communism in relation to world order, nor the future significance of the development of the Soviet bloc and communist China. In spite of discussions with Gide about Russia,[23] he does not envisage the fascination that Marxism was to exert over certain intellectuals in the 1950s, partly, no doubt, as a result of his own rejection of all political parties and ideologies, but also because of his deep scepticism and preference for an 'aristarchy'. Certainly he holds no illusions about government by the people: 'Le prolétaire ne voit pas plus loin que le bout de son pain et ne peut voir au-delà' ('The proletarian doesn't — and can't — see further than his next dinner') (*C*, XXIX, p. 640). By 1929 he perceived that the fervour of popular revolution would eventually run dry and individual rebellion make itself felt: it was likely that communism would suffer the same fate as Christianity and inequality would be re-established (*Œ*, II, pp. 1483–4).

In 1945, however, Valéry wrote a short text on the Russian Army on the occasion of a joint Franco-Russian ceremony. Half a century after 'La Conquête allemande', he develops similar remarks on the victory of the Russian military forces over the Germans. Russia's vast territory, prodigious resources, enormous population and the outstanding quality of its army were, from the outset, a great advantage. Furthermore, it demonstrated its full creative capacity by inventing the new weapons and machinery required for this 'war of our time'. Valéry pronounces too his admiration for the training of the tens of thousands of officers of the Red Army, to whom he attributes the principal responsibility for the strategic victories. Beyond the rhetoric of the occasion, one can perceive his former interest in the military art, in the power that comes from organisation, as well as, perhaps, the sense of a new threat from the East which would be military, this time, rather than economic; it is as though a picture of the imminent 'Cold War' had flickered across his mind:

Une nation capable de [cet] effort d'éducation ... est une nation qui se sent
un avenir d'espèce nouvelle, qu'il est impossible, sans doute, de préciser,
*mais qui ne se résout pas en simples projets de conquêtes ou d'organisation et*
*d'exploitation matérielles des ressources du monde.*[24]

The *Cahiers* of this period are more open to events than in 1914. Now,
the shock of war and defeat is registered strongly. This is no longer a
time for poetry, but for looking at the present-day world. His
pessimism deepens. With totalitarian régimes everywhere installed,
Europe lost, within a brief span of time, so much of its diversity.
Speaking in honour of Voltaire in 1944, Valéry denounces the
horrors committed during the war, introduces the notion of the
'crime against humanity' and calls for the respect of human values as
the only way to preserve Western culture. In 1945 he writes: 'Les
pires excès contre l'humanité sont dus à la foi religieuse, au
patriotisme, – à l'idée de surhomme, c'est-à-dire à des excitants à
*l'infini'* (*C*, XXIX, p. 480).[25]

At the same time, Valéry reflects more than ever upon the future
of the West. In 1919, his vision had been utopic, expectant of a kind
of 'miracle of Cana': obsessed by the myth of a European Napoleon,
he believed that the 'crise de l'esprit' could be resolved by some
individual, by the emergence of a man of genius from among the
unthinking masses. Subsequently his position becomes more realistic, more political. His observation that there remains no great
European nation leads him almost to regret the collapse of
Germany, for that country is seen as vital for the formation of
Europe. In spite of the conflicts, in spite of his latin roots and his
affinity with Italy and Spain, he does not remain fixed upon the old
Mediterranean model, but advocates a Franco-German alliance to
guarantee equilibrium in the face of the development of America
and the Far East.

The only causes to which Valéry fully committed himself – albeit
in utopian rather than militant fashion – arose from his determined
belief in Europe and overall peace; it deeply informed his work at
the League of Nations and the 'Centre universitaire méditerranéen'
which was founded with the aim of opposing fascist ideals. He briefly
cherished the utopian vision of a society of intellectuals which would
ensure world peace and of which he perhaps saw himself as potential
messenger, when he said that he might have achieved something in
the field of politics (*C*, XXVII, p. 800; XXVIII, p. 332). As early as 1924
he wrote that the formation of Europe would require 'la suppression

des barrières douanières et l'effacement de l'histoire' (*C*, IX, p. 835) with all that is implied for economic union and Franco-German friendship.

Valéry hopes that Europe will not suffer its geographical fate and become in Nietzsche's words 'un petit cap du continent asiatique' ('a small cape of the Asian continent') (*Œ*, I, p. 995). He wishes that it would lose its aspiration to be governed by an American commission, even if, in a short article, he portrays America as merely a 'projection de l'esprit européen' ('projection of the European mind') (*Œ*, II, p. 987–90). In the face of Asia and a Europeanised America, Europe itself should remain 'le cerveau d'un vaste corps' ('the brain of an immense body') by helping to establish a balance that would accommodate peacefully the differences between continents. He was resolute in his belief in global co-operation, and saw Europe's role as central to its furtherance. He was aware that any form of politics implies a certain view of man and his destiny, and believed that, rather than disseminating its technology as in the past, if only Europe could re-discover its former spiritual mission and Mediterranean heritage it might have a role in spreading the cause of respect for the individual and the rights of man, which France in particular had championed. Valéry remains confident in the possibilities of achieving a 'politique de l'esprit' ('politics of the mind') which is well-armed and ready to defend its values.

We may perceive in this range of political texts from different periods and of differing importance, various facets of Valéry – the Frenchman, the European, the elitist – as well as the obligations of the conference-speaker and the trace of the events he lived through, each of which must be taken into consideration. But some constant features emerge. The analysis is frequently based on abstract propositions and tackles issues from a general perspective, operating either on a scientific model, such as thermodynamics, or a rhetorical model of parallels and antitheses. His criticism of the notion of equality and the opposition of order and disorder or grandeur and decadence take on particular resonance in this light. Moreover, the antithetical structure (Europe / rest of the world, elite / 'démos informe') itself bears the mark of Western logic, to which he attributes a pre-eminent place.

Overall, the analysis is on a grand scale; Valéry adopts a strategic view, assessing the relationship of forces. This is a matter of equilibrium and the proper functioning of a system, not of the happiness of humanity. He undoubtedly foresaw certain serious problems – and overlooked others. But the lucidity of his analysis certainly sheds light on the major forces driving and disturbing the modern world: economic competition which has replaced territorial conquests, communication, large-scale movements of finance, industrial choices as well as the massive increase in population. To this extent, he traces, in broad brush-strokes, an historical survey such as he might have hoped for from history itself.

Tempered by his profoundly humanist thinking which sees man as an adventure and the present world as an unforeseen and unforeseeable event, Valéry's political writing offers a penetrating analysis of the upheavals, the crises and the difficult choices which mark the end of our century with still greater intensity than they did in his own time.[26]

## NOTES

1    Valéry attempted a synthesis of notes from the *Cahiers*, augmented by further, apparently original, notes, in the dossier 'Histoire Politique' (N.a.f. 19723–31).

2    The expenditure of energy is frequently used as a model in his analysis; it is no doubt thermodynamics that leads him to take a negative view of equality, as a synonym for entropy.

3    'It is said there is a Jewish question. Said and resaid ... Every minority suspected of being too powerful excites or allows others to excite the majority, in this country where public opinion is all more easily excited for believing itself potentially stronger. But opinion is constructed. Money and power get to work on it; instincts lend themselves to it. The principle is envy'.

4    'the fateful consequence, credulity, which is in my view the necessary basis for the most detestable calculations and enterprises' ('Diversité de la France', *Vues* (Paris, La Table ronde, 1948), p. 11).

5    'As a stimulus to intelligence, impurity is more fruitful than purity, enrichment comes from mixing and dissimilarities. One can see that the pure races are intellectually inferior, or at least, incomplete' (BN ms, text written in 1944 and quoted in Philippe-Jean Quillien 'Paul Valéry et l'Allemagne' in M. Allain-Castrillo et al. (eds.), *Paul Valéry et le politique* (Paris, L'Harmattan, 1994), p. 123).

6    'a bureaucratic machine and another machine which smashes and sifts individual wills'

7    'There were loan investment contracts which had greater consequences than the treaty of Westphalia'.

8    'The modern world is governed by Labour and Capital, i.e. by the

absence of ideas — or at least — of all ideas which do not relate to these two allied and enemy factors'.

9 'Politics lines up our masses, gets them to raise their hands or their fists, gets them marching in step, gets them voting'.

10 'Weakmindedness of these politicians ... I have seen the leaders of peoples and was not edified. Vulgar and elementary ideas ...'

11 'Avant-propos' to *Regards sur le monde actuel* (Œ, II, pp. 913–28).

12 'the contrast — from the fifteenth century onwards — between Europe and the rest of the world, resulting from the former's determined pursuit of exact, objective knowledge and from the power it thus acquired'.

13 'Consider what will happen to Europe when through its own efforts there are two dozen Creusots or Essens in Asia'.

14 'Theorem of levelling'; 'The world is getting more equal ... therefore, after a time, nations without physical advantages will be inferior'.

15 'gross material size, statistical elements' ... 'Without thinking we have made strength proportional to mass'.

16 Cf. Œ, I, p. 1006: 'Il faut que notre pensée se développe et il faut qu'elle se conserve. Elle n'avance que par les extrêmes, mais elle ne subsiste que par les moyens. L'ordre extrême, qui est l'automatisme, serait sa perte; le désordre extrême la conduirait encore plus rapidement à l'abîme.' ('Our thought has to develop and maintain itself. It advances thanks to its extremes, but it subsists only by its median values. Extreme order, which is automatism, would destroy it; extreme disorder would lead it even more rapidly towards the precipice.')

17 Valéry, *Vues*, p. 113.

18 'Modernism' is the word used by Valéry for the disorder of the modern world.

19 'Unhappy Europe is prey to an all-too-obvious crisis of stupidity, of credulity and of bestiality'. In 1927, two years before the great economic crisis, he expresses his fears arising from the bankruptcy of European politics: 'La malheureuse Europe — sans "idéal", ne propose rien — propose son état où il n'y a exactement que les sciences de remarquable' ('Unhappy Europe — without ideals — proposes its own condition to others, one in which the only remarkable thing is its science') (*C*, XII, p. 353).

20 'Five religions at least in Europe: catholic, protestant, orthodox, philosophic, and let's also mention the communist religion'. See *C*, XII, p. 252: 'Dans tous les pays, il y aurait à déterminer pour chacun les relations des religions avec les partis politiques' ('In all countries, the respective relationships between religions and political parties would need to be established').

21 'and particularly with those who, subjects or protected peoples of a European power ... find themselves endowed with a culture and artistic or intellectual traditions'.

22 'All colonies in which the workforce is not overwhelmingly European (i.e. able to pass from one nation to another) are declared European and common to Europe'.

23 Discussion noted in the 'cahier' of the period and by Gide in his *Journal*, 26 February 1932.

24 See N. Celeyrette-Pietri, 'Dossier Duhamel / Valéry' in *Bulletin des Etudes valéryennes*, 52 (Nov. 1989), pp. 119–35 (quotation p. 135). This was the last public text written by Valéry and was read for him by Duhamel.

25 'The worst excesses against humanity are due to religious fervour, patriotism, — the idea of the superman, i.e. stimulants without limit'

26 For further reading on the topic of this chapter, please see Bibliography, items 1, 16, 17, 38, 60, 69, 88, 102, 103, 106, 116, 133.

# CHAPTER 15

## Valéry and the Feminine

### Kirsteen Anderson

In the context of what may be termed a phenomenology of creative intelligence, desire finds its embodiment in both masculine and feminine guises. Valéry's particular conception of this distribution of roles within the authorial subjectivity – 'Ma pensée est, je crois, ... toute mâle, ma sensibilité — des féminines' ('My thought, I believe, is ... entirely male, my sensibility — of the feminine type') (C, XXI, p. 884) – authorises a reading which classifies the concern with control, separateness and purity, characteristic of the angelic intelligence, as 'masculine'; while the 'feminine' would describe all that escapes the position of mastery, yearning rather for openness, a relaxation of anxiety concerning ego boundaries and an acceptance of fusion and flow as inevitable.[1]

This conception of a sexual complementarity within the creative consciousness resonates with the dimension of the sacred in Western thought. Several strands in contemporary thinking posit, as a lost yet essential dimension of Western culture and symbolism, the living reality and implications of the androgyny – masculine and feminine components – of the cultural imaginary (cf. C, XIII, p. 315). Luce Irigaray evokes the copula, a renewed interaction of masculine and feminine embracing an awareness of its transcendent function, as a pre-requisite of spiritual regeneration.[2] Jung, similarly, uses the terms 'male' and 'female' as metaphors for the conscious and unconscious aspects of psychological experience and speaks of the spiritual risk incurred by a culture that ignores the dual nature of subjectivity.[3] For Lacan, the androgynous ideal is but one of the myths promoted by the symbolic order with the aim of perpetuating the illusion of an imaginary unity. Yet, interestingly, the dimension of heterogeneity inherent in subjectivity is, in his writings, connoted feminine; and the attempt to experience the supreme bliss which psychoanalytic theory terms *jouissance* functions as an approach to the divine within the human.[4]

251

If Valéry's 'autographical' project is interpreted as the space for the creation of a different self; and if, too, as psychoanalytic theories of aesthetic form suggest,[5] the formal integration of content into a work of art is analogous to the ego's integration of conscious and unconscious functioning, then voice, as a vital, significant form in Valéry's theory and practice, may be read as the *locus* in which the unconscious can be encountered, Irigaray's *copula* enacted, the *mysterium coniunctionis* or divine marriage consummated.

By projecting himself imaginatively into a series of substitute selves or mythic *personae* such as Leonardo, Descartes, Narcisse, Valéry transcends repetitively contingent selfhood in the formalised substance of a purified authorial subjectivity. In the *Cahiers* the voice is theorised as 'mélos', a functioning of time, rhythm and body transposed into language; it is the expression of the ideal self or rhetorically redeemed *ego scriptor* generated in the space–time of writing. The method which animates Valéry's reformulation of the creative subjectivity aims to reconcile fragment and totality, instant and eternity. The desired form of liaison between these two poles is metaphorically conceptualised as the self-imitative mechanism of voice, translated into lasting form: '*La voix communique une imitation de ses conditions d'émission*' ('The voice conveys an imitation of its conditions of production') (*C*, XXIX, p. 76). It is the voice of Faust embodying and expressing, as *alter ego*, a summative experience of the self as simultaneously incarnate yet transcendent being: '[il] sent une *perfection* vouloir se tirer de lui, un produit comme un "mélos", ou une forme — état dans lequel il y a une étrange combinaison du maximum d'égotisme avec le maximum de dépassement de soi et de valeur d'*univers*' (*C*, XXVI, p. 153).[6]

This intelligible and totalising form, derived from the structure and dynamic of the voice (*C*, XXIX, p. 76) is identical to that of the serpent, that Valéryan *imago* par excellence. Rather than limit *ouroboros* to more traditional interpretations which read it in the light of the potentially auto-destructive capacity of analytic self-consciousness, it can be valued for the power accorded it in the symbolism of East and West, as representative of the resources of the psyche for healing its own inner conflicts.[7]

'La mélomanie du serpent' ('the serpent's melomania'), as the vehicle of Valéry's self-poiesis, sings of the desired integration of masculine and feminine within the creative sensibility. The engagement with the imaginal other or serpent-self in his private mythology accords with a Jungian perspective where the collaboration between soul and *imago*, as part of the process of individuation, ensures that the subject remains in contact with the deepest manifestations of its desire.

'Tout homme contient une femme ('every man contains a woman') (*Œ*, I, p. 387); Valéry's sense of the otherness within identity prompts a reaching out beyond present cultural encodings towards more fertile forms of imaginative embrace.[8] Voice, expressive of a potential harmonisation of the polarities involved, symbolizes both the 'origin', a state of lost yet longed-for oneness with the feeling world or matrix of the (m)other; and the *telos* of desire, a utopian or fantasised synthesis of the multiple dimensions of subjectivity. Both aspects are explored in the textually-focused discussion which follows.

Valéry refers to the spatio-temporal chamber of the inventive consciousness as ' "la bouche-oreille" de la conscience' ('the "mouth-ear' of consciousness') (cf. *C*, V, p. 78). Creative desire originates in a 'dédoublement' analysed in terms of auditory phenomena; the internal linguistic exchange guarantees proof of subject status to the consciousness involved (*C*, IV, p. 730). Consciousness as heterogeneity is evoked as a usurping vocal presence (*C*, VIII, p. 98) and it is from this split within the subject that life as vocal vibration, as articulated intelligence, derives its energy and very possibility (*C*, VII, p. 643).

Lacanian theory includes the maternal voice within the category of 'objet (a)', those objects which are the first to be distinguished from the subject's own self yet whose 'otherness' is never very strongly marked. However, the loss of such objects assumes the proportions of an amputation; absent, they come to represent what alone can make good the subject's lack. It is perhaps for this reason that they become the focus of such a powerful fantasy of phenomenal recovery. It may well be that Valéry, in a celebrated *Cahiers* confession where he shares his profound emotional response to a female voice, a contr'alto (*C*, IV, p. 587), is registering an awareness of this kind, the withdrawal of a nourishing vocal presence. Although he does not identify the voice as his mother's, the qualities associated with this primordial listening experience – its location in childhood, his conviction of the absolute and incontrovertible reality of the voice, the urgency of the desire activated in consciousness by the hunger to satisfy his need – entitle one to speak of a displacement of the maternal fantasy from the authentic mother figure onto the voice. In striving as poet towards that 'point délicat de la poésie' ('the tricky thing with poetry') which he identifies as 'l'obtention de la Voix' ('obtaining the Voice') (C, VI, p. 176), Valéry transposes this psycho-physiological experience onto a desire for the metaphorical voice characteristic of the finest poetry, that of 'une femme idéale, Mlle Ame' ('an ideal woman, Mlle Soul')(C, VI, p. 176).

The female voice, however, has paradoxical implications for the structuring of the emergent masculine subject. The dramatisation of acoustic consciousness in 'Poésie' (Charmes) highlights this ambiguous role. Valéry employs the 'mère-nourrisson' ('mother-infant') relationship to represent the delicate balance between control and unconscious prompting in the creative process; yet the poem also enacts a powerful cultural fantasy. Since a child's economy is, at this stage, organised around incorporation – surely the governing image of 'Poésie' – and since it is the auditory field articulated by the mother's voice that the child incorporates, he may be said to hear and experience himself initially in and through that voice. Now, although the maternal voice as sonorous envelope or mobile receptacle serves a positive function in providing an initial containing environment where mother and child are bonded in the fluid bliss of pre-Oedipal *jouissance* – a harmony bordering on ecstasy evoked in the central stanzas – it can also induce a trapping state of impotence.[9]

In initiating the child's own mastery of articulation through the supply of sounds to be imitated, the mother's voice is the force which, rupturing the originary oneness, introduces the child to the realities of the symbolic order: the closing stanzas speak of the disturbing transition which precipitates the infant consciousness into painful awareness of its autonomy. The ambiguous location of the female voice as acoustic mirror, capable of being internalised as well as externalised, has potentially destabilising consequences for masculine subjectivity: 'La voix intérieure est une oreille qui parle. Entendre parle. La conscience est une bouche qui écoute' (C, VIII, p. 378).[10]

The uncertain anchoring of aural events for consciousness may account, in part, for the privileging of the sense of sight as the dominant mode of conceptualisation in the Western philosophic tradition. What Irigaray refers to as the 'scopic economy' privileges sight as the faculty most likely to ensure a desired objectivity. The voice has greater command over space for the developing ego and thus, as psychoanalytic theory argues, boundaries which can be clearly delineated by the visual faculty arc casily overstepped in the world of hearing.

In 'La Pythie' female voice and body are the sites in which the thetic phase, following a Kristevan model, posits the ego as distinct from the maternal *chora* by its assumption in the symbolic order governed by language. The Pythia, in the turbulent fissuring of her substance, confronts the horror of the void, engages in a prolonged agony of textual labour, evoking both a death and a birth. This demanding and psycho-physiologically realistic portrayal of the pain and risk incurred in the creative process can be intriguingly paralleled with Kristeva's view of poetic activity as a deliberately resumed functioning of the semiotic *chora* within the signifying structures of language.[11] The textual voice of Valéry's Pythia (and her bond with the serpent should not be overlooked) embodies the tension which is characteristic of this controlled semiotic breaching of the symbolic and is pulled in two directions: as 'énoncé' it demonstrates, in its respect for form and in the polish of its syntactic coherence, the controlling authority of the masculine subject position, secure within its symbolic parameters. Yet it is aware that the other requires acknowledgement, is tempted by the intuition that the feminine or somatic ground which its mastery implies must also find expression. As 'énonciation' the poem speaks, then, revealingly, through a feminine subject voicing chaotic disruption and disturbing identity, system and control.

Just as Valéry's moving use of a freer, more fluid, searching *écriture* in parts of the *Cahiers* and in fragmentary texts evokes the vulnerability and uncertainty of his indwelling 'secrète soeur' ('secret sister') so, here, the spasmodic voice of the feminine subject reveals the precariousness which is typical of thetic attempts at mastery. In this poetic repositioning of subjectivity in a mediate *rapport* to the (m)other, Valéry distances himself from the radical nature of the experience through the guise of gender exchange. The necessary encounter with difference as the unknown and uncontrollable is disavowed, its threatening formlessness in some measure mitigated by being projected onto a female *persona* whose body and voice bear responsibility for it, and, as such, the Pythia's disturbing confession is a vocal enactment of rejection.

A work of art or poem can function as a substitute or fetish object which stands in for the symbolic order under attack. 'La Poésie' – one such fetish object perhaps – 'est la divinisation de la Voix' ('is the divinisation of the Voice') (*Œ*, I, p. 597). In a suggestive parallel with 'La Pythie', such an object may be either the body or the apparatus eroticised during the vocal utterance or the materiality of language as the predominant object of pleasure. The final statement born in and of Valéry's text, 'Saint LANGAGE, discours prophétique et paré' ('Holy LANGUAGE, prophetic, well-adorned speech') (p. 136), a register of language which has integrated rather than transcended the primal level of organic self-awareness – 'voix de ma substance (primitive). Sensibilité du sensible même' ('voice of my (primitive) substance. Sensitiveness of sensitivity itself') (C, XXVIII, p. 343) – bonds within the voice intelligence and physicality.

In a manuscript jotting for an early poem, Valéry confides the secret urge of his poetic *persona* as 'le rêve d'être un Autre et surtout une femme' ('dream of being another and especially a woman'), that longing to embrace the mystery of absolute otherness within the self.[12]

'Fragments du Narcisse' exploits reflection on both visual and acoustic planes with reference to the male and female protagonists of the Classical myth. Narcisse experiments with possible relations to the feminine as Echo; though the dream of being woman remains unrealised on the level of the scopic economy, it can be more promisingly accommodated in the substance of the voice and its acoustic resonances which overspill the defining limitations of the visual *gestalt*.

The desiring voice of Narcisse encapsulates an encounter between polarities of the psyche which might otherwise remain sundered. The thematics of separation and unity is acted out through a mono-dialogue in which the male voice appeals for some form of satisfaction from a female voice which retorts, in rebuke or mockery, that separateness is insurmountable. In order to overcome painful emotions of anxiety and abandonment similar to those evoked in 'Poésie', Narcisse endeavours to take back into himself, within his own acoustic control and efficacy, that psychic nourishment which is essential to him but which cannot easily be situated within traditional techniques of conceptualisation.[13]

He remains paralysed, however, within the specular logic of identity in which the feminine has no part to play other than as margin or negativity in relation to which the male subject strives to define his identity. As long as subjectivity is conceptualised purely as reflection, whether visual or auditory, it remains, in a sense, unconsummated. Yet there is evidence that voice in its fullness, embracing the limitations which it embodies for Narcisse (C, VIII, p. 385), gestures towards a new economy of desire *in potentia* within the spatio-temporal references of the vocal paradigm. Its mystical resonances are powerful in Valéry's sensibility in its value as the vehicle for a spiritual awareness transcending the present limited conception of subjectivity. The approach to his own divine or spiritual potential envisaged as a more fertile interaction of mind and body (*C*, XVIII, p. 904) entails a fuller integration of his own psychic femininity; despite the tone of regret implied by certain admissions, tellingly placed beneath the rubric 'Faust III' – 'Il est peut-être impossible de rencontrer la forme femelle de cette étrange nature' (*C*, XXIV, p. 375)[14]– the intrinsic value of the attempt is undeniable.

The rational mind may be capable of a kind of totalisation but it lacks the vibrant depth that an integration of its unknown aspects brings to the one-dimensionality of self-reflexive consciousness. For Valéry it is the power of the serpent as self-motivating, self-perpetu-ating impulse, possessed of the capacity to unite male and female, that brings body, flesh, voice back within the compass of the psyche as image and dynamic expressive of its homeopathic power to overcome its alienated state: 'Le cerveau loyal, nu, *pas profond*, toujours trompé par la clarté', Valéry observes, 'enchaîné à ce serpent ou femme nerveuse — qui en sait plus que lui, chacun d'eux y voyant dans un monde inconnu de l'autre ... se continuant l'un l'autre, s'alimentant, s'aidant' (*C*, V, p. 11).[15]

Jung's thinking, rooted deeply in the value of the imagination, offers a number of perspectives which enrich a reading of the voice as expression of the serpent or feminine self. At the heart of his thought lies the concept of individuation, which views the self as the totality of the psyche; the imperceptible process of psychic growth can only come into play when the ego rids itself of its purposive aims, allowing the unconscious to follow its course expressed in symbolic images deriving from personal and collective structures. The goal of completeness depends on the assimilation into the self, not only of the ego, but of the shadow understood both as the primitive or archaic psyche and the animal sphere of instinct. Voice can be interpreted as expressing the imperatives of the specifically Valéryan path of individuation; it speaks to the poet of his shadow self, guiding him towards the more complete state of self-realisation which Jung envisages symbolically in terms of the divine marriage.[16] This image of the hermaphrodite, integrating *animus* and *anima* consciousness in the divine pair, represents the androgynous nature of the creative artist; voice, wedding the Gladiatorial register with all that it excludes, blends these two dimensions in the autobiographical 'mélos' integrating self and personality.

Teste and Emilie, Gladiator and Sémiramis, Leonardo and the Parque, Faust and Lust, Acem and Rachel, partners in the creative quest, can be situated within the framework of the *hierosgamos*, or sacred marriage, considered the goal of the alchemists' research, emblematic of a supreme synthesis. An acknowledgement of the sacred significance of this moment emerges in the aesthetico-mystical *copula* realised through Faust and Lust, a synergy accomplished in and through the voice. The Faustian function in Valéry's autobiographical project was presented earlier as a formalised manifestation of ideal time. Such a form is most accomplished when mind, soul and body are embraced within its scope. Faust lends his body symbolically as container for the transformed relationship with the other in a process of self-embrace which encompasses unconscious realms hitherto distanced as the abject, the feminine or the intolerable (*C*, XXIX, p. 804–5). Faust contains Lust: as voice deploys the topography in which the individuated self comes into being as transformative textuality, so too it is *in* and *as* voice that the embrace with the feminine is accomplished in *Mon Faust*: 'Mais ... voyez-vous que tout mon être n'est qu'une voix' ('But, don't you see, my whole being is but a voice').[17]

One last group of texts remains to be considered in the context of Valéry's alchemical pursuit of integrated selfhood. In *Histoires brisées*, those strange and unfathomable stories, the voice bears witness to its power as pure presence, sufficient in itself as articulation of the mysteries of creative intelligence, expression of the ceaseless modulation of desiring consciousness. These dense texts lend themselves to many forms of interpretation; my own approach focuses on the interplay established between visual and auditory, masculine and feminine, in the framework of an implied mystical or visionary dimension.

The narrative voice communicates the phenomenological awareness of remaining close to the source, to that pure time-consciousness constitutive of identity. It speaks from the interval, 'écart modulé, modelé entre deux *mêmes*' ('modulated distance, fashioned from two *identical parts*') (*C*, XIV, p. 282), expressing desire as presentness to self, as upsurge of imagery, as creative flux emerging from latency. It is, perhaps, the voice of the 'secret sister' in a sequence of feminine embodiments – Calypso, Héra, Emma, Rachel, Sophie, Agar – exploring the space of consciousness as acoustic theatre.[18] And it is not afraid to acknowledge the fragmented, formless and incomplete nature of its utterances.

This is a scenario of orchestrated fluidity, potential chaos, ceaseless transformation of energies and impulses which relates, in part, to the semiotic dimension discussed earlier. It belongs, also, within a psychoanalytic understanding of the visual and acoustic *gestalten*. Male and female protagonists align in a struggle for control; the faculties of vision and speech vie with each other for dominance; clarity, precision and detail are simultaneously undermined by the strangely obscure and enigmatic character of this other space, other time, brought into existence through the experimentation of a textual process which relinquishes all ambition of meaningfulness from the outset, releasing the shadow as it allows the wider creative self to speak of matters which may not conform to the parameters of syntactic control or narrative closure.

It is in *Acem* that the radical otherness of the *Histoires brisées* is encountered in its fullest impact and that the voice, as revelatory of a mystical insight reaching beyond the limits of the real, evokes the accomplishment of selfhood in the form of the quaternity, which ancient symbolism identified as a yet more complex archetypal manifestation of the psyche's nature.[19] The uncertain gender of the protagonist develops further the hermaphroditic potential of Gozon in *L'Ile Xiphos*; his voice registers, as does that of Faust, the ineffability of the real and yet, when it comes into its own, orchestrates a thematic complex of extraordinary significance. It speaks, in the tones of a child, of love and tenderness, summoning into the time of the text an embodiment of the androgyny as a young man and woman seat themselves on either side of Acem. As the observing level of consciousness relaxes its hold, relinquishing scopic mastery, the voice can give full measure in bringing into being the vision of the quaternity:

Je compris ou j'imaginai que les trois personnes qui composaient cette masse devaient avoir les yeux fermés … Moi-même, je me sentais comme insidieusement contraint de fermer mes yeux. L'évanouissement de la lumière me faisait sentir je ne sais quel besoin de suivre ou de simuler sans le vouloir une diminution de ma faculté de regarder …. Bientôt nous étions QUATRE, sans doute, dans les pleines ténèbres (*Œ*, II, p. 457).[20]

In this exchange of voices between male and female, brother and sister, desire interrogates the foundations of its being. The young man asks: 'Qu'as-tu fait des semences précieuses de ton vouloir créateur? Et pourquoi n'as-tu pas jeté dans la balance féminine de notre sort tout le poids des énergies de la perfection?' (p. 455).[21] This, the voice of self-reproach in Valéry, awakens its own response as the young girl answers: 'Nous sommes frère et soeur, et tout ce que nous sommes voudrait que nous partagions la même couche, et qu'il n'y ait entre nous que ce qu'il faut de différence pour aliment des divins efforts de l'union' ('We are brother and sister, and all that we are would have us share the same bed and be only sufficiently different as to feed the divine labour of the union') (p. 456). Valéry's autobiographical journey leads towards this visionary acceptance of the value of the other within the self as an essentially different, creatively necessary participant: 'C'est pourquoi le vrai créateur doit avoir les deux sexes' ('That is why the true creator must be of both sexes') (C, XIX, p. 135).[22]

NOTES

1 See the suggestive discussion of this question in T. Brennan (ed.), *Between Feminism and Psychoanalysis* (London, Routledge, 1989).
2 Luce Irigaray, *Ethique de la différence sexuelle* (Paris, Minuit, 1984).
3 C. G. Jung, *Psychology and Religion* (New Haven, Yale University Press, 1938), pp. 18–19.
4 See Jacques Lacan, 'Dieu et la jouissance de la femme', *Le Séminaire, 20, Encore* (Paris, Seuil, 1975).
5 See Allan Roland (ed.), *Psychoanalysis, Creativity and Literature* (Columbia University Press, 1978).
6 'he feels that something perfect wants to be drawn out of him, a product like a 'melos' or a form — a state which curiously combines the maximum egoism and the maximum self-transcendence'.
7 I am indebted to earlier critics for pointing in this direction: Peter Boa, 'Valéry's "Ego Poeta": Towards a Biography of the Authorial Self', *Neophilologus* 62 (1978), pp. 51–62; Elizabeth Sewell, *Paul Valéry: The Mind In The Mirror* (Cambridge, Bowes and Bowes, 1952), pp. 52–3.
8 In her analysis of the dominant masculine imaginary of Western culture, governed by the logic of identity, Irigaray argues that its speculative processes require, as the ground which enables them to operate, a dark backing analogous to that which ensures the mirror's reflective function. This marginalised or repressed dimension, the other of the Western subject, is the location of the feminine imaginary. See *Ce Sexe qui n'en est pas un* (Paris, Minuit, 1997).

9 For discussion of the importance of acoustic perception in the foetus and the new-born infant see Guy Rosolato, 'La Voix: entre corps et langage' in *La Relation d'inconnu* (Paris, Gallimard, 1978) and Kaja Silverman, *The Acoustic Mirror: The Female Voice in Psychoanalysis and Cinema* (Bloomington, Indiana University Press, 1988).

10 'The inner voice is a speaking ear. Hearing speaks. Consciousness is a listening mouth'.

11 Many Valéryan descriptions of inner language intuit a level of psychosomatic activity, generating yet distinguishing itself from verbal articulation, which come close to Kristevan definitions of the semiotic as mark or imprint embodying the condensing and displacement of energies within the body (C, X, p. 547; XVIII, p. 56).

12 Unpublished sonnet, *Artifice* (1890), quoted in Céline Sabbagh, 'Transformations textuelles: le sourire funèbre', in Jean Levaillant (ed.), *Ecriture et génétique textuelle: Valéry à l'œuvre* (Lille, PUL, 1982), p. 135.

13 The first stages of Valéry's expansion of the Narcisse theme from the early sonnet *Narcisse Parle* to its ampler development in *Fragments du Narcisse* were jotted on the same pages which carry the *brouillons* of 'Poésie' (*Narcisse* ms II, fos. 127, 129).

14 'It is perhaps impossible to encounter the female form of this strange nature'.

15 'The loyal brain, naked and *superficial*, always taken in by clarity... tied to this serpent or nervous woman — who knows more about it than he does, each of them looking into a world unknown to the other ... perpetuating each other, feeding and succouring each other'.

16 See C. G. Jung, *The Psychology Of Thought Transference* (London, Routledge and Kegan Paul, 1983).

17 'Textes inédits. Quatrième acte de "Lust"', *Cahiers Paul Valéry 2. 'Mes théâtres'* (Paris, Gallimard, 1977), p. 60.

18 See N. Celeyrette-Pietri's study *'Agathe' ou 'Le Manuscrit trouvé dans une cervelle' de Valéry* (Paris, Minard, 1981).

19 For Jung's discussion of the fourfold structure of the psyche see C. G. Jung *et al.*, *Man And his Symbols* (1964; London, Aldus Books, 1979), p. 185 and *Psychology And Religion* (New Haven, Yale University Press, 1938), p. 76.

20 'I understood or imagined that the three figures who made up this mass must have had their eyes closed ... I, too, felt insidiously obliged to close my eyes. The fading of the light made me feel I don't know what urge to follow or to feign unwillingly a decrease in my own capacity to see ... Soon, no doubt, there were FOUR of us, in full darkness.'

21 'What have you done with the precious seeds of your creative will? Why haven't you thrown the whole weight of perfecting energies into the feminine side of the scales?'

22 For further reading on the topic of this chapter, see Bibliography, items 2, 6, 10, 18, 27, 39, 42, 51, 70, 104, 114.

CHAPTER 16

# *Dream and the Unconscious*

## Malcolm Bowie

No great European poet has provided his readers with a richer prose hinterland than Valéry in his notebooks, essays, dialogues, lectures and occasional writings. It would be a straightforward matter to conclude from the copiousness of these, and from the finesse of Valéry's remarks on the art of poetry in particular, that everything the reader of *La Jeune Parque* and *Charmes* could possibly require by way of background knowledge or exegetical commentary had already been supplied by Valéry's own ever-generous pen. When it comes to Valéry's writings on dream and the unconscious, however, the relationship between his works in prose and those in verse has major elements of strangeness and tension. So much so that the entire topic could be examined in terms of the failures of 'fit' that exist between what the prose works seem to promise and what the verse provides. To put matters in an excessively simple preliminary form: nothing in the rest of Valéry quite prepares us for the turbulent dreamscape of *La Jeune Parque*.

Valéry wrote at great length about dreams. It was one of the subjects that exerted a continuous gravitational pull upon him as he wrote his *Cahiers*, and much that is to be found in his reflections upon consciousness and the self relies for its clarity of definition on dream as a necessary *repoussoir* notion. The characteristic structures and movements of consciousness were to be found where dream was not: 'Au fond — aussi — avec ma théorie de la conscience — n'ai-je pas — cherché surtout une délimitation de l'inconscient' (*C1*, p. 333).[1] It is at first sight odd, therefore, that he should so often have written in a scornful or indignant tone about Freud's contribution to the study of unconscious mental functioning, for Freud's theory also has room within it for a great deal of contrastive play between conscious and unconscious 'systems' and may seem to the modern reader strikingly close to Valéry's own views.

Yet Valéry described himself as 'le moins Freudien des hommes' ('the least Freudian of men') (*LQ*, p. 225) and wrote with an un-mistakable tremor of disgust about Freud's account of infantile sexuality. In *Propos me concernant*, Freud is joined by Proust in Valéry's target zone:

Ce n'est pas moi qui rechercherais le Temps perdu! Encore moins approuverais-je ces absurdes analyses qui inculquent aux gens les rébus les plus obscènes, qu'ils auraient déjà composés dès le sein de leur mère (*Œ*, II, p. 1508, cf. 223).[2]

To some extent, Valéry is accurately characterising one central tendency of Freud's thinking about mental development. Freud, like Proust for that matter, did indeed keep on reminding grown-up human beings of the desire-worlds which they had once inhabited as infants, and of the sometimes disabling legacies which unresolved childhood conflicts and unhealed childhood wounds could hand down to adult experience. And when Freud came to describe the work of artists and intellectuals he did indeed relate their *Wisstrieb* or 'desire-to-know' to an early phase of infantile sexual research. Yet where others have drawn comfort from Freud's view of the 'child as father of the man', and from the continuities he proposes between the dependent infant at the breast and the self-determining adult agent, Valéry sometimes seems to recoil in panic and disarray. Puzzles that have a desire-driven infant as their solution are 'obscene'. Psychoanalysis proceeds by imposing 'une simple "saleté" ou égoïsme brut, etc au cœur des hommes' ('a mere nastiness or brute egoism etc at the heart of mankind') (*C*, IV, p. 289).

The evidence of his writings and of his personal library suggests Valéry never seriously attempted to read Freud, either in the original or in translation, which is uncharacteristic of his openness to new ideas (he did read all of Nietzsche, for instance, and enthused over *Das Kapital*). It is regrettable that, relying upon hearsay, he thus closed off the possibility of discovering just how close his own highly inflected account of the human mind was to Freud's successive models of what he bizarrely termed the 'psychical apparatus'. For Valéry, the essential difference between the psychoanalytic account of dreams and his own was that Freud studied meanings where he himself studied structures:

Il y a des siècles que je m'occupe du rêve. Depuis, vinrent les thèses de Freud et C^ie qui sont toutes différentes — puisque c'est la possibilité et les

caractères intrinsèques du phén[omène] qui m'intéressent; et eux, sa
signification, son rapport à l'histoire du sujet — de quoi je ne me soucie pas
(*C*2, 174).[3]

Valéry returns often to this defiant distinction in the *Cahiers*, and
Judith Robinson-Valéry gives it a powerful inaugural role in the
chapter that she devoted to dreams and the analysis of consciousness
in her splendid *L'Analyse de l'esprit dans les 'Cahiers' de Valéry* (1963).[4]
The problem, and not just for admirers of Freud, is that Valéry's
remarks in this vein, in so far as they purport to describe *The
Interpretation of Dreams*, are seriously flawed. As a clinician, Freud was
of course concerned with the life-histories of his patients, and he
took pains to situate their symptoms along a historical axis; but as a
theorist he paid constant attention to the underlying structures of
mental life, and to the characteristic modes of functioning that
decisively separated the 'system' of the unconscious from that of
perception and consciousness. *The Interpretation of Dreams* stages an
interminable dialogue between, on the one hand, case material,
dream-narratives and psychoanalytic interpretations, and, on the
other, the parsimonious principles required by an emerging science
of the unconscious in order to hold all that diffuse consulting-room
talk in check. Freud's extraordinary volume is the record of an ever-
renewed journey from meaning to structure, and the bedrock on
which much of its subsidiary argumentation is built is the distinction
between 'condensation' (*Verdichtung*) and 'displacement' (*Verschiebung*):
the unconscious has just two underlying structural proclivities and
all its processes, including dreaming, can be understood in terms of
their interplay.

By far the most instructive of Valéry's misrepresentations of
Freudian theory involves the relationship between the alternative
zones, regions, systems or agencies into which the mind may be
divided:

Ce qui me prouve que les théories du rêve à la Freud sont vaines, c'est que
l'analyse s'y porte sur des choses descriptibles en termes ordinaires —
tandis que le rêve devrait être *indescriptible* — ou descriptible par des
contradictions ou des partitions (comme — *il y avait un cheval, mais je savais
que ce n'était pas un cheval* — — ) (*C*2, p. 177).[5]

For Freud himself, however, the unconscious as revealed by dreams
was a foreign country, and they did things differently there. Valéry's
horse that is also not a horse would be entirely at home in the world

of Freudian dream-narrative and interpretation. Ordinary language was all that patient and analyst had when they came to do their collaborative work upon the productions of the unconscious, but this did not mean that such language was adequate to the task: it was only by placing a singular pressure upon familiar words and sentence-structures, by thwarting and flummoxing them, by opening them up to paradox and contradiction, that the oddity, the impropriety and the insatiable desirousness of the unconscious could be grasped. When Freud came to summarise his own theory in the metapsychological paper entitled 'The Unconscious' (1915), he placed a constant emphasis upon the split between mental territories which was also a split between logics. The unconscious could never be expected to speak peaceably to consciousness because it spoke its own language and would not translate.

It is when Freud lists the specific characters of the unconscious that readers of Valéry's *Cahiers* will begin to rediscover their bearings. 'There are in this system no negation, no doubt, no degrees of certainty', Freud announces, and wishful impulses 'are exempt from mutual contradiction'.[6] In addition, the processes of the unconscious are timeless in that 'they are not ordered temporally, are not altered by the passage of time'. The degree of convergence between Freud and Valéry on these matters is so remarkable that it is tempting to speak of simultaneous discovery:

Le rêve met l'implicite [. . .] *en scène* [. . .] Ce qui dort est la négation (*C*2, p. 177).

rêves, états dans lesquels il arrive qu'il n'y a point de *Si* – point d'hypothèses (p. 156).

Peu ou point de *possible* dans le rêve (p. 177).

Le rêve est le règne de l'instant (p. 143).[7]

– J'incline à croire que la loi suprême du rêve, sa loi et condition d'existence est l'*instantané*, et qu'il vit sous la pression du besoin de réponse immédiate (p. 192).

Numerous other detailed points of comparison and overlap could be adduced. Where Valéry, for example, speaks of the association of ideas as reigning supreme in the dreamworld (*C*2, p. 173), Freud speaks, as we have seen, of condensation and displacement, which are the same process of association in two contrasting guises. But the overarching common tendency of their writings on dream is the creation and maintenance of a separation between the unconscious and conscious portions of the mind. Each of them dramatises this difference and polices the borders between two irreconcilable worlds.

It is only when this broad area of agreement between Valéry and Freud has been mapped that their major divergence begins to come into focus. And although this divergence is not the one that Valéry's impatient remarks on psychoanalysis strive to suggest, it is none the less real and profound. Where Freud in appointing himself as a curator of the unconscious, as a guardian of its specificity, had the further goal of locating the sources of mental suffering, Valéry's interest in the unconscious belonged more to cognitive science (though, as we shall glimpse later, he is deeply and necessarily engaged with the residue of mental pain irreducible to his formal calculus of mental functioning). Valéry's theory of consciousness sprang into being by back-formation from his observation of the dreaming mind, and even in its most developed forms still bore the trace of that which it was not. If the procession of dream-images had an unavoidable liquidity about it, if dream itself was a 'domaine sans cloisons, d'un seul tenant, homogène, de proche en proche, purement combinatoire' (*C*2, p. 23),[8] consciousness was to be understood architecturally, in terms of the separable and recombinable elements that it could manipulate at once. If dream was associative, consciousness was integrative. Degrees of consciousness could be expressed in terms of the number of ideas or conceptual frameworks that could be interconnected:

Le degré de conscience n'est d'ailleurs que le degré ou nombre de dimensions d'un *espace*, ce nombre correspondant à des changements indépendants plus ou moins nombreux [...] *Ce nombre de dimensions est le nombre des corps ou points ou lieux distincts de références* — à chaque nombre correspond un nombre de connexions (*C*2, pp. 229–30).[9]

In writing of this kind, we glimpse a distinctive feature of Valéry's speculative style. Just as the highest achievement of consciousness, according to this view, would lie in the highest level of organised complexity to which the human mind could ascend, so the inveterate re-thinker of thought seeks his own most conspicuous success in his capacity to separate yet integrate the languages of the various intellectual disciplines at his disposal. He will not settle for innocuous propositions to which, say, physics, geometry, biology and rhetoric could all amicably subscribe, but places those disciplines in conditions of tense creative adjacency, making each of them re-thinkable in the light of the others and deriving a multi-dimensional thought-map from their interplay. Where dreams have a lazy fluidity about them consciousness works hard, striving always towards the fullest and most discriminating exercise of its own powers. Valéry's own 'Dream', in short, is one of awakening from – remaking in the fullest lucidity of consciousness – all the dream-like states and processes recognised as characteristic of the human mind.

By choosing to model consciousness in active contrast with dream, Valéry appears, then, to be revealing a one-way philosophical propensity: he thrives upon the heterogeneity intrinsic in mental activity and militates on behalf of organised complexity. Consciousness must distinguish itself from dream because the dreaming mind is acquiescent through and through, sunk deep in its own desires and their hallucinatory fulfilments. Consciousness aspires to a perpetual mobile attentiveness and dream is its desolate shadow.

Yet there is for Valéry something deeply unsatisfactory as well as something necessary and nourishing about an ethic of mental development such as this. The emancipation of consciousness from dream cannot be allowed to be too successful. In part this counter-current within Valéry's thinking has to do with the inner world of memory and potentiality that each human being harbours: 'Il y a toute une foule de capacités, de ressources, de sensations et modifications *potentielles*, de tous ordres, dont les événements font paraître *à chaque instant* les effets actuels' (*C*, XXII, p. 109). Dream is a form of remembrance and at the same time a future-driven actualisation of what had previously been merely possible worlds. Besides, dream is a natural resource: it takes its cues from the appetitive life of the body and is coloured by an entire range of emotions. As a devoted student of the formal intricacies of nature wherever these are to be found, Valéry has no wish to exclude from his field of enquiry a product of the human mind that is as ingeniously structured as a sea-shell or a tree.

A recurrent motif in the *Cahiers* suggests, however, that there is something more than benign scientific curiosity in the scrutiny that Valéry brings to bear on dreams. What I have in mind is his symptomatic over-insistence that any attempt to retell dreams in a conventional narrative mode is an absurdity and an aberration:

*Tous les récits de rêve sont grossièrement faux* — ne représentent plus des *rêves*. J'entends aussi des récits que n[ou]s n[ou]s faisons de nos propres rêves. Même nos souvenirs (*C2*, p. 164).

La traduction en langage de veille *tue nécessairement* la vraie substance phénoménale du rêve (p. 172)

Le rêve probable et le langage sont incompatibles. Tout récit de rêve est faux — ne peut pas représenter ce qui doit être l'essence du rêve — s'il existe (p. 192).[10]

And so Valéry's refrain continues, as if some demonic temptation to narrate were always falling short of complete exorcism. This is to a limited extent a rebellion on Valéry's part against the merely picturesque literature of dreams that had been much favoured in the nineteenth century, and to a greater extent, as we have seen, an aspect of his campaign against psychoanalysis, which had turned the narrating, re-narrating and wholesale prosifying of dreams into what was claimed as a bold new therapeutic technique. But such motives do not in themselves explain the vehemence of Valéry's attack on the *récit de rêve*, or the doggedness with which he appoints and re-appoints himself as the protector of a threatened mental species. Dream represents for him, or so it would seem, a singular power, a *daimon* of the mental life, an untameable and unnameable force whose blessing the creative writer cannot and should not dispense with. In its refusal of language and its resistance to narrative the succession of dream-images is not simply suggesting an alternative form of organisation for mental contents but taking us to the brink of an ineffable and contentless internal realm – a place where curiosity, ratiocination and Valéry's entire log-book of self-conscious speculation somehow no longer matter.

What is it that dreams contain which stimulates yet endlessly undermines the narrative impulse? Why is it reprehensible for us to turn our dreams into stories, either for the benefit of others or as a mnemonic device for purely internal use, as a way of remaining in touch with nocturnal experiences which may have moved, excited or terrified us and which we have no wish to lose? If creative thought involves a movement between mental levels or registers, or an inward translation between idioms, or a cross-hatching between different kinds of ideation, why not allow dream materials to be turned into tales? The answer to questions of this kind begins to emerge when we remind ourselves of the meanings of *rêve, rêver, songe* and *songer* in *Charmes*.

In a number of cases these terms are synonymous with reverie and suggest not night dreams but the characteristic fantasy-tinged movement of a relaxed wakefulness. 'Les Grenades', for example, culminates upon a moment of sensuous delight that is also an occasion for free-floating introspective enquiry:

> Cette lumineuse rupture
> Fait rêver une âme que j'eus
> De sa secrète architecture. ($Œ$, I, p. 146)[11]

Very different from such a compelling brief account of creative reverie are the *rêves* that appear in 'La Pythie' as the very instrument of extremity and excess:

> Ah! brise les portes vivantes!
> Fais craquer les vains scellements,
> Epais troupeau des épouvantes,
> Hérissé d'étincellements!
> Surgis des étables funèbres
> Où te nourissaient mes ténèbres
> De leur fabuleuse foison!
> Bondis, de rêves trop repue,
> Ô horde épineuse et crépue,
> Et viens fumer dans l'or, Toison! (*P*, ll. 201–10)[12]

'La Pythie' is an ingenious experiment in exacerbated erotic imagining, and these closing lines of the priestess's monologue bring an already supercharged scene of pain, terror and delight to its culminating moment of intensity. Sex is represented not just as a matter of brutish appetite and procreative drive but as a series of textured surfaces that belong to the bodies of animals and to mobile animal populations: prickles, spikes, frizzy body-hair and a fleece form one associative sequence and a flock, a swarm and a horde another. The final *Toison* is both the Golden Fleece and a crinkled pubic covering. The Pythia has reached a moment of ecstatic self-surrender that is also one of opening up and evacuation. Orgasm and giving birth have been conflated into a supreme feminine life-event, and that event has been located in a fantasmal, animalised human body. And what has produced this moment of surfeit and repletion, this huge internal pressure, this straining outwards against barriers and sealed partitions, if not dream itself? – 'de rêves trop repue'. Dreams are a dangerous food, an energy-source that drives the human organism towards an intolerable pleasure and a monstrous, uncontainable fecundity. Small wonder that the author of the

*Cahiers* should not want them to be narrativised and subjected to closure, for they are the emblems, the enactments upon an internal stage, of an unassuageable natural force. Dreams are the home territory of Eros. Staying in touch with them and refusing to dispel their enigmas are essential to the poetic calling.

   The dreamworld as Valéry evokes it both in his notebooks and in his poems is, then, very far from being a safe haven or a *hortus conclusus*. It contains monsters. When he comes to describe the dreamer's familiar experience of discovering that his or her emotions are somehow immanent in the dream-images themselves, his chosen example has its own sombre eloquence:

En rêve la différence du vu et du pensé (ou senti) est infiniment petite. Peur et monstre se confondent, s'échangent (*C2*, p. 48).[13]

And when he discusses dream-images as metaphors 'taken literally', the best metaphor for metaphor itself proves to be that of the mythical composite beast:

Considère métaph[ore] etc. comme combinaison ... de plusieurs choses pour exprimer 1 seule, et qu'au lieu de lire de la sorte cette expression, tu la regardes comme mixture, monstre, chimère ou griffon — tu la signifies par un être hybride et *équivoque*.
   Le monstre non viable, incohérent et étant — est comme l'opposite, le contraire de la loi, de l'abstraction, — du sens résultant. Et l'un est marque du rêve, comme l'autre de la réflexion (*C2*, p. 59).[14]

The monster is both a puzzle for the analytic intellect and a dangerous, intractable combination of desire and rage which threatens to disable the intellect before it can set to work. But Valéry, far from withdrawing in delicate distaste from these dream-creatures and seeking refuge among salubrious hypotheses and theorems, lingers in their unsettling company. Indeed, he goes further: when he sets about constructing poetic soliloquies, it is often as a monster that he steps forward to speak. Whether as a pythoness, or as the serpent in Eden, or as the eponymous heroine of *La Jeune Parque*, he presents himself as an assemblage of body-parts, a concoction of psychological characteristics and an uneasy amalgam of conflicting desires. And if the narcissism of Narcissus reveals itself as a monstrous internal hybridity (cf. *FN*, ll. 86–9), it is taking on a quality that belongs to all couples and all acts of coupling:

                    La Terre appelle doucement
           Ces grands corps chancelants, qui luttent bouche à bouche,

Et qui, du vierge sable osant battre la couche,
Composeront d'amour un monstre qui se meurt....

(*FN*, ll. 184–7)[15]

Lovers, as their bodies interlock, are creating a new chimera or a new griffon, and finding themselves drawn into a phantasmagoria. Such is the price one pays for the patronage of Eros, and poets have no option but to pay it. The poetic voice must stay close to the equivocal hybrids that dwell in dreams, or risk being lost to the safe and seemly elaborations of propositional prose. The worst that Valéry can say of the attempt to translate dreams into the language of the waking state is that it is 'comme la poésie traduite en prose' ('like poetry translated into prose') (*C*2, p. 172).

The tension between the waking and dreaming states is a powerful and productive one for Valéry the poet, and nowhere more so than in *La Jeune Parque*. Whereas as a theoretical writer he veers between the challenge of consciousness and the incitements of dream, and establishes on this basis a leisurely contest between two different kinds of mental process, as the author of *La Jeune Parque* he creates from the same fundamental contrast a dramatic structure that is all urgency and impulsive movement.

In one sense, the poem is a triumph of the story-teller's art: it narrates a single grand adventure of consciousness, beginning with the least and ending with the most that can be expected of an individual human mind. While in the opening lines of the work, a singular voice gradually becomes audible within the impersonal sound-world of nature (*JP*, ll. 1–3), the closing lines find that same voice speaking with the amplitude of apparently complete self-certainty (ll. 508–12). The poem ends 'well', upon an act of consciousness which embraces all earlier acts and raises them to a new power. Violent self-wounding and tender self-giving mark out the extreme emotional horizons of an interiority that has become vast and many-mansioned. In the course of the monologue, the Parque has become a working model of the natural world, a theatre in which its creative and destructive energies conduct their mighty battle. The new dilated human selfhood upon which the poem ends brings the speaker to the threshold of the non-differentiation from which she departed, but with this difference: that self-loss is now chosen rather than enforced, an opportunity rather than a limitation.

At the simplest level, however, the narrative design of the poem is undermined by the narrator's seeming impatience with her own slow scheme. She steals her own thunder. For example, the funereal landscapes in which the Parque's last exertions occur, and the desire for death which shadows her final celebration of the senses and of intelligent life, have been memorably present during numerous earlier episodes. The 'délicieux linceuls' with which she swathes herself at the beginning of the poem's last verse-paragraph, and the tomb into which her flesh twice threatens to melt (*JP*, I, ll. 468, 491), have been anticipated much earlier, in such sensuous inventions as

> Rien ne me murmurait qu'un désir de mourir
> Dans cette blonde pulpe au soleil pût mûrir      (ll. 115-6)[16]

The dark intimation which the Parque's negative proposition attempts to defer is already being accepted by her deliquescent image of vegetable growth and decay, and by Valéry's over-ripe profusion of sound effects. Clearly, when she says 'no' to death, she also means 'yes'. Similarly, when the Parque figures herself towards the end of the work as a

> victime entr'ouverte,
> Pâle, qui se résigne et saigne sans regret      (*JP*, ll. 386-7)[17]

she is continuing to play variations on an idea which has been present from the first paragraph onwards. This is the idea of a pleasurable violence – a goad, a bite, a rupture – from which the benefits of self-knowledge are expected to flow. The final line of the first section 'J'y suivis un serpent qui venait de me mordre' (l. 37)[18] provides a thematic cell from which countless further portraits of intellectually sanctified wounding and torture are to be derived: 'ma lourde plaie' ('my heavy wound'), 'cette morsure fine' ('this subtle bite'), 'ma jeune blessure' ('my young hurt') (ll. 48, 98, 289), and many more elaborate scenarios in the same vein, echo and re-inforce each other in such a way as to subvert any grand narrative design. Or rather we might wish to say, mimicking Valéry on dreams, that the story of an emergent consciousness is being allowed to liquefy, to lose its internal partitions, to become an associative texture rather than a hierarchical arrangement of levels, and that narrative time has been reduced to a sequence of luminous, self-contained instants. The poem's larger sense of dramatic outcome is perpetually being teased by an always precocious desire to have done, to receive now rather than at some appointed later time its 'lumineuse rupture'. How can a poem culminate properly and end well when all the events that it records have this tendency to become pre-echoes or prematurities?

What makes the poem particularly liquescent, despite the arsenal of causal and chronometrical notions that it also deploys, is the insistent sexual content of its images. The notebooks and drafts from which the final text eventually emerged tell us that the intellectual drama came first, and that it was only as a series of humanising afterthoughts that sex arrived on the scene: 'tout le sexuel est surajouté' ('all the sexual bit is added'), Valéry confided (*LQ*, p. 124). But the process is not as artificial as his phrase, read in isolation, makes it sound, for certain of his favourite terms already moved amphibiously between the cognitive and sexual spheres. *Pur, vierge, nu* and their cognates, for example, had formed themselves into a lexical cluster many years before, during the composition of the early poems collected as *Album de vers anciens*, and now had a practised versatility about them.

What Valéry did, however, as he 'superadded' sexual suggestion to his abstract philosophical diction was literalise a range of implications that were already present in the early drafts. And he did this by constructing overt scenes of arousal and gratification and by giving free rein to a fascination with the female breasts and genitalia:

> Elle [mon âme] sait, sur mon ombre égarant ses tourments,
> De mon sein, dans les nuits, mordre les rocs charmants;
> Elle y suce longtemps le lait des rêveries ...      (*JP*, ll. 55–8)[19]

> Poreuse à l'éternel qui me semblait m'enclore,
> Je m'offrais dans mon fruit de velours qu'il dévore      (ll. 113–4)[20]

> Et vous, beaux fruits d'amour,
> Les dieux m'ont-ils formé ce maternel contour
> Et ces bords sinueux, ces plis et ces calices,
> Pour que la vie embrasse un autel de délices,
> Où mêlant l'âme étrange aux éternels retours,
> La semence, le lait, le sang coulent toujours!      (ll. 259–64)[21]

> Il [le Cygne-Dieu] eût connu pourtant le plus tendre des nids!
> Car toute à la faveur de mes membres unis,
> Vierge, je fus dans l'ombre une adorable offrande ...      (ll. 431–3)[22]

Each of these images is so powerfully realised in itself, and so intricately woven into the associative texture of the poem as a whole, that elements added by the poet at a late stage become major bearers of its meaning. Valéry has given us not a series of

allegorical links between the dynamics of self-awareness and the
sexual anatomy of human beings, but a fantasmal sexual body
which has become the very instrument of thought. This body spans
the entire poem in the manner of a dislocated female Gulliver. It is
broken into parts and scattered, but nonetheless retains an uncanny
power of cohesion. Breasts and vulva are joined at intervals by a
throng of further features (throat, temple, shoulder, knee, foot and
many more), and although these body-parts do not add up to a
whole person they provide thinking with its necessary site and with
a first inkling of its characteristic shapes. Wherever the Parque's
attention comes to rest upon her *corps morcelé*, sexual and cognitive
responses are triggered indissociably. M. Teste had reported on
bodily pains as a 'geometry', as a series of figures inscribed in
human flesh, 'qui ressemblent tout à fait à des idées' ('which look
absolutely like ideas') (*Œ*, II, p. 24). In *La Jeune Parque* this geometry
is extended to pleasure as well as pain, and to the intermediate
states of the human organism upon which the sexual imagination
thrives. Kissing, biting, penetrating, self-pleasuring and exhibitio-
nistic self-display become the elementary forms of thought. Just as
'fear' and 'monster' could become consubstantial during a night-
mare, sexual reverie and speculation on the higher functions of self-
awareness came to flow into each other in the final form of *La Jeune
Parque*. Sex in this work is a liquefying agent not simply because
Valéry is fascinated by fluidic motions and bodily secretions, but
because it is presented as the inexhaustible energy which animates
all the modulations and transformations of which the mind at large
is capable. It is the power-source of dreams harnessed for poetic
use.

Major elements in Valéry's poetic project seem, then, to be much
closer to Freudian theory than Valéry himself could comfortably
have acknowledged. Valéry is nowhere closer to the transformational
processes of the Freudian dream-work than in the sheets of preparatory notes that he devoted to the sleep of the Parque. The third
section of the third sheet quoted by Nadal, for example, seems to
belong both to the world of the Freudian unconscious and, presciently, to the Lacanian idiom as well:

Mélange — méprise — confusion                    les battements
Substitution — Modulation  autre  module    le Même   l'Autre
                        ↓        adule
                     méconnue[23]

The convergences between this text and the bare bones of psycho-analytic model-building are remarkable. Two contrasting transformational processes – substitution and modulation – are specified as the key components of a minimal mental economy. Emphasis is placed both on the mechanisms of identification between subject and other (adulation is the identificatory urge running wild), and upon the presence of wishful mistakes and misrecognitions in all intersubjective transactions. The subject's perilous indecision between desiring the other and desiring to *become* the other, present throughout Freud's discussion of dream, is placed beneath the sign – 'les battements' – of a hesitation and a rhythmicity that are immanent in the life of the mind. But above all Valéry's notes take us into a realm of transformation or 'processiveness' without term. This is the seamless, partitionless unconscious which never imposes closure and stays immersed in the onrushing stream of its own desire.

Yet if *La Jeune Parque* is thought of merely as a tense and rhythmically fluctuating encounter between two different textual dispositions – between dream and narrativity, as we might briefly say – one special strangeness of the work remains unaccounted for, and one further link with Freud's theory unexplored. Although desire, in Freud's account, can absorb all the 'shreds and patches' of personal experience into its fabric, there are past events, mental residues, that are no longer readily available to the person concerned. These are the painful and disturbing experiences that have been repressed, and that can be recovered and deprived of their power to hurt only by indirect and usually very slow routes. Psychoanalytic therapy is one such route, and *repression* is its theoretical watchword.

Freud's fundamental concept cannot, I think, help us very much in understanding what Valéry's poem is 'about', and is certainly too blunt an instrument to meet the requirements of detailed exegesis. It can, however, shed light on the diction and the tone of the work. Valéry is acutely conscious of his classical forebears, and proudly imports a Racinian model of eloquence into a cultural climate marked by world war and feverish literary experimentation. The *arioso* style of Gluck's recitatives was also an important stimulus, its highly inflected continuity of line, and the malleable emotions for which that line was the vehicle, offering a further model for the vatic incantation of the Parque's speech. This speech was to be, in part at least, stately, seemly and oblique. Valéry's cultivation of these qualities went hand in hand with his self-conscious attempt to attenuate the severity of his early outline schemes. The poem being born needed to be given its own tenderness, and there must have seemed no simpler way of imparting this quality than by naming it often:

> cette gorge de miel,
> Dont la *tendre* naissance accomplissait le ciel          (*JP*, ll. 119–20)
>
> *Tendre* lueur d'un soir brisé de bras confus ...                   (l. 208)
>
> Que si ma *tendre* odeur grise ta tête creuse                    (l. 218)
>
> Un fleuve *tendre*, ô mort, et caché sous les herbes
> (ll. 242 cf. 269, 289, 379–80)[24]

These moments are echoed and re-inforced in countless other indications of softness, gentleness, calm, appeasement and half-light, and, removed from the text in this way, may seem to offer a modern version of Madeleine de Scudéry's celebrated *Carte du Tendre*, a portable guide to the more refined and less energetic amorous emotions. But in their context the effect is quite different. This is tenderness under duress, a region of the human heart that has as its neighbouring territories violence, disgust and destructiveness.

It would be fruitless to suggest that something is being repressed in *La Jeune Parque*, and that if only the clear-headed reader could discover what this was – what trauma, mental lesion or primal scene – this most complex of Valéry's long poems would begin to yield up its secrets. What happens in the text is far subtler than this. The classicising Valéry who pays his long homage to Racine, and the Valéry who seeks obliqueness and *attendrissement* by way of the long *legato* movement of his characteristic verse-paragraph, is also a master of suddenness and surprise. *La Jeune Parque* creates by these means, operating jointly, an astonishing mimesis of repression enforced and then lifted, of key insights being lost and then returning. The alternating directness and indirectness of his verse textures create a dense interlace of different affects and intensities. The 'monster' that belongs to dream and the unconscious, and can never finally be ousted, is present in the poem as a perpetual threat:

> L'âme avare s'entr'ouvre, et du monstre s'émeut
> Qui se tord sur le pas d'une porte de feu ...          (*JP*, ll. 75–6)[25]

but as a benevolent promise of meaning too. The lucid constructions of the waking mind gain their urgency and their animation from the dangerous mental company they keep. Valéry's poetic text is an infinitely resourceful portrait of a thinking creature who dreams, desires and dies; 'la Jeune Parque' is a self-perfecting consciousness, a disciple of complexity and integration, but one which nevertheless remains in contact with the monsters of the dreamworld to the point of becoming monstrous itself.

The relationship between dreams and waking mental activity is, for Valéry, therefore, a troubled one, and there is no single place in his *œuvre* where it is fully resolved or harmonised. What is remarkable about his presentation of this *psychomachia* is that it should have so little Romantic pathos in it, and be accompanied by so little special pleading for the susceptibilities of the individual desiring self. The *daimon* of self-diversifying and self-integrating consciousness, like the *daimon* of dreams, is situated within a very powerful general model of natural process; which makes possible the phenomenon of which Lacan spoke, and which Freud equally might have acknowledged: 'L'artiste *s'avère savoir sans moi ce que j'enseigne*'.[26] Whether we approach this model by way of the prose 'hinterland' of the *Cahiers* or by way of the haunting poetic textures of *La Jeune Parque*, the generality, objectivity and disinterestedness of Valéry's project are secure. Dreams offer him neither a picturesque, hidden corner of desire-driven subjectivity nor a stage on which individual emotional histories are endlessly replayed, but a long perspective on to nature at large and on to the uneasy place of *homo sapiens* and *homo cogitans* within it.[27]

NOTES

1  'At bottom — I, too — with my theory of consciousness — haven't I been seeking above all a way of delimiting the unconscious?'
2  'I'm not one to be looking for Time lost! Still less would I approve these absurd analyses which drill into people the most obscene riddles, which they are supposed to have acquired at their mother's breast'.
3  'I've been thinking about dream for ages. In the meantime, the theses of Freud and Co. came along and they are quite different — since what interests me is the possibility and the intrinsic characteristics of the phenomenon; and what interests them is the meaning, its relation to the history of the subject – which I'm not bothered about'.
4  Judith Robinson-Valéry, *L'Analyse de l'esprit dans les 'Cahiers' de Valéry* (Paris, Corti, 1963), pp. 104–33.

5 'What proves to me that Freud's theories on dream are vain is that the analysis concerns things describable in ordinary terms — whereas dream should be *indescribable* — or describable by contradictions or divisions (as in — there was a horse, but I knew it wasn't a horse — — )'.

6 'The Unconscious', *Standard Edition of the Complete Psychological Works*, trans. and ed. James Strachey (Hogarth Press and Institute of Psycho-Analysis, 1953–74), vol. 14, pp. 186–9.

7 'Dream *stages* the implicit. What is asleep is the negating function'.

'dreams, states in which it happens that there are no Ifs — no hypotheses'.

'Little or zero *possibility* in dream'.

'Dream is the reign of the instant'.

'I am inclined to think that the supreme law of dreaming, its law and condition is the *instantaneous*' and that it lives under pressure of the need for immediate answers'.

8 'undivided domain, all of one piece, homogeneous and continuous, purely combinatory'

9 'the degree of consciousness is moreover only the degree or number of dimensions of a *space*, this number corresponding to more or less frequent independent changes ... *This number of dimensions is the number of bodies or points* or *distinct places of reference* — to each number corresponds a number of connections'.

10 '*All dream narratives are crudely false* — no longer represent what the dream was. I mean the accounts we give ourselves of our own dreams as well. Even our memories'.

'The translation into waking language necessarily kills the true phenomenal substance of dream'.

'The probable dream and language are incompatible. Every dream narrative is false — cannot represent what must be the essence of dream if it exists'.

11 'This luminous breaking / Made an erstwhile soul of mine / Dream of its secret architecture'.

12 'Ah! Break down the living doors! / Crack open the vain seals! / Thick pack of dreads, / Fraught with mental fire! / Arise out of deathly stables / Where my dark places nourish you / With their fabulous fleece! / Leap up, too charged with dreams, / Ye spiny, hairy horde / Come up to sunlight, / Fuming monstrously, the famous Fleece!'

13 'In dream, the difference between what is seen and what is thought (or felt) is infinitely small. Fear and monster are run together, become interchangeable'.

14 'Consider metaph[or] etc. as a combination ... of several things to express one thing, consider that instead of reading this expression in that way, you regard it as a mixture, monster, chimera or griffon — you signify it by a hybrid and *equivocal* being.

'The monster which is non-viable, incoherent and existing — is, so to speak, the opposite of the law, of abstraction and the resulting sense. And one is the mark of dream, as the other is of reflection'.

15 'The earth calls gently, / To these teetering bodies, wrestling mouth to mouth, / And they, beating the couch of virgin sand, / Make up of love a monster who will die'.

16 'Nothing murmured that a death wish could / Beneath the sun in that blonde pulp wax strong'.

17 'gaping victim, pale / Who, resigned, surrendering, bleeds without regret'

18 'I followed there a serpent who'd just bitten me'

19 'She [my soul] knows how, o'er inner shadows, wandering, tormenting me / Of my breast at night the charming mounds to suck / She long draws there the milk of many a dream ...'

20 'Porous to eternity which seemed to envelop me, / I gave for his devouring the velvet fruit, my flesh'

21 'And you fine fruits of love, / Did heaven make this form maternal, / This contour sinuous, these folds and chalices, / That life embrace an altar of delights, / And mixing the strange soul with the return of things, / The seed, the milk, the blood should always flow!'

22 'He [the swan-god] would yet have known / The tenderest nest! For shielded by my folded limbs, / I was, in shadow, virginal, an offering adorable'

23 'Mixture — mistake — confusion — heart-beatings
Substitution — transformation        other module    the Same    the Other
                    ↓        adulates
                    ill-known'
(quoted by O. Nadal in *'La Jeune Parque' de Paul Valéry, avec états successifs et brouillons inédits du poème* (Paris, Gallimard, 1992), p. 200.)

24 'this honeyed breast / Whose tender springing did heaven delight' ... 'tender gleamings of an evening of mingled arms, confused' ... 'If then my tender scent rises to intoxicate your empty head' ... 'A tender stream, oh death, and hidden 'neath the grass'

25 'The secret soul stands cautiously ajar, and, troubled, glimpses in herself / The guardian monster writhing at the fiery gate ...'

26 Lacan repeats this dictum of Valéry, to whom he gave a dedicated copy of his doctoral thesis of 1932. See A. Ménard, 'Place des références à Paul Valéry dans l'œuvre de Lacan', *Bulletin des études valéryennes*, 45 (June 1987), pp. 45–52.

27 For further reading on the topic of this chapter, please see Bibliography, items 15, 21, 49, 83, 89, 112, 114, 130.

# CHAPTER 17

# Self and Other: Valéry's 'lost object of desire'

## Paul Gifford

The purpose of this last chapter is to explore something of the dynamic set of tensions at the heart of Valéry's self-science: the problematic relationship between Self and Other. Neither of these terms is unequivocal or transparent. We might say that the object of Valéry's lifelong quest is to possess clearly the sense of the first. The sense of the second term is variable (it is a category word): the 'Other' means the non-self insofar as it acquires importance for the self relationally, whether object or person, external to the subject's own universe of consciousness or, most interestingly, as we shall see, intrinsic to it (the self experienced *as* other).

In its purest form, Valéry's 'self-science' is a declaration of autonomy, a dismissal of other selves:

> Mais moi, Narcisse aimé, je ne suis curieux
> Que de ma seule essence;
> Tout autre n'a pour moi qu'un coeur mystérieux,
> Tout autre n'est qu'absence          (*FN*, ll. 231–4)[1]

The adventure of Valéry's Narcissus is dominated by the marvelling discovery of the mirroring power of human consciousness, taken as 'source' of identity and selfhood. When set beside the protagonist's central desire for self-apprehension, self-seizure and self-coincidence, the lovers' all-too-human dreams of a communion-in-alterity seem remote and irrelevant. The only interiority to which there is immediate access is one's own; the most immediate, the most perfectible, other-reciprocity available, therefore – or so it seems – is with oneself.

Valéryan autocentricity is not, of course, to be equated with navel-gazing self-concern. Characteristically and reasonably, Valéry defends himself against just such a charge, not infrequently made in his own lifetime, by pointing to the bio-structural fact that one's eyes form the centre of one's circle of view (*C*, VIII, p. 55). In some sense, a 'self' cannot be other than 'self-centred'. And yet so resolute and consistent a centering of self upon self is set to create acute and dynamic tensions within the world of the human subject; particularly if we choose to consider the 'self' (as the 'Fragments du Narcisse' give us every encouragement to do), as the subject, not simply of conscious awareness, but, more intimately and fundamentally, of desire.

Genetically speaking, Valéry's 'System' was invented in the founding crisis of 1891–2 by way of defensive reaction to a violently wounding experience of the Other, in both the erotic and metaphysical senses which adolescence so readily links together. To observe how this occurs is to be alert to the permanent solidarity of these two senses throughout Valéry's work.

'Un regard m'a rendu si bête que je ne suis plus ... L'idéaliste agonise. Le monde existerait-il?' (*GV*, p. 107).[2] The Other glimpsed is the least substantial or reliable of possible 'others': never encountered, never spoken to, forbidden by her married status, wrapped in ideality – still, essentially, a dream, albeit it an invasive and profoundly disturbing one. Though the impinging feminine glance (almost!) persuades the youthful idealist of the reality of the real world, it would certainly be hard to imagine an 'other-presence' less likely to encourage him to confide himself to it, or to find in other-directed love a positive path to self-discovery.

Instead, the phantasmatic 'Méduse' of 1891–2 alerts Valéry to the secret presence and disruptive power of psycho-sexual eros, experienced as Another within. 'Dieux! Dans ma lourde plaie une secrète sœur / Brûle ...' ('Ye gods! Within my heavy wound a secret sister / Burns ...') (*JP*, l. 48) : so the Parque will say in reviewing her moment of initiation and awakening. That the 'Other within' is said to emerge out of the cavity or quick of a 'grievous wound' is a highly suggestive pointer in deciphering the wider crisis of Valéry's twenty-first year. From this most central of poetic myths, in which the poet recognised a virtue of spiritual autobiography, it is clear that the wound is, structurally, that of the self's own *dédoublement* and inner division. The mutation involved in the Parque's awakening has torn her away – fatefully and against the deepest gravitation of the heart – from a state of unitary being-in-the-world, which is nostalgically celebrated in the hymn to the lost paradise of the 'Harmonieuse

MOI' (*JP*, ll. 102–48 ). Hence the protagonist's first appearance in disarray, under night skies, chilled with horror and constricted with the sea-swell of her own imminent 'tears of the mind'. She speaks here for the primal Valéryan intuition that, to awakening conscious-ness, the world itself is strange – *other* in precisely the negative (existentialist-absurdist) sense that has come to dominate the litera-ture and thought of the century.

The poetic myth thus points discreetly but firmly to an underlying substratum of metaphysical and religious anguish, hence to a deeper level of the crisis of 1891–2. This insight is remarkably confirmed in a – still unpublished – prose poem of 1888, dedicated to Mallarmé and entitled 'Enterrement de Dieu'. As the earth falls on the illustrious Coffin, which a heedless generation of *fin de siècle* merry-makers is consigning to the earth, the consternation of the young witness and narrator of this Event-in-culture takes on the propor-tions of a cataclysm in nature:

C'est alors que le Soleil, après un dernier éclat pâlit et disparut. Quelque chose m'avertit qu'il ne reviendrait plus et qu'on ne le reverrait pas.
  Elle-même la lune s'était fondue dans les cieux. Le firmament sombre n'avait pas d'étoiles. C'etait un trou noir et froid. Et à ce moment je sentis tomber sur mes mains de là-haut quelques gouttes glacées semblables à des diamants fondus et je compris que tous ces astres venaient de se détacher et que je voyais couler les larmes du Ciel . . .
  Un grand cri déchira l'air.
  Un grand vent fit voler les feuilles qui couvraient la Terre . . . Et il me semblait que ce vent soufflait en moi et éteignait mon Etre.[3]

The adventure of modernity, of human consciousness alone and autonomous, is glimpsed here under the sign of Absence. Yet it would be hard to imagine a less Nietzschean salute to the ways of liberty than this cry of dereliction of the Romantic heart, stricken with horror at the absurdity of existing in a cosmos without *logos*, ontologically insubstantial and void, negative to the relational desire for light, life and love of which the writer is the subject. The *anima religiosa* in Valéry is here widowed: deprived of her assumed Other, hence of the assurance founding her own identity.

If we take the measure of this underlying crisis, the violence of Valéry's defensive reaction to the Medusa, with its decisive and irradiating effects, is less opaque than it often seems from many of Valéry's own later accounts.[4] The 'absurd' disproportion between objective cause and subjective effect is seen to be supercharged with a more central sense of void, a more fundamental absurdity. Hence, the radiating effects of the first love-crisis: the temptation to suicide (*GV* p. 40); the radical destruction of all the idols of his youth (not only literature, but also symbolist religiosity and liturgism, esoterism, and the platonising mystique of friendship): nocturnal 'doubles' all, undermined by the loss of the idealist-spiritualist *arrière-monde*. It explains above all the quasi-'conversion' outlined in the illuminative 'Nuit de Gênes' and the permanently determining form of analytical and critical reflexivity imparted to a thinking life. Speaking with the deeper, synthetic 'truth' of poetry, the Parque will say: 'L'horreur m'illumine' ('horror illumines me') (*JP*, ll. 265).

The affective trauma at the origin of the System constitutes a global crisis of assurance about the value and reality of the non-self; a crisis dismantling the persona of the subject as previously constituted and inaugurating a new one. For M. Teste, the Other represents a Sartrean *pour autrui*. It is the domain of social appearing and pleasing, hence also of intellectual diminishment, of mystification and inauthenticity: 'Je me suis préféré' ('I gave myself preference') (*Œ*, II, p. 15). Conversely, the theme of the proud singularity of the powerful mind and its pure self-transcendence runs through the *Cahiers* like the key-signature of Valéryan egotism. *A fortiori* and crucially, the bid for spiritual self-sufficiency now repudiates any metaphysical Other – to the point where Valéry can write recapitulatively: 'Spiritualité – croyance à la possibilité de l'esprit de *se suffire*' ('Spirituality – belief in the possibility for the mind to be self-sufficient').[5] In all respects, the self-writing subject of the *Cahiers*, by strategic decision and perpetually exercised choice, constitutes a sphere of attentive self-presence, variously compared to a citadelle, a laboratory, an island; it is even, in respect of the 'vertical' or 'projective' dimension of selfhood, the temple elevated to an autonomous 'mystique sans Dieu'.[6] He is 'un ordre fermé, un édifice complet en soi' ('a closed order, an edifice complete in itself' (*C*, IX, p. 258).

What is fundamentally questioned by the lifelong practice of analytical reflexivity here pursued is '*the* Self', considered as a natural hypostasis, and manipulated as such, subtly or naively, by rationalist philosophers, religious systems, Romantic poets and writers of the 'culte du Moi'. For the analyst, the notations 'I' and 'me' are functions of the purely psychological act of what Paul Ricœur has recently called *idem*-recognition, i.e. the identification of

selfhood by the criterion of sameness.[7] In this sense, the 'Self' is a
fiction answering 'la nécessité où nous sommes de rapporter finale-
ment à un unique *objet* toujours le *même* toutes choses' (*C*, IX, p. 65,
cf. *C*, VIII, p. 531).[8] Thanks to this dubious cipher-word, we purchase
the illusion of unity and referrability at the price of falsifying the
world of the psyche. (In much the same way, the 'generalised Self'
we call 'God' is said by Valéry to effect a suspect 'clôture imaginaire
des choses' ('imaginary closure of things') – *C*, IX, p. 235.)

In the new autocentred construct of identity, the relational
structure of self-and-other does not, of course, disappear. It is
immediately re-located within the 'autosphere' itself, and remodelled
on the reflexive duality 'Je / me':

*Narcisse* — La confrontation du Moi et de la Personnalité. Le conflit du
souvenir, du *nom*, des habitudes, des penchants, de la forme mirée, de l'être
arrêté, fixé, inscrit — de l'histoire, du *particulier* avec — le centre universel,
la capacité de changement, la jeunesse éternelle de *l'oubli*, le Protée (*C*, IV,
p. 181)[9]

The term 'personality' or 'person' is always taken by Valéry to
mean the sum of the contingent qualities pre-defining an individual
— in short, the negated Other. By contrast, the 'pure Self' is always
the identifier-liberator: the function placing our true identity else-
where-and-beyond in the very act of recognising – and rejecting – all
particularity; it restores to selfhood a character of free potentiality,
open dynamism, human transcendence. Here is a structural invariant and *idem*-effector which, paradoxically enough, opens up the
hypostasised self towards a transformational, multi-dimensional,
creative future (cf. *C*, XX, p. 295). There is a more latent paradox: it
lies in the fact that the impossibility, in Valéry's system, of coinciding
with one's empirical persona implies, at least structurally, that the
Other-function will, sooner or later, be seen as the key to subject
identity: 'L'homme ne SE reconnaît que ... *dans un Autre!*' ('Man
recognises HIMSELF... only in Another' (*C*2, p. 333).

Does this reflexive and functional duality, however, give any
acknowledgement to a human vocation for genuine exchange, real
encounter? Interestingly, it does so in two different but secretly
complementary ways. On the one hand, the functional reality of
what we term 'thought' is increasingly defined by Valéry in terms of
an inner dialogue. 'JE et ME — Dialogue — à une voix / Ces deux
inconnus, dont le discours est connaissance' (*C*1, pp. 129, 440).[10] The
theological analogy that suggests itself here is Christian and

trinitarian: 'le système indivisible *Parler-entendre* ... produit une Dualité-Une, une *Binité* en 2 personnes qui s'exprimerait par cette formule théologique: il y a deux personnes en Moi' (*C*1, p. 467).[11] Nor is the analyst of the *Cahiers* inclined to underrate the importance of this inner dialogue structurally inherent in human consciousness. It is the enabling condition of interpersonal exchange (*C*2, p. 240) and a standing invitation to seek a complement outside the self (cf. *C*, VIII, p. 549). In love, this virtuality is realised: 'hors de soi le chemin de soi' ('outside oneself the road to oneself') (*C*1, p. 430). The mono-dialogue of subject identity here develops a higher dimension, comparable, suggests Valéry, to the development of 'la connaissance consciente' ('conscious knowledge') (*C*2, p. 519). In short, 'l'homme communique avec — soi, par les mêmes moyens qu'il a de communiquer avec l'*autre*. / La conscience a besoin d'un *autre fictif* — d'une extériorité — elle se développe en développant cette *altérité*' (*C*1, p. 978, cf. *C*2, p. 241).[12]

Despite the remarkable qualifier 'fictif', betraying the potency of Valéry's residual idealist persuasion, the incursion of the word 'altérité' already represents an implicit breach in the proud autarchy of the Valéryan system. Moreover, it is a breach which has a powerful subterranean resonance in the personal and affective ego. Strategically, it offers a consonance-in-desire with the vaulting dream to which it beckons: that of a communion with a genuine — ontologically different — Other, realising a supreme degree of exchange and intimacy.

Often, Valéry speaks in just these terms of friendship:

Dialogue total, système de consciences nues ... Mon idée était que cette 'amitié' fût une expérience vitale, presque 'métaphysique' puisque la volonté d'approximation de Deux Moi – c'est-à-dire de deux UNique – par voie d'échanges de plus en plus précis s'y développât aux dépens de tout (*C*1, p. 165 cf. *C*2, pp. 1315–6)[13]

Even before the encounter of 1920–1, the same dream of an extreme intimacy between separate consciousnesses also envisages a complementarity-in-love with a feminine Other. His rigour in self-awareness, his physiological sense 'et ce mysticisme sans objet qui est en moi' ('this mysticism devoid of any object which is in me') might, says Valéry, have made something of love, had destiny granted him a partner of like mind and senses, possessing 'une fureur intelligente et expérimentale, un pressentiment de la volupté comme *moyen*' (*C*2, p. 401).[14] Reviewing at a later stage his experimental attempts in this same genre, he writes similarly of an extreme development of the faculty of sympathy, an attraction between human individuals which would stand to ordinary sexual attractions rather as passionate research in the arts or sciences stands to the quest for some instinctual or material satisfaction (*C*, XII, p. 200).

More surprisingly, perhaps, the thought of an intimate communion with a metaphysical Other is never quite purged or perfectly excluded from Valéry's autosphere: 'S'il y avait un Dieu, je ne vivrais que pour lui — quelle curiosité, quelle passion m'inspirerait un si grand être — — quelle science autre que la Sienne?' (*C*, VII, p. 544).[15] In 1925, Valéry can even note of his entire adventure of self-writing: '... que si penser à tout ceci, ce fût penser à Dieu ...?' ('... suppose thinking of all this were thinking of God?' ) (*C*, XI, p. 192).

Characteristically, we notice, Valéry's confidences delving into the most intimate region of his desiring human sensibility remain in the mode of hypothesis or regret, rehearsing an ideal high enough to condemn the mediocrity of actual relationships, yet too soaring to figure other than as conceptions incapable of actual incarnation: 'sentiments très anciens qui sont demeurés à l'état réservé, parmi les possibilités impossibles, les idéaux sans place' (*C*, XXII, p. 199).[16] Valéry's unpublished 'Dialogue of divine things' expresses this unresolved residue of transcendent aspiration allusively, in the symbolic figure of 'la Divine Mélancholie'. She bears, too deep for words, a burden of tears 'de ce qui n'a pas été, de ce qui n'a pu être ... d'une tendresse sans réponse'. She is 'une ... *vivante injure au Dieu*, car toute la Toute-Puissance ne peut rien pour racheter ce qui ne fut pas — et la tromperie du monde créé à l'égard des humains' (*C*2, pp. 1336–7). [17]

Elsewhere, this same zone of sensibility appears fraught with a less containable charge of spiritual exaltation and resentment. Reconformed to a living bi-polarity during the love-affair of 1920–1, the autocentric citadelle resonates briefly with a hymn to the splendour of loving which memorably re-evaluates this human relation as such. A secret spring opens 'la vraie demeure de mon âme' ('the true dwelling-place of my soul') (C, VII, p. 778). The verb 'to be' is strangely reconjugated: 'Mon esprit a trouvé ceci de monstrueux, de neuf, de monstrueusement neuf — que vous êtes — Tu es. J'ai trouvé que Tu Sum ... Je suis est inconjugable. Ou plutôt se conjugue: Je suis, tu suis ...'.[18] Such declarations turn inside out and upside-down Narcisse's science of subject-identity or selfhood ... Love indeed 'changes everything'.

Most strikingly, perhaps, Valéry engages at this point in what he elsewhere refers to sarcastically as the romantic lover's propensity to think himself privy to the 'politics of the universe' (*C2*, p. 404). To be profoundly loved, was this not 'le but impossible de Dieu' ('the impossible goal of God') (*C*, VII, p. 659)? Fleetingly, in the glow of the 'gloire amoureuse', Valéry glimpses the novelty, the persuasive possibility, of that other-centred gift-love predicated of the Christian God:

> Quelle nouveauté, quelle étrangeté que de rattacher au Dieu la bonté, la justice, la vérité ... Tendresse et univers. Tristesse et toute-puissance. Idée de sacrifice, non plus de l'homme à Dieu, mais de Dieu à Dieu (*C*, VII, p. 801).[19]

Yet, the amorous alchemy fails; at which point, the dereliction experienced – and the knots of metaphysical resentment laid bare – are proportional to the splendour of the Other-directed excursus:

> Solitude, échange interne — ô Vie. Il faut avouer que le Moi — n'est qu'un Echo (*C*, VIII, p. 385)[20]

> O seul. O le plus seul ... Pourquoi n'y a-t-il pas de Dieu? ... Il n'y a rien de pareil. Ces mondes n'existent pas. Nous les tirons précisément de leur inexistence. Le Dieu est fait de notre impuissance, de notre abandon, de notre imperfection, de notre détresse, prises en sens contraire. Mais *s'il était, nous-mêmes ne serions pas* (p. 466).[21]

Valéry's intimate spectre of ontological disppointment re-emerges here, and with it, an ever-prompt essentialism of spiritual imagination. The knot of logical incompatibility he posits between divine and human subjects invokes implicitly a transcendental Subject – absolute Mind or Spirit – as envisaged by all nineteenth-century idealist systems (e.g. Schopenhauer, Hegel). The reactive self-objection that precedes and prepares it, incriminating the naive 'complements' of his own desiring sensibility, is quintessentially Valéryan, an exact harmonic of his entire thought on 'les choses divines'.

This set of insistent relational nostalgias – indeed, the entire dynamics of spiritual negativity in Valéry – reminds us centrally of Lacan's 'lost object of Desire': the unknowable Object, without image or metalanguage, which is posited in all desiring and which engenders a perpetually metonymic quest of 'partial objects'.[22] Valéry's poetic myths consistently evoke or invoke just such an object. Sometimes, they do so in exactly Freudian terms (the lost breast of 'ma mère Intelligence' in 'Poésie'), sometimes in the terms of the romantic-symbolist myth of the 'golden age' shot through with images borrowed from St John of the Cross (the lost paradise of the 'Harmonieuse MOI') or of Biblical myth (the Eden of 'Ebauche d'un Serpent'). There are also more anecdotal personal myths (such as the lost 'contr'alto' (CI, p. 53) which Valéry posits, somewhat vaguely, as the 'musical' origin of his particular tension desiring ideality.

Such objects of relational nostalgia have their counterparts in objects of expectancy, which are 'lost' in the related sense that they, too, are denied to – or at least, by infinite deferral, withheld from – the possessive or fusional desire of the subject: thus, the perfectly noumenal 'beau soleil, vrai Soleil' towards which the Icarus-flight of 'Le Cimetière marin' vainly aspires; the ideally beautiful Other of a transfigured or essential subject-identity which Narcisse attempts – and fails – to grasp; the 'Source où cesse même un nom' ('Source where even a name ceases') in 'Le Rameur'; and the 'Personne pure, ombre divine' ('Pure person, shadow divine') of 'Les Pas'.

Lacan's account of the 'lost object' of course refers to the purely immanent world of an unconscious structured like a language, rather to a transcendent – and, in Lacan, 'barred' – world of Forms. It is nevertheless recognisably related to the deficiency which Plato already identifies as centrally characteristic of *eros*.[23] Valéry's poetic images and structures certainly establish him as a native-born Platonist, as we might expect from his Romantic-Symbolist ante- cedents. (More radically, one might enquire whether platonism itself is not some sort of universal first language of psychic desire as reflexively apprehended by the subject.) Equally clearly, the essenti- alist in him is amputated of the *arrière-monde*, and in consequence powerfully aware of the broken correspondence of sign and referent, mind and reality; he is also painfully forewarned of the distorting powers of the imaginary ('le ficudiaire', 'le mythe').

The trauma of scission and suspicion in which his thought is rooted does nevertheless produce its own characteristic relational structure: that of desire contained – and of expectancy sustained – in the mode of indefinitely deferred consumation. In one of his finest prose poems, 'Station sur la terrasse' the writer of the *Cahiers* speaks memorably of the 'pure', para-mystical tension of sublime (or 'spiritual' or 'mystic') Desire that survives in an 'archipure rationalist':

Si tu veux, ma Raison, je dirai — (tu me laisseras dire) — que mon Ame, qui est la tienne aussi, se sentait comme la forme *creuse* d'un écrin, ou le creux d'une moule et ce vide *s'éprouvait* attendre un objet admirable — une sorte d'épouse matérielle qui ne pouvait pas exister — car cette forme divine, cette absence complète, cet Etre qui n'était que Non-Etre, et comme l'Etre de ce qui ne peut Etre — exigeait justement une *matière* impossible, et le creux vivant de cette forme *savait* que cette substance manquait et manquerait à jamais au monde des corps — et des actes. (*C2*, p. 689)[24]

The remainder of the passage directly compares this mysticism of the lost Object to the sense of presence-absence inhabiting the religious believer, who designates 'God' the centre of the sphere of subjectivity he experiences himself to be. (The image of the sphere is Pascal's; Valéry's suspicion here is precisely that theistic belief projects a metaphysical Other conceptually extrapolated from the dynamic deficiency of the self – 'un *autre* fictif'.)

The latter part of Valéry's thinking life from 1921 onwards is very centrally concerned with the deconstructive *critique* – but also the re-thinking and the re-invention – of the two major, inherited sets of discourses of the 'lost Object'. He questions intensively all forms of mystico-religious belief, on the one hand, and, on the other, the erotico-romantic passion of love. The functional analogy between these two human phenomena is frequently stressed (cf. *C2*, pp. 453, 499; *C*, VII, p. 50; *C*, XI, p. 20 ). They follow the same fomula of psychogenetic production: that of 'idolopoésie', instituting the one-and-only object as 'la clef qui ouvre pour moi le Moi' ('the key that opens for me the Self') (*C2*, p. 481). Both expand and explore human potential (*C2*, p. 471). Both evince a need for transcendence of the empirical ego, and the quest for a heightened power of being: 'une excitation vers ce réel complet que presque tous les sens essaient de composer au moyen de X. Et non seulement les sens, mais tout ce qui réclame reponse en nous — depuis le besoin du tendre jusqu'à l'appétit métaphysique' (*C2*, p. 489).[25] 'Je suis, dit-elle, l'Etre réel dont celui qui t'est connu, que tu aimes, que tu édifies en toi, qui te déchire et te ravit — n'est que le songe. Eveille-toi. Dissipe mon fantôme. Tu verras quelle je suis' (*C2*, p. 487). [26]

The 'metaphysical' substratum of amorous desire is brilliantly illuminated by these remarks. What love desires is indeed 'le réel complet' – 'l'Etre' – not as conceptual deliverance, but as experienced reality. But, we notice, appetitively so, in the mode of deficiency and need; and to profoundly ambiguous effect. For, to awaken from the mind-made phantom we construct of the Other may be to discover the plenitude of a 'real' Object, satisfying the whole measure of the hungry need-god within us, but it may also be to be fall from this hope, and to encounter the Other in his / her 'real' imperfection and contingency. The greatest hope may also be the most appalling trap – 'le piège épouvantable de la tendresse' ('the appalling trap of tenderness') (C 2, p. 481). The spectre of this deep-seated Valéryan fear of Disappointment haunts the finale of 'Fragments du Narcisse' and the manuscript drafts of 'Les Pas'.[27]

At bottom, *amour-passion* and religious mysticism are felt as doubly transgressive in Valéry's system of thinking; each challenges both the inherited ideological and moral codes set up to contain them, but also the autocentric order of enfolding lucidity by which it is 'understood' within the 'System'.

The theme of *voluptas ab opprobriis vindicata* (C, VII, p. 748) has particular resonance and density in this context. In the traditional Catholic regulation of sexuality known to him, Valéry sees a travesty to be resisted and corrected. Sexual delight (he dismisses the word 'pleasure') is vigorously defended against moral condemnation, spiritualistic scorn and confusion with procreative function. Insistently, Valéry presents it as a sign of true humanity and of true human transcendence (C2, pp. 538–9). It is indeed a 'sacrement', a mystical 'sign' or 'figure'. For if only procreation is at stake, 'toute la partie psychique et super-affective de l'amour ... — ne s'explique pas' ('the whole psychic and super-affective part of love is inexplicable') (C2, pp. 556–7).

This is no vain boast. In one curious and vibrant anagogic tale sketched in the *Cahiers*, an appearing Angel reproaches two lovers with having sinfully stolen from the Lord by fornication 'ce qu'il y avait en vous de puissance de feu' ('what there was in you of divine fire'). He is told with dignity that the fulguration of sexual eros is the only sign vouchsafed to mortal man of a God who might be unlike anything to found in the world. In short, it is a far better theistic sign – there can be no question of *proof* – than the classic 'five ways' of Aquinas! (C2, pp. 536–7).

Just as characteristic as Valéry's defence of human *eros*, and perhaps reciprocal to it, is the almost total elimination from his cross-examination of Christian doctrine of other-centred gift-love (technically called *Agape*). At every point where this motif might have been invoked – in his reflexions on the themes of Creation, Incarnation, Revelation, or Sacrifice, for instance – it is very signally absent. The notion that such Love is, rather than an attribute, the very nature (*ipse*) of God, is not formally considered and dismissed in the *Cahiers*. Yet it is clear that, in a more oblique way, Valéry, for most of his life, did think of this notion as an after-thought or late addition to the divine 'poem' developed by religious humanity, as an all-too-human attempt to give the world the affective depth it is felt to lack or to refurbish an otherwise unacceptable image of the Divine (*C*, XXV, p. 415 ).

A typical expression of this oblique view can be found in 'Ebauche d'un Serpent'. The God who creates does so, not out of exuberant, other-centred generosity, but as a debile gesture of vanity, from a need to exist 'pour autrui'. The inexpert demiurge Valéry imagines destroys his own autarchic Perfection, setting up inadvertently an 'Other-consciousness' whose critical mirror must objectify, relativise and destroy him as 'true God' . . .

It will be seen that Valéry's self-science remembers – not primarily Judeo-Christianity – but the attributes of divinity, as understood in a long tradition of hellenic essentialism running from Plato and Aristotle: a model uniting coincidence of being and knowing, autarchic self-completion, perfection, detachment, serenity, *apatheia*. This implicit model of subjectivity or selfhood appears clearly in the 'Tête complète et parfait diadème' ('Head complete and perfect diadem') of 'Le Cimetière marin', to which the protagonist aspires as 'récompense', at the limit of the act of pure thought; it is this controlling model of subject identity, we may say, which leaves in Valéry's account of 'Self and Other' its subsistent shadow of idealist psycho-theology.

Valéry's last work, *Mon Faust*, attempts a recapitulative decipherment of the deepening enigma of Self and Other. 'Le Solitaire' grapples with the isolated self, seen as inner duality and as reflexive equation; Faust is 'resolved' (i.e., destroyed) by his own immanant principle of transcendence or 'Moi pur'. Inversely, in a famous scene of 'Lust', Act II, Faust yields to the melting beauty of sunset and a sweet-scented Garden, secretly charged with the energising presence of a life-enhancing feminine Other. His famous hymn to Living (recalling the supreme 'instant' of Goethe's protagonist) expresses a moment of perfect, quasi-mystical self-coincidence and plenitude, in which all the lack and longing of Desire seem to be cancelled.

Yet by an exquisite irony, the Faustian 'instant' is presented as a
masterpiece of the solitary Mind. At Faust's definition of 'reality' –
'Je touche, je suis touché' ('I touch, I am touched') – Lust acquiesces
with a gentle hand laid on his shoulder, solliciting exchange between
them of the deepest feeling of living, offering a higher dimension of
contact with reality. Faust hesitates between intimacy and distance,
the 'tu' and the 'vous', then retracts, fearful of the devastating
'totality' involved in sexual intimacy and the dependency of the
heart. He consents, finally, to share the peach plucked from the Tree,
thus entering into the ambiguous and troubled logic of relational
exchange. 'Je me sentais œuvre parfaite' – he will say in the Duo of
Act IV – 'mais vous étiez près de moi' (*MF* ms III, fo. 59).[28]

In the unfinished fourth act,[29] Lust sollicits the consent of Self to
Other which loving always entails, the gift by which alone can exist
the 'douceur d'être et de n'être pas' ('sweetness of being and not
being'). Faust, reactively, defers the promise which he fears cannot
be kept ('ne hâte pas cet acte tendre' ('do not hasten this tender
act')). His refusal to love invokes all the phantoms of 'idolopoésie',
and the absence of any ultimate safeguard against the spectre of
idealist Disappointment. If Lust's voice nevertheless prevails, it is in
so far as she expresses, with a force of strangeness ever less reducible
to the translation operated by the logocentrism of Faust, the prayer
for Life which is latent also in him:

> Rien n'a pu ressembler à cela: une force sans nom, et que le mot Amour
> voile plus qu'il ne désigne ... C'est elle que j'implore. Je prie ce que je puis.
> Je prie ce que je sens de tout mon être devoir être prié ... O mon principe
> de Moi qui êtes dans Faust, faites ceci: Je voudrais qu'il s'aime comme je
> m'aime, et qu'il m'aime comme je l'aime (fo. 12)[30]

We are unsurprised to find Lust declaring that her exigency 'va si
loin, si haut, que je ne puis me l'avouer à moi-même' ('runs so far, so
high, that I cannot confess it to myself') (fo. 63). What she seeks in
love is an 'absolute' realisation of I–Thou reciprocities, a veritable
re-creation of love restoring its potential for 'le réel complet'.

If she is ultimately heard, it is that the Faustian intellect consents
at the last to recognise, in its alterity, the obscurely mystical
expectancy at the wellsprings of the poem or prayer that love always
is:

> Fille, enfant de ce qui se faisait dans l'ombre de ma pensée lucide ...
> tandis que je croyais penser, toi la force de penser (fo. 92)[31]

Relève-toi petite Lust ... Tu es grande petite Lust, très grande. Et j'ai beau te saisir de toute ma pensée, te comprendre de toute mon expérience, prévoir tes mouvements, moi à qui rien d'humain n'échappe, moi que rien d'humain ne peut désormais surprendre et toucher, toutefois ...

Oui, voici que c'est à présent un amour comme il n'y en eut point de pareil (fo. 65).[32]

This recognition of the Other within, hence of the infra- and ultra-rational determinants of Intellect, is unparalleled in Valéry. We may recognise here a 'turning point'[33] upon which pivots the sense and intent of the unfinished Act IV.

Is the Poem of a 'higher love' destined to remain, ironically, a splendid burst of mystico-poetic fireworks emprisoned in the mirror of self-writing? Or is the intimate music of Presence it celebrates a better-than-illusory promise, an allusive presentment of the 'admirable Object' secretly expected and waited upon by our whole psychic being? Valéry's writing of the veiled figure human desire and its 'lost Object' pushes in these manuscripts towards a discernable alternative of metaphysical import, a sort of crisis.

The fourth Act of *Lust* remains unfinished, its crux undecidable. A series of written traces of Valéry's own inner steps however give it echo in the *Cahiers*. A testimentary entry 'Où je me resume' ('In which I summarise myself') speaks of an apocalypse of the heart: 'Il triomphe. *Plus fort que tout*, que l'esprit, que l'organisme. Voilà le *fait* ... Le plus obscur des faits. Plus fort que le vouloir vivre et que le pouvoir comprendre est donc ce sacré C[oeur]' (*C*, XXIX, p. 909).[34] The penultimate entry, uncertainly decipherable, probably reads: 'Refaire Thêta' ('Rework Theta') (*C*, XXIX, p. 911), that is to say the Platonic dialogue 'On things divine'. The last trace reads simply: 'Le mot Amour ne s'est trouvé associé au nom de Dieu que depuis le Xrist' (*C*, XXIX, p. 911).[35]

To many of Valéry's commentators, this coda given to the twenty-six thousand pages of the *Cahiers* has seemed embarassing, problematic or simply opaque; so much so that it is frequently treated as absent from the record. 'Hélas! de mes pieds nus qui trouvera la trace / Cessera-t-il longtemps de ne songer qu'à soi?' (*JP* ll. 322–3).[36] The opacity, at least, is substantially lessened when it is seen against the lifelong search of the self-enfolding intellect for a lost Object of relational desire. If the last traces are seen to answer the structures of expectancy, reversal and liquidation visible in all Valéry's crises, then they cannot well be considered negligeable. If, finally, we are able to discern here a distinction, at last acquired and operative, between essentialist *eros* and Christian *agape*, then the record Valéry in fact leaves us may well offer a profoundly receivable sense, answering his own intuition that the human subject 'ne SE reconnaît que ... *dans un Autre.*' (*C*2, p. 333).

What may be concluded with assurance is that all forms of relational desire are seen, ever more clearly, to proceed from the same 'figure voilée' of the Other within the psyche. Towards the decipherment of this most 'mystérieuse Moi', all major force-lines of Valéry's reflexive adventure recede; to it, his Odyssey in the universe of mental forms is, perhaps, ultimately addressed.[37]

NOTES

1 'Yet I, beloved Narcissus, am curious / Alone and solely of my essence; / All others have for me a heart opaque, / All others are but absence'
2 'A glance has made me so stupid that I no longer exist ... The idealist is expiring. Does the external world really exist?'
3 'Then it was that the sun, after a final brightness, paled and disappeared. Something warned me that it would not return and that we would not see it more. / The moon itself had melted in the skies. The dark firmament held no stars. It was a dark, black hole. And at that moment I felt falling on my hands from above a few icy drops like melted diamonds and I understood that all those stars had come unstuck and that I was watching the tears of heaven flow ... / A great cry rent the air / A great wind stirred up the leaves that covered the earth ... And it seemed to me that this wind blew within me and extinguished my Being' ( BN ms Proses anciennes I, fos. 115–6).
4 See e.g., 'Propos me concernant' (*Œ*, II, pp. 1507–38).
5 BN ms dossier Mallarmé, 'Traité des choses hautes et passions de l'esprit', fo. 167.
6 This expression first occurs in 1906 (*C*, III, p. 856) and is officialised in 1924 (cf. *Œ*, II, p. 34).
7 See Ricœur's distinction between '*idem*-identity' and '*ipse*-identity', *Soi-même comme un autre* (Paris, Seuil, 1990).
8 'the need we have to relate everything finally to a single object, always the same'
9 '*Narcisse* — The confrontation of the Self and the Personality. The conflict of memory, the name, habits, inclinations, the mirrored form, the being immobilised, fixed, inscribed — of history, of the *particular* with — the universal centre, the capacity for change, eternal youthfulness of forgetting, the Proteus'

10 'I and ME — Dialogue — of one voice / These two unknowns whose discourse is knowledge'.

11 'the indivisible *Speaking-hearing* system … produces a duality in One, a Binity in two persons which could be expressed by this theological formula: there are two persons in me'

12 'man communicates with — himself, by the same means he has for communicating with *the other* / Consciousness needs a fictive other — an exteriority — it develops only in developing that *alterity.*'

13 'Total dialogue, system of naked consciousnesses … My idea was that this "friendship" would be a vital, almost a 'metaphysical' experiment since the will to approximate Two Selves – that is, two unique singularities – by means of increasingly precise exchanges would develop at the expense of all else'

14 'an intelligent and experimental fury, a presentment of sexual delight as a means'

15 'If there were a God, I would live only for him — what science, what passion so great a being would inspire in me — — what other science than his?'

16 'very ancient feelings which have remained in reserve, among the impossible possibilities, the ideals with no place'

17 'for what was not, could not be … for a tenderness without answer … *a living insult to the god,* for all Omnipotence can do nothing to redeem what was not – and the fraud practised by the created world upon human beings'.

18 'My mind has discovered this monstrous thing, this novel thing — that you are, – you Karin are. I have found that You *Sum* … I am is undeclinable. Or rather is conjugated: I am, you am …' (Unpublished letter of 9 April 1922 [Bibliothèque nationale]).

19 'What novelty, what strangeness to link God to goodness, justice, truth … Then this strange thing. Tenderness and universe. Idea of sacrifice, no longer by man to god, but of God to God.'

20 'Solitude, inward exchange — oh, Life! … One has to admit that the self — — is just an Echo'

21 'Oh, alone. Oh, the most alone … Why is there no God? … There is nothing of this kind. These worlds do not exist. We draw them precisely from their inexistence. The god is made up of our impotence, our abandonment, our imperfection, our distress, understood in reverse. But *if he were, we ourselves would not be*'.

22 See 'L'instance de la lettre dans l'inconscient ou la raison depuis Freud', *Ecrits 1*, (Paris, Seuil, 1966), pp. 249–89.

23 See *Symposium* 201 and its echoes in Valéry: *C*, VIII, p. 201; XVII, p. 665; *Œ*, I, p. 1275, etc.

24 'If you will, Reason of mine, I will say — (you will let me say) — that my soul, which is yours also, felt itself to be the *hollowed* form of a jewel-casket, or the hollow of a mould and that this *vacancy* experienced itself as

waiting for an admirable Object – a sort of material spouse who could not exist – for this divine form, this utter absence, this Being which was nothing other than Non-Being, called precisely for an impossible *matter*, and the living quick of this form *knew* that such substance was lacking, and would forever be lacking, from the world of bodies — and of acts'.

25 'an excitement towards the entirely real which almost all the senses attempt to compose by means of X. And not just the senses, but everything that demands response in us — from the need for tenderness to metaphysical appetite'.

26 'I am, says she, the real Being of which the being you love, which you edify within yourself, which tears and ravishes you — is but the dream. Wake up. Dispel my phantom. You will see which I am.'

27 Cf. *Ch.* ms I, fo. 30:

> Surgi des drames / terreurs / fureurs de ma couche
> Aux ténèbres tendre par ma bouche
> Donne-moi ce que tu voudras!

28 'I felt myself a perfect work ... but you were near me'.

29 See extracts published by Jean Ballard (*Œ*, II, pp. 1410–15) and by Ned Bastet, in 'Mes Théâtres', *Cahiers Paul Valéry 2* (Paris, Gallimard, 1977), pp. 51–88.

30 'Nothing can have resembled that: a force without name, which the word love veils rather than points to ... It is this I implore. I pray to whatever I can. I pray to what I feel with my whole being should be prayed to ... Oh, my principle of me who art in Faust, do this: I would that he love himself as I love myself and that he should love me as I love him.'

31 'Daughter, child of what proceeded in the shadow of my lucid thought ... while I thought to think, you [were] the power of thinking'.

32 'Rise up, little Lust ... You are great, little Lust. And though I seize you with my whole thought, understand you with all my experience, foresee your movements, I whom nothing human escapes, I whom nothing human can henceforth surprise and touch, yet ...

   Yes, here now is a love the like of which there never was ...'

33 This expression figures (in English) as title in one of the last of Valéry's notebooks (cf. *C*, XXIX, pp. 783–876).

34 'It triumphs. Stronger than everything, than the mind than the organism. There is the fact. The most obscure of facts. Stronger than the will-to-live, than the power-to-understand, is then this damn / sacralising H[eart]'.

35 'The word Love has been associated with the name of God only since Xrist [Christ]'. See my commentary in *Valéry – le Dialogue des choses divines* (Paris, Corti, 1989), pp. 155–90; 400–6.

36 'Alas, of my naked feet whoever finds the steps / Will he long cease to think but of himself?'

37 For further reading on the topic of this chapter, please see Bibliography, items 2, 6, 7, 9, 15, 18, 27, 39, 41, 44, 82.

# Conclusion

## Paul Gifford and Brian Stimpson

The readings in the present volume have proposed, not another set of re-interpretations of the same material, reviewed according to the latest critical modes, but, more radically, an engagement with the process of Valéry's unique thinking and writing practice viewed in the perspective of the 'unitary spirit' proper to it. The diverse but determined critical reassessment proceeding here has sought to shift the focus of attention – and, first of all, the textual corpus considered – so as to redefine the terms of the debate in conformity with the deeper logic of Valéry's singular enterprise of the mind.

Shifting the definition of 'the work' and displacing its centre of gravity leads one away from earlier, schematic divisions between unrelated continents of the mind: published texts and private notes, lyric expression and canonic art, abstract intelligence and the various modes of pre- or trans-rational apprehension of things, the shock of the new and the continuity with tradition, as also between theory and practice in numerous sectors of this uniquely awakened and wide-ranging mind. For Valéry too, 'le temps du monde fini commence' ('the time of the finite world is beginning'); and we may henceforth circulate freely within it.

The finite world is a place of inter-relations. The lyrical writing of *La Jeune Parque* is, we observe, deeply informed both by the long-practised precision of inner analytical observation and by the resurgent forces of the deep psyche. We see that divisions of genre are artificial and that the margins, the contiguities, the subterranean continuities between them are rich with discovery; that aesthetic, political and scientific theories alike are founded in the experience of the perceiving subject; that the dynamics of Self and Other impinge upon whole areas of Valéry's thinking, from inherited notions of selfhood, to mythical models, feminism and the political and social implications of human being-in-the-world.

Valéry seems, in fact, to have understood more profoundly than most that the era of relativity in physics presages, in the universe of mind-made phenomena, not so much cultural 'relativism' merely, but rather, added to his theory of 'points of view', a profound and inexhaustible 'relationality'. Not only so; but we discover in reading him 'whole' that his apparent aversion to so much of the 'modernity' of his age and the public adoption of values that seem to hark back to earlier, more stable, periods of Western civilisation, are simultaneously subverted and counter-balanced by the radical re-definition of terms, the pointing of problems which leap forward beyond his own generation, addressing issues that continue to preoccupy us at the end of the twentieth century. Does any other of the 'masters of modernity', one wonders, look so consistently – and so reversibly – backwards-and-forwards, stripping down and sifting more rigorously the European inheritance of the mind, while inventing more boldly over such a range of human concerns? Is there a more fully assumed vocation at the quick of the modern crisis of culture; in short, a more pivotal figure?

Correspondingly, fresh, or at least previously undervalued, areas of his work emerge as offering new avenues of exploration: the lyricism that is to be found in the prose poetry and the *Cahiers*; the insights afforded by the manuscripts into the genetic process; the whole range of experimental forms of prose writing; the chapters of the Pléiade *Cahiers* (on Dream, on Science, Self and Personality, Eros, Thêta and so many more ...); the reflections upon writing that go far beyond attempts to view the process as quasi-autonomous and self-justifying, and see it rather as the enactment through writing of the inexaustibly mysterious and fascinating subject of Desire (one of the most significant new emphases of the present set of re-evaluations). There is too, in these essays, a sense of the changes of form and focus in Valéry's preoccupations: of the mind as an evolving process, with its own 'biography', and, consequently, of the significance of the *dual* movement of *repetition and renewal* in all his work.

How will Valéry be read in the new century? Certainly no one approach, no overriding method, no single all-embracing formula suggests itself, any more than Valéry himself was able to fashion an all-encompassing statement of his own 'system'. Yet there are valuable pointers in the essays collected here.

Supremely among modern writers, it seems, Valéry is to be read as a series of articulated opposites, in the paradoxical play of opposing forces: between heterogeneity and system; between the 'œuvre ouverte' and the 'œuvre fermée'; between the mobility of intellectual forms and surfaces and the desiring depths of the psyche; between intelligible continuity and the discontinuities of intellection or of experience; between the reflexive subjectivity (or 'self') and an external other (whether natural world, human collectivity or personal complement), but also between the agent-self and the constitutive 'other' consistently rediscovered within.

The opposition of public and private may be instanced as generating one of the most fruitful lines of reassessment: it underpins many crucial areas of Valéry's activity, including language itself, the function of writing, the published and unpublished production and the contrast between his perceived positions on a series of issues and his 'reserved' thinking. What Valéry tells the Révérend Père Gillet in 1927 of his religious enquiry is more broadly true: 'il m'est arrivé de chercher à mon tour, à ma guise, – fort timidement en public, – trop hardiment, peut-être, dans le privé de ma pensée' (*LQ*, ll. 163–4).[1]

The dynamic interrelation of these contrasting movements could not be equitably comprehended in the past; only now, with our considerably more complete knowledge of the submerged bulk of the iceberg of Valéry's writing, can we take their full measure and – more importantly – begin to assess the issues in the perspective of Valéry's own way of looking at things.

This primary tension in turn accentuates another constitutive paradox: that of the comprehensive analytical gaze, over-arching in its generality yet rooted in the specificity of a particular subject. In the late twentieth century, we stand very much where Valéry in his own time so presciently stood: far removed from a vision of a metaphysically significant subjectivity wrapped in the veils of Romanticism; accepting that the 'author' is desacralised; admitting that the integrity and unity of the 'personality' has been systematically undone, the hypostasised 'Self' issuing from four centuries of anthropocentic humanism of Greek and Judeo-Christian antecedence fundamentally deconstructed. We can only refer, then, as he did, to the questing experience of the subject in its phenomenological perception of selfhood, within-body, within-world.

'Le Moi pur', on this acccount, seems to epitomise a notion of selfhood conceived at the fault-line between two phases of culture, a concept looking both backwards and forwards. In some respects, it is a mythical centre of reference replacing in immanentist terms a lost 'essence' or 'absolute' of the hypostasised Self (Valéry speaks in just this way of 'le Singulier-universel' (C2, p. 428)). Yet it is also, for Valéry and for us, a functional entity and a necessary reactive process by which the reflexive subject transforms limitation and enclosure into the hope of a universality geared onto the real. If the individuated 'I' can indeed mirror the non-self, react to it and creatively interact with it, this can only occur by first exploring the universe of representation carried within. The motif of hesitation running through Valéry's sense of modernity ('malgré moi-même, il le faut, ô Soleil') indicates sufficiently – more perceptively, perhaps, and more honestly than many declared 'post-moderns' – that this is less than the full reality of being we desire. Yet the compensation is a rich one: the mirror of the mind then holds all questions, permits all invention and re-invention of necessary answers – just as it also bears witness to our failure to bridge the gulf between 'knowing' and 'being', or even between 'knowing' and 'understanding'.

We accede here to the strategic pertinence of Valéryan universality. This dimension is highlighted by a number of contributors: Valéry, we are told, is not so much an observer of political-social actuality as a witness and decipherer of the human adventure in history; not so much the inventor of an impersonal science of literature, but of a concretely rooted, reader-related poetics; not so much a practitioner of art or music criticism, but an explorer of the enunciated seeing and hearing of the aesthetic subject; not so much a thinker who insists in putting all reality into one theory-laden head, but someone who steadily and freshly takes the measure of the knowable and the unknowable.

The *tabula rasa* of re-thinking everything from observable first-hand data, out of tangible experience, invoking genuinely available resources, while seeking the functional patterns and interactions of human activity, means that what Valéry offers us above all, perhaps, is an experimental art of strategic rethinking. At the very time when the inherited framework of civilised life undergoes a profound sea-change, his unblinking lucidity, his unfailing reference to the real possibilities and limits of the system 'Body-Mind-World', his sense of balance, his unwillingness to repress or exclude what he cannot reduce to intelligibility, offer an uncommon glimpse of the potential of awakened, self-cognisant thought.

The intellectual and spiritual radicalism of such a stance is not to be underestimated. 'Perpetual lucidity' alone drives the thinker resolutely towards an extreme point of despair at the human condition, to a searing experience of existential anguish in face of the insufficiency of simply ... *being*. In an argument that clearly echoes that of the Serpent in 'Ebauche d'un Serpent', Eryximaque suggests – hellenically – in l'*Ame et la danse* that Creation itself was a response to the Almighty's 'effroi d'être ce qui est' ('fright at being what is'); and that we in turn are driven by our desire for knowledge never to be satisfied with that which simply *is*: 'connaître ... *c'est assurément n'être point ce que l'on est*' ('knowing is *assuredly not being what one is*') (*Œ*, II, p. 167).

However, as so frequently in Valéry, the sheerly devastating lucidity of this confrontation with the bedrock of existence launches a dynamic of creativity and renewal. What answers are there, Socrate asks Eryximaque, to this supreme 'ennui' (that of 'la vie toute nue quand elle se regarde clairement' ('life stripped naked and viewing itself clearly'))? The latter can suggest only the consolations or distractions of intoxication, love, hatred, greed. No, there is one more, says Socrate (who has clearly been manipulating the entire rhetorical strategy): it is 'l'ivresse due à des actes' ('intoxication produced by acts') and especially the acts which engage the movements of the body. The dance of Athikté becomes an image of the Phoenix not simply rising from the flame but capturing in and for itself the elemental powers and virtues of fire itself:

cette exaltation et cette vibration de la vie ... cette suprématie de la tension, et ce ravissement dans le plus agile que l'on puisse obtenir de soi-même, ont les vertus et les puissances de la flamme ... [font] briller ... ce qu'il y a de divin dans une mortelle (p. 170).[2]

Athikté's dance may be seen as a symbol of the self-transcending capacity for renewal of the modern mind; her body – totally engulfed by and identified with its own centripetal gyrations – seeks to attain 'une possession entière de soi-même, et ... un point de gloire surnaturel' ('an entire self-possession and ... a pinnacle of supernatural glory') (p. 172). But – and this, it is suggested, is the most strikingly resonant aspect of Valéry's modernity – this highest and ultimate aspiration, this seeming coincidence of self as subject and self as object is at once sublime and doomed. The body's efforts to possess itself mirror the soul's aspiration for divine profundity and fullness of being; yet in both cases the insights and glimpses of knowledge so attained 'ne sont et ne peuvent être que des moments, des éclairs, des fragments d'un temps étranger, des bonds désespérés hors de sa forme ...' (p. 172)[3]

A gulf is fixed which no romantic striving can transgress and no 'post-modern ethics of play' can conceal or dissolve into insignificance. The subject, entrapped within its own psychic closure, may not break out; our very overbids betray us as the – finally impotent – creatures of unlimited Desire. Within the untransgressible limits, Valéry pursues an experimental extremism (in which he is not unique among twentieth-century writers); and yet – which is much rarer – it is an extremism which is consciously controlled, monitored, reactively adjusted. His writing practice is a continual, determined, obsessive exploration of this limit: the writing of the limit and of the tensions of that situation articulated between nullity and creative renewal is what provided the dynamic force of his entire mental project:

J'ai voulu «écrire» pour moi, et en moi, pour me servir de cette connaissance, les conditions de limite ou fermeture, ou (ce qui revient au même) celles d'unification de tout ce qui vient s'y heurter; et donc aussi celles qui font qu'on ne les perçoit ordinairement pas, et que la pensée se fait des domaines illusoires situés au delà de la Borne (Œ, II, p. 467).[4]

This is the frame within which everything is called into question and everything is written anew. It commands the scriptural processes themselves: the necessary interaction of retrospection and prospection, looking back in order to look forward; the relationship articulated between 'RE' and 'BLE', between 'Répétabilité' and 'Possibilité' (C, XXVII, p. 706); the instability, the incompletion and the negative dynamics of his analytical writing; but it is to be found too in the poetic writing, and especially the manuscripts, where one can trace the experimental forms adopted as the poetic voice seems to invent itself as it writes, moving through successive approximations towards a greater coherence of articulation while at the same time listening back to the source of its own song: the writer proceeds, says Valéry 'comme s'il essayait de se souvenir de la suite encore à naître' ('as though trying to remember the sequel still to emerge' (C, IV, p. 886).

The confrontation with the extreme limit of experience provides the frame for the problematising of all things human. As readers, we can thus recognise in the Cahiers, as also in their intimate dynamic relation to the diversity of the published works, an *evolving project*, *process* rather than *product*, a constantly renewed exploration of the territory of the mind. The writings may have become a 'corpus' in retrospect, but this is to impose a unitary – and essentially static – vision: the impetus of 'the thinking-writing act' and its continued value for us lies in its capacity to problematise issues, to propose links, contrasts and challenges, to revert to the source of a question and ask it anew.

The thinking-writing subject is constantly, in the daily space of the *Cahiers* placing himself at the farthest point, at the extreme limit of experience – up against the 'Limite', 'Borne' or 'mur' designated in 'La Révélation Anagogique' – and asking: what, then, is possible? The whole Valéryan enterprise, indeed, asks what is possible to the human mind, without, beyond or before metaphysics.

All these features of singularity and of pertinence point us towards the nature of Valéry's 'universe in mind'. We are offered, not the oneness of an all-encompassing totality of sense – systematicity in the nineteenth century, Hegelian, sense is the perfect antipode of Valéry – but a form of universalism which is founded in relativity, since it both inscribes the observer into the equation and proposes an infinitely resonant interconnectedness or relationality.

A number of classic objections to Valéry's work wither and fade at this point. It was once objected that the da Vincian search for an 'attitude centrale à partir de laquelle les entreprises de la connaissance et les opérations de l'art sont également possibles' (*Œ*, I, p. 1201)[5] was a form of vain theorising which led to little by way of creative practical realisations in the fields of the sciences or the arts. Along with that view went a certain critical mistrust of 'amateurishness', of a breadth of reference purchased, it was supposed, at the expense of superficiality, largely thanks to Valéry's gifts for analogy. Did not such analogical thinking merely circulate metaphors from one domain to another?

Where Valéry was often seen, from the nether shore of his visible public writings, as an 'universaliste manqué', he can now more accurately be seen as a master of the partial, provisional, fragmentary tissue of our contemporary intelligibilities; the master, that is, of an order that is constantly destabilised, of an incoherence on which the mind is constantly struggling to impose a frame born of itself, fitting to itself and which it is simultaneously and tirelessly concerned to re-draw.

If Valéry continues to speak to the end of the twentieth century, as he so clearly does to the authors of these essays, it is because he has the uncanny knack of asking the right questions, of revealing their interconnectedness, and of enacting in his writing the possibilities, the explorations, the aspirations and sublimations of the mind, momentarily captured in its act of thinking.

The individual mind can offer a mirror upon the universe with the possibility of observing the structures and movements on a grand scale within the patterns of its own workings:

> 'L'esprit' est ce qui peut former (ou feindre) toute chose par ses combinaisons internes. Et il n'est rien qui ne soit comparable à un jeu de l'esprit.[6]

Yet the inner text, contrary to the idealisms of nineteenth century thought, is not held to be continuous with or directly reciprocal to the text of reality itself. Valéry's 'universe in mind' integrally assumes the broken modern correlation of sign and referent; it implies rather an essentially problematising dialectic of enquiry, tributary, as we have seen, to Poincaré and Einstein.

If it progresses in elucidation, invention, self-correction and re-invention, its ever-open dialectic renounces any final synthesis of a conceptual or theoretical order, any nomination in the order of common nouns – any 'dernière pensée'. The gaze within the inner space of subject-consciousness operates according to a negating dynamic, perceiving relationships in the very process of its own divisions and fractures:

> Ma parole intérieure peut me surprendre — et je ne puis la prévoir. Quand elle parle, (quand Il est parlé) j'appelle Moi non ce qui parle, il terzo incommodo, — mais l'auditeur. Le Moi est le premier auditeur de la parole—non celui qui répond — mais celui qui va répondre. Dès qu'Il répond, il cesse d'être Moi.
>
> Le Temps, consiste à reconnaître cet auditeur fictif ou cette situation, *relation d'audition*.
>
> Ce Moi ne se reconnaît dans rien, ne se trouve dans nulle chose et ne peut se mirer étant négation de toute chose fixe. Et si quelqu'un l'imitait parfaitement il ne s'en distinguerait pas.
>
> Mes singularités les plus rares, si je les soupçonne, tombent de moi.
>
> Tout ce que je vois n'est pas *moi*. Tout ce que je puis voir n'est pas moi, ou cessera de l'être.[7]

Here, ultimately, is the source of the awakening bite and regenerative savour of Valéry's mind. And here, too, is the possibility of constantly renewed readings of his work.

NOTES

1   'I have on occasion sought, in my turn, in my own way, — very timidly in public — too boldly perhaps in the privacy of my own thought'.

2   'this exaltation and vibrancy of life ... this supreme tension, and this delight in the greatest agility to be obtained from oneself, have the virtues and powers of the flame ... cause to shine forth ... what is divine in a mortal being'.

3   'are and can only be moments, flashes, fragments of a foreign time, desperate leaps beyond its own form'.

4   'I wanted to "write" for myself, and in myself, to use this knowledge, the conditions of limitation or closure, or (which comes to the same thing) the conditions unifying all that comes up against them; and therefore also the conditions which mean that they are not always perceived, and that thought makes for itself illusory domains situated beyond the Boundary'.

5   'the central attitude from which the enterprises of knowledge and the operations of art are equally possible'

6   ' "The mind" is what can form (or feign) everything by its internal combinations. And there is nothing which is not comparable to the play of the mind' (Dossier 'Esprit-Conscience-Intelligence', circa 1908, N.a.f. 19468, fo. 231.)

7   'My inner speech may surprise me — and I cannot predict it. When it speaks (when He is spoken) I call Myself not the speaking agent, an intrusive third party — but the listener. The 'I' is the first to hear what is said — not the one who replies — but the one who is about to reply. As soon as HE replies, it is no longer Me.

Time consists in recognising this fictitious listener or the situation, the listening relationship.

This 'I' does not recognise itself in anything, does not find itself in anything and cannot look upon itself since it is a negation of any fixed thing. If someone were to copy it exactly it would not be any different.

The things that are most exceptionally peculiar to me, if I view them with suspicion, fall away from me.

Everything that I see is not *me*. Everything I am able to see is not me, or will become so' (*Ibid.*, fo. 380).

# Select Bibliography

The following list of critical works has been compiled with the help of contributors, who were asked to identify the most significant reading for their topic. The final note in each chapter refers to the numbered items listed below. The editors have added some important general works.

1. Allain-Castrillo, Monique, Philippe-Jean Quillien, François Valéry and Serge Bourjea (eds.), *Paul Valéry et le politique*, Paris, L'Harmattan, 1994.
2. Anderson, Kirsteen, 'Valéry et la voix mystique: la rencontre avec le féminin' in P. Gifford and B. Stimpson (eds.), *Paul Valéry. Musique, mystique, mathématique*, Lille, PUL, 1993, pp. 277–92.
3. Aquien, Michèle, 'Les deux faces du langage dans les *Cahiers* (1894–1903)' in *Paul Valéry: L'Avenir d'une écriture, Remanences*, 4–5 (June 1995), pp. 85–96.
4. Bastet, Ned, 'Œuvre ouverte et œuvre fermée chez Valéry', *Annales de la Faculté des lettres et sciences humaines de Nice*, 4th term, 1967, pp. 103–20.
5. Bastet, Ned, 'Valéry et la voix poétique', *Annales de la Faculté des lettres et sciences humaines de Nice*, 15 (1971), pp. 42–9.
6. Bastet, Ned, 'Ulysse et la Sirène', *Cahiers Paul Valéry* 2, Paris, Gallimard, 1977, pp. 49–141.
7. Bastet, Ned, 'Le même avec le même: le dialogue unitif valéryen et le troisième Acte du *Solitaire*', *Bulletin des études valéryennes*, 28 (1981), pp. 19–40.
8. Bastet, Ned, 'La contemplation "esthétique"' in A. Guyaux and J. Lawler (eds.), *Littérature moderne, 2, no. Paul Valéry*, Paris-Genève, Slatkine-Champion, 1991, pp. 17–28.
9. Bastet, Ned, 'Apocalypte Teste' in *Paul Valéry, Convergenze al testo, Micromégas*, 2–3 (1983), Roma, Bulzoni Editore, pp. 87–103.
10. Bertholet, Denis, *Paul Valéry*, Paris, Plon, 1995.
11. Blüher, Karl-Alfred, 'Valéry et la sémiotique du théâtre' in K.-A. Blüher (ed.), *Paul Valéry: Perspectives de la réception*, Œuvres et critiques 9, 1, Paris, J.-M. Place, 1984, pp. 181–209.
12. Blüher, Karl-Alfred and Jürgen Schmidt-Radefeldt (eds.), *Valéry und die Philosophie, Forschungen zu Paul Valéry*, 5 (1992).

13. Blüher, Karl-Alfred and Jürgen Schmidt-Radefeldt (eds.), *Paul Valéry: Le Cycle de Mon Faust devant la sémiotique théâtrale et l'analyse textuelle*, Tübingen, Gunter Narr Verlag, 1991.

14. Bourjea, Serge, 'La Comminution valéryenne', *Poétique*, 62 (1985), pp. 159–78.

15. Bourjea, Serge, *Le Sujet de l'écriture*, Paris, L'Harmattan, 1997.

16. *Bulletin des Etudes Valéryennes, numéro spécial «Japon»*, 56–7 (June 1991).

17. *Bulletin des Etudes Valéryennes, numéro spécial «Amérique»*, 76 (November 1997).

18. Celeyrette-Pietri, Nicole, *Valéry et le Moi. Des 'Cahiers' à l'œuvre*, Paris, Klincksieck, 1979.

19. Celeyrette-Pietri, Nicole, *'Agathe' ou le manuscrit trouvé dans une cervelle*, Paris, Minard, 1981.

20. Celeyrette-Pietri, Nicole (ed.), *Lecture des premiers Cahiers de Paul Valéry*, Paris, Université Paris Val de Marne et Didier-Erudition, 1983.

21. Celeyrette-Pietri, Nicole, 'La psychanalyse et le cas Valéry' in K.-A. Blüher (ed.), *Paul Valéry: Perspectives de la réception*, Œuvres et critiques 9, 1, Paris, J.-M. Place, 1984, pp. 103–126.

22. Celeyrette-Pietri, Nicole, 'L'ecriture brève', in A. Mairesse-Landes, and S. Bourjea (eds.), *Valéry, aujourd'hui, Actes du colloque de San Francisco, Bulletin des études valéryennes*, 72–3 (November 1996), pp. 29–40.

23. Celeyrette-Pietri, Nicole, 'L'écriture et la voix' in K-A. Blüher and J. Schmidt-Radefeldt (eds.), *Poétique et Communication, Cahiers du XXe siècle*, 11, Paris, Klincksieck, 1979, pp. 207–27.

24. Celeyrette-Pietri Nicole and Antonia Soulez (eds.), *Valéry, la logique et le langage*, Arles, Actes Sud, 1988.

25. Celeyrette-Pietri, Nicole and Brian Stimpson (eds.), *Un Nouveau regard sur Valéry*, Paul Valéry 8, Paris, Minard, 1995.

26. Celeyrette-Pietri, Nicole, 'La "Connaissance de la connaissance"' in N. Celeyrette-Pietri, and B. Stimpson (eds.), *Un Nouveau regard sur Valéry*, Paris, Minard, 1995, pp. 273–89.

27. Crow, Christine, *Paul Valéry, Consciousness and Nature*, Cambridge University Press, 1972.

28. Crow, Christine, *Valéry and the Poetry of Voice*, Cambridge University Press, 1982.

29. Deguy, Michel, 'Deux poétiques de Valéry', *Nouvelle Revue Française*, August 1971, pp. 1–11.

30. Derrida, Jacques, 'Qual Quelle' in *Marges de la philosophie*, Paris: Minuit, 1972, pp. 325–63.

31. Derrida, Jacques, 'Valéry boucheoreille' in *Le Langage et l'homme 18*, Paris, 1972.

32. Duchesne-Guillemin, 'Les Dialogues de Paul Valéry', *Cahiers de l'Association internationale des études françaises*, 34 (1972), pp. 73–91.

33. Franklin, Ursula, 'Valéry et le poème en prose' in *Bulletin des études valéryennes*, 21 (June 1979), pp. 33–49.

34. Franklin, Ursula, *The Rhetoric of Valéry's prose 'Aubades'*, University of Toronto Press, 1979.
35. Fromilhague, René, 'La Jeune Parque et l'autobiographie dans la forme', in J. Levaillant et M. Parent (eds.), *Paul Valéry contemporain*, Paris, Klincksieck, 1974, pp. 209–35.
36. Gaède, Edouard, *Valéry et Nietzsche*, Paris, Gallimard, 1962.
37. Genette, Gérard, 'La littérature comme telle', in *Figures I*, Paris, Seuil, 1966, pp. 253–65.
38. Ghebali, Victor-Yves, 'Politique et antipolitique' in M. Jarrety (ed.), *Valéry pour quoi?*, Paris, Les Impressions nouvelles, 1987, pp. 209–224.
39. Gifford, P., 'Animus et Anima. Valéry et la mystique de l'amour supérieur' in P. Gifford and B. Stimpson (eds), *Paul Valéry. Musique, mystique, mathématique*, Lille, PUL, 1993, pp. 293–14.
40. Gifford, P., *Paul Valéry – le dialogue des choses divines*, Paris, Corti, 1989.
41. Gifford, P., 'Le Dialogue des choses divines: une genèse résorbée' in *Paul Valéry*, Paris, Champion, 1991, pp. 29–41.
42. Gifford P. and B. Stimpson (eds.), *Paul Valéry: Musique, mystique, mathématique*, Lille, PUL, 1993.
43. Gifford, P., *Paul Valéry. 'Charmes'*, Glasgow Introductory Guides to French Literature, 30, 1995.
44. Gifford, P., 'Eros, Mythos, Logos: Valéry et la mythopoésie du désir' in N. Celeyrette-Pietri and B. Stimpson (eds.), *Un Nouveau regard sur Valéry*, Paris, Minard, 1995, pp. 121–40.
45. Grésillon, Almuth, *Elements de critique génétique*, Paris, Presses universitaires de France, 1995.
46. Guyaux, André and James Lawler (eds.), *Littérature moderne 2, no. Paul Valéry*, Paris-Genève, Champion-Slatkine, 1991.
47. Hainault, Jean (ed.), *Valéry: Le Partage de midi – 'Midi le juste'*, Actes du *Colloque international tenu au Collège de France le 18 novembre 1995*, Paris and Geneva, Champion-Slatkine, 1997.
48. Houpert, Jean-Marc, *Paul Valéry: Lumière, écriture et tragique*, Paris, Méridiens Klincksieck, 1986.
49. Houpert, Jean-Marc, 'Ecrire comme on efface' in N. Celeyrette-Pietri and B. Stimpson (eds.), *Un Nouveau regard sur Paul Valéry*, Paris, Minard, 1995, pp. 101–19.
50. Howe, Elisabeth A., *Stages of Self: The dramatic monologues of Laforgue, Mallarmé, and Valéry*, Athens, Ohio University Press, 1990.
51. Howe, Elisabeth, A., ' "Blood, milk, tears": L'écriture féminine et le refus du maternel dans *La Jeune Parque* de Valéry et dans le *Book of Thel* de William Blake' in A. Mairesse-Landes and S. Bourjea (eds.), *Valéry aujourd'hui*, Colloque de San Francisco, *Bulletin des études valéryennes*, 72–3 (November 1996), pp. 253–6.
52. Hytier, Jean, *La Poétique de Valéry*, 1953; Paris, Colin, 1970.
53. Ince, Walter, *The Poetic Theory of Paul Valéry: Inspiration and technique*, Leicester University Press, 1961.

54. Ince, Walter, 'La Promenade avec Monsieur Teste', *Yale French Studies*, 44 (1970), pp. 169–84.
55. Ince, Walter, 'La poétique de Valéry' in K.-A. Blüher (ed.), *Paul Valéry: Perspectives de la réception, Œuvres et critiques 9*, 1, Paris, J.-M. Place, 1984, pp. 155–70.
56. Jallat, Jeannine, *Introduction aux figures valéryennes*, Pisa, Pacini, 1982.
57. Jallat, Jeannine, 'Suivre Léonard ou la question du récit' in R. Pietra (ed.), *Valéry: La Philosophie, les arts, le langage*, Grenoble, Université des Sciences Sociales de Grenoble, 1989, pp. 119–26.
58. Jarrety, Michel (ed.), *Valéry pour quoi?*, Paris, Les Impressions nouvelles, 1987.
59. Jarrety, Michel, *Valéry devant la littérature. Mesure de la limite*, Paris, Presses universitaires de France, 1991.
60. Jarrety, 'Réflexions sur une politique de l'esprit', *Secolul 20* (1995), pp. 7–12.
61. Jarrety, Michel, *Paul Valéry*, 'Portraits littéraires', Paris, Hachette Supérieur, 1992.
62. Kao, Shuhsi, 'Valéry et la critique américaine', *Bulletin des études valéryennes*, 48–9 (November 1988), pp. 137–47.
63. Kao, Shuhsi, *Lire Valéry*, Paris, Corti, 1985.
64. Köhler, Hartmut, 'Valéry et Husserl: Le moi et son œuvre', in K. Blüher and J. Schmidt-Radefeldt (eds.), *Poétique et Communication, Cahiers du XXe siècle*, 11, Paris, Klincksieck, 1979.
65. Köhler, Hartmut, *Poésie et connaissance. L'œuvre lyrique à la lumière des 'Cahiers'*, Paris, Klincksieck, 1985.
66. Köhler, Hartmut, 'La physique du corps: le dépassement dépassé?' in N. Celeyrette-Pietri and B. Stimpson (eds.), *Un Nouveau regard sur Valéry*, Paris, Minard, 1995, pp. 257–71.
67. Kluback William, *Paul Valéry: Philosophical Reflections*, New York, Peter Lang, 1987.
68. Kluback William, *Paul Valéry: The search for intelligence*, New York, Peter Lang, 1993.
69. Kluback, William, *Paul Valéry: Illusions of civilization*, New York, Peter Lang, 1996.
70. Kluback, William, *Paul Valéry: The continuous search for reality*, New York, Peter Lang 1997.
71. Lantieri, Simon, 'Valéry et la philosophie' in K.-A. Blüher (ed.), *Paul Valéry: Perspectives de la réception, Œuvres et critiques 9*, *1*, Paris, *J.*-M. Place, *1984*, pp. 47–80.
72. Laurenti, Huguette, *Valéry et le théâtre*, Paris, Gallimard, 1973.
73. Laurenti, Huguette (ed.), *Recherches sur 'La Jeune Parque'*, Les Lettres Modernes, Paul Valéry 2, Paris, Minard, 1977.
74. Laurenti, Huguette (ed.), *Approches du 'Système'*, Revue des Lettres modernes, Paul Valéry 3, Paris, Minard, 1979.

75. Laurenti, Huguette (ed.), *Musique et architecture*, Revue des Lettres modernes, Paul Valéry 5, Paris, Minard, 1987.
76. Laurenti, Huguette (ed.), *Lectures de 'Charmes'*, Revue des Lettres Modernes, Paul Valéry 6, Paris: Minard, 1974.
77. Laurenti, Huguette (ed.), *Paul Valéry: «Ovide chez les Scythes»: étude génétique d'un manuscrit inédit*, Montpellier, Centre d'Etude du XXe siècle, Université de Montpellier, 1997.
78. Lawler, James, *Lecture de Valéry: une étude de 'Charmes'*, Paris, Presses Universitaires de France, 1963.
79. Lawler, James, *The Poet as Analyst. Essays on Paul Valéry*, University of California Press, 1974.
80. Levaillant, Jean, *Genèse et signification de 'La Soirée avec Monsieur Teste'*. Thesis 2 vols. (Université de la Sorbonne – Paris IV), 1966.
81. Levaillant, Jean and Agathe Rouart-Valéry (eds.), *Poétique et poésie*, *Cahiers Paul Valéry 1*, Paris, Gallimard, 1975.
82. Levaillant, Jean and Agathe Rouart-Valéry (eds.), *'Mes théâtres'*, *Cahiers Paul Valéry 2*, Paris, Gallimard, 1977.
83. Levaillant, Jean and Agathe Rouart-Valéry (eds.), *Questions du rêve*, *Cahiers Paul Valéry 3*, Paris, Gallimard, 1979.
84. Levaillant, Jean, *Ecriture et génétique textuelle. Valéry à l'œuvre*, Lille, PUL, 1982.
85. Levaillant, Jean, 'Inachèvement, invention, écriture', in L. Hay (ed.), *Le manuscrit inachevé*, Paris, CNRS, 1986, pp. 101–125.
86. Lussy, Florence de, *Charmes, d'après les manuscrits de Paul Valéry. Histoire d'une métamorphose*, 2 vols. Paris, Les Lettres Modernes, 1990–6.
87. Lussy, Florence de, *La Genèse de «La Jeune Parque» de Paul Valéry*, Paris, Minard, 1975.
88. Mairesse-Landes, A. and S. Bourjea (eds.), *Valéry aujourd'hui*, Actes du colloque de San Francisco, *Bulletin des Etudes valéryennes*, 72–3 (November 1996).
89. Ménard, A., 'Place des références à Paul Valéry dans l'œuvre de Lacan', *Bulletin des études valéryennes*, 45 (June 1987), pp. 45–52.
90. Nadal, Octave, 'Poèmes en prose', *A mesure haute*, Paris, Mercure de France, 1964.
91. Nadal, Octave, *La Jeune Parque: Manuscrit autographe*, Paris, Gallimard, Le Club du Meilleur Livre, 1957.
92. Nash, Suzanne, *Paul Valéry's 'Album de vers anciens': A past transfigured*, Princeton University Press, 1983.
93. Pickering, Robert, *Genèse du concept valéryen – 'pouvoir' et 'conquête méthodique' de l'écriture*, Paris, Lettres Modernes (Archives des Lettres Modernes 243, 'Archives Paul Valéry' no. 8), 1990.
94. Pickering, Robert, *Paul Valéry, poète en prose. La prose lyrique abstraite des 'Cahiers'*, Paris, Minard, 1983.
95. Pickering, Robert, '«Ebauche» et écriture de la présence d'absence' in

B. Stimpson (ed.), *Lecture plurielle d'«Ebauche d'un Serpent»*, *Bulletin des Etudes valéryennes*, 50–1 (June 1989), pp. 57–66.

96. Pickering, Robert, '«Dessiner un discours perdu»: parcours scripturaux dans l'*Alphabet*' in A. Guyaux and J. Lawler (eds.), *Littérature moderne*, 2, no. Paul Valéry, Paris and Geneva, Champion-Slatkine, 1991, pp. 169–85.

97. Pickering, Robert (ed.), *Paul Valéry. Se faire ou se refaire. Lecture génétique d'un cahier (1943)*, Clermont-Ferrand, Centre de recherches sur les littératures modernes et contemporaines, 1996.

98. Pickering, Robert, *Paul Valéry, la page, l'écriture*, Clermont-Ferrand, Centre de recherches sur les littératures modernes et contemporaines, 1996.

99. Pietra, Régine, *Valéry. Directions spatiales et parcours verbal*, Paris, Les Lettres modernes, Minard, 1981.

100. Pietra, Régine, 'L'Architecte assassiné, ou la coquille du philosophe', in A. Guyaux and J. Lawler (eds.), *Littérature moderne*, 2, no. Paul Valéry, Paris and Geneva, Champion-Slatkine, 1991, pp. 79–89.

101. Pietra, Régine (ed.), *Valéry: La Philosophie, les arts, le langage*, Grenoble, Université des Sciences Sociales de Grenoble, 1989.

102. Quillien, Philippe-Jean, *Histoire et politique de Paul Valéry*, thèse de l'Institut d'Etudes politiques de Paris, 2 vols., 1990.

103. Quillien, Philippe-Jean, 'Paul Valéry et l'Allemagne', in M. Allain-Castrillo, P.-J. Quillien, F. Valéry and S. Bourjea (eds.), *Paul Valéry et le Politique*, Paris, L'Harmattan, 1994, pp. 51–137.

104. Pozzi, Catherine, *Journal*, Claire Paulhan (ed.), Paris, Ramsey, 1987.

105. Rey, Jean-Michel, *Paul Valéry: L'aventure d'une œuvre*, Paris, Seuil, 1991.

106. Rey, Jean-Michel, 'Valéry et "le temps du monde . . . "' in *Fini et infini*, Paris, Seuil, 1992, pp. 24–5.

107. Ribis, M. (ed.), *Paul Valéry et les Arts*, Arles, Actes Sud, 1995.

108. Robinson, Judith, *L'Analyse de l'esprit dans les 'Cahiers' de Valéry*, Paris, Corti, 1963.

109. Robinson, Judith, 'Un nouveau visage de *La Jeune Parque*: le poème commenté par son auteur', *Bulletin des Etudes valéryennes*, 25 (October 1980), pp. 47–65.

110. Robinson-Valéry, Judith, 'L'Œuvre de Valéry comme dialogue', *Bulletin des études valéryennes*, 29 (March 1982), pp. 31–41.

111. Robinson-Valéry, Judith (ed.), *Fonctions de l'esprit. Treize savants redécouvrent Paul Valéry*, Paris, Hermann, 1983.

112. Robinson, Judith, 'Les cris refoulés de *La Jeune Parque:* le rôle de l'autocensure dans l'écriture, in M. Bowie and A. Finch (eds.), *Baudelaire, Mallarmé, Valéry. New essays in honour of Lloyd Austin*, Cambridge University Press, 1982, pp. 411–32.

113. Robinson-Valéry, Judith, 'Les *Cahiers* de Valéry: œuvre préparée ou non?' in L. Hay (ed.), *Carnets d'écrivains I*, Paris, éditions du CNRS, 1990, pp. 131–50.

114. Robinson-Valéry, Judith, 'Mallarmé, le «père idéal»', in *Littérature, no. spéc. Paul Valéry,* 56, (1984), pp. 104–18.

115. Robinson-Valéry, Judith, 'Valéry et la science', in K.-A. Blüher (ed.), *Paul Valéry: Perspectives de la réception,* Œuvres et critiques, 94, 1, Paris, J.-M. Place, 1984.

116. Roulin, Pierre, *Paul Valéry, témoin et juge du monde moderne,* Neuchatel, La Baconnière, 1964.

117. Romer, Stephen, 'Paul Valéry et T. S. Eliot' in P. Gifford and B. Stimpson (eds.), *Paul Valéry. Musique, mystique, mathématique,* Lille, PUL, 1993, pp. 113–25.

118. Schmidt-Radefeldt, Jürgen, *Paul Valéry linguiste dans les Cahiers,* Paris, Klincksieck, 1970.

119. Schmidt-Radefeldt, Jürgen, 'Valéry et les sciences du Langage', *Poétique,* 31 (1977).

120. Schmidt-Radefeldt, Jürgen, 'Sémiologie et langage' in K.-A. Blüher, *Paul Valéry: Perspectives de la réception,* Œuvres et critiques 9, 1, Paris, J.-M. Place, 1984, pp. 153–72.

121. Starobinski, Jean 'Monsieur Teste face à la douleur' in M. Jarrety (ed.), *Valéry pour quoi?* Paris, Les Impressions nouvelles, 1987, pp. 93–119.

122. Starobinski, Jean, Préface aux *Cahiers 1894–1914,* Paris, Gallimard, 1990, vol. 3.

123. Stimpson, Brian, *Paul Valéry and Music: A study of the techniques of composition in Valéry's poetry,* Cambridge University Press, 1984.

124. Stimpson, Brian, '*Langage musical, langage poétique: Valéry à la recherche de son chinois poétique*' in R. Pietra (ed.), *Valéry: la philosophie, les arts, le langage,* Grenoble, Université des Sciences Sociales de Grenoble, 1989, pp. 249–63.

125. Stimpson, Brian, '«Insulaire que tu es, Ile – »: Valéry, the Robinson Crusoe of the Mind', in L. Spaas and B. Stimpson (eds.), *Robinson Crusoe: Myths and metamorphoses,* London, Macmillan, 1996, pp. 294–315.

126. Stimpson, Brian, (ed.), *Lecture plurielle d'«Ebauche d'un Serpent»,* Bulletin des Etudes valéryennes, 50–1 (June 1989).

127. Stimpson, Brian, 'Toute la modulation de l'être: la musique qui est en moi', in P. Gifford and B. Stimpson (eds), *Musique, mystique, mathématique,* Lille, PUL, 1993, pp. 37–57.

128. Stimpson, Brian, 'Composer continu et discontinu: modulation et fragmentation dans l'écriture valéryenne' in N. Celeyrette-Pietri and B. Stimpson (eds.), *Un Nouveau regard sur Valéry,* Paris, Minard, 1995, pp. 121–40.

129. Stimpson, Brian, 'A Rendez-vous with Myself: Valéry à Londres', in S. Bourjea (ed.), *Paul Valéry, 1894: L'avenir d'une écriture, Remanences,* 4–5 (1995), pp. 31–48.

130. Tsukamoto, Masanori, 'A l'état naissant, tout est rêve – Le rêve et la

poésie chez Valéry', *Bulletin des études valéryennes*, 71 (March 1996), pp. 23–36.

131. Tsunekawa, Kunio, 'Essai d'une analyse de *La Soirée avec Monsieur Teste*', *Bulletin d'études valéryennes*, 56–7 (1991).

132. Tsunekawa, Kunio, '«Agathe», utopie de la pulsion sémiotique valéryenne' in N. Celeyrette-Pietri and B. Stimpson (eds.), *Un Nouveau regard sur Valéry*, Paris, Minard, 1995, pp. 141–9.

133. Tsunekawa, Kunio, *Rencontres Occident-Orient sous le regard de Paul Valéry. Colloque de Tokyo*, Paris, Minard, 1998.

134. Valéry, François (ed.), *Paul Valéry et la politique, suivi de Paul Valéry, 'Principes d'anarchie pure et appliquée'*, Paris, Gallimard, 1984.

135. *Paul Valéry, L'avenir d'une écriture*, special no. of the review *Rémanences*, 4–5, June 1995.

136. Valéry, Paul, *Vues*, Paris, La Table ronde, 1948.

137. Yeschua, Silvio, *Valéry, le roman et l'œuvre à faire*, Paris, Minard, 1977.

# Index

love (*cont.*)
 amour-passion and 'idolopoésie', 289–90
 'l'amour supérieur', 292–3; (*see also Desire, Sexuality*)
Loyola (S Ignace de), 48, 66
Lucretius, 87
Lulle, Raymond, 91

Mach, Ernst, 86, 99 n. 1
Mallarmé, Stéphane, 6,22, 30, 66, 129, 133, 187, 188, 190, 191, 192, 196, 209, 219
Manet, Edouard, 220
Mathews, Jackson, 5
Maxwell, James Clerk, 74, 75, 77
Merleau Ponty, 129, 130, 135 n. 19
metaphysics, 86–8, 281–2, 291
 ontological disappointment, 282, 287
Michael-Angelo, 220
Moltke, Helmuth, von, 65, 238
*Mon Faust* ('Lust', 'Le Solitaire'), 17, 31, 162–4, 291–4
Monet, Claude, 220, 230
Morisot, Berthe, 220, 221, 227, 230
Mozart, Wolfgang Amadeus, 225
music, 20, 26, 73, 109, 219, 223–7
 modulation in *La Jeune Parque*, 20, 173–77
 in 'La Pythie', 180
'Mystique sans Dieu', 8, 26, 32–3, 48–9, 60–1, 175–6, 283
myth, as sublimation, 20, 49, 180
 as paradigm of self-construction, 53–68
 critique of 'fiduciarity', 93–8

narrativity
 and fiction, 141–5
 and dream, 267–71
 and poetry, 110, 271–7
Nietzsche, Friedrich, 2, 5, 28, 45, 91, 98, 237, 239, 247, 263
*Note et Digression*, 56, 59–61, 67
'Nuit de Gênes', 23, 171, 283

'Other', the, 10, 280
 alterity within, 50, 157, 179–80, 281
 feminine Other, 141, 146, 202, 203, 210–12, 285–6
 metaphysical Other, 280, 281–2, 294, 299
Ovid, 25, 193

Pascal, Blaise, 6, 87, 96, 99–100 n. 4, 130, 196, 289
Pasteur, Louis, 228
perception ('manières de voir')
 Leonardo as model, 57–9
 perception in painting, 227–32

phenomenology of poetic sensibility, 128–32
Pétain, Marshal Philippe, 238
'Petits Poèmes abstraits' ('PPA'), 121–34
Picard, Emile, 78
Piéron, Henri, 78–9
Perrin, Jean, 77, 78
Picasso, Pablo, 2, 219
Plato, 90, 93, 160, 209, 291
Plotinus, 48, 90
Poe, Edgar, 7, 22, 66, 74, 159, 188, 196
poetics
 literary, 4, 44, 47, 105–19
 generalised psychopoetics, 44
'Points de vue', 8, 43, 70, 86, 99 note 3, 227
Poincaré, Henri, 66, 145, 304
Pozzi, Catherine ('Béatrice', 'Karin', 'CK'), 25, 160
Presocratics (The), 90
Prigogine, Illya, 79
*Propos me concernant*, 18
Proust, Marcel, 20, 138, 263

Raphael, 220, 221
Racine, Jean, 188, 219, 276
Rembrandt, 220
Renan, Ernest, 164
Renoir, Pierre Auguste, 220
religion
 critique of religion, 48–9, 96–7
 Judeo-Christianity, 290–1, 293–4
 the sacred, 128–31, 179, 251, 282
 Valéry's 'Enterrement de Dieu', 202
Rhodes, Cecil, 66, 237–8
Riemann, Bernhard, 74
Rimbaud, Arthur, 22, 66, 132
Robbe-Grillet, Alain, 2
Rousseau, Jean-Jacques, 95
Russell, Bertrand, 71
Ruysbroek, 48

Sartre, Jean-Paul, 2,
Schoenberg, Arnold, 219
Schopenhauer, Arthur, 90, 287
science
 entropy, 65, 232, 243
 mathematics, 42–3, 73–4, 78, 140
 neurosciences, 78–9
 physics, 74–6, 77–8
 relativity theory, 80–2
 scientific modelling of the self, 70–1
self (le Moi)
 dialectics of selfhood 173–7
 'Ego', rubric of the *Cahiers*, 18–19, 50
 'le moi caché' (the unconscious), 19–20, 33, 262–77

CAMBRIDGE STUDIES IN FRENCH

GENERAL EDITOR: Michael Sheringham (*Royal Holloway, London*)
EDITORIAL BOARD: R. Howard Bloch (*Columbia University*), Malcolm
Bowie (*All Souls College, Oxford*), Terence Cave (*St. John's College, Oxford*),
Ross Chambers (*University of Michigan*), Antoine Compagnon (*Columbia
University*), Peter France (*University of Edinburgh*), Christie McDonald (*Harvard
University*), Toril Moi (*Duke University*), Naomi Schor (*Harvard University*).